OPERATION PLUM

TEXAS A&M UNIVERSITY MILITARY HISTORY SERIES

117

OPERATION PLUM

THE ILL-FATED 27TH BOMBARDMENT GROUP AND THE FIGHT FOR THE WESTERN PACIFIC

Adrian R. Martin

and Larry W. Stephenson

Texas A&M University Press
College Station

This paper meets the requirements of ANSI/NISO Z39.48-1992
(Permanence of Paper).
Binding materials have been chosen for durability.

Library of Congress Cataloging-in-Publication Data

Martin, Adrian R. (Adrian Robert), 1944–
    Operation Plum : the ill-fated 27th Bombardment Group and the fight for the Western
Pacific / Adrian R. Martin and Larry W. Stephenson. — 1st ed.
        p. cm. — (Texas A&M University military history series ; #117)
    Includes bibliographical references and index.
    ISBN-13: 978-1-60344-019-6 (cloth : alk. paper)
    ISBN-10: 1-60344-019-4 (cloth : alk. paper)
    1. United States. Army Air Forces. Bombardment Group (Light), 27th 2. World War,
1939–1945—Aerial operations, American. 3. World War, 1939–1945—Campaigns—Pacific
Area. 4. World War, 1939–1945—Regimental histories—United States. I. Stephenson,
Larry W. II. Title.
D790.25327th .M37 2008
940.54'2599—dc22

                                                                          2007048110

Being anxious to retain for ourselves a narrative of the activities of the 27th Bomb Group from the time it left America until it was rendered inactive by the War Department due to the almost complete depletion of its personnel in the Philippines and the activities of the few remaining survivors in Australia, I have asked Captain McAfee, the Group Intelligence Officer, to allot certain phases or periods of time to you to report on.

Col. John H. Davies

Contents

Illustrations

Maps

Photographs

ILLUSTRATIONS

Preface

GLENWOOD STEPHENSON HAS always been considered something of a hero among the members and descendents of his family. In the summer of 1934, at the height of the Depression, Glen left his home in Wisconsin to seek a better life. What began as a nomadic odyssey of riding the rails and picking up odd jobs just to stay alive culminated in his graduation from the U.S. Military Academy at West Point and subsequent death in action as a U.S. Army Air Corps pilot in World War II.

Glen's family did not know much about his last years of life, nor were they able to obtain many details of his untimely death. After learning from officials that his son had died in a bomber crash in Australia in April 1942, Gordon Stephenson wrote to the army and to Glen's fellow officers seeking information regarding his son's military experience, though without much success. Other family members continued writing letters for years after the war and eventually were told that a fire in 1973 at the National Personnel Records Center in St. Louis was responsible for the lack of information.

In 1995 Glen's nephew Larry, the son of his brother Clyde, made what became a fortuitous trip to Australia. As a heart surgeon, he had been asked to speak at the annual meeting of the Cardiac Society of Australia and New Zealand in Canberra. Knowing that his uncle had been killed in Australia and that the family had sought more detailed information, Larry devoted his spare time to researching at the National Military Museum. He did not find much, but his curiosity was piqued.

Back home he looked through the file that the family had accumulated on Glenwood and noticed an almost unreadable photocopy of a 1943 newspaper article listing the names of some surviving pilots who were known to have flown with his uncle. Checking the West Point yearbook, Larry discovered that two of those pilots had been in Glen's 1940 graduation class. He contacted the Military Academy Alumni Office, which agreed to pass letters of inquiry to the two men, providing they were still alive. One of them, Julius B. "Zeke" Summers, responded and gave Larry a possible explanation as to why it had been so difficult to find information on Glen and his fellow airmen in the 27th Bombardment Group. 1,209 men had arrived in the Philippines in November 1941; one year later only twenty returned to the United States. The rest, according to Summers, were dead or in Japanese prison camps. Further complicating research efforts was the fact that the 27th was consistently involved in America's early World War II losses in the Philippines, Java, Australia, and New Guinea. Recordkeeping under those conditions had been a low- to nonexistent priority, and documents the units did have were often lost or had to be destroyed to prevent capture.

Even so, Larry recognized that he held an ace for his research: He had spent twenty-one years in the army and reserves, retiring as a colonel, and as such would have access to records and personnel that civilians might not. Thus began literally years of letters, phone calls, and e-mails that slowly started to produce results. Glenwood's service record began to take shape. A certain excitement was building.

In 2000 Larry's father, Clyde, met Adrian Martin. Adrian had written a book, *Brothers from Bataan,* about his own uncle who had been in the Philippines at the same time as Glen and had survived the Bataan Death March but died in a POW camp. Clyde, a Marine Corps veteran of World War II, believed, and Adrian agreed, that a book should be written about the 27th Bombardment Group. Almost immediately, Adrian began an investigation into the subject, with Larry sharing his accumulated information. After eight years of collaboration and further intense research, the story has emerged.

For most Americans, the war in the Pacific began at Pearl Harbor and continued with our costly but slow-and-steady march to Japan and victory. The shock and confusion of those early months of the war and the horrendous losses sustained by the 27th Bombardment Group and others were not events that the U.S. military wished to share with the home front. Once the tide had turned, the weeks and months of lost battles and lost lives were quickly forgotten in the rush to report every success. It is now recognized that units such as the 27th played a major role in the eventual defeat of the Japanese by delaying their progress and thus allowing America's military production and troop training to gear up. This is a story worth telling. We wish this book to be a fitting memorial to Glenwood Stephenson and his comrades in arms, who should no longer be the forgotten soldiers of the Pacific.

The epigraph that appears at the beginning of this book was written by

Col. John H. Davies, commanding officer of the 3rd Bombardment Group, U.S. Army Air Corps, writing at Charters Towers, Australia. Taken from the introduction to a fifty-nine-page typewritten monograph, *The 27th Bombardment Group Reports,* which deals with the 27th Bombardment Group, it was completed in September 1942. The authors were U.S. Army Air Corps pilots from the 27th who had gotten out of the Philippines before Bataan fell. Photographs and many official military documents such as troop lists, orders, and reports are included. Excerpts from this unpublished monograph are quoted throughout this book and referred to each time as the *27th Reports.* At the time it was written, the authors only knew that U.S. forces on Bataan and Corregidor had surrendered but beyond that did not know their fate, which included that of most of their comrades in the 27th.

Acknowledgments

As this project developed during the past six years, three former members of the 27th Bombardment Group have rendered invaluable assistance: Brig. Gen. William G. Hipps, USAF (ret.); Col. Ronald D. Hubbard, USAF (ret.); and Col. J. Harrison Mangan, USAF (ret.). They were always willing to give of their time to answer questions and provide explanations when necessary. Each also reviewed the manuscript during various stages of preparation.

Chief MSgt. Paul H. Lankford, USAF (ret.), who has led the 27th Alumni Group over the past several years, has not only been helpful in answering questions and explaining various issues but also has provided us with introductions and access to other 27th alumni and their families. Other former members of the 27th and 3rd Bombardment Groups who have been particularly helpful include Ralph Harrell, Jack Heyn, George Kane, Dick Launder, and Lt. Col. Warren G. Stirling, USAF (ret.).

Gus Breymann, whose uncle Gus Heiss was a pilot with both the 27th and 3rd, could always be relied upon to provide advice, track down a fact, or provide other information from his large collection on the subject. We appreciate the help of Mary Catherine May, author of *The Steadfast Line,* which focuses primarily on the 27th at Bataan, by providing troop lists and other group-related documents. We thank historian Noel Tunny, author of *Fight Back from the North* and *Gateway to Victory,* for his help and suggestions. Edward Rogers gave us documents, photographs, and good advice.

We are indebted to author-historian William Bartsch, on whose two excellent books on the U.S. Army Air Corps in the Philippines, *Doomed at the Start* and *December 8, 1941: MacArthur's Pearl Harbor,* we greatly relied on for critical information. He was always available to answer questions, supply documents and photographs, and make corrections and suggestions as well as critically reviewing the resulting manuscript.

Two of the most important source books for our project were *They Fought with What They Had,* by Walter Edmonds, and *Fall of the Philippines,* by Louis Morton. Significant Internet sources were Peter Dunn's Web site, Australia at War (www.ozatwar.com), and G. Wayne Dow's genealogical site, which includes "Unit History—27th Bomb Group (L)" (www.lindadow.net/unit_history-27th_bomb_gp_lt.htm).

We would like to thank those who reviewed the manuscript and made helpful suggestions: Richard Best; Gus Breymann; Ray Brown; Gen. Ralph Eberhart, USAF (ret.); Jack Heyn; Ross Kogel; Jennifer Stephenson Mathews; Col. Paul Poberezny, USAF (ret.), Experimental Aircraft Association founder; Jim Ramsey; Ben Scheiwe; Clyde Stephenson; Robert Stephenson; Dave Stringham; Murray Thomas, M.D.; Australians Michael Marsh, M.D.; Michael Merlini; and Peter Dunn; Philippine-born and educated Lourdes Andaya, M.D.; Gervacio Laqui, PT, MTC; Erlinda de Leon, CSM, MSM; and Cesar Rosales Jr.

We also thank those who allowed us to use diaries or memoirs, including Mrs. Frank Bender; Ron Hubbard; J. Harrison Mangan; and James McAfee Jr. People who provided photographs were William Bartsch; Bill Beck; James Bollich; Gus Breymann; Patrick Callahan (on behalf of Maj. Gen. John Henebry); Mrs. Oliver Doan; Ken Farmer; James Gautier; Henry Gundling; Tom Gerrity Jr.; Ralph Harrell; Jay Harrelson; Jack Heyn; William Hipps Jr.; David Hochman, M.D.; Ron Hubbard; Hilton Keeter; Louis Kolger; Richard Launder; James Lee; Granville Prewett; Henry Rose Jr.; Al Tisonyai; Noel Tunny; Robert Wolfersberger; James Zobel (from the Gen. Douglas MacArthur Foundation); and the National Archives. Robert Hammond helped us with photo editing and graphics. D. James Miller, Ph.D. and Tony Kirk were instrumental in obtaining the use of the painting of Royce's Raid by Richard Taylor that appears on the cover. Our thanks also to the Military Gallery, Wendover, U.K. for permitting its use.

We appreciate the help of Scott Maher, World War II aircraft expert from the Experimental Aircraft Association, and Japan-born and educated Choichi Sugawa, M.D., for checking some of the factual content. We are grateful for the research done on the crash of B-25 #41-12455 by Ralph Harrell and James V. Lee Jr. and Australians Garth Gray, Robert L. Jago, Russ Morrison, George Perkins, Lido Poppi, Stephen Rowley, Karl Stager, Noel Tunny, and Alan Wakeham.

Thanks to Laura Archer and Donna Hammond for editorial assistance and to Carol Stephenson, wife of Larry, for editing and other suggestions. We thank Glenwood's brother Clyde and Clyde's daughter Patti for their Internet research efforts as well as providing other sources of information and suggestions. Finally, we wish to thank editor Thom Lemmons and copyeditor Kevin Brock for their skillful editing of the manuscript after it was submitted to Texas A&M University Press.

OPERATION PLUM

Nearing the Brink of World Conflict

B Y THE SUMMER OF 1940, the world was poised for global war. But no one was certain exactly when and where it would break out. During the prior twelve months, Europe had become engulfed in war. In the Far East, Japan was becoming progressively more belligerent toward its neighbors. Its armies had already invaded the Asian mainland, and by 1940 Japan controlled most of eastern China. Meanwhile, the United States, in its own search for world order, juggled several neutrality acts along with the Ludlow Amendment, which required a national referendum before Congress could declare war except in case of invasion. That summer two isolationist groups, America First and the Ohio (Over the Hill in October) Movement, floated propaganda through print and radio that the nation should stay out of these conflicts. But the longer the United States remained uncommitted, the more one-sided the struggles on the other side of the oceans became.

Although land and naval strength were important, several strategists predicted that air power would win the next Great War. In response, the army and navy accelerated the training of U.S. military pilots in anticipation of America's military involvement somewhere in the world. At the same time, the number of warplanes coming off West Coast assembly lines vastly increased.

Glenwood Stephenson

It is easy to imagine a dusty Plymouth Road King coupe rolling up to the gate of the U.S. Army flight school at Maynor Field near Tuscaloosa, Alabama, in July 1940. Peering inside, the MP on duty spotted the shiny gold bar on the collar of the driver's khaki uniform and delivered a crisp salute.

The gesture should not have taken 2nd Lt. Glenwood "Glen" Gordon Stephenson by surprise, but it did. It was his first salute as a commissioned officer since graduation from one of the finest colleges in the nation the previous month. In his checkered earlier life, Stephenson had been continually penniless, a hobo who rode railroad freight cars, a "dogface" private in the army, and most recently that lowest of human forms, a cadet at the U.S. Military Academy. Salutes were something he was accustomed to giving, not receiving.

Recovering, Stephenson returned the salute and showed his orders. Receiving permission to continue from the guard (and another salute), he put the Plymouth in gear, let out the clutch, and steered it through the gate to his new quarters. He was once again about to put himself on the trainee end of the military pecking order. But the young lieutenant was not dreading the experience—quite the contrary. Just prior to graduation, Stephenson learned that he had been accepted as a student in the U.S. Army Air Corps's primary flight school. Now here in central Alabama, he was reporting for training duty once again.

His aim was to become a pilot. This was one more step along a challenging, fateful path. In June he had completed the four-year course at the Military Academy at West Point, New York, and achieved the ultimate goal of every cadet, which is to earn a bachelor of science degree and be commissioned a second lieutenant, U.S. Army.

Stephenson was born in 1914 in Milwaukee, Wisconsin, to middle-class parents, Gordon and Hazel; his father was a successful electrical engineer. As a youth Stephenson displayed a sense of adventure. Twice, when things did not go his way, he tried running away. He spent hours in the fields and valley near his home searching for mischief with other neighborhood boys. Other times the boy enjoyed riding the streetcar from one end of Milwaukee County to the other alone. A Boy Scout, he financed his streetcar trips by delivering newspapers.

When Stephenson was in seventh grade, his comfortable life in Milwaukee came to an abrupt end. A doctor told his father that the dust at Cutler-Hammer, a manufacturer of electrical devices, and the dampness from nearby Lake Michigan were aggravating his asthma and he should move to the country. The family sold their city house in the spring of 1927. Gordon Stephenson closed on eighty acres of land near Arpin in central Wisconsin and became a farmer.

The family's new home was nothing like their comfortable Milwaukee residence. The house had no electricity or indoor plumbing, a shallow twenty-foot well provided water of dubious quality, and a round oak stove in the downstairs living room provided the only heat; the upstairs bedrooms in winter seemed as cold as the outdoors. The family never had a telephone.

Years of fighting asthma made his father rather frail, weak, and unable to perform strenuous physical activity, so Stephenson and his three brothers, Stuart (two years younger), Roland (four years younger), and Clyde (six years younger), supplied most of the farm labor. Fifteen cows provided milk that the family sold to a nearby cheese factory. Fifty chickens provided eggs, and a large vegetable garden provided food for canning. Grain was planted in the fields, and the trees at the back of the property furnished wood for heat. In the autumn of 1927, Stephenson began making the daily one-mile hike to the single-room Meadowbrook School, which had fewer students in all eight grades than there had been in one grade at his Milwaukee school. A year later he was a freshman at Auburndale High School north of Arpin. Because he lived on a farm, Stephenson drove his family Ford to school.

It was about this time that the Stephensons' finances took a turn for the worse because of the onset of the Great Depression. Profits from the sale of the Milwaukee house had been invested in the stock market, which collapsed in October 1929, destroying all of the family's investments. The wood the four boys cut now was sold to pay their mounting grocery debts. This and their other morning chores before school took a couple of hours minimum. The boys cleaned the cow stalls each morning, milked the cows, and fed them silage from the silo. They cooled the metal cans of milk to prevent spoiling before they delivered the milk to the cheese factory. Then they fed the horses and hitched them to the wagon. The milk cans were loaded afterward, and each, when full, weighed about eighty-five pounds. After the boys emptied them at the factory, the cans were filled with whey, a cheese byproduct, which the brothers fed to the hogs at home. They also had to feed other animals before finally heading off to class. After school, they had other farm chores, which often took hours to complete.

Stephenson applied any extra energy to extracurricular school activities. He played on the varsity basketball team his junior and senior years and participated in school plays as well as the glee club. Academically, teachers lauded his skills but lamented that he seldom used them. During his senior year, the school principal appointed him president of the student council. The twenty seniors in Stephenson's Auburndale High School Class of 1932 graduated that June. Herbert Hoover was still president. *The New York Times* index on the stock market was at its lowest, farm income was down $7 billion, and even college graduates were having difficulty finding work. That was the world confronting Stephenson.

Because of family finances, a four-year college was out of the question. For those interested in becoming teachers, there were one-year programs offered at schools like WOCONO (Wood County Normal) in nearby Wisconsin Rapids. Stephenson moved in with the Fischers, who owned a creamery in which he worked for room and board while attending school. After a semester of teacher methods courses, he did classroom observations for six weeks and then was sent to a rural grade school for two months of actual teaching. Stephenson graduated with his twenty-six classmates in June 1933, but only five found teaching jobs. School districts were not hiring new teachers, and some were even cutting veteran teachers' salaries.

The young man often heard discouraging stories of the Depression from hobos who stopped at the creamery. In a letter to his family, he mentioned that "about a half dozen bums [hobos] a day stop in here for a drink of buttermilk. Everywhere, the general trend seems to be the same. Most of them have traveled to each of the government work projects that are supposed to be for the unemployed, but they say in nearly every instance, the work is done by contract."

Shortly after graduation, in another letter to his parents Stephenson described the bleak job situation in education and industry, suggesting that maybe he should look for "something different" to do. By July he was a member of Battery E, 120th Artillery, Wisconsin National Guard, which was part of the 32nd Division. He was paid a dollar a month per meeting, with two weeks of summer camp required. He continued to work at the Fischer Creamery until the end of August. That month he drove to Waukesha, just west of Milwaukee, to see about enrolling in Carroll College but was unable to find a job to pay for his room, board, and tuition. In November rumors began that the Wood County Civil Works Administration (CWA) might be hiring five hundred men in December to work on new road construction. Even unskilled workers in the CWA were making more than rural schoolteachers. By the end of the year he found employment at Richville Gravel Pit a few miles west of the family farm. During this time, Stephenson's mother showed signs and symptoms of mental illness, and because of this, his sickly father, who was often ill-tempered, spent much of his time taking care of Lillian (seven and a half years old) and David (four years old), the youngest of the six children. In June 1934 Stephenson decided to head west in search of a job either along the way or along the West Coast.

Hobos, those traveling vagabonds of the 1930s, were riding the rails looking for work. By the summer of 1934 estimates stated that 25,000 families and more than 200,000 young adults were wandering through the United States seeking food, clothing, shelter, and a job. Stephenson bought a camera, rolled up his few clothes in a bundle, and hitched a ride to the Green Bay and

4

Western tracks in Wisconsin Rapids, where he hopped a westbound freight. He knew he had to be careful during his journey. Hobos usually hung out in "jungles" where trains stopped or where one line intersected with another heading in a different direction. They were not a criminal element during the Depression. Many, like Stephenson, were educated folks down on their luck and looking for work and adventure; some even referred to themselves as "Knights of the Road." Hobos usually looked out for each other and even developed their own symbol language, using chalk to mark sidewalks, trees, walls, fences, or doors to help their fellow travelers find work, food, or a safe shelter in difficult and dangerous environments. The symbols represented a particular direction or a warning such as "beware of dangerous dog," "a kind lady lives here," "people here will give you food for work," "this is a safe place to camp," "jail good but prisoners starve," "police hostile to tramps," or "bad man lives here."

As Stephenson rode west on the rails, he finally found a job in central Washington as a gandy dancer (one who installs or repairs railroad tracks), which lasted for a good part of the summer. In September the repairs were completed, and the railroad no longer needed the extra workers. He then made his way to California, where he found jobs just as scarce as anywhere. During this time, he wrote to his old high-school sweetheart, Maggie Zwaschka, and described himself as probably "the biggest flop in the class so far."

Stephenson eventually enlisted in the army in November and was sent to Fort McDowell on Angel Island in San Francisco Bay, where he awaited transfer to the Philippines in January 1935. Arriving at Fort McKinley near Manila later that month, the fresh recruit was assigned to Company A, 31st Infantry Regiment and spent most of his time drilling and learning the craft of the soldier.

Back in Arpin, life for his family was not going well. The Stephensons were having a difficult time paying their bills. His father's temperament, fueled by worsening asthma, his wife's mental illness, and the poor economy, was not pleasant. That spring Gordon Stephenson filed a quitclaim deed and turned over the farm to the man who held the mortgage. Also at this time, Stephenson's mother was committed to the Mendota State Hospital in Madison. After hearing of the family problems, Stephenson wrote, "I'm sorry I can't help out financially, as I am still in the hole myself." In late May his family left Arpin and rented a farm near Little Suamico, ten miles north of Green Bay.

Within six months his maturity and intelligence had become evident to several of the company officers. They suggested that he attend the West Point

Prep School at Fort McKinley and then apply for an appointment to the military academy.

For once, Lady Luck was on Stephenson's side. That fall the Philippines held their first national election and selected Manuel Quezon as president. The United States sent a forty-three-member congressional delegation to attend the inauguration, which included Wisconsin senator F. Ryan Duffy. While touring the military installation at Fort McKinley, Senator Duffy met Stephenson, who impressed him, and he encouraged the serviceman to apply to West Point. Afterward Stephenson soldiered on, but in a February 1936 letter the War Department informed him that he was the principal-at-large nominee of Senator Duffy. In May Stephenson left for New York by ship via California and the Panama Canal.

That summer the prototype of the new four-engine Boeing B-17 bomber was being evaluated. The air corps wanted it for coastal defense, its primary mission at that time, as well as for strategic bombardment if that was needed. The Army General Staff, however, had already cut the production order from sixty-five to thirteen airplanes and in June had vetoed a request by the air corps for additional planes. The army brass thought the range of this future super-bomber was excessive, one of the generals telling the airmen, "A couple hundred miles of range was enough to satisfy the interest of any Army commander."[1]

On Wednesday, July 1, 1936, on the plain of West Point, Stephenson took the oath of "Duty, Honor, and Country." Finances plagued him the first year there. He did not realize that once accepted to the academy, he or his family had to deposit $300 to cover the cost of the plebe uniforms, books, and other necessities. The new cadet was both embarrassed and apologetic when his father received the bill, but fortunately, he was able to borrow part of the money from one of his aunts. Also, to economize, he had to miss many varsity football games and social events. Stephenson often referred to himself at West Point as a "dog face," a nickname for lowly infantry grunts, which he had been in the Philippines.

Near the end of Stephenson's sophomore year, the Army Air Corps decided to test its navigational skills with the new long-range bomber, practicing the interception of an enemy fleet sailing toward the East Coast. An Italian ocean liner, *Rex,* en route to New York served as the target for this exercise. Three B-17s were dispatched on the mission, locating the *Rex* 625 miles at sea. The liner was photographed and a message was dropped on her deck. The flight on May 12 was broadcast on radio coast to coast and made front-page headlines across the country the next day. Naval officers, however, were incensed by this intrusion into their territory. The navy reminded the Army General Staff of a rule promulgated by the War Department on September 1, 1936, at the apparent insistence of the navy, that limited Army Air Corps operations to an area within 100 miles of the continental coast. This rule would now be enforced, and the army promised to keep its airmen on a tighter leash.[2]

After successfully completing his first two years at West Point, the cadets were given the summer of 1938 off. Stephenson had not seen his family or friends back home in the four years since he had left Wisconsin as a hobo.

Much had changed for the Gordon Stephenson family since the last time the eldest son saw them. The Stephensons now lived near Little Suamico, a rural community just north of Green Bay, prompting Cadet Stephenson to write home for directions. Brothers Stuart, Roland, and Clyde were now taller than Stephenson, and Lillian and David could not remember what their absent brother looked like. And his mother was now confined permanently to a mental institution. But one thing remained constant for the family; although never on relief, their struggle to survive the Depression was a daily challenge. Even though Stuart, Roland, and Clyde were good students, each had to drop out of school for at least a year at one time or another to help support the family. That summer, the cadet worked as a hired hand at a farm less than a mile from his family's place, receiving twenty dollars a month plus room and board. He visited his family frequently and his mother at the mental institution.

Clyde Stephenson later remembered: "I don't recall Glen being any different the summer he was home from West Point—although he was more mature. I couldn't see Glen acting big time because he came from such a poor family like ours. Glen had a good sense of humor, an outgoing personality, was adventurous, and definitely a leader."

On August 22 Cadet Stephenson's visit came to an end. He said goodbye to his family and boarded a train, figuring it would be only twenty-one months before he would see them all again following graduation. That summer, however, was the last time his close relatives and Wisconsin friends ever saw Stephenson.

During his junior year, he started showing an interest in flying.

U.S. Army Air Corps

U.S. Army pilots had been in airplanes since before Stephenson was born, in fact beginning only eight years after the Wright brothers' first successful flight. The army purchased three Wright Flyers and two Curtiss aircraft in 1911, its criteria for these heavier-than-air flying machines including that they carry two men aloft for at least one hour at a speed of forty miles per hour. Two second lieutenants, Henry "Hap" Arnold and Thomas Milling, were sent to Dayton, Ohio, to begin flying lessons at the Wrights' flying school that May. In June they became the first army officers to complete the course and returned to their base in Maryland. Wright Model B Military Flyers soon followed, crated in a railroad boxcar.[3]

After America entered World War I in 1917, the U.S. Army Air Service (which later became the Army Air Corps) swelled to more than 150,000 officers and enlisted men. Hap Arnold, who was a captain when the war began, rose to the temporary rank of colonel, serving at army headquarters in Washington as the executive officer of the Air Division, which was then part of the Signal Corps. By June 1919, with postwar demobilization, the air service shrunk to 5,500 officers and 21,500 enlisted men. In 1924 the air service conducted the first successful flight around the world, which began in Seattle on April 6 with four Douglas World Cruisers; two aircraft finished the journey 175 days later. Two years after this the Army Air Service became the Army Air Corps. In 1938 Major General Arnold, a member of the West Point Class of 1907, was made chief of the Army Air Corps.[4] His World War I duties had included dealing with aircraft and engine production as well as pilot training. This experience well prepared him for things to come.[5]

Just as Stephenson was beginning his senior year, Germany invaded Poland on September 1, 1939. Two days later France and Great Britain declared war on Germany. Within the next several days, many of the countries belonging to Britain's Commonwealth of Nations, including Australia, Canada, India, Newfoundland, New Zealand, and South Africa, also declared war on Germany. On November 30 Russian troops invaded Finland. Germany attacked Denmark and Norway five months later.

Pres. Franklin Delano Roosevelt was a proponent of a strong air force and on May 16, 1940, endorsed the expansion of the air corps by 2,748 flying cadets and 7,000 enlisted men.[6] One former air corps pilot recently recalled about this buildup: "General Hap Arnold, Chief of the Army Air Corps, was smart as hell. He decided that the only way that the President would have enough pilots for all the aircraft that were being built was to recruit them early. I went to every college town and explained that I was in town by orders of President Roosevelt, and I'd want to interview people about going into the Air Corps."[7] Those selected were put on a roster so that when the flying schools opened, men were ready to attend immediately.

On May 19 Germany invaded Belgium, Luxembourg, and the Netherlands. As the Nazi regime continued to roll through Europe, Stephenson told his brother Stuart in a letter that the United States "would be damned fools to sit back, doing nothing, and watch other democracies fall." In another letter home he wrote, "We are encouraged not to express too much in the way of opinions relative to government policies concerning the war in Europe, so consequently, I don't say much—nor do any of us—even though we think quite a bit and draw conclusions among ourselves."

Right before his June graduation, Stephenson obtained a low-cost military loan and bought a 1940 Plymouth Road King coupe for $739.40. He had survived the academy's four rigorous years and probably thought the tough times were behind him. But they had not yet begun. General Arnold's eldest son, Henry H. "Hank" Arnold Jr., was also a member of the West Point Class of 1940, but unlike Stephenson, he was denied air corps training because of poor eyesight.

On June 22 France surrendered to Germany. The fall of France eliminated most congressional disagreement about the need for massive expansion of national defense. Arnold and his air corps were soon given $1.5 billion with instructions to "get an air force."[8] During the second week of August, the Germans began massive air attacks on England.

Army Air Corps Pilot Training

It was an intense environment that Stephenson stepped into that summer in Alabama. Primary Flight School lasted about three months. Much of that time was spent flying with instructors in the primary trainer, a Stearman biplane. The wings, the fuselage, and the tail assembly of the aircraft were covered with cloth fabric instead of metal, the wings painted bright yellow and the fuselage a bright blue. There were two cockpits in tandem, each with a single seat, from which the plane could be flown; the instructor would be seated in the back and the student pilot in the front. These airplanes took off and landed at a speed of 40–50 mph and cruised between 60–90 mph. Students learned not only to fly during this phase but also some acrobatics to get a better feel for the plane. Classroom sessions followed daily early morning physical-fitness workouts.

By the end of the week, the weary pilots were looking for excitement. Fellow flying cadet and West Point classmate Warren Stirling recalled: "Tuscaloosa County was dry. But 30 miles south in the next county, alcohol was permitted. Just across the county line was a bar called the Cotton Patch. Every Friday night, each student would migrate—as if it were a magnet—to the Cotton Patch to drink beer. They had a juke box in the corner that played continuously."

While the flyers were listening to tunes like "In the Mood," "Georgia on My Mind," "Moonlight Serenade," and "Let's Dance," a controversial presidential election was approaching. Roosevelt was seeking an unprecedented third term, and before the election he urged the passage of the Selective Training and Service Act. The return of the draft was a risky political move. In September 1940 Congress passed the measure, which provided for the annual induction into the military of 900,000 men between the ages of twenty-one and thirty-six. This was the first draft or conscription law enacted in the United States during peacetime.[9]

Also that month, Japan entered into the Tripartite Pact with Germany and Italy. The latter two had already agreed to come to each other's aid in the so-called Pact of Steel. This considerably strengthened Japan's hand in dealing with America, as the alliance bound the three powers to assist one another if attacked by a power not yet engaged in the European or Asiatic wars.

In Washington, Roosevelt engineered a destroyers-for-naval-bases deal with Great Britain. Britain got fifty U.S. Navy destroyers, while the United States received ninety-nine-year leases on several naval and air bases in the Atlantic and Caribbean. This was a major departure, many critics cried, from America's position of neutrality. Shortly before the election, Roosevelt calmed voters who feared he was a warmonger by declaring in a Boston speech, "Your boys are not going into any foreign wars." He was reelected with 84 percent of the electoral vote.[10]

Weeks later, while on a vacation cruise on the USS *Tuscaloosa,* the president received an urgent message from British prime minister Winston Churchill. To defeat Germany, Churchill said England needed every imaginable piece of war equipment plus seven thousand combat planes. Roosevelt's response became the basis for the eventual Lend-Lease Act. His theory was that if the United States gave them the needed goods, England could defeat fascism and America would not have to get involved by sending manpower. After the war was over, they would return the materials that were lent to them. After all, Roosevelt had declared, "We must be the great arsenal of democracy."

By November, Stephenson had completed sixty-five hours of flying and the first phase of his pilot training. He would have been quite pleased with himself, for if you were going to flunk out, it usually happened during Primary Flight School. Washouts were those who lacked the necessary flying skills, especially those related to landing. Stephenson and his colleagues next moved on to the Southeast Air Corps Basic Flying School at Maxwell Field in Montgomery, Alabama. Leaving Tuscaloosa, the cadet pilots stopped at the Cotton Patch one last time for some of their delicious country-fried chicken.

Maxwell Field, according to Stirling, was "one of the finest facilities of the Air Corps." The men now entered Basic Flying School, which emphasized instrument flying, navigational training, weather study, and day/night flying in BT-13s and BT-14s. These trainer aircraft were sturdier aluminum-skinned monoplanes (having a single set of wings). They had an enclosed cockpit with two seats, one behind the other, with flight controls with each. The student pilot would sometimes sit in the back and the instructor in the front seat, at other times the reverse, but after the students became familiar with the plane, they often flew solo. BT-13s and BT-14s, mounting a 450-hp Pratt and Whitney engine, were much faster than the earlier Stearman biplanes. The cadet pilots also spent time in the Link Trainer, which was a mechanical mockup of a cockpit in which instrument flying could be practiced without leaving the ground. In a fall letter Stephenson described the intensified training as "busy all the time getting up at 5:30 to drill the flying cadets at 6:30. Then ground school all morning, and fly from 12:00 to 5:00 every day. Have to keep awake all the time as we have about 50 instruments and plenty of power and speed. Often twenty or more ships try to land at the same time."

Getting leave time was next to impossible. Each flying-school session usually lasted about four months but now was compressed to two to three months because of the need for more pilots with the expected outbreak of war. Thanksgiving furlough was canceled. Fortunately, Stirling and his wife, Florence, invited Stephenson and his roommates, Bert Hoffman and Jim Downing—all bachelors and members of the West Point Class of 1940—over for a turkey dinner. In many ways this was an ill-fated dining party, for Stephenson, Hoffman, and Downing would all die in air crashes during the war, and their host would spend three and a half years as a POW. But that was in the future. Of more immediate concern for the men, all four completed Basic in late December.

On December 28 they began their final phase of flight instruction, Advanced Flying School, also at Maxwell. Pilots used AT-6 trainer airplanes, and the emphasis turned to night flying, instrument flying, cross-country flying, and aerial gunnery. Flying the advanced trainer, with its 600-hp supercharged engine, retractable landing gear, and .30-caliber Browning machine gun, was more similar to flying a fighter of that time. Aerial gunnery consisted of in-flight target practice with some stationary targets on the ground and others towed behind another plane. The .30-caliber machine gun fired twenty rounds per second. The aerial target, about twenty feet long, made out of cloth, and resembling a big windsock with the larger end of the cone closest to the towing plane, was attached by a steel cable. When bullets hit it, the target would ripple. Every so often the gun fired a tracer so the pilot could observe the path of the shots. It was not uncommon to find bullet holes in the tow plane after target practice. The seating arrangement in the AT-6 was the same as the basic trainer, where the instructor sat in one seat either in front of or behind the student pilot.

On March 14 Stephenson graduated in the Class of 41-C with an aeronautical rating of Pilot. After the three flying schools, he had 201 hours of flying time, 64 percent of it flying solo, and a flying grade of C, very satisfactory. In his ground-school subjects he had a 92.6 percent average.

Becoming an army pilot was not an easy task. From the time Stephenson entered flight school until after the end of the war, the washout rate for this training regimen was 60 percent. Student pilots who did not make it often became navigators or bombardiers.[11] Upon his graduation, Stephenson was ordered to report to the 27th Bombardment Group in Savannah, Georgia. West Point classmates Stirling (of Philadelphia, Pennsylvania), James McAfee (of Charlotte, North Carolina), and Julius B. "Zeke" Summers (of Somerville, Tennessee) were also assigned to the unit. A new adventure was about to begin.

Savannah and Hunter Field

Its official name was the 27th Bombardment Group (Light, or L). The "L" designation at the end of its name indicated that the unit was equipped with smaller types of bombers, which were often more nimble and used in close support of ground troops. The aircraft needed to be fast and maneuverable, equipped with both forward- and rear-firing guns, and able to carry a relatively large payload.[12] They would swoop in low with their machine guns blazing and drop their ordnance. The airplanes themselves were referred to as "attack aircraft" and had the prefix "A" (attack) as part of the model number. The 27th at this time flew single-engine Northrop A-17s and twin-engine Curtiss A-18s. It was also referred to as a "Bomb Group" and an "Attack Group," the latter being the name of Army Air Corps units flying these types of aircraft up until the late 1930s. In addition, 27th pilots flew Douglas B-18s, which were twin-engine medium bombers and had been considered state of the art in the mid 1930s. The designation "Medium," or "M," indicated a group that primarily flew medium bombers such as twin-engine B-18s, B-25s, and B-26s. The designation "Heavy," or "H," meant a unit flew larger four-engine bombers like the B-17s, B-24s, and later B-29s.

The 27th Bombardment Group was constituted on December 22, 1939, and activated on February 1, 1940, when the elite 3rd Bombardment Group

1. 1940 West Point graduates (top, L to R) James McAfee, Glenwood Stephenson, (bottom, L to R) Warren Stirling, and Julius "Zeke" Summers. *Courtesy* USMA Howitzer

was split in two at Barksdale Field in Louisiana. In October the 27th and the 3rd moved to Hunter Field in Savannah, Georgia, so the airmen could practice low-level attacks against ships off the Atlantic coast. The 27th originally consisted of the 15th, 16th, 17th, and Headquarters Squadrons, but the 15th was sent to Lawson Field at Fort Benning, Georgia, then replaced by the 91st Squadron. Savannah's civil airfield had recently been named for hometown World War I flying ace Frank Hunter. In ninety days more than three thousand Savannah-area workers changed the city airport into an army air base, adding barracks, hangars, and runways. Although civilian flights continued temporarily at Hunter, local officials recognized that a new commercial airport was needed. Eventually, a new facility emerged northwest of the city, but in 1941 all air activity was at Hunter, or as the Army Air Corps called it at the time, the Savannah Air Base.

About the time Stephenson motored to Savannah, the 27th had received twin-engine Douglas A-20 Havoc attack bombers fresh from the assembly line in California. Pilots took trains and sometimes Douglas DC-3 twin-engine transports to the plant at Long Beach and ferried the A-20s to Savannah, flying in formation and making stops along the way. In his memoir pilot Ron Hubbard said about the thrill of flying these brand-new high-performance warbirds: "The feeling of power and speed, it was the first modern plane that I had flown. When the air speed crept up over 200 mph, I screamed exultantly. It would seem slow now, but at the time it was wild. I was in love with the plane. The thrill was greater than when I checked out much later in the jet fighters."

Hubbard was a first lieutenant in the Headquarters Squadron at the time. He had grown up in Warren, Ohio, and spent the year after high school graduation working in a steel mill to earn money to attend college. After two and a half years at nearby Hiram College, he dropped out when his funds ran out and joined the Army Air Corps, with the intent of earning enough money to return to school and obtain a degree in mathematics. The army sent him to San Antonio, where he completed his primary and basic courses at Randolph Field, nicknamed the "West Point of the Army Air Corps." He graduated from the advance course at nearby Kelly Field in October 1938, then served as a pilot in attack squadrons in Hawaii until his transfer to the Headquarters Squadron in 1941.

Stephenson's first flights in Savannah were in the older, slower B-18 bomber. In a letter home he described his often-dangerous flights: "Cruise at about 150–180 mph and land at 90–100 mph. Last Sunday, I made an ordered flight to Louisville, Kentucky, and we almost didn't get back as one

2. Pilots Gus Heiss and Tom Gerrity with A-20s in background, summer 1941. *Courtesy Gus Breymann*

of the props got to throwing oil from the engine. Lost 14 gallons in 3 hours, which is a lot of oil." In the same letter he mentioned that fuel put in his plane contained some water, causing his engines to quit before he got on the runway. Another plane fueled at the same time crashed just after takeoff, injuring the crew.

Sand was also tough on the planes in Savannah. Stephenson noted that it was "especially hard on the airplane engines, even the cars. We're lucky here if we get half the normal life out of an engine before it is ready for a complete overhaul." Sometimes sod was laid to cut down on the blowing sand. Pfc. Paul Lankford of the 16th Squadron remembered that because of the soft soil, the pilots would have to rev the engines to almost maximum power to jockey the big planes into their parking space. "The air base commander was giving twenty young Southern belles a tour of our airbase. As the pilot turned the plane to park it, he throttled the engines to full rev. The skirts and petticoats went almost straight up over their heads and the ladies had all they could do to try and pull them down. It was quite a sight!"

Lankford, who was from Gadsden, Alabama, was typical of the younger enlisted men in the 27th. He had joined the army in October 1939 shortly after graduating from high school. Following in-processing, he was sent to Barksdale Field and attended a six-week Army Air Corps training course taught by 1st Lt. William Hipps of the 3rd Bomb Group, who, like Lankford in February 1940, would soon find himself in the 16th Squadron of the 27th. He was sent to Love Field in Dallas, Texas, where he completed a six-month aircraft-engine maintenance course in March 1941 and then returned to the 27th.

Stephenson's job with the 27th, besides being a pilot, was as engineering officer for the 16th Squadron. He was third in command for a squadron of fifteen officers, 190 enlisted men, and eighteen planes. There were many split ups of the 27th as the Army Air Corps expanded and some personnel were sent elsewhere to form new units. New men arrived daily from various mechanical and specialist schools. Stephenson observed in a letter that everyone had their yellow-fever shots and one unit expected to be sent to the Caribbean. He thought his unit might be next. They even had classes in Spanish on the base, which further fueled that speculation.

The 27th and Airborne Artillery

After the success of the Nazi Stuka dive bombers early in the war, the army and the air corps decided that they needed dive bombers too. In late spring of 1941, the 27th would be one of the first units to receive them. The German Junkers 87, better known as the Stuka, made its World War II debut over Poland and was the most conspicuous element in the fearsome Blitzkrieg. While Luftwaffe fighter pilots controlled the air over many European countries, Stukas flew precision-bombing missions in support of the rapidly advancing German armies, functioning as the field commander's airborne artillery.[13] Although these planes proved highly effective, the U.S. Army prior to the war had little interest in this form of bombing, mainly because of performance limitations, which they had found inherent in the design of such airplanes.[14] They were developing larger two- and four-engine aircraft that could fly longer distances and carry greater bomb loads. The U.S. Navy, however, found dive bombers effective for precision bombing and for attacking maneuvering ships. These planes typically carried one large bomb, which was capable of crippling or even sinking a ship, attached to the underbelly of its fuselage.[15] After the pilot initiated the dive, the closer he got to the target before releasing his weapon, the more accurate he tended to be (but he still had to allow enough altitude to safely pull out of the dive). Although the accuracy of the bomb-delivery system increased the closer the plane got to the target, unfortunately for the pilot, so did the effectiveness of antiaircraft and other defensive fire.

3. Douglas A-24 in dive. Note the perforated dive brakes deployed on the wings. *Courtesy University of Chicago Press*

The U.S. Navy had dive bombers. In May 1941 the 27th Bombardment Group started getting these single-engine aircraft, which were called SBD (Scout Bomber Douglas)-2s and SBD-3s. The army referred to them as the Douglas A-24 Dauntless dive bomber. Some came directly from the navy, and others came from the Douglas factory in Long Beach. Pilots from the 27th would travel to California, then fly the planes back to Georgia.

Stephenson's real ambition, however, was to fly one of the new twin-engine A-20 light bombers. He remarked in a letter that he might have to go to McDill Field in Tampa to be checked out in one. Because of a one-pilot compartment, the first flight was solo, and the men needed room for possible error. McDill had 7,000-foot-long runways that were 360 feet wide; Hunter's were only around 4,000 feet. The light bombers could cruise at 300 mph and landed at from 110 to 130 mph. When Stephenson returned to Savannah, the 27th was preparing for maneuvers. But he was not going. He was one of a handful of group pilots instead detailed to "Ferrying Command" duties.

Air Ferrying Command

President Roosevelt signed the Lend-Lease Act into law on March 11, 1941, just about the time Stephenson was graduating from flight school at Maxwell. The bill went well beyond the destroyers-for-bases deal of a few months previous. Congress appropriated $7 billion to initiate the arrangement. Ships, tanks, guns, and planes were now headed to Britain. The United States remained neutral in name only and inched closer to entering the European war.

England needed bombers, and the Douglas Long Beach plant was producing them at a rapid rate. What were needed were trained pilots to fly them from the West Coast to the East Coast for shipment overseas. On May 29 the air corps created the Air Ferrying Command to fly aircraft from U.S. factories to Canadian and American Atlantic ports for delivery. At first factory crews delivered the planes, but by mid-July the ferrying task was in the hands of the Army Air Corps. Some aircraft destined for the British, such as four-engine B-17 bombers, were flown directly to England using air-ferrying routes with refueling stops along the way.

The war continued to spread. On June 22 Germany invaded the Soviet Union.

At the beginning of July, Stephenson, James McAfee, Robert Ruegg, Arthur Rush, Robert Stafford, and possibly a few others from the 16th Squadron were ordered to California. Initially staying at the Hotel Carmel in Santa Monica, Stephenson sent a postcard to his brother Clyde indicating that his assignment of flying one plane a week across the country would probably take forty-five days. In a letter to his brother Stuart, he described these flights: "made the last trip from Long Beach to New York City in 2–1/2 days [actually fourteen hours of flying time]. We have to cruise around 200 mph to conserve gasoline as we get the best hourly consumption rate at that speed."

The Long Beach Airport (Mines Field) was where the men usually boarded the Douglas aircraft. The company, however, was having difficulty producing enough planes, and Boeing took up the slack. Some pilots would go to a location near Seattle to ferry the Boeing-built planes to the East Coast.

The aircraft being delivered were similar to the A-20s the 27th were flying. The British designated them the DB-7B Havoc. The paint color of the Royal Air Force was slightly different than the American A-20s, using the RAF red, white, and blue roundel instead of the American white star. Most shuttle crews for the DB-7Bs consisted of only one person, the pilot. Sometimes a group would fly in formation, other times the men just kept visual contact with one another. Depending on which route the DB-7B pilots took determined where they stopped to refuel on their way to Floyd Bennett Field in New York City. Montreal, Canada, also received planes, and British pilots were on hand to fly some of them to England by a northern route.

Pilots often chose their own course and altitude cross-country. The rules were somewhat restrictive as the planes were not to be flown at night or under instrument conditions. Occasionally, the men even got to have fun with the planes. Ruegg recalled that one time he and others flew close to the ground and chased antelope across the prairie.

Frank "Pete" Bender, who had grown up in Brooklyn, New York, was another pilot assigned to the Ferrying Command. He attended Hobart College in upstate New York, making the All-American lacrosse team. He joined the Army Air Corps in 1939 and completed his primary pilot's course in Tuscaloosa. Bender was then sent to Randolph Field for his basic course and then to Kelly Field. Upon graduation in May 1940, he was assigned to the 3rd Bomb Group in Savannah.

After completing his Ferrying Command duties and returning to Savannah in September, Bender was reassigned to Stephenson's 16th Squadron of the 27th. In his memoir he reveals that the ferrying trips "were relatively leisurely, and while not boring, were not really challenging to us 'hot pilots.' But boys will be boys, and we quickly learned that we could avoid any boredom that might have bothered us en route by performing some mild aerobatics, such as slow rolls, which would keep boredom at bay."[16]

Often, when one plane was delivered, the pilots had to immediately hop on a commercial airliner to return to the West Coast. Stephenson complained once in a letter about landing at Floyd Bennett Field and then making a mad dash across Brooklyn to get to La Guardia, where they were holding a West Coast–bound plane for him.

Returning to Long Beach was sometimes an adventure. On one occasion poor weather kept Stephenson's flight grounded in Denver, so he took a train to Salt Lake City and caught another plane to Long Beach. Problems also developed heading east. After staying overnight in El Paso, the next leg of the trip found him grounded in St. Louis because of a structural problem. Afterward, all DB-7Bs were temporarily grounded.

Several times Stephenson flew into Chicago on his way back to California and hoped he could visit his family in Wisconsin. Each time his day off was denied. By the winter of 1940–41, the Stephenson family had given up on being farmers. His brother Roland was then an engineering student at the University of Wisconsin in Madison, and his younger brother Clyde had joined the Marines and was stationed with the U.S. Pacific Fleet at Pearl Harbor. Money continued to be a problem. In August, however, Stephenson was able to send Roland thirty dollars to buy a new suit and also sent brother Stuart a ten-dollar check to "buy something nice for the family."

In mid-September Stephenson learned that he would be returning to the 27th in Savannah by October 1. He fully expected to move to a new station shortly thereafter. While he was away, the 27th went to Louisiana on maneuvers in August and had a good opportunity to test their A-20s and dive bombers.

Louisiana Maneuvers

Heat, humidity, dust, chiggers, mosquitoes, malaria, snakes, and mud were daily fare in Louisiana for the 27th as they and other units began the largest U.S. military maneuvers to that time. More than 350,000 soldiers—nineteen full divisions—and fifty thousand vehicles participated. War games were a vital training tool in preparation for the war everyone thought was coming but no one wanted to discuss. The 27th was involved in two training maneuvers, one at Barksdale Field near Shreveport and the other at Lake Charles in the Louisiana bayous. While foot soldiers of the "Red Army" and the "Blue Army" fought through swamps and mud on the ground, the air corps practiced bombing, strafing, and air support for both sides. There were a few accidents, as evidenced by this excerpt from the *27th Reports:*

> The entire first phase went well with only one or two minor mishaps. Harry Mangan on a test flight in an A-20 had one engine go out

on the take-off and landed in the Red River, a little wet and a little wiser. Dick Birnn tore out six high-tension lines and blacked out 7 towns, coming out O. K. except for a power company complaint. Then, too, there was the episode told of the 27th when they bombed and routed their own cavalry. But who can tell which side one's on when he's on both.

Fortunately the errant bombs did not injure anyone on the ground; they were only flour sacks. In the first week alone, seventeen soldiers died—seven by motor accidents, one by suicide, two by drowning, two by disease, and five by airplanes. Later a few others succumbed to coral-snake bites.[17]

Practicing without real weapons was far from ideal. Besides the flour sacks for bombs, according to Ron Hubbard, trucks and jeeps simulated tanks and stovepipes became antitank guns. Soldiers fired blanks. Most of the time the men slept on drenched soil.

The 27th flew more missions than any other group at the maneuvers. It was during this time that they used the airplane they were supposed to take overseas—A-24 dive bombers. By October the entire group was back in Savannah, where Stephenson rejoined the unit. In a late September letter sent to his brother Stuart from Long Beach, Stephenson included some unexpected news. "May get married if I get moved off to Texas or some such place so don't be surprised. Not promising anything." His family did not even know that he was dating.

Ann Grace Nail

This abrupt two-sentence mention of marriage in the middle of a four-page letter to Stuart jolted the Stephenson clan. There was no way to question Stephenson by phone, for the family did not have one. By the time a letter arrived seeking answers, Glenwood Stephenson and Ann Grace Nail of Savannah already had their marriage license.

His romance in one sense should not have caused surprise. The girls at Auburndale High School had adored him, female classmates at Wood County Normal found him good looking, there were numerous pictures of him at West Point with elegantly dressed young ladies by Lake Delafield and Flirtation Walk, and he constantly questioned his brothers about their love lives. Yet in his letters he never once mentioned dating anyone.

Ann Nail was a slender beauty with radiant brown hair who possessed an engaging smile and was almost five years younger than Stephenson. She was eighteen in 1938 and an usherette at the historic Lucas Theatre. Two years

4. Bob Wolfersberger preparing to "wind up" an A-24 dive bomber at Lake Charles, Louisiana, August 1941. Note the leather helmet, standard for both the pilot and rear gunner. *Courtesy Bob Wolfersberger*

later she ran the cash register at Morrison's Cafeteria a few blocks away. Both spots were popular with the air-base officers. In the early months at the new base, the food was not very good, and officers often drove downtown for a good meal and entertainment. Capt. William Hipps had introduced Nail to Stephenson at the Officers Club at Hunter in March 1941. The two hit it off immediately.

Nail's family came to Savannah from Reidsville, a small town forty miles west of Savannah. By the time Stephenson came into the family picture, the parents had separated. She continued to live with her mother and on occasion brought her new pilot-boyfriend home.

Her mother adored Stephenson. He was a West Point graduate, good looking, humorous, and steadily employed. He represented a secure future for her daughter, who already had suffered through an impulsive and secretive first marriage. When she was eighteen, Nail had eloped one night in April 1938 and was married before a judge. The union lasted only two weeks before the young bride was living back home. Stephenson's whirlwind courtship slowed in July, when he was assigned to the Ferrying Command. Cards and letters from the various cities he flew into and an occasional visit to Savannah kept the relationship going. When he returned in late September, Stephenson was convinced that no matter where he was going to be sent next, he would get married.

The couple exchanged vows on October 6 in a quiet Monday afternoon ceremony at the home of Rev. Arthur Jackson, the pastor of the First Baptist Church. After the wedding, the couple toured New York City, visited the Catskills, and even spent a day at West Point. The honeymoon, however, was short. The 27th had received its secret orders. They were to be part of Operation PLUM and were scheduled to leave around October 19. While on his honeymoon, Stephenson was promoted to first lieutenant.

"This Rumor Has Gone Too Far!"

ACRONYMS AND CODE NAMES played a big role in the military lexicon of World War II. "Radar," "OVERLORD," and "D-Day" all had an additional life once the war was over. One name, however, seemed to fade away not long after its birth. That was Operation PLUM. The word "PLUM" was stamped on every piece of equipment and footlocker in October after the 27th received their secret orders. The reason this term has received little attention decades later is that for many it came to mean death, for most three and a half years as a POW, and for all an experience with extreme frustration.

When Stephenson returned from his brief honeymoon trip to New York, most of the officers knew where the 27th was headed—the Philippines. Enlisted men like SSgt. Louis Kolger considered this a chance for travel and great adventure. "Our destination was supposed to be secret, and when the subject came up at Hunter Air Base, people would tell you so. On the other hand, you could go to any saloon in Savannah, and they would tell you that the 27th was being sent to the Philippines."

Operation PLUM

Although many members of the 27th thought that PLUM was an acronym and meant either "Philippines-Luzon-Unaccompanied-Manila" or "Philippines-Luzon-Manila," it was actually a code name for the "U.S. Army in the Philippines."[1] Pfc. Leland Sims of the Headquarters Squadron recalled that as a joke he and several others informed their families that PLUM stood for "Places Lost Unto Man." Those who jokingly called it "PLUM to Hell," however, would turn out to have the most accurate description of what was to follow.

Some who had initially signed on escaped the assignment by pure luck. Pvt. Ralph Harrell had been with the 3rd Bombardment Group at Barksdale

Field in Louisiana and moved with them to Savannah. He missed the Louisiana maneuvers in September because he was attending a technical school. A week before the 27th left for the Philippines, one of his hometown buddies in the 3rd, Pvt. Granville "Buck" Prewett, said, "Ralph, if you get out now and don't go overseas, you will miss all of the excitement, and have nothing to talk about." Prewett had just signed up for the 27th on a bulletin board in the cafeteria. Harrell also went over and put his name on the list. Later that day, however, his girlfriend in Savannah talked him out of it, and he crossed off his name. A day later the orders were cut, and those on the list were in the 27th and no longer part of the 3rd. By going to the Philippines, Buck definitely had something to talk about. He would endure the Bataan Death March and three and a half years in Japanese prison camps.

Many looked back on that month of October as being one of utter confusion. New men were suddenly assigned to the 27th. There were a few desertions by those who did not want to go overseas. Unfortunately, much equipment needed for the Philippines was left behind. Kolger was told to leave all his supplies and equipment in Savannah with the understanding that it would be replaced when he got to his new base. He left Savannah without as much as a screwdriver to service a bomb group.

Some took items that seemed illogical at first. Hubbard got some advice from a friend when he brought his wife to her parents' home in Ohio. "Ran into an old retired army officer who had served in the Far East. Inspired by his stories of the hunting possibilities in the Philippines, I visited the local sporting goods store and bought the only big game rifle they had, a Winchester 348." Since most of the officers and enlisted men assumed they were going to a warm climate, they packed such items as golf clubs and swimming suits. Gus Heiss, a pilot in the 17th Squadron from Houston, Texas, packed a small, but good, phonograph and his library of classical records.

Despite the uncertainty over what to take, one thing seemed certain—the 27th would have A-24 dive bombers in the Philippines. Many of the pilots had only a few flights in the plane before they left Hunter. The promise was that the bombers would be there for them when they arrived in Manila.

Majs. Reginald F. C. Vance and John "Big Jim" Davies, the two senior officers in the 27th, went out to California ahead of the group and visited Sacramento, where they saw "Pop" Liggett, who commanded the Army Air Corps depot there. The officers tried to expedite the process of getting their bombers transported to the West Coast and then to the Philippines. The planes had to be disassembled, crated, and shipped by rail to California, where they would then be loaded on a ship.

Major Vance had recently returned from England, where he had been an observer for the Army Air Corps during the Battle of Britain. After his arrival, he was assigned to command a squadron of observation planes in Savannah, which was not part of the 27th Bomb Group. When it was determined that the 27th would be sent to the Philippines, Vance, who was senior to Davies in both age and years in the military, was then assigned to the unit as its new commander. Major Davies, who was the operations officer of the 27th, became assistant commander. Davies's nickname, "Big Jim," was well deserved as he was said to have stood six feet, four and a half inches tall by some and six feet, six inches by others. He was born in Piedmont, California, in 1903 and attended the University of California, where he earned a varsity letter as a javelin thrower. Soon after graduation in 1928, he joined the Army Air Corps and obtained his pilot training in California and San Antonio. Among his numerous previous air-corps assignments was a stint with the 3rd Attack (Bomb) Group in the mid-1930s.

By October 21 the five troop trains were loaded, and supposedly all took different routes to avoid sabotage.[2] The A-24s were to meet them in California. The next day the men were moving west. The 16th Squadron boarded their train around noon. It was raining hard, and the men felt mixed emotions at their departure. Stephenson shared a compartment with fellow pilot Pete Bender. Leland Sims recalled that a five-day trip in a crowded train without the opportunity for a shower was more than quite annoying. Many thought the military would arrange a trip like those advertised in magazines. The reality was far from this ideal. Hubbard in his memoir states: "lured by the remembrance of a couple of train trips in the past, I decided to volunteer to travel with the troop train. It was a very bad mistake. Stops were at isolated sidings way off in the boondocks with bored hours of waiting for the tracks to clear. Food or drink, when it did come, was mainly dried out sandwiches and cold coffee." The trains arrived in San Francisco between October 26 and 29, but not all of the men rode the rails. Several officers went by car, while a few others flew.

On Angel Island the men each received numerous vaccinations for prevention of the various diseases they might encounter in the tropics. While the *President Coolidge* was being loaded with equipment, the officers toured San Francisco. A foreshadowing of the disaster awaiting the 27th in the Philippines occurred while loading the ship. On October 29 a boxcar waiting on a siding of the pier, which contained the personal belongings of the officers, somehow broke loose and rolled off the dock and into the bay. A crane and a barge had to be procured. It took a day to retrieve the boxcar and another day to unload it. Each officer claimed his belongings, which were spread out on the dock to dry and included suits, uniforms, coats, boots, shoes, books, golf clubs, a Winchester 348, and probably Gus Heiss's phonograph and record collection. Because of the damp weather, those soggy items that were still salvageable were later taken to Angel Island, where attempts were made to further dry them before repacking them for the voyage. Finally the day came for departure to their not-so-secret destination. Ferry boats transported troops from Angel Island to the *Coolidge,* moored on the east side of Pier 45 in San Francisco Harbor:

> The men started down the Angel Island Hill on a dreary, drizzling
> November 1st. It somehow befitted the mood of the time. Everyone
> was naturally sad at leaving their friends and families, but each had
> an inner conviction that he was doing the right thing. Sad, perhaps,
> but the men were really sure of themselves. On to the small ferry-
> boats the Squadron passed. Each man was checked before he got on
> the boat. Finally loaded, the little vessel poked into the harbor and
> the first famous words of the 27th were uttered by Willie Eubank,
> "This rumor has gone too far." Then at once laughter and jeers broke
> out relieving the tension. That made the ferry land midst a great deal
> of kidding and laughter. Up the gangplanks into the U.S.S. Coolidge
> poured the 27th Group, young men, elderly men, eager men,
> anxious men, sad men, but all men. They were really a wonderful
> crew and the Group Commander had reason to feel proud. At last
> the whistle blew, people waved, and the great ship shuddered as her
> props dug into the water and headed for the Golden Gate Bridge.
> Everyone craned a neck for a last look. Then into the Pacific Ocean
> the ship slipped. The 27th Group was Philippine Islands bound.[3]

The remark that had gotten the troops laughing was made by twenty-nine-year-old 1st Lt. William Eubank Jr. from Bluefield, West Virginia. He was the leader of the 91st Squadron and had been a member of the 3rd Bomb Group before being assigned to the 27th.

Another pilot, Harrison "Harry" Mangan, commented about departure day: "I recall my mother standing on the dock waving good-bye—a forlorn figure if I ever saw one. She had said good-bye to my step-father just a few months before from that same spot!" Mangan was born in Nogales, Arizona, located on the Mexican border, where his family owned property. His step-father, Walter, was an army colonel and a graduate of West Point, whose career had taken him to many different places so that Harry had attended thirteen different schools by the time he graduated from high school in North Carolina. Mangan then attended college for two years at the Citadel (the military college of South Carolina) before quitting to join the Army Air Corps. Wanting to be a "flyboy," he was initially too young to be a pilot, so his unit trained him as a bombardier. At age twenty-one he began pilot training at the Dallas School of Aviation in 1940 and completed the subsequent two courses at Randolph and Kelly Fields. He was then assigned to the 3rd Bomb Group in Savannah and reassigned to the 27th in January 1941.

Parting in Savannah on October 22 had been difficult for the Stephensons, newlyweds of only fifteen days. He tried to make the best of it. In his long distance calls and letters to his wife, he tried to remain cheerful. His first letter, written aboard the ship bound for the Philippines, expressed his true feelings: "I tried not to show how much it hurt when we parted, but somehow, today I feel worse than ever about it all, and I do miss you more than I ever thought possible. I never thought I'd ever settle down and be really contented and happy. Seems like a dream now, but I can thank Heaven I do have you to come back to."

The Passage to the Philippines

Despite the anguish of leaving friends and families, the trip on the *President Coolidge* was a rather pleasant experience. The ten-year-old cruise ship had been taken over by the army in 1941 to transport troops eight thousand miles to the Philippines and return to San Francisco with American military dependents, who were being evacuated because of a potential war with Japan. The *Coolidge* had been partially gutted to make room for all the soldiers but still retained some of the elements of leisure, including a swimming pool and theater. A ship of the American Presidents Lines, the *Coolidge* had huge eagles painted on its smokestacks, and being relatively new, it had speed.

The senior officers were arranged three to a stateroom, while the younger officers had bunk beds or cots on the breezy screened-in decks. Enlisted men bunked below decks. Stephenson roomed with experienced officers Louis Hobbs and Ed Backus, who were both about to be promoted to captain. Their stateroom was one of the larger cabins, so many of the other officers used it to hold bull sessions and for loafing. It was a leisurely, comfortable cruise. To prevent boredom, some read, some wrote letters home, some played cards, and some participated in the various recreational programs available. Swimming, deck tennis, and boxing were the favorites. Pfc. James Bollich of the 16th Squadron participated in boxing and recalled that the winner received

5. Officers of the 16th Squadron aboard the *President Coolidge,* November 1, 1941:
1) 2nd Lt. Leroy W. Cowart Jr.; 2) 2nd Lt. Phil R. Downey; 3) 1st Lt. David A. Hoch-
man; 4) 1st Lt. Ralph L. L. Schmidt; 5) 2nd Lt. Charles M. Cannon Jr.; 6) 1st Lt. Julius B.
Summers; 7) Flying Cadet John A. Ryan; 8) 1st Lt. Robert F. McClure; 9) 2nd Lt. Robert
G. Ruegg; 10) 1st Lt. James B. McAfee; 11) 1st Lt. Glenwood G. Stephenson; 12) Capt.
William G. Hipps; 13) 2nd Lt. Harry R. Roth; 14) 1st Lt. Frank P. "Pete" Bender; 15) 2nd Lt.
Columbus "Doc" Savage; 16) 1st Lt. Paul E. Mitchler; 17) 2nd Lt. Oliver C. Doan; 18) 2nd
Lt. Samuel H. Dillard III; 19) 2nd Lt. Richard B. Donnewald; 20) 2nd Lt. Henry J. Rose;
21) 2nd Lt. Alexander R. Salvatore. The only officer missing from this photograph is 2nd Lt.
Robert F. Stafford. *Courtesy Jay B. Harrelson*

three dollars for his efforts and the loser two dollars. Bender remembered in
his memoir that "a ring was set up on the deck. Ruegg and I were the fly-
weights. It was not until about 25 years later that we discussed this fight and
each of us thought we lost it based on the beating that each of us endured.
We really went at it with vigor." At least the troops were entertained.

There were two army nurses as well as army physicians and dentists
onboard who looked after the troops' health needs and conducted sick call
each morning. The 27th had its own dentist, Dr. Claude Daniels, and each
squadron had a physician assigned. Capt. William Marrocco was the senior
physician and assigned to the Headquarters Squadron. First Lt. Carl Mango

was assigned to the 17th, 1st Lt. Elack Schultz to the 91st, and 1st Lt. David Hochman to the 16th. Hochman's training and the circumstances that led him to the 16th typified that of the younger physicians onboard. Originally from New York City, he graduated from New York University and then attended medical school at the Royal College of Physicians in Edinburgh, Scotland. After that he served a two-year internship in New York City before being drafted and assigned to the 16th Squadron, 27th Bombardment Group in July 1941. Although he had no military training whatsoever, he was given the title of flight surgeon.

The one thing that most of the men remembered about the trip was that the food was great. The cruise ship's dinner menu, different every night, offered nine distinct appetizers, multiple soups, steaks, prime rib, salmon, roast duck, and five types of vegetables plus desserts. In his diary James McAfee compared the mess to "the kitchen of Henry VIII." Little did those feasting like royalty know that, in a few short months, they would be starving on Bataan and considering themselves fortunate whenever they were able to obtain a morsel of meat from a monkey, water buffalo, or army mule.

Stephenson took the menus, colorfully decorated with Far East scenes, and wrote on the back letters to Ann every night on the first leg of the trip to Honolulu. Although the *Coolidge* had plenty of bars, none was open. Many of the officers, however, smuggled on their own liquor. For a price, the ship's stewards could also supply alcohol. One of the party scenes was Stephenson's stateroom. In a letter to his wife, he mentioned that one of his roommates smuggled a gallon of whiskey onboard and spent an inebriated evening drinking numerous toasts to Stephenson's picture of Ann.

But the trip was not just one big party. There was still soldiering to do. Each morning saw roll call followed by physical training exercises. The huge, comfortable lounge was the perfect spot for lectures from several officers who had prior Philippine experience. They provided an overview of what to expect in Manila and elsewhere in the islands. Capt. William Hipps lectured on dive-bombing techniques.

Hipps had become leader of the 16th Squadron during the summer of 1941. He was born in Lumber City, Pennsylvania, in 1912 and had graduated from West Point in 1937. He obtained his pilot training at Army Air Corps schools in San Antonio and was then assigned to the 3rd Attack (Bomb) Group. When the 3rd was split in 1940 to form the 27th Bomb Group, Hipps was transferred into the new unit. At about the time they boarded the *Coolidge*, officials decided that the 16th Squadron was "top heavy" with West Pointers; the 17th Squadron already had Warren Stirling. Summers was

6. 27th Bomb Group physicians at Waikiki Beach, Hawaii, November 6, 1941. Standing, L to R: Drs. Elack Schultz, Carl Mango, William Marrocco. Kneeling: Dr. David Hochman. *Courtesy David Hochman, M.D.*

therefore transferred to the 91st Squadron while onboard the *Coolidge*, leaving Hipps, Stephenson, and McAfee in the 16th.

Besides games of poker, bridge, and double-deck pinochle, many listened to radio station KGEI from San Francisco, which was broadcast over the ship's PA system each evening. Pilot Columbus "Doc" Savage from the 16th Squadron remembered one of the sergeants was listening to the popular tune "Georgia on My Mind." The sergeant told him, "Hmm, Georgia on my mind. What I really want is Georgia under my feet." Homesickness set in for many. One officer had deserted and never boarded the ship. McAfee said in his diary that he missed his wife, Julia, so much that he thought of getting off the boat in Hawaii and returning home. Most of the married men could hardly wait for Hawaii so they could mail their letters and call home.

Finally, on the morning of November 6, Diamond Head came into view. Major Davies granted shore-leave passes with the warning that everyone had to be back onboard by 2:00 P.M. Some rushed for phones while others hurried to the Waikiki bars. Everyone tried to pack as much fun into these six hours of freedom as they could. McAfee and "Zeke" Summers got a tour of the island from a friend. Savage toured Oahu by taxi. Mangan and another group went to the famous Royal Hawaiian Hotel on Waikiki Beach for drinks; later he walked the beach and was disappointed that it was all gravel and rocks. Some bought Hawaiian clothes, and some purchased cameras with which to take pictures to send home.

Stephenson, unfortunately, missed meeting up with his younger brother Clyde, who was stationed on the USS *California* at Pearl Harbor, because his battleship was out at sea; the brothers had last seen each other during the summer of 1938. After mailing the letters to Ann and calling her, Stephenson and others returned to the ship loaded with "hair tonic" for their nightly "slug" parties. Bender and friends wandered into a bar for some refreshment, had a few drinks of gin and coconut milk, and after enough of this libation, thought it good enough to help out for the rest of their cruise. They purchased a case of gin and a bag of coconuts. Although they believed that they had enough to last the rest of the trip, they were spotted coming up the gangplank with their purchases, and their room became the place to be for a few days.

Blackouts to Manila

By the time the men of the 27th slept off the effects of their six-hour shore leave, they noticed distinct differences during the ensuing fourteen-day journey to the Philippines. The air was warmer, the seas calmer, and the two army nurses onboard suddenly got better looking—a rumor soon spread that the two women were movie stars Greta Garbo and Betty Grable incognito. But something else was also distinctly different.

The convoy, which included the transport ship USAT *Winfield S. Scott,* loaded with tanks and men of the 192nd Tank Battalion, was now being escorted by the cruiser *Louisville* because of suspected Nazi submarines or raiders in the Pacific. Blackout conditions prevailed at night. All portholes, windows, and doors were covered, and there was no smoking on deck. To aid in identification, men had to draw a silhouette of the escorting cruiser.

Everyone, however, was a bit more on edge after the *Louisville* suddenly left the convoy one day. Hubbard in his memoir wrote: "the *Louisville* one afternoon heeled over and went roaring off at full speed toward a small dot on the southern horizon. Word spread that it was a Nazi Raider and everyone crowded on deck to watch a gun battle, but nothing happened." The Nazi raider turned out to be the Norwegian ship *M. S. Talisman.*

Because of Stephenson's earlier overseas military experience, when his turn came to lecture, he was assigned to familiarize the men with the Philippines. He might have started by reminding them that Adm. George Dewey's victory in May 1898 over the Spanish forces in Manila Bay during the Spanish-American War contributed to the United States obtaining the islands. By December of that year, the Treaty of Paris ended hostilities, and as part of the deal, Spain sold the Philippines to the United States for twenty million dollars. To preserve America's interest, a military presence became necessary. After a recent decade or so of harmonious relationship between the two countries, leaders on both sides of the Pacific believed that the Philippines were ready for independence. In 1934 Congress passed the Tydings-McDuffie Act, which called for a transition to full independence over a ten-year period. During this time, the U.S. military would be allowed to maintain army and naval bases as it saw fit. Stephenson likely told them that his old unit, the 31st Infantry Regiment, was stationed at Fort McKinley there.

After the inauguration of Pres. Manuel Quezon in November 1935, the challenge of preparing a Filipino military to withstand foreign aggressors fell into the hands of Gen. Douglas MacArthur, who had left his position as U.S. Army chief of staff in Washington, as a four-star general, to become the military advisor to Quezon. As military advisor he was still on active duty with the U.S. Army, but his new rank was now only major general (two stars). MacArthur, with the help of his handpicked staff officers, Maj. Dwight D. Eisenhower and Maj. James B. Ord, devised a ten-year plan to significantly upgrade the military of the new Filipino government. Some doubted at the time that it could be done. Two years later MacArthur retired from the U.S. Army and shortly thereafter was made grand field marshal of the Philippine Army, charged to continue the army's development. With the passage of the National Defense Act, MacArthur envisioned that in ten years a strong Filipino army, quick torpedo boats, and fast dive bombers would make an invasion so costly in lives lost on the beaches that no foreign country would dare attack the islands.

Up until the summer of 1941, U.S. Army units in the Philippines and the Philippine Scouts were part of the U.S. Philippine Department. The Philippine Army, which MacArthur commanded, remained separate, though over time many American officers served in advisory positions in its newly formed units.

By 1940 thirty thousand Japanese citizens were living in the Philippines. Many were working undercover for the Imperial Japanese Army Headquarters, posing as businessmen, servants, and tourists. President Quezon would recall that "only later did I discover that my gardener was a Japanese major and my masseur a Japanese colonel."[4] About half of the Japanese males living in Manila were Japanese military reservists.[5] Commercial planes of Nippon Airways, manned by military pilots and observers, flew seven photographic missions over Luzon in November and December 1940. Extensive aerial photo reconnaissance included potential landing areas for invasion operations.[6]

Why were the Philippine Islands important to the Japanese? In order to secure the oil fields in the Dutch (or Netherlands) East Indies, Japanese military planners knew they had to capture the Philippines because the American units based there would be a threat to Japan's flanks as its troops proceeded south to invade Southeast Asia.[7] They also wanted to seize the Philippines to facilitate air and sea travel between these new conquests and Japan proper. In addition, they intended to use the islands for intermediate staging areas and supply bases, which would facilitate military operations farther south.[8]

Because of the continuous breakdown in negotiations between Washington and Tokyo, most suspected that war in the Pacific would eventually happen. The only question was where and when. What the men of the 27th were really concerned with, however, was where were their planes? They fully expected their dive bombers to be with the convoy escorted by the heavy cruiser USS *Pensacola* and were confident that the planes were right behind them. What they did not know was that the *Meigs*, loaded with their planes and ammunition, was still in port in San Francisco on November 13. By the time the 27th reached Manila, the *Pensacola* convoy, which included the *Meigs*, still had not reached Honolulu.

In hindsight, military overconfidence and unpreparedness hindered the U.S. war effort from the start. Sims remembers some of the 27th enlisted men saying, "If we get into a war, we will just have to tear them a new one." Another private remembered: "Nervous about Japan? No! Our own propaganda had us pretty well convinced we could whip the little myopic bastards in a couple of weeks when, not if, they attacked." McAfee, in his diary entry of November 18, noted a word of caution: "There has been a great deal of discussion about the U.S. and Japan. Most everyone seems to believe that the U.S. has Japan licked and that irritates the hell out of me. Japan's Navy is bound to be bigger than ours out here and that could decide the issue. The darn Japs ought to know that if I do. [If war breaks out], it will take airplanes, big naval concentrations, and lots of guys with guns."

None of these necessary items was in great supply in the Philippines in November 1941.

War Plan Orange and Rainbow 5

Military strategists had argued for decades about what to do with the Philippines in case of war with Japan. The Joint Planning Commission of the War Department had plans in place for potential wars with various countries. Each potential adversary and subsequent war plan was assigned a color code name. War Plan Orange (WPO) become the code name for a possible conflict with Japan. One contingency of WPO called for American and Filipino troops to retreat to the Bataan Peninsula if there were a successful Japanese invasion of Luzon, the main island of the Philippines. Accordingly, food, ammunition, and medicine were stored there. While Bataan protected the nearby fortified island of Corregidor, Corregidor in turn protected the entrance to Manila Bay, and if the U.S. held both, any Japanese attack would be costly. The battle for Bataan would be a defensive one as the Japanese struggled against not only the American and Filipino troops but also the rugged mountains and dense jungle terrain. Meanwhile, the U.S. Navy would steam from Pearl Harbor, sink the Imperial Japanese Navy in the South China Sea, and within six months enter Manila Bay to save the fighters on Bataan. Although this looked good on paper, many naval experts said that realistically it would take two years, not six months, to reach Manila Bay.[9]

MacArthur thought that War Plan Orange was too conservative. He visualized the American and Filipino troops defeating the Japanese on the beaches; many scoffed at this overconfident assessment. But to fulfill his plan, MacArthur needed additional air power. To help defend the beaches during an invasion, Army Air Corps leaders in Washington sent dive bombers—

the 27th Bombardment Group. Also included in the September voyage of the *Coolidge* were New Mexico's 200th Coast Artillery and the 194th Tank Battalion to provide protection for the airfields. MacArthur fully expected the Japanese invasion to come in April 1942, and by that time everything he needed to defend the Philippines would be in place.

In contrast to the color war plans, the Rainbow war plans contemplated confrontation with multiple enemies versus a single foe. In January 1941 the United States and Great Britain had held secret meetings in Washington to discuss strategies for the impending world conflict. They decided that Germany, not Japan, was the main enemy.[10] Victory in Europe would come first. Rainbow 5, which was the plan the United States was adhering to by the summer of 1941, called for the protection of the Western Hemisphere and ultimately sending task forces to the eastern Atlantic, Africa, and/or Europe.[11] Army and naval forces already positioned in the Pacific would therefore have to fight the Japanese with whatever supplies and reinforcements could be spared.

The War Department, however, turned its policy 180 degrees regarding the defense of the Philippines in the summer of 1941 after they realized that the B-17 bombers just coming off the assembly lines had sufficient range to strike southern Japan from bases in the northern Philippines. Now they decided to develop the Philippines as an offensive base from which to threaten the Japanese mainland with these long-range bombers if Japan did not stop its southern aggression. The War Department therefore started a rapid buildup of men and materiel there.[12]

During this time, the War Department made an important change in the command of the Army Air Corps, giving Hap Arnold much more power. Prior to this, the chief of the Army Air Corps was in charge of procurement, training, and supply, while the chief of the General Headquarters Air Force was in charge of operating and directing air-combat units. Neither man had authority over the other, and both reported directly to the chief of staff of the army. In June the U.S. Army Air Forces was created by combining the Combat Command (formerly the General Headquarters Air Force) and the Army Air Corps. The new organization was placed under the command of Arnold.[13]

Also in June the Japanese military decided to set up bases and airfields in southern Indochina and Thailand, even if that action "risked war with Britain and the United States." Then, following negotiations with Vichy France, more than forty thousand Japanese troops began occupying French Indochina without incident on July 25.[14]

On July 26 President Roosevelt issued an executive order freezing Japanese assets in the United States, thus halting all trade with Japan as well as banning its ships from using the Panama Canal. This was mainly an oil embargo, however, and was followed by similar restrictions by the British and Dutch. American leaders thought this would force the Japanese either to drop their long-term aggressive strategy in Southeast Asia or to seize the Dutch East Indies to meet their oil needs—a move that would lead to war.[15] As part of this get-tough policy by Roosevelt, a new army command was created in the Philippines, the U.S. Army Forces in the Far East (USAFFE). On July 26 sixty-one-year-old MacArthur was called back to active duty in the U.S. Army, quickly promoted to the rank of lieutenant general (three stars), and given command of the USAFFE. In August the Philippine Army, which MacArthur had so recently headed and belonged to the Philippine Commonwealth, was inducted into the service of the United States.

MacArthur had known about Washington's war plans all along and wanted Rainbow 5 changed to allow him to defend all of the Philippines, not just the Manila Bay area. Thus he was delighted to learn in November 1941 of the revision of Rainbow 5 allowing him to do just that.[16] Estimates of army strength that month ranged from 120,000 to 130,000 troops, of which about 31,000 were U.S. Army troops. This contingent contained many types of units, including the 27th Bombardment Group and all other Army Air Corps commands. The only infantry unit consisting entirely of Americans was Stephenson's old 31st Regiment, which had 2,100 men. The 11,957 men of the Philippine Scouts, considered fearless fighters, were part of the U.S. Army and had American officers commanding the Filipino enlisted men. The other 90,000–100,000 troops were members of the Philippine Army. Many of them were poorly equipped and poorly trained, some having been drafted into the army just weeks or months before war broke out. For many of the new recruits, the first time they would fire a rifle would be in combat. Compounding the problem was that over sixty-five dialects were spoken in the islands. In 1941 only 27 percent of Filipinos spoke English, so Filipino troops from one island had difficulty understanding those from another island, not to mention their American officers.[17]

U.S. advisors also served with Philippine Army units. Just before war broke out, Maj. Gen. Jonathan Wainwright was put in charge of the North Luzon Force, 28,000 troops, which was responsible for defending the island north of Manila. Brig. Gen. George Parker Jr. commanded the 15,000 troops of the South Luzon Force, which was to defend the southern portion. Brig. Gen. William Sharp commanded the Visayan-Mindanao Force, which

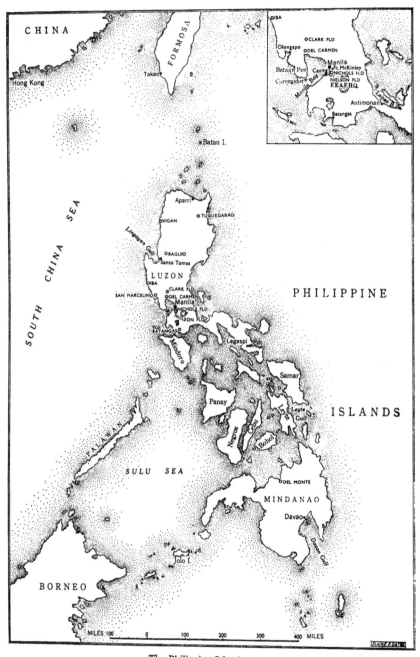

The Philippine Islands

I. Philippine Islands. *Courtesy Australia War Memorial*

included most of the Philippine Islands south of Luzon, with about 25,000 troops on Mindanao and another 20,000 spread out among the other islands under his authority. Wainwright's command had the bulk of the military assets; much of the remainder was assigned to Generals Parker and Sharp. MacArthur's Reserve Force was headquartered in Manila and directly under his command.[18] Brig. Gen. George B. Moore commanded the Manila Harbor defenses, Maj. Gen. Edward P. King Jr. was chief of artillery, and Maj. Gen. Lewis H. Brereton was MacArthur's air commander.

As the 27th continued their journey to Manila, only a handful of men knew of the Rainbow plan, and none of them were on the *Coolidge.* There were a few in the group who saw the eventuality of the war with Japan well before the Pearl Harbor attack. For months Japan's actions in the Far East were headlines in the newspapers. During the weeks before the war, the men heard about the strained diplomatic relations between Japan and the United States. Most, however, thought the United States would first be involved in the war in Europe. Onboard the *Coolidge,* men recalled Captain Hipps's lecture on the inevitability of war with Japan. But few thought it would begin at Pearl Harbor. Some realized the tough road ahead. Leland Sims of the motor pool wrote prophetically in his last letter home, "I will walk through Hell before I return."

The men of the 27th continued to lounge in the sun during the day, listen to lectures in the early evening, and have their slug parties late into the night. Like the biblical Goliath, they considered themselves unbeatable—the Japanese did not stand a chance.

The Lull before the Storm

It was a clear, sunny Thanksgiving Thursday when the *Coolidge* steamed into Manila Bay on November 20. Bollich, who had the option of remaining behind and attending flight school, recalled that the transport sailed within the couple of miles between the Bataan Peninsula and Corregidor in the mouth of the bay. "Both places appeared as tropical paradises. It all looked like a place that I would really enjoy. I decided that I had made the right choice by coming along with my squadron."

The Philippines had that effect on people. During the 1930s, an assignment there was considered the softest duty in the U.S. military. Even with war raging in Europe and Japan creating problems in the Far East, career soldiers stationed around the islands did not appear overly concerned that war would touch them. Many considered the monthly arrival of men, tanks, and guns as only precautionary measures. That overconfident attitude toward hostilities with Japan had been in place for years when the *Coolidge* docked at Pier Seven.

Everyone on the ship was in a holiday mood that morning. Two P-40 fighter aircraft greeted them with a flyby, and the 31st Infantry Regiment Band from Fort McKinley belted out rousing military tunes. Hours later the men disembarked, climbed on trucks, and began a ten-mile ride to Fort McKinley. The trucks rolled along Dewey Boulevard and then through a squalid slum neighborhood. Here young Filipino boys gave them the V-sign while saying the standard "Hi Joe." Finally the trucks filed past the gates and into Fort McKinley.

Rosters indicate that the troop strength of the 27th Bombardment Group stood at 1,209 men. This included eighty-two officers, three flying cadets, and 712 enlisted men from the 27th itself, plus two additional units that were attached to the group. The 48th Materiel Squadron from Savannah, with its fifteen officers and 211 enlisted men, was to provide maintenance work, including mechanics of all types, parachute riggers, radiomen, sheet-metal workers, armorers, and welders. The 48th also supplied parts and performed other duties. The 454th Ordnance Company, Aviation (Bomb), was also referred to as an ordnance "squadron" because it was an Army Air Corps unit. Activated in Savannah, it numbered six officers and 180 enlisted men, whose function was to manage the group's bombs and ammunition.[19]

The 27th Bombardment Group and the 48th and 454th Squadrons were slated for the new airfield at San Marcelino on the western coast north of Bataan. The runway had been laid and the barracks were just being completed, but the water supply had not yet been installed.[20] Since the expected aircraft had not arrived, the runway received little use. Whereas some troops were sent out to the new airfield, most of the 27th remained at Fort McKinley. The enlisted men and some of the officers lived in tents erected on the parade grounds, polo field, golf course, and rifle range. The majority of the officers were placed five or six to a dwelling in the now-empty married officers quarters (the families having departed for the States earlier). General Wainwright gave the welcoming speech to the 27th. He had graduated first in his class at West Point in 1906, participated in a campaign to put down the Philippines insurrection of 1909–10, and had served in France during World War I. According to John Whitman, a U.S. Army historian, during the latter part of the 1930s, Wainwright's drinking problem became too obvious to ignore, so the War Department put him out to pasture by sending him to the then-quiet Philippines (though his tenure would turn out much different than the military had anticipated).[21] The general told the men of the 27th that the Filipino soldiers wore their uniforms in better military fashion than they did. According to 27th pilot Francis Timlin, Wainwright "gave us a stern lecture on how to behave in the tropics [and anywhere else]."[22] Mangan in his diary wrote: "Meant to mention that the general of the post welcomed us the other day. Not one word as to any island defenses or our part in any movement of the sort. Instead, 30 minutes of what would happen to us if we didn't wear clean, proper uniforms at all times and correct evening wear."

Because many in the 27th were camped on the parade ground, Wainwright initially ordered that they all wear their Class A uniforms (coat and collared shirt with tie) while camped there in tents. Major Vance, then the commander of the group, went over to the general's headquarters and boldly questioned this order. Wainwright told him he understood his reasoning and rescinded the edict.[23]

Manila night life was in demand those first few days. The posh Army-Navy Club, the Alazar Club, and the Manila Hotel were all frequented by the officers of the 27th as were the many dives like the Grass Shack and the Bamboo Hut. McAfee found the Filipino habit of letting the customers pour their own drinks a little unsettling—his arm was too strong. Bender's memoir reveals: "Our crowd went to the Army-Navy club and the Jai Alai building for the high brow entertainment or the Casa Manana for nightclubbing or the Bamboo Hut for noisy singing and dancing. It was indeed surprising to see how some of the people of Manila went on with business as usual in spite of the tenseness that one was now able to feel in the air." Hubbard's favorite place was "Tom's Dixie Kitchen. Not an upscale spot, but it had loud jazz, cheap drinks, and good oriental food plus southern fried chicken, fish, and hush puppies."

According to the *27th Reports,* the Jai Alai Club was known for "bets, beers, babes, and [ending up] broke." Many lost money gambling. Ron Hubbard was not one of them: "I spent several evenings in the club lounge on a leather chair overlooking the court. Beside each of the dozen chairs was a small end table and a waiter to serve that chair. The waiter stood by to keep the glass full and take a bet down to the window. If you won, he brought the winnings back knowing a good tip awaited."

Increased Army Air Corps Presence in the Philippines

As part of the U.S. buildup in the Philippines, military leaders had decided that dive bombers were needed. The 27th was the only combat-ready dive-bomber unit in the Army Air Corps at the time. Gen. George Marshall, chief of staff of the army, and Hap Arnold had decided to send the 27th Bombard-

7. Curtiss P-40 fighter. *Courtesy University of Chicago*

ment Group and its A-24s following a conversation they had on September 25, 1941.[24] Although the U.S. Asiatic Fleet was stationed in Manila Bay, it did not have any aircraft carriers. The reason for locating the 27th at San Marcelino was to defend against an amphibious assault against either Manila or the Lingayen Gulf. Both places were assumed to be major objectives of any invasion force. The Japanese needed to capture Manila to control its harbor and excellent port facilities, while the shores of Lingayen Gulf, with their low, sloping beaches, were well suited to land men and offload equipment. In addition, from Lingayen a plain extended about 120 miles to Manila Bay and was most favorable for mobile warfare.[25]

Two other large Army Air Corps units were also part of this buildup of American forces. One was another bomber unit, the 19th Bombardment Group, while the other was a fighter command, the 24th Pursuit Group. Both units were headquartered at Clark Army Airfield about fifty miles north of Manila.

The 24th Pursuit Group was formed in September 1941 in the Philippines from three pursuit squadrons already there, two of which had arrived at the end of 1940. Maj. Orrin S. Grover commanded the group. The unit had its own three squadrons as well as two more attached (in November) that had

8. B-17 Flying Fortresses at Port Moresby, en route to the Philippines, September 10, 1941. *Courtesy Australian War Memorial*

arrived with the 27th Group on the *Coolidge.* Four squadrons eventually obtained the modern P-40 fighters before December 7, while one squadron still flew older, slower P-35s. One squadron each was located at Clark, Iba, and Del Carmen Army Airfields and two at Nichols. The 19th Bombardment Group had thirty-five Boeing B-17 bombers. One squadron had arrived in the Philippines during September 1941, while the rest arrived in October–November, all flown to the Philippines from the United States. Lt. Col. Eugene L. Eubank (not to be confused with William R. Eubank Jr., who led the 91st Squadron of the 27th) commanded this unit, which was stationed at Clark.[26]

Since the 27th, unlike the other two Army Air Corps groups, were still without its airplanes, its headquarters until December 8 was in Quarters 4 at Fort McKinley, then until December 24 in a thirty-by-sixty-foot tent in a ravine behind Quarters 4. The men quickly discovered that being a flying outfit without planes could be quite boring. Whereas the officers could leave Fort McKinley at night, the enlisted men were not always as lucky. Keeping them occupied during this time was not easy. Some enlisted men were kept busy digging drainage ditches around McKinley, while others built revetments, a protective wall usually of earth, sand, or stone, to shelter the expected airplanes. Hubbard in his memoir reveals that Major Davies "wanted to start building revetments for the planes when they arrived. We put in a requisition for sandbags and managed to get enough for a good start on the first one but were then told that no more were available. The Quartermaster explained that there was no emergency and no reason to justify spending money for local procurement."

There was also the issue of flight time. None of the pilots had their November flying time in, and that additional flight pay was important to their families back in the States. According to Hubbard, "The 27th managed a reluctant loan of four obsolete and very decrepit B-18 two-engine bombers from the 19th Bomb Group." Everyone got his four hours' minimum flight time in, though not without some adventure. McAfee recalled, "The ships were in extremely sad shape—parts were held together with baling wire and other parts held together with what appeared to be only gravity."

Flying them was a challenge, as Stephenson and McAfee found out. The November 26 entry in McAfee's diary discloses: "flew with Glen to Clark Field in a B-18 this afternoon. First time either of us had flown since the States, and we both narrowly missed piling up on taking off. [clipped some tree tops] We were both at fault, and it was much too close for comfort."[27]

Some flew over to San Marcelino to check on their new base from the air. It looked pretty remote to the pilots, so they pooled their money and rented a house in Manila to serve as their Officers' Club. They planned on flying down for weekends later. Meanwhile, they used the house for storage.[28]

Back home, the pace of rearmament and mobilization, which gained momentum earlier in the year, was starting to slow down. Understandably, Americans did not want to get involved in another world war. The public and congressional sentiment still held to the hope that any immediate belligerent showdown with Japan or Germany could be avoided. They simply did not want to send their young men into harm's way, as evidenced by a near defeat of the bill to extend Selective Service, continuation of a prohibition against sending draftees outside the Western Hemisphere, and apathetic public response to submarine attacks on U.S. destroyers in September and October.[29]

Softball was another activity that kept the 27th occupied in the Philippines. The 16th and 17th Squadrons faced each other often during their first two weeks on Luzon. They selected an all-star team to face the Manila Polo Club team on December 7. The game was the start of a hectic and memorable twenty-four hours: "The game began at 2:00 P.M. and by 4:00 P.M. the score was 19–2 in favor of the Polo Club. The game gradually shifted to the bar at the club where everyone got stiff in preparation for the dinner at the Manila hotel the Group was giving in honor of Major General Lewis H. Brereton who had just recently replaced Brigadier General Claggett as the commanding general of the Far East Air Force. Gen. Brereton was our Base C. O. at Savannah at one time."[30] Brereton arrived in the Philippines on November 4 on a Pan American Clipper to assume command of the newly created Far East Air Force (FEAF), headquartered at Nielson Field just south of Manila. Prior to this he had commanded the Third Air Force at Tampa, Florida, and before that had commanded the Army Air Corps bomb wing in Savannah, which included the 27th and 3rd Bombardment Groups. Summoned to Washington in October 1941, Brereton received his new assignment from Hap Arnold and learned of the military and political problems that existed in the Far East.

Brereton quickly recognized the urgency of preparing a strong air force in the Philippines. His first days were spent upgrading FEAF Headquarters at Nielson Field and inspecting the airbases on the islands of Luzon and Mindanao. He surmised that only two fields—Clark Field on Luzon and Del Monte Plantation on the far north side of Mindanao near the coastal town of Cagayan, about five hundred miles south of Manila—were adequate for B-17 heavy bombers during the wet season.

Located on a plateau two thousand feet above sea level, the Del Monte plantation itself was famous for producing pineapples and other fruits for canning.[31] The natural meadows in the area were ideal for runways. Their compacted soil alleviated the need for extensive grading, and basic lawn cutting sufficed to carve out runways. By November army engineers directing a workforce of fifteen hundred men had built a number of short runways there as well as a mile-long runway to accommodate the large B-17s.[32]

But additional airfields were needed elsewhere as well as more pilots, more planes, and more equipment. Twelve days after his arrival, Brereton left for Australia to inspect facilities there necessary for the air-ferrying route that would supply the Philippines in the future. To avoid publicity, the general and his group wore civilian clothes and no military titles were used, though apparently nobody was fooled. Tokyo broadcasts reported Brereton's visit with most of the details of his business.[33] All three of his recommendations from this tour—establishing more airfields for the air-ferrying route, creating more bases in Australia to accommodate U.S. planes, and providing for additional pilot training in Australia—were approved by MacArthur and

Washington. They later proved critical for the United States and its allies in winning the Pacific War.[34]

Earlier, in September 1941, MacArthur had approached General Wainwright, who was then in charge of an infantry division in Manila, and asked him to agree to command the planned North Luzon Force, to be headquartered at Fort Stotsenberg, north of Manila and adjacent to Clark Field. On November 25 he directed Wainwright to assume his new duties at Stotsenberg, which would become basically a command-and-control headquarters for a number of army units. Upon arrival at his new post three days later, he found his staff consisted of an adjutant (personnel officer), a supply officer, and a surgeon. The means of communications between his headquarters and various subordinate units would be the local telephone and telegraph system.[35] Anticipating the heightened state of alert of U.S. military forces in the Pacific, one would assume that at least fifty top staff officers and enlisted men would have already been in place there to aid Wainwright. Yet just a day or two earlier MacArthur had told a group of high-ranking officials, "it would be impossible for the Japanese to attack before the following April."[36]

That same day the general and other U.S. commanders in the field received a secret priority message from Secretary of War Henry Stimson containing the following information:

> Negotiations with Japan appear to be terminated to all practical purposes with only the barest possibility that the Japanese government might come back and offer to continue. Japanese future action unpredictable. But hostile action possible at any moment. If hostilities cannot, repeat, cannot be avoided the United States desires that Japan commit the first overt act. This policy should not, repeat, not be construed as restricting you to a course of action that might jeopardize your defense. Prior to hostile Japanese action, you are directed to take such reconnaissance and other measures as you deem necessary.[37]

MacArthur informed Brereton, who had returned to Manila on November 26, about the contents of the cablegram. Because of the escalating tensions, Brereton issued a twenty-four-hour-alert order to all of his units.[38] Also, as a result of this warning message to MacArthur and a similar one the Navy Department dispatched to the naval command in the Philippines two days earlier, emergency precautions were immediately put into place. U.S. High Commissioner Francis B. Sarye called MacArthur and Adm. Thomas

Hart, his navy counterpart in command of U.S. Asiatic Fleet, into a conference. Afterward, air-reconnaissance patrols intensified. The following day all leaves were canceled, and all army units in the Philippines were placed on war alert. Two infantry divisions were dispatched to the beach positions around the Lingayen Gulf and two more positioned along the Batangas coast. A few days later Hart and MacArthur decided that army B-17s would patrol the northern offshore area as far as Japanese-occupied Formosa (now Taiwan). They believed that the B-17s, with greater speed and a higher ceiling than the navy PBY flying boats, would have a better chance of coping with any Japanese fighters they might encounter. Navy planes would patrol to the south and west, including long-range missions as far as the Indochina coast. These planes eventually reported on a large number of Japanese transport and cargo ships at sea. The British, Australians, and Dutch were also flying reconnaissance missions farther south out of Malaya and the Dutch East Indies. They too had sighted Japanese transports and some warships as well as Japanese military aircraft. By December 6 MacArthur had established a final alert. Airplanes were dispersed and guarded. Defenses were manned with normal guards increased. Counter-subversive measures began.[39]

Vice Adm. Tom Phillips, newly appointed commander of the British Far East Fleet based at Singapore, was in Manila conferring with Hart and MacArthur at that time about mutual defense issues and trying to borrow four American destroyers to beef up the fighting capabilities of the relatively few ships he had there. At 6:00 P.M. on December 6, a message came in that reconnaissance planes from Singapore had sighted a large Japanese convoy off the coast of Siam (Thailand) heading in the direction of Malaya. Phillips mentioned he would be returning to Singapore in the morning. Hart replied, "If you want to be there when the war starts, I suggest you take off right now."[40]

Bender in his memoir notes: "We had heard Brereton had suggested that aerial photography missions be flown over the Japanese stronghold at Formosa, but MacArthur did not go along with this suggestion for whatever reason." Bender happened to be at the Bamboo Hut on the night of December 6 and had a chat with Brereton, who kept looking out the window of this large nipa bamboo-and-grass building. Bender could not help asking the general what he was thinking at that time. "His reply was simply to the effect that he expected the Japanese attack to start within the next day or so."

The next night, December 7 (December 6 in Hawaii), Brereton was at the Manila Hotel attending the dinner held in his honor by the 27th Bombardment Group, but he did little partying. He was in constant touch with Mac-

Arthur's staff and his air commanders. None of the pilots at Clark attended, for Brereton had them on alert. All in attendance had a grand time. Following the dinner, the pilots adjourned to the hotel bar for more festivities, finding their way back to Fort McKinley by 2:00 A.M. It was December 8 in Manila. Because of the International Date Line, it was still the early morning of December 7 at Pearl Harbor in Hawaii. The *Pensacola* convoy, with the 27th's much-needed airplanes, was on the Pacific Ocean five thousand miles and more than eight sailing days away.

X-Day

By late October 1941, Japanese strategists had completed their preparations for the invasion of the Dutch East Indies, Thailand, Malaya, Hong Kong, and Singapore as well as the U.S. Pacific island possessions, including Wake, Guam, and the Philippines. Adm. Isoroku Yamamoto, commander in chief of the Japanese Navy, gave his planners only six months after hostilities began within which to defeat the U.S. Navy.[41] Their initial strategy was formulated with the dual purpose of gaining swift control of the economic resources of the targeted territories, essential to the prosecution of the war, and eliminating British and American military bases that might be used either to block the way to these resources or to launch a counteroffensive. To ensure that the needed oil resources were obtained intact, Japan intended to capture the main oil-producing centers in Dutch and British Borneo soon after the start of hostilities and, as soon as airbases were secured in Malaya, to take Palembang on Sumatra by airborne assault.[42]

By November 1941 the Japanese military had fairly accurate knowledge of ground, air, and naval strength in the targeted regions thanks to reconnaissance and espionage. This included locations of airfields and fortifications as well as terrain and climatic conditions in which their troops would have to fight.[43] In the Philippines they knew U.S. and Filipino Army troop strengths, number and types of U.S. Navy ships, and the types and number of aircraft on hand and where they were located.[44]

At the time the Imperial Japanese Army consisted of fifty-one divisions spread throughout the Far East. Each division formed a basic ground-fighting unit and typically consisted of fifteen thousand to twenty thousand infantry troops, though there could be more or less depending on various factors. Within a division were generally, in decreasing size, brigades or regiments, followed by battalions, companies, and platoons. Often, divisions were organized into larger commands, typically a corps, which then formed armies (though some armies consisted of divisions rather than corps). During large

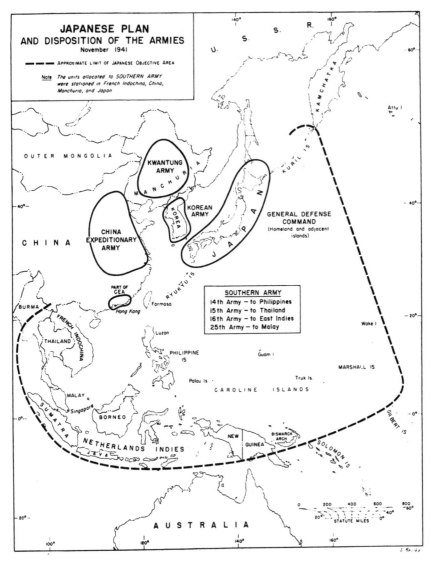

JAPANESE PLAN
AND DISPOSITION OF THE ARMIES
November 1941

— — — APPROXIMATE LIMIT OF JAPANESE OBJECTIVE AREA

<u>Note</u> *The units allocated to SOUTHERN ARMY were stationed in French Indochina, China, Manchuria, and Japan*

OUTER MONGOLIA

KWANTUNG ARMY

KOREAN ARMY

GENERAL DEFENSE COMMAND
(Homeland and adjacent islands)

CHINA EXPEDITIONARY ARMY

C H I N A

PART OF CEA

BURMA

Hong Kong

Formosa

SOUTHERN ARMY
14th Army — to Philippines
15th Army — to Thailand
16th Army — to East Indies
25th Army — to Malay

Luzon

THAILAND

FRENCH INDOCHINA

PHILIPPINE IS

Guam I

Palau Is

Truk Is.

Wake I

MARSHALL IS

MALAY

Singapore

BORNEO

CAROLINE   ISLANDS

SUMATRA

N E T H E R L A N D S   I N D I E S

JAVA

NEW GUINEA

BISMARCK ARCH.

SOLOMON IS

GILBERT IS

A U S T R A L I A

200   400   600   800
STATUTE MILES

2. Japanese plan and disposition of armies, November 1941. *Courtesy U.S. Army*

battle-front situations, armies are sometimes gathered into larger commands typically referred to as army groups.

In early November the Japanese army notified their major tactical commanders of their assignments for the upcoming Southeast Asia invasions. Lt. Gen. Masaharu Homma, fifty-four years old and considered by the Imperial Army as one of their most brilliant strategists, was notified on November 2 that he would direct the Fourteenth Army against MacArthur in the Philippines. He was told at the time, "The troops opposed to you are third class and unworthy to face us in battle." War with the United States, Britain, and their allies would begin in the next several weeks, with surprise air attacks against Malaya, Hong Kong, Wake, Midway, Guam, the Philippines, and the U.S. Navy Pacific Fleet anchorage at Pearl Harbor. These attacks on air and naval installations "would crush their power in one fell swoop." Homma, who was told that these surprise attacks would commence on X-Day, and the rest of the Imperial Japanese Forces eagerly awaited further orders.[45]

3

War Begins

COL. HAROLD H. GEORGE, the chief of staff of the 5th Interceptor Command, spoke to his fighter pilots at Nichols Field outside Manila. "Men," he said, "you are not a suicide squadron yet, but you are damn close to it. There will be war with Japan in a very few days. It may come in a matter of hours."[1] Later that morning George gave a similar speech to the pilots at Clark Field and added that a great Japanese fleet was drifting slowly south along the western reaches of the South China Sea, destination unknown.[2] Allied reconnaissance flights sighted many Japanese warships and troop transports southwest of the Philippines headed in a southerly direction on December 6.[3] If the 27th Bombardment Group pilots had been present for the colonel's warnings, they might not have partied into the morning hours of December 8. As it was, most had only a few hours of sleep before they heard of the Japanese attack on Pearl Harbor. Details of the bombing were sketchy at best. So what if Japan attacked Hawaii, they thought, certainly our navy destroyed them. But what concerned the men more at that moment was the rumor that the Philippines would be hit next. Without their airplanes, what would the 27th fight with?

Information in the military is usually directed through the chain of command from the higher-ranking officers down to the enlisted personnel. The attack on Pearl Harbor started at 7:55 on Sunday morning, December 7, which was 2:25 A.M. Manila time, Monday, December 8 (the International Dateline is between Hawaii and the Philippines). At 3:40 A.M. MacArthur's chief of staff, Brig. Gen. Richard Sutherland, received the news of the Pearl Harbor raid and, in turn, immediately notified MacArthur, who had difficulty believing that the Japanese had struck Hawaii (having expected the initial attack to be against the Philippines). By 5:00 A.M. Admiral Hart hurried to MacArthur's office to confer on strategies. Meanwhile, General Brereton was outside, waiting to tell MacArthur that he wanted his planes armed and in the air and to seek permission to bomb Formosa. But the USAFFE commander was too busy to see him. Brereton was told to go back to his office at Nielson Field and await further orders.

The air commander had earlier informed Majs. Reginald Vance and John Davies about the Pearl Harbor attack, and they, in turn, informed their officers. The *27th Reports* records these first hours of hostilities:

> At 4:30 A.M., Major Davies, our Commanding Officer [would become CO that day] got a phone call. Pearl Harbor had been bombed. War had come. Twenty-three years of peace and a phone call at an ungodly hour stating that peace was no more. We were stunned. We couldn't believe it. And all we could do was sit tight and hope our ships [planes] arrived. At. 8:00 A.M. reports started coming in of other raids and most of them in the Philippines. Nobody knew what to do. The only thing we knew how to fight with was planes, and we had none. Capt. Hipps started the men off on small arms drill, and we went about the unimportant details in a daze.[4]

Most of the pilots of the 27th were sleeping off the effects of the wild party the night before. At 6:45 A.M. (December 8 in Manila), while James McAfee was getting dressed for breakfast, he heard the tail end of a radio broadcast about Pearl Harbor. Ron Hubbard, lying in bed, heard the commotion, covered his ears, and went back to sleep. At 8:00 A.M. Hubbard was on his way to the shower when someone ran in and shouted that Major Davies wanted to see him immediately.

Frank Bender writes in his memoir about the attack on Pearl Harbor: "We did not seem to worry about it [the War] too much, and we conjured up the thought that lasted throughout the days until the Philippines fell into the hands of the enemy, that there would almost immediately be an immense convoy sailing to deliver to us the goods and wherewithal to finish this debacle in our favor and come home." Bender's reason for confidence was partially correct. In preparation for a potential war, U.S. Army troop strength had swelled from 188,565 in 1939 to 1,460,998 by December 1941.[5] The problem was that most of these men, including pilots, were still being trained and combat units still needed to be assembled and equipped.

In his diary McAfee voices concern about his brother, Lt. Stanley McAfee, who was stationed on the minelayer USS *Oglala* at Pearl Harbor. It was difficult in the early hours sorting out what information was the truth from what was only rumor. Being an officer, he had more access to the real information about what had happened at Pearl Harbor than the enlisted men. Even so, three days after the sneak attack, McAfee observed, "They say we weren't hurt much at Pearl Harbor but I wouldn't be surprised if the whole fleet was sunk." Glen Stephenson knew his brother Clyde was stationed on the USS *California* and probably heard in the first few days that the battleship was listing to one side. What he did not know was that Clyde was not aboard when the Japanese attacked.

Pearl Harbor

Although the conquest of Hawaii was not an initial goal of the Japanese military, naval leaders knew that if war came with the United States, the U.S. Pacific Fleet stationed at Pearl Harbor would have to be dealt with quickly and decisively. If they failed, those warships would be a major threat to the Japanese conquest of the island nations of the western Pacific. When the attack came, news of it was flashed around the world.

Within a few days, newspapers carried the picture of the burning USS *Arizona* settled on the bottom of Pearl Harbor. The story with the picture also told of the damage to Clyde's battleship, the *California*. Glen had exchanged letters with Clyde since his younger brother had joined the Marine Corps in January 1940. While ferrying bombers in the summer of 1941, Glen had just missed him in Long Beach. On the way to the Philippines in November, he again just missed him in Honolulu. What Glen never learned was that Clyde had a ringside seat for American's entrance into World War II.

The *California* returned to port a few weeks before the attack after gunnery maneuvers at sea. This target practice developed ominous signs when submarines that were not American were noticed in the area. The battleship received orders to put live ammunition in all of its guns, the first time Clyde could remember that happening. The guns remained loaded until the *California* returned to port. A week before the air raid, Clyde's new temporary assignment took him onshore. He was among nine marines selected from each battleship and sent to Fort Weaver at the entrance to Pearl Harbor to teach machine-gun and automatic-rifle firing to sailors. "On Sunday morning we got up early, had breakfast, and went back to the tents and sat down and played some cards. All of a sudden, we had a lot of planes going overhead. A few seconds later, we heard explosions. It didn't take long to figure out what was happening."

Japanese dive bombers began their attacks from high altitudes over the ships, but the torpedo bombers made lower runs only five hundred feet off the ground. On their way to launch torpedoes against the ships in harbor, they passed over the marines. Clyde remembered: "Directly overhead was at least a squadron of torpedo bombers. The torpedoes could be seen shining in the sunlight." A nearby armory stored rifles and machine guns. The Marines tore the wooden door off, grabbed weapons, and started peppering away at the planes. The first air strike lasted about an hour. Fortunately, no bombs fell in Clyde's area; the maps the aviators were using probably did not even include Fort Weaver. During the half-hour lull before the second attack, the marines organized and started to look for a possible Japanese landing. These men could not see Battleship Row, trees blocking their view, but they could see enemy planes and hear explosions. From the noise and billowing smoke, they knew their navy was devastated. The second attack, which included much strafing, lasted about another hour. The marines continued to fire at the Japanese aircraft and to watch for amphibious landings. Clyde commented, "One plane came right down the 500-yard rifle range at us flying very low, and I believe, was hit considerably, although probably not vitally, as he headed away in good order."

For two days the marines stayed on the beach at Fort Weaver looking for an invasion force. On Tuesday, December 9, Clyde was finally ordered to return to the *California*. His ship had been moored at the southern-most area of Battleship Row, closest to the harbor entrance, on December 7. Shortly after the attack began, a bomb hit and exploded a magazine of antiaircraft ammunition that was stored below decks, killing about fifty men. A second bomb destroyed the battleship's bow plates, and the incoming water could not be held back. The *California* sank into the muck, with only her superstructure remaining visible.[6] According to Clyde, "Our ship was hit with a couple of torpedoes and couple of bombs and it sank right at the piling it was tied up to. It set down in 30 feet of mud at a slight angle to port. The upper decks were out of water and everything under the water line was flooded."

Approximately 186 vessels, including yard craft, were anchored at Pearl Harbor at the time of the Japanese attack, roughly half of the U.S. Pacific Fleet. No aircraft carriers were in port. The battleships *California, Oklahoma, West Virginia, Arizona, Nevada,* and *Utah* were sunk. The *Tennessee, Maryland,* and *Pennsylvania* were moderately damaged. Additionally, three light cruisers, three destroyers, and four auxiliary craft were either sunk or significantly damaged. More than two hundred airplanes were destroyed or damaged. Those killed, missing, and who died of wounds numbered 2,403 men, while another 1,178 wounded survived.[7]

Clyde Stephenson and Stanley McAfee, whose ships were sunk, witnessed one of the two most one-sided battles of the Pacific War. Little did they realize at the time that their older brothers Glen and Jim were present for the other—the Battle for the Philippines.

In addition to Pearl Harbor and the Philippines, the Japanese also attacked U.S. military garrisons on the islands of Guam, Wake, and Midway, as well as the British in Singapore, the Malayan peninsula, and Hong Kong that day.[8] Historians debate the exact date World War II started, as many consider the German invasion of Poland in September 1939 as the origin date. Others suggest Japan's attack on Manchuria in September 1931 as an even earlier beginning. The abundant natural resources and good strategic position Japan acquired allowed for the empire's continued expansion.[9] In 1937 Japan invaded China and began occupying French Indochina in 1940.

With the development of the Greater East Asia Co-Prosperity Sphere, Japan's intentions were clearly the conquest and subjugation of all lands and peoples on the western rim of the Pacific Ocean, extending from the Aleutian Islands in the north to as far south as New Guinea and the Solomon Islands. The scope of Japan's imperial vision included the Philippines, Hong Kong, Burma, Malaya, the Dutch East Indies, French Indochina, and Thailand. Whether it intended to also conquer Australia and New Zealand had not yet been fully determined by December 1941.

December 8: Confusion on Luzon

Right here was where the 27th had their first run in with that all powerful hunk of paper called the T.B.A. [Table of Basic Allowances, which describes how many and what type of weapons, other equipment, and personnel a particular type of unit can have.] The T. B. A. said no rifles and no machine guns and that the Material Squadron at an Air Base was supposed to do our protecting for us. What Material Squadron and what Air Base weren't specified [their field at San Marcelino was not ready yet] and that ended that. We learned fast enough though and with a little aid and some fast paper work that was never proven, 450 rifles appeared on the scene and the Group started training.[10]

In his memoir Hubbard recalls "rumors everywhere, but no real facts. We expected to be attacked at any moment. The rest of the day was total chaos. Air raid alarms but no attacks. Rumors everywhere but no real news. We were to furnish three crews for B-18s at Nichols Field to bomb Formosa at night." But the mission to bomb Formosa did not happen. Reasons given included the lack of reconnaissance information about enemy positions, the need for the Japanese to attack the Philippines first before offensive air action could be initiated, and MacArthur's unfamiliarity with strategic air capabilities.[11]

Some in the 27th were even beginning to doubt if Pearl Harbor had really been attacked and that the United States was really at war. After the noon hour, however, such doubts were erased. Iba Field and Clark Field were attacked.

Iba Field was next to the village of Iba, about 85 miles northwest of Manila on the western coast of Luzon. The airfield had a grass runway and a run-down army barracks, which housed the personnel. The 3rd Pursuit Squadron was located there as well as an army air-warning-system (AWS) detachment, which had arrived on October 18 and set up a SCR-270 B radar installation. This station consisted of electronic equipment and an oscilloscope housed in an operating truck, which was connected to another truck that provided the power supply, with an antenna mounted on a large trailer. Both vehicles were hidden under tarps. The radar had a 150-mile tracking limit. But unlike those being used by the British and Germans as well as some back in the States, this unit could not determine the altitude of any targets it tracked. Since November 29 the AWS detachment had been operating their radar station continuously, working each of the three crews in eight-hour shifts.[12]

On a number of occasions, Iba radar had picked up blips of what the operators suspected were waves of Japanese planes over the South China Sea heading toward Clark Field or Manila. These radar sightings usually occurred at night, so when P-40s were directed to the location of the bogey, the pilots were unable to make the intercept because it was dark and were usually flying at a different altitude. The blips that the Iba radar was tracking then would turn around and head back over the open sea. At the time some believed that these hits were merely the radar malfunctioning.[13]

The Japanese soon determined that Iba Field was operating in conjunction with some form of advanced aircraft-detection system, which alerted the fighter squadron there. A naval communications unit monitored AWS personnel using voice and Morse code to vector P-40s toward the approaching aircraft. Japanese spies working on Luzon may also have reported on the radar unit at Iba. Although these flights over Luzon were for reconnaissance, many now believe that some were merely a test to see how close aircraft could advance toward the Philippines before being detected. At a meeting held at 1:00 A.M. on December 8, Japanese naval air headquarters on Formosa decided to alter their bombing plans for their initial raids that morning, changing the targets from Clark and Nichols Fields to Clark and Iba. Based on their intelligence estimates, Japanese headquarters now realized that the

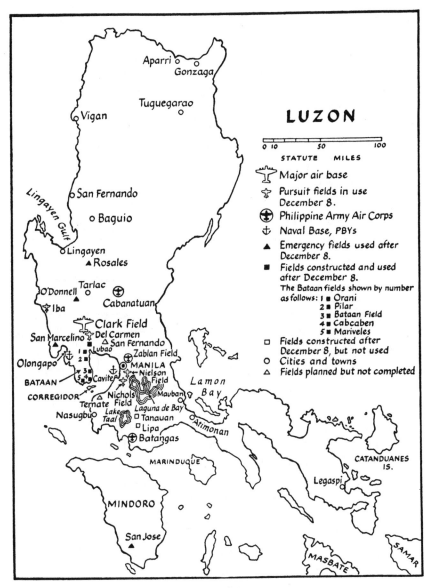

3. Airfields on Luzon. *Courtesy Little, Brown, and Co.*

P-40s at Iba would be waiting for their strike force as it flew south from Formosa against Clark and Nichols Fields and would also be ready to attack the returning bombers.[14]

Brereton, whose request for offensive action was denied earlier that morning, heard that the Japanese had raided Baguio in northern Luzon about 8:30 A.M. This strike, he believed, constituted an attack on the Philippines, and he again requested authority to begin offensive operations. What he received from MacArthur's headquarters was permission to conduct reconnaissance only over Formosa.

The Japanese attacks on Pearl Harbor and the Philippines were very well planned and executed. The raids on the Philippines involved 252 modern aircraft for an overwhelming aerial assault.[15] The U.S. Army Air Corps had on Luzon only 125 modern aircraft, including about ninety P-40 fighters and thirty-five B-17 bombers; sixteen of those B-17s had been appropriately sent five hundred miles south to Del Monte Plantation on December 6 so they would be out of harm's way in case of a surprise air attack.

The morning of December 8 found the FEAF fighter squadrons on high alert and ready to take off, together with most of the B-17 bombers at Clark Field. Three other B-17s were undergoing maintenance and consequently grounded.

Soon after dawn on December 8, small numbers of carrier-based aircraft made attacks on the Davao Airfield at Mindanao in the southern Philippines, inflicting minor damage.[16] Major attacks on Luzon were set to begin about that time, while the Japanese airplanes on Formosa were about four hundred miles north of the northern tip of Luzon. Army bombers were already in the air and attacked a minor airfield in northern Luzon at about 8:30 A.M. Another group of aircraft bombed Camp John Hay, the army's summer retreat in the town of Baguio a couple of hundred miles north of Manila, apparently hoping to catch MacArthur spending time there.[17] Philippine president Quezon was at his summer residence in the hills near Camp John Hay convalescing from tuberculosis. When he heard the planes thundering over his house, he had his secretary call the general's headquarters in Manila.[18] None of the planes was intercepted.

Most of the American fighters from the various Luzon airfields were patrolling much of the morning, looking for enemy aircraft or providing protection for the airfields, the naval base, and Manila, in many cases responding to false alarms. All of the B-17s, except the three being serviced, were in the air. A few of these were sent on reconnaissance missions looking for Japanese aircraft and naval vessels, while the rest circled Luzon so they would not be caught on the ground. The main strike force of Japanese aircraft, navy bombers and fighter planes, were scheduled to take off at 2:30 A.M. and arrive over their targets shortly after dawn.[19] Because of a dense fog at airfields in western Formosa, they were not able to begin taking off until about 8:18 A.M. Meanwhile, as the morning wore on, the American fighters had returned to their bases for refueling and the B-17s were called back. At about 10:14 A.M. MacArthur telephoned Brereton and gave him permission to bomb Formosa.[20]

Around 11:30 A.M. the radar station at Iba Field picked up what appeared to be a large flight of aircraft, numbers unknown, coming from the north and headed toward Luzon.[21] All U.S. fighter squadrons were notified. As the enemy aircraft neared the coast, it appeared that one group was headed toward Iba and the other toward the Manila area, possibly to bomb the city, the large naval base at Cavite, or one of the nearby airfields. Colonel George ordered all fighters to either intercept the enemy or fly protective patterns over airfields and other potential targets.

U.S. fighter pilots encountered problems all morning. One was responding to false alarms, which would continue throughout the day. Another involved the communication systems—radio, telephone, and telegraph— which did not always function correctly between the various airfields, the command center, and pilots in the air, thus interfering with in-flight coordination of aircraft and properly vectoring them to intercept the enemy. Since the radar at Iba Field had been active only a few weeks, at times there were doubts concerning if it was functioning appropriately. In addition, when fighters took off from some airfields, they stirred up so much dust that, after a few launched, the rest would have to either wait for the dust to settle or take off from a different direction, and then only with diminished visibility. The takeoff delays also added further confusion, and some squadrons never assembled once they became airborne.

Capt. William "Ed" Dyess of Albany, Texas, was the twenty-five-year-old commanding officer of the 21st Pursuit Squadron, which had been located at Hamilton Field, California, and was sent over on the *Coolidge* with the 27th Bombardment Group. Upon his squadron's arrival at Nichols Field in late November, his men were issued some well-worn P-35 fighters. About a week later they began receiving the new P-40s. According to Dyess, none of the guns in the new planes had been fired. The unit had to install and bore sight them, which basically means adjusting the gun sights. Only a few rounds were issued for the test purposes because of a shortage of .50-caliber ammunition. "Some of the planes had not ever been in the air. The gun barrels still were packed with cosmoline [a protective grease put on guns when in storage]. The Filipino mechanics assigned to help us prepare for the eventualities were more hindrance than help. Many of them [young pilots] were only a few months out of flying school. They knew the zero hour was at hand."[22]

After circling Luzon for a few hours, the B-17s were called back before noon, refueled, and dispersed. Their pilots broke for lunch. As they were eating, everyone had a chuckle as Don Bell, the popular Manila radio announcer, came on the air and reported that Clark Field had been bombed. Bell was reporting from the top of a downtown Manila hotel.

Bandits over the Philippines

As the pilots headed back to their bombers, the ominous drone of the Japanese armada could be heard in the distance. Some joyously thought the overhead planes were from the U.S. Navy. Their enthusiasm was short lived when they noticed bomb-bay doors opening.

The Japanese pilots expected all hell to break loose around them as they neared Clark, with P-40s and flak thick in the sky and minimal aircraft targets on the ground. But what they found at the airbase was "a target rich environment." Men on the ground were enjoying lunch, and many planes fully loaded with fuel and munitions were sitting in dispersal areas.

But two significant factors kept the American bombers and fighters on the ground at Clark Field. The B-17s had been out that morning and had just returned for refueling and arming for a possible bombing mission to Formosa. Colonel George had issued orders to the fighter squadrons through their group headquarters to intercept any oncoming Japanese aircraft. The planes were fully fueled and the pilots in their cockpits, but the group commander at Clark, Maj. Orrin Grover, kept them on the ground. Trying to sort out some of the confusion and false alarms, Grover wanted to wait until he had an exact bead on the enemy bombers before sending up his planes. Unfortunately, he kept them on the ground too long.

Two formations of bombers were sighted approaching the air field at about 20,000 feet and flying in V-formations of twenty-seven and twenty-six planes. At this, Joe Moore, the leader of the 20th Pursuit Squadron, could wait no more and gave the order to take off.[23] Moore and Grover did not know that the Japanese fighters were already high over Clark Field, circling and waiting to cover the bombers as they arrived. Moore and two other P-40s had just taken off as the bombers passed over the field, dropping their ordnance in an almost perfect pattern. The three fighter pilots were gaining altitude as they looked back to see the field covered with smoke, explosions, and burning aircraft. In a matter of minutes, the Japanese had dropped 636 bombs on Clark, not one which landed more than 200 feet outside the border of the field.[24] After the bombers had passed over, the Japanese fighters came down and strafed what was left. First, a group of thirty-four Zeros, which had been escorting the bombers, attacked the airfield for twenty-two minutes. After they left at 1:00 P.M., another group of fifty-one Zeros arrived and strafed Clark Field until 1:15 P.M.[25]

Two other bomber formations, also totaling fifty-three aircraft, attacked Iba at 12:44 P.M. They inflicted major damage on the airfield and its installations in a matter of minutes, dropping 480 132-pound bombs and 26 1,100-pound bombs.[26] Most importantly, they destroyed the only functioning U.S. Army radar in the Philippines.[27] After the bombers left, forty-two Zeros strafed Iba until 1:05 P.M.

Although these major attacks had been planned for much earlier in the day and were delayed because of fog on Formosa, as it turned out, the timing, particularly at Clark Field, could not have been better for the Japanese. Eighteen of the nineteen B-17s there were either destroyed or significantly damaged; one was still out on patrol and escaped damaged. Through repair and salvage, six of the damaged bombers were later made operational.[28] Also, about thirty-four P-40 fighters were destroyed, twenty of them on the ground at Clark.[29]

American fighters had difficulties with high-altitude flying during the opening days of the war. The P-40s did not have supercharged engines and were relatively heavy, so they had difficulty reaching the higher altitudes where the Japanese bombers flew. Once there, the fighters' maneuverability above 20,000 feet was quite limited. Another problem was that oxygen-tank adapters had not been installed in many of the P-40s. According to Dyess: "We learned that day what it is like to fly for hours at 15,000 feet and above without oxygen. There was none [oxygen] at Clark Field. Without it, that night found me so done in, I doubt I could have seen a Jap even if he had been in the cockpit with me."[30] The adapters, needed for transferring stored oxygen from the tanks to the fighters for use by the pilots, had not yet arrived, and this severely limited the time that pilots could function above 15,000 feet. When the Americans did reach these altitudes and got near the Japanese bombers, they first met escorting fighters. And on this count, many of the P-40 pilots experienced malfunctions of some or all of their six .50-caliber machine guns because of defective parts.[31]

Another reason the Japanese chose to bomb from 20,000 feet was that that altitude was 2,000 feet beyond the range of the Americans' antiquated 3-inch antiaircraft guns. This turned out to be an unnecessary precaution. The 200th Coast Artillery, responsible for Clark's antiaircraft defenses, could manage to explode only one out of six of their 3-inch shells at the correct altitude; those that did so still fell 2,000–4,000 feet short of the high-flying bombers.[32] As would be expected, especially on the opening day of the war, a certain amount of damage was also inflicted on the P-40s by friendly fire.

Finally, in the few minutes it took to bomb Clark and Iba fields, most means of communication were destroyed or damaged. The result was that fighter pilots flying protection over the Manila area could not be contacted and directed to intercept the enemy aircraft. Many of those pilots never saw an enemy warplane that day.

Up until December 7 and 8, army pilots thought that Japanese aircraft were vastly inferior, but they quickly learned this was certainly not the case. The Zeros proved much more maneuverable than the P-40, though the latter were slightly faster, and that the P-35s many used that day were no match.

Alleged to be Wingtip to Wingtip

The military had several hours after the raid on Pearl Harbor to prepare for a possible strike on the Philippines, and yet historians have often stated that MacArthur and Brereton inadvertently left their airplanes lined up in neat rows, wingtip to wingtip, making them sitting ducks for the Japanese air attack. In fact the Army Air Corps in the Philippines lost about half of its modern airplanes that morning. MacArthur and Brereton gave different reasons for this in subsequent years. Determining which one of them was really at fault may never be resolved conclusively. Historian William Bartsch has performed an autopsy of sorts on the day (December 8) in the Philippines in an attempt to establish the etiology (or cause) of and the responsibility for the loss of planes on the ground at Clark Field. As a result of his detailed dissection, he finds that MacArthur, Brereton, and other leaders shared the blame for some aspect of the day's disaster. But he also castigates certain personnel at Clark for not getting the 20th Pursuit Squadron airborne in a timely fashion and for not passing along to the headquarters of Eubank's B-17 force a warning about the approaching enemy aircraft the airfield received.[33]

December 8 Continues

Six of the pilots from the 27th—Tom Gerrity, Robert Ruegg, Gus Heiss, Alexander Salvatore, Bender, and Harry Roth—volunteered to go on a mission flying the old B-18 bombers. The men were not sure where they were going, but they thought they would probably be attacking Japanese bases on Formosa. They flew from Nielson Field over to Nichols Field to have bombs loaded. While at Nichols, the air-raid sirens went off. Heiss's and Bender's planes were able to get off the ground, but Gerrity, piloting the third plane, was trying to get his engines started when a bomb exploded nearby and injured his hand. Heiss and Bender flew around for about two and a half hours until they thought it was safe to return, but when they could not get an all clear over Nichols, they headed to Batangas, a Filipino army airfield farther south of Manila. Bender observes in his memoir: "Their Filipino outfit was equipped with P-26 aircraft which were ancient fighters equipped with .30 caliber guns, slow, and long disregarded by our forces. Nonetheless, Captain Jesus Villamor led his group of valiant men, and distinguished himself, as did his men, as long as they had a ship to fly."

On December 8 Major Vance was officially transferred to Brereton's headquarters and made intelligence officer. Davies then assumed command of the 27th.[34]

Later that afternoon, when reports of the destruction at Iba and Clark filtered into Manila, the men of the 27th assumed that Fort McKinley would be next. For the rest of the day, the enlisted men dug foxholes, manned machine-gun posts at Nichols Field, and watched the skies as the air-raid sirens screamed false alarms every couple of hours.

Finally in the middle of the night, the Japanese attacked them. "The first air raid was quite an experience. It came at 0300 Dec. 9th with no warning at all and after two or three false alarms. Brother Hubbard got so tangled up in his mosquito net he thought it was made of flypaper, and Bert Bank went through the porch screen without bothering to find the door." For Hubbard, the "bombs were thunderous and lifted me out of bed right through the mosquito net. As I went out, I noticed someone had gone through the screen door without bothering to open it." McAfee told a similar tale: "Last night was a Lulu! The first bomb hit about 1/2 mile away and several more fell in quick succession. I went through the mosquito bar just a flyin' and hit outside the house in one jump. After it was over, I realized that somehow I had a pair of underwear shorts on, my pistol, tin hat, and shoes. Nothing else!"[35]

It must not have taken over a few seconds to get out of bed, because as we were getting out, we were almost stepped on by rushing, half-naked men. About the time you could get up, you'd be pushed back down again by another person. The Filipinos (a skittish bunch) having set up machine guns throughout the area, were shooting tracer bullets every place. The first impression was that the end had come and stars were shooting every place. Bits of hot shrapnel were falling all around. It looked like a great Fourth of July celebration.[36]

Bender recalled: "When they [the Filipino soldiers] heard the Jap planes, they all started shooting in every which direction that the guns would point. It seemed that everyone who possessed a gun of any sort, including American sidearms, was wildly shooting into the air." The first 27th death was Pfc. Jackson P. Chitwood from the 16th Squadron, killed by a bomb while manning a machine gun at Nichols Field.[37]

Anything and everything that could fire shells and bullets into the sky were used during the bombing raids. The local citizens futilely used pistols. Hubbard got out the .348-caliber rifle with a magnum load that he planned to use for big-game hunting. Because of the dunking his footlocker took in San Francisco Bay, some shells misfired. But perhaps all this fire helped the Japanese achieve nighttime bombing accuracy at Fort McKinley and nearby Nielson and Nichols Fields during blackouts. In addition, McAfee observed: "When the Japs bombed, there must have been 10,000 flares shot up by 5th columnists. Dirty Bastards!"

Manila under Attack

It took a while for the destruction at Pearl Harbor, Iba Field, and Clark Field to sink in. Those first few days of disbelief led to some inaction. The 27th without planes was practically useless. Air-raid warnings continued to be an everyday occurrence, and rumors abounded: "their planes had arrived and were being assembled on Dewey Boulevard"; "the Japanese were landing everywhere"; and "help was on the way." Amid this hurricane of confusion, the pilots of the 27th somehow wanted a crack at the Japanese. On December 10 Davies sent Lieutenants Stirling, Savage, Summers, and seven others to Clark Field to function as pilots. The orders to report to Clark came with Davies's recommendation: "they are damn good pilots and officers." The pat on the back did not help; none of them got to fly. Some salvaged parts, others moved into communications and transportation, and a few served as lookouts. Stephenson, along with Hipps, McAfee, and Ruegg, were sent to Nielson Field to work at Brereton's headquarters.

Captain Hipps was officially assigned to FEAF headquarters, and Stephenson became the new leader of the 16th. In the 17th Squadron Herman Lowery, the commanding officer, was sent to Nichols to work in the G-2 section (intelligence) for Vance, and Mangan replaced him. Mangan, a second lieutenant, had second thoughts about becoming a squadron commander. "I had trouble over time trying to keep the morale of the troops up. We weren't really doing anything. We had no real mission. Trying to keep people busy under conditions as they were was not a pleasant task."

[Lt. Robert W.] Whipple and [Lt. Richard R.] Birnn had the sweet job of sitting on top of one of the hangars as lookouts. It was a nice job if you didn't care about Jap planes and bombs. Every time they sighted something, they had to run up a red flag and then run or fall down about 100 steps and dive into a bomb hole. Whipple used to look at his watch and tell us he had only 12 hours to live. Seems he guarded his life from the time he got off duty until he went back to work. One day while getting ready to take Birnn's place as a flag pole sitter on top of the hangar, Whipple watched Birnn put up the red flag and lead his men down the stairs to safety. Always before, Whipple had let his men go first, but he decided that Birnn had the right idea about leading his men instead of following them. He thought he could move a lot faster than they could under such conditions.[38]

Dyess described taking off on December 10 from Clark Field during one of the scrambles in his P-40: "I was half-way through the take-off, running in an opaque dust cloud before I realized that I had left my goggles, helmet, and parachute behind. When I shot out of the dust into the dazzling sunlight, I almost jumped out of the cockpit. Right beside me was another P-40—Buzz [Wagner]. He recognized me at the same time. He laughed like a hyena."[39] Lt. Boyd D. "Buzz" Wagner commanded the 17th Pursuit Squadron.[40] Another P-40 pilot became disoriented taking off in the dust from Clark that morning and plowed into a B-17.[41] Other pilots were killed or injured and planes destroyed by hitting bomb craters either while landing or taking off.

Zeros and P-40s continued to have dogfights over Manila, and the bombing of Nichols, Nielson, and McKinley continued. McAfee managed the situation map for General Brereton, observing: "It would be bad if the Japs knew they had practically knocked out our air force. Our B-17 force is cut in half and the P-40s about as bad. I remember telling Julia [in a letter] that we would lose a third of our forces learning how to fight. It was more than half!"[42]

A day or so after Fort McKinley was bombed, 27th pilots Heiss and Francis Timlin were ordered to fly an old, beat-up B-18 to attack a convoy of cargo and troop-transport ships off the northern tip of Luzon. They dropped their bombs on the vessels and encountered no enemy fighters. After that they were sent on various other missions. But one evening after returning to Clark Field, their bomber was strafed and destroyed. Heiss and Timlin were issued another battered B-18 and continued to have various adventures with that aircraft until flying it to Australia.

December 10 turned out to be a doubly bad day for the Allies in the western Pacific. The U.S. garrison on the island of Guam, just fifteen hundred miles east of the Philippines, surrendered to the Japanese. That same day the Royal Navy's mightiest and newest battleship, HMS *Prince of Wales,* along with the battlecruiser HMS *Repulse* were sunk in less than two hours by Japanese air attacks. The two capital ships were being escorted by three destroyers—all the Royal Navy could muster for the mission—and were to attack the naval task force landing Japanese troops in Malaya four hundred miles north of Singapore. The British ships had virtually no air support, though an aircraft carrier, HMS *Indomitable,* at that time undergoing repair, was meant to be part of Admiral Phillips's fleet. The *Prince of Wales,* nicknamed "HMS *Unsinkable,*" and the *Repulse* had just arrived in Singapore eight days earlier to support the garrison there and to serve as a deterrent to enemy aggression in the area. Phillips was among the sailors lost with *Prince of Wales.*[43]

On December 13 a group of fifty-two volunteers, all from the 48th Materiel Squadron of the 27th, was sent on a secret mission. They boarded an inter-island boat, the *Palawan,* loaded with 90,000 gallons of aviation fuel and, under the cover of darkness, cautiously headed south to San Jose on the island of Mindoro. There they maintained a grass landing field 150 miles south of Manila. P-40s and bombers could refuel there on their way north to Luzon or on their way south to Del Monte Plantation on Mindanao or to Australia. These men became known as the Mindoro Detachment.

> All three squadrons were merely sitting at Fort McKinley waiting for orders—120 men from the group were assigned to McAfee at Nielson Field. Several of the officers from all squadrons had various jobs at Air Force Headquarters, and a few men were manning machine guns at Nichols Field. Corporal Bandish, 16th Squadron, distinguished himself first in shooting down a Zero that was strafing Nichols Field. He didn't hit the Zero, but shot the pilot through the head, and the Zero ended up in the graveyard along McKinley-Manila road. Several others later got partial credit for shooting down strafing Zeros.[44]

The following day, when FEAF headquarters abandoned Nielson Field for the "safety" of Fort McKinley, McAfee was placed in charge of the airfield. "I guess they figured nobody but a low-ranking 1st Lieutenant would be dumb enough to stay on that field—it's going to be bombed to hell. We're having a terrible time camouflaging them. There's no cover here." High-ranking officers drove by the base, according to McAfee, and "then retreated to a safe place and called me and gave me hell for not hiding the planes better. You can't make them invisible."

Harry Mangan's tenure as a squadron leader came to an abrupt end on December 17, after the *Pensacola* convoy was found. The USS *Meigs,* loaded with the 27th's dive bombers, never docked at Pier Seven in Manila Bay as expected. It and the other vessels of the convoy were headed for Brisbane, Australia. Only twenty-three pilots and two enlisted men from the 27th were selected to fly to Australia to get the planes. One of them was Mangan.

The Great Escape

Mangan was told by Major Davies, "I want to see you in my quarters at 2:00 this afternoon and bring a parachute and a change of clothes and don't tell anybody anything." Later he ran into about eight other people who had been given the same message. Soon after, they all were told that as soon as it got dark, they were going to Nichols Field to board an airplane.

Hubbard recalled: "We were to assemble at Nichols Field for a 3:00 A.M. take off. Two B-18s and a C-39 [two-engine transport plane] were to get us there. They were all on their last legs, held together with hope and bailing wire." Secrecy was of the utmost importance, especially with Japanese spies and collaborators in the area. Pilots were not told of their destination until the last minute.

> Several officers were secretly called to headquarters. They were all scared to death. No one knew what he had done or what he was going to do. They were told they would all go to Nichols Field about 7:00 P.M. and would receive orders there. Everyone was guessing where he might be going. Everyone had ideas it would be south, but due to the fact that they were only allowed to bring 30 lbs. of luggage, they thought it couldn't be very far south. They fully expected to be back within two weeks with planes and equipment for combat.[45]

Summers returned in the early evening of the seventeenth from Clark Field and was met by Davies. "He said hello to me, and he also told the Adjutant to put my name back on the list. He left, and I asked the Adjutant just what I had volunteered for and he told me that I was one of the pilots who had been chosen to fly to Brisbane."[46] The two enlisted men going from the 27th were MSgt. William Wesley and SSgt. William Hewitt, the line and communication chiefs. (See appendix 1 for list of 27th pilots who left for Australia.)

The pilots had to take off in the dark because the Japanese had air superiority over the entire area. The airfield was entirely blacked out, and the
2,500-foot runway was pocked with bomb craters.

Nichols Field was black as pitch and a rather grim, quiet group of
men moved over the small bridge leading to the living quarters of
Nichols Field proper. They knew their future hopes and plans. They
had been thoroughly briefed that afternoon at a secret session at Fort
McKinley. Now that crew moved silently to a chosen rendezvous
at Nichols Field. And what a rendezvous! A set of quarters near the
flying field itself had been chosen as the meeting place but it had also
been chosen by the Nips as a target. It showed the effect.

A bomb had hit directly in the back yard and had halved a huge
tree standing there. The effects of the bomb extended to the house
itself and the entire rear had been demolished. Debris lay all about in
the living room where the gang was to assemble. The weird glow of a
candle disclosed maps scattered on the floor.

"Gus" Heiss and F. E. Timlin had just come in with their battered
B-18 and were bending over the maps. Jack Caldwell was speaking
softly and the pilots around heard the plan. "Salvy" Salvatore and
Fred Hoffman [from the Philippine Air Depot] were to fly the C-39.
Strong [possibly Allison Strauss] and his co-pilot, the B-18. "Gus"
and "Tim," the other B-18. Plans called for a 3:00 A.M. take off for
Darwin, Australia.

The men went to various rooms of the house to grab a bit of
sleep. The mosquitoes were terrific and sleeping hard at best. Some
went out in front and stayed awake.

Finally 3:00 A.M. came. The band moved as one for the field talking quietly and trying not to notice the stench of dead horses and
people buried in the wreckage of native dwellings nearby. A broken
gas main lent its own odor. The shattered hangars cast a weird frame-
work in the glow of fires on their floors.

Hoffman and "Salvy" led their boys to the C-39 and everyone
piled aboard. Sal had never seen the inside of a C-39 but co-pilot he
was. Hoffman studied the engines and Grant Mahony [a P-40 pilot]
went ahead with a flashlight to lead Hoffman to the runway. Finally
at the runway, Hoffman turned and faced the ship down the runway.
Grant crawled in, maps were checked, and everyone tensed for the
take-off. After all, a blacked out field with a 2500-ft. bomb-marked

runway and an overload is no breeze. A mechanic stood at the end of the strip and blinked a flashlight—the signal to go. The engines broke into a roar; the ship started moving. Down the runway it thundered and headed for the trees at the far end. An eternity passed and the end of the runway came fast. At last Fred pulled the overloaded ship into the air and the 27th's representatives of hope were Australia bound. At the meeting they heard their much sought after A-24s were docked in Australia and after them they were. Oh Lord, how the Philippines needed those planes.[47]

But the men surely wondered why their planes were in Australia and not Manila. And many were concerned about the condition in which they would find them.

The Pensacola *Convoy and Politics*

On November 14 the flotilla known as the *Pensacola* convoy set sail from San Francisco for the Philippines. Seven transport and cargo vessels, including the *Meigs,* which carried the much needed fifty-two A-24 dive bombers, were escorted by the heavy cruiser *Pensacola* and the submarine chaser *Niagara.*[48] The ships also carried two regiments of artillery, large quantities of ammunition, unassigned army pilots, personnel from the 7th Bombardment Group, and eighteen P-40s. Back in November, many in the 27th thought the convoy at most was two days behind them, not the two weeks it actually was. Since convoys were required to zigzag at the speed of its slowest ship, the group lost ground every day against its expected time of arrival.

After stopping in Honolulu, the *Pensacola* convoy left on November 30 for its trek across the Pacific by way of the slower, longer, but safer southern route. When the ships received word of the attack on Pearl Harbor, paint cans emerged and the vessels were painted battleship gray. Weapons and ammunition were removed from the holds, lookouts were posted, and the crewmen wore life jackets at all times.[49]

Meanwhile, a tug of war developed as to what to do with the convoy. Adm. Richard Turner, director of the navy's War Plans Division, wanted it to return to reinforce Hawaii. Gen. Leonard T. Gerow, head of the army's War Plans Division, wanted it to return to the States. Gen. George C. Marshall, chief of staff of the U.S. Army, thought it should continue to Manila to aid MacArthur. And there was the rumor that others thought it should head to England to help the British.[50] While the argument raged, the convoy was ordered to put into Suva in the Fiji Islands until further notice.

Even though prudent military strategists in Washington believed that the war in Europe had to be won first and thus the convoy should return to the United States, President Roosevelt felt obligated to help MacArthur and the Philippines. The islands were, after all, a possession of the United States, and the general was popular. The sentiment of the American public after Pearl Harbor was strongly in favor of helping the Philippines. On December 12 the convoy was finally ordered to Brisbane. A "Most Secret" Australian message indicated the approximate arrival time of the convoy as December 16 or 17. Thus, Davies needed to get his pilots to Australia as soon as possible.

Hipps, who was working at FEAF headquarters, remembered that when Brereton heard that the convoy was to proceed to Brisbane: "He went directly to MacArthur and told him that he thought the entire 27th Bombardment Group should be immediately sent by ship to Australia so that the dive bombers could be reassembled and brought back. He also explained to MacArthur that the enlisted men were highly trained and experienced and the pilots of the 27th were top notch." But MacArthur reportedly replied, "the airmen are able-bodied and should make damn good infantrymen." Hipps believed that not sending the entire unit to Australia was a big mistake.

The reality was that, despite what MacArthur is alleged to have told Brereton, he needed those A-24s as much as anyone, and he needed them as soon as possible. Also, the planes were useless without the 27th pilots, who had been trained to operate them under combat conditions. The quickest way to get the aircraft to Luzon was to fly the pilots and mechanics to Australia and then fly the dive bombers back. In fact, a plan to that effect had been put together rapidly. Whether it was MacArthur's, Brereton's, or someone else's idea is not known. A document dated December 13 from the 27th's headquarters, addressed to "Commanding General [Brereton], FEAF," and marked "Secret" lists fifty-four pilots and fifty-seven enlisted men by name who were to go, presumably by air, to retrieve the rerouted planes.

MacArthur was elated at the news that the *Pensacola* convoy would not turn back to Hawaii, even believing that with a strong naval escort, the transports and freighters could make Manila.[51] On about December 18 he and Admiral Hart held a meeting in Hart's office to discuss the convoy. Hart did not share the general's optimism. He and his colleagues believed that retaining the Philippines was no longer possible and that resources should be saved to "defend the defensible."[52] With the Japanese in control of the air, Hart also wondered how the ships would safely unload their men and cargo if they got through to Manila.

On December 21, before the convoy arrived in Brisbane, MacArthur contacted Brig. Gen. Julian F. Barnes, in charge of the army troops in the transports. He instructed him to unload the airplanes in Australia and have the air-corps personnel assemble them there. Afterward, the rest of the troops and equipment would proceed to the Philippines if a naval escort could be secured.

Moving cautiously, the convoy reached Brisbane on December 22, about five days later than expected (at which time the 27th's pilots, led by Major Davies, were more than seventeen hundred miles away in Darwin). Unfortunately, the ships had been loaded without any tactical purpose, and all manifests were hopelessly confused.[53] After docking, every hold had to be entirely emptied and then reloaded, leaving behind the aircraft and airmen. The convoy then started for the Philippines on December 28. Yet when Maj. Gen. George Brett arrived to assume command of all U.S. troops in Australia, one of his first acts was to reroute it to Darwin and notify MacArthur on January 1, 1942, that the tactical situation would not allow the ships to press on to Manila.[54]

Early Weeks of the War

The war in the Philippines continued as a one-sided affair during the balance of December 1941. The Japanese continued bombing airfields and other military installations on a daily basis, while MacArthur's air force wilted. The remaining planes in service were often damaged and needed constant maintenance and repair; because of the dwindling numbers, the P-40s were mainly used for reconnaissance and only occasionally to challenge the Japanese planes. The antiaircraft efforts of the 200th and 515th Coast Artillery were moderately successful despite the fact that they were firing obsolete, corroded ammunition. If the Japanese had realized in these early days just how bad MacArthur's situation was, they might have initiated their invasion sooner.

The 5th Bomber Command sent B-17s from the 19th Bombardment Group on missions against the Japanese from Del Monte. But by December 20 the last of the remaining fourteen bombers were transferred to Batchelor Field near Darwin, Australia. From there they continued to fly missions against targets in the Philippines.

The enemy continued to bomb Clark Field once or more daily followed by strafing runs. Most of the buildings had been destroyed, and most of the men were living in the rifle butts (protective areas where targets were placed during rifle practice) at the edge of the field. Conditions were bleak. The men often wore the same clothes for weeks. Pete Bender and Harry Roth were assigned to fly a B-18 at night and take personnel and supplies from Clark to Del Monte. They flew without navigational aids, and a blackout was in effect throughout the Philippines. Their flights during these very dark nights were often punctuated by severe thunderstorms.

Bender recalled about one of the Clark Field bombings: "We saw them open the bomb-bay doors and then the bombs started falling. It looked like the end for us, because we were able to actually see the bombs from the time they left the aircraft. It was a strange feeling, almost like seeing it in slow motion. Because we were in a hole, we could not take our eyes off the bombs as they seemed to be coming directly towards us." Fortunately the bombs dropped no closer than fifty feet from him. "The field had been hit and burned so many times that it was nothing more than ruins and a burnt odor was ever present in the air."

Although a handful of pilots did fly and some ground support staff actually worked on the few aircraft available, the bulk of the 27th tried to keep busy the best they could. Some men built revetments at Nielson Field for the anticipated A-24s. Others became laborers, digging slit trenches and foxholes; functioned as radiomen; or manned machine-gun outposts at Nielson. As optimism increased for the A-24s arrival from Brisbane, higher headquarters ordered the 27th to work on airfields at San Fernando and San Marcelino to the north of Manila and at Lipa to the south.

Most of the men, however, learned how to become infantry soldiers. Cpl. Robert Wolfersberger of the 27th recalled, "We all got issued 30-06 rifles which had to be de-cosmolined and then we were instructed how to use them." These Enfield rifles were leftover World War I issue, and most had not been fired in years. The men were further divided into platoons and hurriedly given instructions on how to disassemble, clean, and reassemble the rifle by officers who probably had little training in the matter.

Army Air Corps headquarters repeatedly requested groups of officers from the 27th for assignments at various airfields where P-40 squadrons were located. In each case the pilots eagerly volunteered because they thought they would be getting to fly combat missions in the fighters. They were disappointed, however, when they arrived at the airfields and found out that their duties would be administrative.

The Invasion

After the initial bombing on December 8, the Japanese followed up with a small invasion force on December 10 at Vigan and Aparri in northern Luzon, approximately 200 miles north of Manila. Another small landing

4. Sequence of Japanese landings on Luzon, December 1941. *Courtesy Little, Brown, and Co.*

soon followed at Legaspi 150 miles southwest of the capital. The invaders met brief resistance from the battered air corps and little from the infantry. The Japanese used these incursions to secure airfields so their aircraft could more easily attack targets on Luzon and provide support for the main invasion later that month.

The landings at Lingayen Gulf came as no surprise. Everyone knew the Japanese Army was coming. It was not a matter of if, but when and where.

"When" was the early morning of December 22. "Where" turned out to be a stroke of luck for the Japanese. American and Filipino leaders had already anticipated where the Japanese landing site would be and had the 11th and 21st Divisions of the Philippine Army waiting for them. But a navigational error placed the invasion convoy four miles south of the intended beachhead and the American defenders.[55] The huge invasion force entered Lingayen Gulf in three transport echelons, with escorting warships in support of seventy-six transports. Onboard was the Fourteenth Army, commanded by Lieutenant General Homma.[56] The Japanese landed at three points, and only on one beach did they meet significant resistance.[57] By the end of the day, more than 43,000 troops, many veterans of the China war, were ashore. Their supplies, along with artillery and tanks, were also on Lingayen beaches. MacArthur instructed his commanders that there would be "no withdrawal from the beach positions," which were to "be held at all costs."[58]

The Fourteenth Has Landed

Homma landed two divisions at Lingayen, the 16th and the 48th, which opposed the two Filipino divisions along with the Philippine Scouts of the 26th Cavalry.[59] MacArthur had always insisted, "The Filipino, if well trained, made an excellent, courageous soldier," but many of the soldiers had little training by this time, and being unorganized, they often fled under the pressure of fire from enemy planes, tanks, and artillery.[60] Resistance against the advancing Japanese was minimal in many areas. The Philippine Scouts were an exception. They were highly trained, motivated soldiers. Wherever their units were deployed, they tenaciously defended their ground.

The fighting on the first day was confused and indecisive. Many Filipino units melted away into the hills. But American troops, the Philippine Scouts, and some other Filipino units kept fighting, which slowed down Homma, a cautious commander.[61] Major General Wainwright requested permission to withdraw the North Luzon Force behind the Agno River, which MacArthur granted.

On December 23 the Japanese made significant advances into American-

and Filipino-held areas, and by evening MacArthur made the decision to pull back to the Bataan Peninsula, which effectively put WPO-3 (War Plan Orange) into action. The withdrawal to Bataan was well organized, with a series of defensive lines temporarily established as well as rear-guard actions to slow down enemy forces so that key roads could be kept open for an orderly retreat.[62]

The next day another 7,000 soldiers of Homma's army landed on the shores of Lamon Bay, seventy-five miles southeast of Manila, as the second arm in an enveloping attack to capture the city. Caught between the two advancing fronts, one from the northwest about one hundred miles from the capital and one from the southeast about seventy-five miles away, were the North and South Luzon Forces, including the 27th Bombardment Group.

Because of Japanese naval and air supremacy, the Philippines were cut off from almost any aid from the United States, Hawaii, or Australia. Thus, according to MacArthur: "General Wainwright quickly developed a pattern of defense to cause a maximum of delay to the enemy. He would hold long enough to force the Japanese to take time to deploy in full force, then he would slowly give way, leaving the engineers under General Casey to dynamite bridges and construct road blocks to bar the way."[63] Brigadier General Parker, commanding the South Luzon Force, went to Bataan to organize the defenses while Brig. Gen. Albert Jones conducted the retreat. Jones used similar delaying maneuvers to slow the Japanese forces coming from the shores of Lamon Bay so that his troops could also reach Bataan.

Commercial buses and other motor vehicles were commandeered to speed up the withdrawal of the South Luzon Force while also moving goods, ammunition, equipment, and medical supplies from Manila to Bataan. The Filipino buses must have been interesting targets for the Zeros. They were typically painted bright orange, yellow, or other colors of the rainbow and covered with advertisements also in bright colors. Each had names painted all over it, including that of the driver's favorite girlfriend.[64]

Homma and his staff had debated as to whether their air forces should bomb the many bridges connecting roads to Bataan, but they decided to leave them intact so they could be used later.[65] MacArthur's forces, however, destroyed 184 bridges during their retreat.[66]

The U.S. Asiatic Fleet

MacArthur's plan for the defense of the Philippines depended heavily on the cooperation of the naval and air-corps leadership, but Admiral Hart, the commander of the U.S. Asiatic Fleet, did not share MacArthur's enthusiasm for the aggressive defense of the Philippines. After the devastation of FEAF on Luzon and his own base at Cavite in Manila Bay, Hart realized that defending the islands was nearly hopeless. MacArthur needed the supply lines from Hawaii and Australia kept open, and the navy was responsible. He was of the opinion that the Japanese blockade of Manila Bay was rather loose.[67] He had also thought that the navy would play a major role in intercepting the Japanese invasion in the Lingayen Gulf.

Hart, a four-star admiral, had not been on the same page with Mac-Arthur, then a three-star general, on many issues, including the notion that the Japanese would wait until April 1942 to attack. He recognized in November, as did his naval superiors, that the deteriorating diplomatic situation between the United States and Japan signaled that war was imminent. In fact, like Brereton, he too had thought the perfect day for such an attack was the day of the Army-Navy game, when American officers, caught up in the emotion of this gridiron rivalry, might have their guard down.[68] Unlike what happened at Pearl Harbor and Clark Field, Hart dispersed many of his ships beyond the range of the Japanese bombers. After the destruction of the Cavite base during the first week of the war, he ordered most of his remaining vessels other than submarines south. After the successful invasions on December 22, he saw the writing on the wall for the Philippines.

Hart also knew his small fleet, which had arrived in Manila Bay from China in the autumn of 1940, was no match against the Japanese Combined Fleet. The U.S. Asiatic Fleet consisted of one heavy cruiser, *Houston,* one light cruiser, *Marblehead,* thirteen aging destroyers and their tender, twenty-nine submarines and their three tenders, twenty-four navy PBY reconnaissance seaplanes, and a dozen or so auxiliary vessels, including six wooden PT boats.[69] At that time the Combined Fleet consisted of ten battleships, thirty-five cruisers, ten modern aircraft carriers, 111 destroyers, and sixty-four submarines.[70] Hart knew that at any time, most of these warships could be in Philippine waters. The admiral himself left Manila on December 26 aboard the submarine *Shark.*

Another problem adding to the American frustration of defending the Philippines was that many torpedoes carried by the U.S. submarines were defective. Only a single transport, the *Hayo Maru,* was sunk by a sub during the invasions of December 22–24.[71]

The 4th Marine Regiment, which consisted of two battalions, was also under Hart's command. The unit had recently arrived at the Olongapo Naval Station at Subic Bay from Shanghai. There was another battalion of marines at the Cavite Naval Base. During the Japanese invasion, the 4th Marines was transferred to Corregidor, where it was given a crucial role in the island's beach defenses. The marine battalion at Cavite was transferred to the Navy Section Base at Mariveles to help in its defense. MacArthur requested that he be given command of these marine units since all would stay behind when much of the navy left. Hart agreed.

When the U.S. Navy Hospital near Cavite was forced to close in late December, some doctors, corpsmen, and other medical personnel were sent to the naval facility at Mariveles while others staffed first-aid stations on Corregidor in support of the marines there. Still others were given jobs at the hospital on Corregidor. A significant portion of this medical staff also remained behind when Hart and the ships left.

Lipa Airfield

Although twenty-three pilots had left to get the A-24s, the majority of fliers remained behind. Davies put Maj. John Sewell in charge of the 27th during his absence. William Eubank continued to lead the 91st Squadron. Glen Stephenson had been put in charge of the 16th Squadron shortly after the war broke out, and Warren Stirling took charge of the 17th Squadron when Lowery and Mangan left for Australia.

Initially, Stephenson, Eubank, and Stirling had been among the fifty-four pilots and fifty-seven enlisted men selected to fly to Australia for the A-24s. The enlisted men would have served as mechanics and in other key technical roles while in Australia, then as rear gunners for the dive bombers on the way back. Between December 13 and 17, the list was reduced because of a lack of available transportation.

Mangan noted about Stephenson's taking over the 16th: "He was a soldier—West Point, career, regular, and a dealer with men. We ROTC [Reserve Officer Training Corps] types were throttle jockeys. We wanted flying hours. I think that influenced Davies' thinking in leaving McAfee, Stirling, and other Pointers with the 27th."

> On December 21st, all Squadrons [16th, 17th, and 91st] were notified
> from Hq that they were to move to new stations to prepare fields
> for the reception of the A-24s which Major Davies and the other
> pilots had gone to Australia to fetch. This was quite a joke, though a
> serious one, to us because we felt that the new stations would all be
> occupied by the enemy very shortly since the war in northern and
> southern Luzon was going badly. The 16th Squadron was supposed
> to go to Lipa 40 miles south of Manila.[72]

When Stephenson and his squadron arrived at Lipa on the twenty-second, at long last the men felt they were doing something constructive, though some thought their work pointless. The Japanese that day had begun their major invasion at Lingayen, north of Manila. Cpl. Robert Wolfersberger observed: "We were ordered to load up our trucks with our equipment, and move from our tents on the parade grounds of Ft. McKinley and go to Lipa in Batangas Province 40 miles south of Manila Bay. There in a sugar cane field next to a coconut grove, the engineers cut a landing strip for our airplanes [A-24s] rumored to be arriving soon."

Bender in his diary captured these thoughts: "We arrived at Lipa toward evening. We worked tirelessly and had about 3,000 natives helping us especially in transplanting grass for the field that was to be our home base after our aircraft arrived. We never knew what the outside world was doing—no telephones or communications."

While the 16th was camped near Lipa for two days with their tents pitched in the coconut grove next to the airstrip, all hell was breaking loose on Luzon. The Japanese army was advancing from both the north and south toward Manila. The enemy to the south of the city was moving rapidly up Highway 1, just east of Lipa.

4

Fighting on Bataan

THE JAPANESE LANDINGS of December 22 and 24 both north and south of Manila had met little resistance. MacArthur learned quickly that the untested North and South Luzon Forces were no match for Homma's Fourteenth Army and its accompanying air and naval superiority.

MacArthur knew that if his troops stayed in Manila and central Luzon, they would rapidly be caught in the Japanese pincer movement. He decided to declare Manila an open city to spare it from destruction.[1] The general moved his headquarters to the island fortress of Corregidor at the mouth of Manila Bay. All American and Filipino troops under his command on Luzon were ordered to retreat to the Bataan Peninsula.

Retreat of the 27th Bombardment Group

Momentous orders such as this one usually move down the chain of command, from the generals at headquarters to generals in the field and then to their subordinate commanders—colonels, lieutenant colonels, majors, captains, and finally the lowly lieutenants. It is never an instantaneous process and sometimes takes hours or longer. Not all of it can be done by telephone, radio, or letter. Sometimes orders have to be transferred by word of mouth or even rumor.

That is exactly what happened to the 27th Bombardment Group on December 24. Verbal orders issued were: "With what you can carry on your backs, be at Pier 7 at 1930 hours [7:30 P.M.]."[2] McAfee observed: "I'll never forget this day. I've never heard of one more snafu. At 1:30 Hipps called and said for me to send all my men to the docks [Manila] to load on a boat. I commandeered enough trucks to transport them [my men]. Everyone was running for their life—I got the impression the Japs were only a few miles away."

The 27th still had two squadrons out in the field—the 91st, led by Lieutenant Eubank, and the 16th, under Lieutenant Stephenson. Eubank at San Fernando, directly north of Manila, received a phone call informing him of the capital's open-city status and to report to the docks. Lieutenant Stirling, commanding the 17th at Fort McKinley, was informed of the movement and arranged for trucks to transport his men directly to the docks.

Meanwhile at Lipa, Stephenson and more than one hundred men of the 16th Squadron were just finishing lunch. The day was hot, the field dusty, and the air filled with rumors. They were on edge after hearing of the successful Japanese landing just to their south near Highway 1. As the men were preparing to go back to work, the distant drone of a car engine speeding toward them caught their attention. Cpl. Robert Wolfersberger recalled that an army staff car raced down the road and slid to a dusty halt at the campsite, where an army colonel inquired for the squadron commander: "The colonel breathlessly told Lt. Stephenson to load up his men and take off for Manila and leave everything [behind] because the Japs had landed at a seaport about 20 miles down the road and were proceeding steadily up towards our site with tanks and infantry." Stephenson, however, got 1st Sgt. J. B. Scruggs and told him to assemble the squadron. The men reloaded all of their gear and proceeded to Manila. But other organizations did just as the colonel suggested—they roared off and left their supplies.

Dr. David Hochman recalled that Capt. Mark Wohlfeld, the executive officer of the 27th, also arrived on a motorcycle that day to warn the unit about the rapidly advancing Japanese, saying, "Get the hell out of here! Go immediately to Manila Harbor!" The *27th Reports* corroborates the general rush to evacuate: "Anyhow, the greatest haste [amounting to nearly a rout] and speed were urged. You couldn't take anymore luggage and equipment than you could carry and no specific things were designated to be taken. Air Force Headquarters just quit work and disappeared all at once. Every officer and enlisted man had to leave all his personal belongings and nothing but the barest essentials were taken." In his memoir Frank Bender writes: "Christmas Eve and what a day! We got a telegram from Manila. 'Get your outfit back to Manila immediately.' Naturally, we tried to imagine why the suddenness of the thing, and we didn't know whether to bother to pack up all the equipment we had, or whether to leave it. Glen had the usual level head, and began to systematically get things packed."

Meanwhile, Bender went into Lipa looking for any form of transportation. With the help of the mayor, he returned with two sedans and six trucks. "The trucks were loaded with equipment and the men were sprawled all over the equipment with a rifle in hand and ready for any emergency," he recalled. "I had never seen men work so hard with so little to eat and almost no sleep at all."

Against orders, the 16th loaded everything they had, from tools to ammunition to food, and in the late afternoon began the forty-mile trek to the Manila docks with their cars and trucks. Some also remember that a school bus was commandeered from a nearby village so everyone had a ride. The men arrived amid confusion, expecting to meet up with the 27th headquarters detachment and McAfee and his men from Nielson. McAfee, who had a shorter trip than the two squadrons working at the other airfields, was delayed at Nielson because of incoming aircraft that had to be refueled.

At 4:00, 9 P-40s from Clark Field landed at Nielson and one poor devil flew through the hangar wall and caught fire. The pilot got out OK. Another landed on the barricaded runway and tore his ship all to pieces. All personnel with the exception of McAfee, Dillard, Stafford, Owen [actually Harrelson] and four enlisted men had left the field, but they gassed up the P-40s to get them away. At the same time the gas storage and houses at Nichols were set afire and other demolition work was going on. Pappy Gunn [an older, legendary aviator] flew in and then out when he found General Brereton wasn't there. Dillard, Stafford, and Owen took off in 3 O-49s [single-engine observation planes] on a road behind the field. The road was lined with trees but they made it okay. Their destination was Corregidor. No one knew whether they would make it or not without being shot down.[3]

Besides flying an unfamiliar airplane, the destination was also unfamiliar to one pilot. Second Lt. Robert Stafford recalled: "I had never flown an O-49 before. I asked where Corregidor was and McAfee just pointed in the direction of Manila Bay and said, 'It's out there.'" 2nd Lt. Jay B. Harrelson remembered: "Stafford and Dillard had never flown into Corregidor before. I told them that the landing strip there had an elbow in it, so they had to slow down quickly and then make a turn just after they landed."

McAfee could not fly to Corregidor as planned, so he had no choice but to head for the Manila docks. There, at 8:00 P.M., he ran into Stephenson and his weary 16th Squadron. The 17th under Stirling and the 91st under Eubank had yet to arrive. The orders they received were for the 27th Bomb Group to sail for Bataan. Boats were at a minimum, confusion ran rampant, and in the distance fires and explosions lighted the sky as ammunition, gasoline, and supplies were destroyed so that the Japanese could not use them.

The "normal" chain of command for the 27th was in complete disarray. General Brereton, the Army Air Corps commander, had received orders from MacArthur to set up FEAF Headquarters in Australia. By 4:00 P.M. he was on his way to rendezvous with the plane—a navy PBY seaplane—that would take him there.[4] Captain Hipps and others from FEAF Headquarters left at midnight on December 24 in two twin-engine Beechcrafts on loan from Philippine Airlines.[5]

Not long after arriving in Manila, Stephenson and McAfee realized that they were on their own and directly responsible for the welfare of their men.

All Roads Lead to Bataan

English writer John Milton, in his epic poem *Paradise Lost,* describes in his lengthy verse about the Fall of Adam and Eve one of the hells as a place of enormous confusion, with devils flying around chaotically at breakneck speed. Milton titled that hell "Pandemonium." The same word probably best describes what Stephenson and the 27th experienced as their convoy, with lights doused, drove down Dewey Boulevard in the early evening and screeched to a halt at the Manila Pier. Sgt. Sam Moody from the 91st Squadron noted: "Confusion ran wild. It would be hard to call the rush of men a retreat. It was more like a disorganized group of individuals. An Army without leadership and discipline is a mob. The rush to the ships in the bay could be described in no other way. Each man was put on his own to care for himself as best he could."[6]

Boats of all shapes and sizes were coming and going. Trucks of all shapes and sizes were dropping off soldiers and other military personnel. Officers from various units were scurrying about looking for orders or giving them. No one was really sure who was in charge or where they were to go. Some clung to the hope that the boats waiting for them were to take them to Australia. But when they saw small ferryboats moored to the docks, they forgot that idea.

The 16th pulled into the Manila dock area at 8:00 P.M. and Stephenson had, against orders, brought all of his food and equipment in the Squadron. This turned out to be a big break later. Glen and McAfee got together on the docks and decided that since everything was so tied up that they would just take care of themselves. The situation was that the Group was supposed to evacuate to Bataan. This move was to be accomplished by boat. Glen and Mac decided to hell with this since it meant leaving all the trucks and equipment on the docks. Glen took the trucks and half the men around to Bataan by road and Mac took the other half of the 16th over to Bataan by boat.[7]

Bender remembers: "The confusion there was terrific. The pier itself was a solid mass of humanity and the lack of information was demoralizing. Trucks were crowded on the pier, which was too narrow for them to turn around on, so after a few trucks were unloaded, they were abandoned in place." At about 10:00 P.M. that night, they finally learned that they were bound for Bataan. The men had no information as to whether the enemy was on the ground in the area, and there was no way to find out. They were put under the temporary command of McAfee.

Even though McAfee's group left under the cover of darkness, it was a harrowing trip. There were all kinds of boats and even submarines traversing Manila Bay in the dark. Most ran without lights to avoid detection. McAfee's boat, an inter-island steamer, was loaded with more tired, weary men than it could possibly hold. Few had life jackets. Perhaps fewer had any sleep or had eaten much that day. All each man carried was a laundry bag across his shoulders filled with his military clothes. Some were not even aware of their destination until 11:00 P.M., when they set off for Bataan.

The almost silent, blacked-out voyage was a nightmare. Bender recalled that the quiet was suddenly broken by a call from the darkness out over the water some distance away:

Caller: "Hallo o!" [voice obviously using a megaphone]
Our Captain: "Hallo o!"
Caller: "Do you know where you are?"
Our Captain: "No!"
Caller: "You are in the middle of a minefield! Turn to the south."
Our Captain: "We are proceeding in a southerly direction!"

According to McAfee, at 8:00 A.M. this launch docked at Mariveles Harbor on the extreme southern tip of Bataan, and "they unloaded to the tune of a bunch of [Japanese] bombers."

The Bataan Peninsula is almost thirty miles long and twenty miles at its widest point. The southern tip is only a couple of miles from Corregidor. The west side has steep cliffs plunging down to the South China Sea. The east side faces Manila Bay. The land along the bay, extending inland for about two miles, is relatively flat and swampy, with many rice paddies and fish ponds. One road ran along its eastern coast and another met that road at the tip of the peninsula and ran in a northerly direction along the west side. Bataan's interior remains a dense jungle, with deep ravines, small streams, and rugged mountains, and at the time had trails, not roads, except for a few that crossed the peninsula from east to west. Few if any in the 27th had ever been there. Its geographic features, however, made it an ideal place to take up defensive positions against an attacking foe. The landscape would be as much an obstacle to the Japanese as American weapons.

Stephenson realized that all the equipment, tools, and food he brought from Lipa would likely be needed on Bataan, and besides, it would all fall in the enemy's hands if he left it behind. There was hardly enough room on the boat for just the men. Many truck convoys stopped at Manila filling stations and got road maps. Roads were narrow, two-lane blacktop or in some places dirt, especially the East Road that ran along Manila Bay to the southern tip of Bataan. The drivers traveled with their lights off to prevent the Japanese from spotting them from the air. Few knew the way. Proceeding in the dark, trucks occasionally got lost or ran off the road into the ditch.

Pfc. Paul Lankford of the 16th Squadron said: "To get around Manila Bay, you first had to go west and then north to get around the swampland. We had our tool chests and a big metal dolly and other equipment and supplies on the trucks, and our men were piled on top of the equipment and also hanging onto the running board so that everybody had a ride."

Leaving Manila, Stephenson came across the 515th Coast Artillery, whose job it was to protect Manila from air attacks. They too were preparing to withdraw. Stephenson stopped and talked to a first sergeant about whether there were any delays ahead. Fortunately there were few. The lieutenant learned, however, that the NCO was Adrian Martin from DePere, Wisconsin, just south of Green Bay. Stephenson told him that his family had lived in Suamico just north of Green Bay. Both agreed that they would be much better off in frigid Wisconsin watching the Green Bay Packers finish their season than where they were headed.

Dr. Hochman remembered of the overland journey: "We had come to the south of a little town called San Fernando where the Japanese were supposedly bivouacked. Suddenly we made the turn into Bataan. We all had to be very quiet this entire trip. It was very nerve-wracking, scary, and dark as hell. One of the trucks did tip over." Lankford added: "My truck had a

Filipino driver. I think he fell asleep at the wheel and drove into a rice paddy. The truck turned over. I was unconscious and they took me to the hospital. I stayed there a couple of days."

Second Lt. Tom Gerrity from Chicago was a pilot with the 17th Squadron and assigned to General Wainwright's headquarters. He commandeered a new car and had a Filipino drive him to Bataan. The driver was terrible and almost immediately crashed into the rear of one of the trucks. Gerrity got out and hitchhiked the rest of the way to Bataan.[8]

The 91st, led by Eubank, finally arrived at the docks in Manila. Transportation supposedly had been sent earlier in the day, but none arrived. The men later went into San Fernando and commandeered cars, trucks, and busses. By the time the squadron arrived in the Port Area, no boats were available. The men then proceeded back to San Fernando and on to Bataan. Wisely, they loaded their trucks with as much food as possible.

Later on Christmas Eve, Warren Stirling pulled up to the docks with the 17th and boarded the *Lamao*. The boat was in the middle of the bay when the sun came up, and he immediately knew they would be sitting ducks for Japanese bombers that might fly over. But they too landed safely at Mariveles. The *Lamao* was overcrowded beyond belief. It sat at anchor on Christmas morning until about 10:00 A.M. while waves of Japanese bombers entertained its passengers, swooping and doing acrobatics overhead. Finally, barges took the men ashore, and within minutes three Japanese dive bombers sank the *Lamao*.

But not every unit was fortunate to have leaders with foresight. There were literally tons of food, medicine, and equipment abandoned in Manila and in Central Luzon. Col. E. B. Miller, a tank commander in the 194th Tank Battalion from Brainerd, Minnesota, recalled that most of the trucks racing to Bataan were empty as they passed over the Calumpit Bridge, the gateway to the peninsula.[9] To survive there and delay the Japanese as envisioned in War Plan Orange, American and Filipino forces would need all of the supplies that had been left behind.

It was Christmas when Stephenson, McAfee, Eubank, and Stirling arrived on Bataan by either boat or truck and immediately began looking for one another. They needed to get organized and find out what was happening. McAfee got his men together and double-timed them down the road: "No breakfast and where are we going? No lunch and we hiked six miles carrying our laundry bags. The men suspect I don't know what to do. At last found a man who knows where the 16th is. Sent a sgt. to tell Glen to send a couple of trucks for us." Later in the day, McAfee's found the squadron, had some coffee, and slept on the ground that night.

Bender recalled: "The entire day of Christmas was spent in walking up the road, and trying desperately to advise the men the little we knew of our situation, especially as we were as ignorant as they were. Very few of us had anything to eat at all from Christmas Eve to the morning of December 26." Eventually the 16th's officers found a place on the bank of a fine stream, which seemed the best location available.

> By 5:00 P.M., the entire 16th Squadron had assembled in a ravine
> close to Cabcaben on Bataan and proceeded to have their first meal
> [Christmas dinner] since noon the day before. It consisted of bread
> and hot coffee. Everyone's spirits got a lift from the coffee, and a
> little Christmas cheer crept into the crowd. During this "coffee
> hour" a rabble of men piled out of trucks on the road and descended
> upon the 16th. This rabble turned out to be the 17th led by "Goon"
> [a West Point nickname] Stirling. It was a terrible Christmas from
> every angle—no food, no idea of the war situation, no place to sleep,
> no orders, the Group scattered to the four winds, and prospects for
> getting our airplanes and into the war were *NIL*.[10]

December 25 was a terrible day for the 27th's men and their comrades, but it was a great day for the Japanese Army. They had MacArthur's forces on Luzon in full retreat. Manila had fallen—all they had to do was occupy it. Also, the Japanese had just captured the port city of Davao on the south side of the island of Mindanao and the island of Jolo farther south. These two locations would be used as bases for their conquest of the nearby oil-producing island of Borneo. By capturing Davao and Jolo, they could also prevent supplies coming to MacArthur's troops from Allied bases farther south. This also put the American air base at Del Monte in jeopardy.[11] That same day the British surrendered Hong Kong, their crown colony, with its large naval base and excellent harbor, to the Japanese. Two days earlier the U.S. garrison on Wake Island surrendered. This too would affect the troops fighting in the Philippines because it temporarily closed the Pacific air-ferrying route for heavy bombers from the United States to Australia and beyond.

During the retreat, Wainwright's North Luzon Force had dwindled from 28,000 to 16,000 men. Most of the 12,000 lost were Filipino soldiers who had deserted. Parker's South Luzon Force only lost 1,000 of its 15,000 troops on the retreat.[12] Some of the Filipino units, however, got cut off by the rapidly advancing Japanese and were unable to make it to Bataan.[13]

Bender recalled that it "turned out that moving this small group [of the 16th Squadron] to Bataan with its kitchen equipment was a smart move. December 26, and I take my hat off to our cooks. They made breakfast for all personnel in our own squadron plus I don't know how many transients that had been separated from their own outfits." His group then spent the rest of the day digging foxholes.

In the days after Christmas, the 27th eventually organized itself. Headquarters set up near Limay, about eight miles or more north of the 16th's position. Each squadron camped near creeks so that they had a water supply and under tree cover so as not to be observed by Japanese pilots. But outfits without jobs were not worth much on Bataan. Fortunately, Stephenson and McAfee had a plan.

Bataan Airfield

On December 28, Stephenson and McAfee went up to Air Force HQ and talked to Colonel George [after Brereton's departure, Col. Harold H. George was placed in charge of the air units] about getting a job for the 16th. They had success as Col. George assigned that squadron to Bataan Field and ordered the 16th to take charge of the servicing and maintenance of some P-40s that were coming in, and also, they would be on hand if the dive bombers came in. They were to build revetments for the expected A-24s.[14]

James Bollich of the 16th Squadron stated: "We did not abandon our tools for working on the aircraft. It is good that we didn't because they were the only tools that we had for working on the planes on Bataan. Because of our tools, we were given the job of taking care of the few remaining planes that we had. That kept a lot of us off the front lines."

Getting bombed on a daily basis would become routine for the 16th, especially after December 28. Also on that day word came from Corregidor that many of the men in the air corps, including the entire 27th Bombardment Group, should be prepared at once to move out and carry seven days' rations. They were to board ships for Mindanao in the southern Philippines, where the air bases at Del Monte would be used for air operations against occupied Luzon. The following day, however, they received word that only one inter-island vessel, the *Mayon,* was available, so only the 19th Bombardment Group, with its 650 enlisted men and officers, would be taken to Mindanao. The 27th remained on Bataan.[15]

On December 29 the Japanese turned their attention to Corregidor after learning that it was now MacArthur's headquarters and, they assumed, the nerve center for his army. They staged an air attack, with more than 130 bombers, that lasted three hours.[16] Most of the 27th sat on the beach and watched the fireworks. Second Lt. Tom Gerrity from the 17th Squadron, General Wainwright's air-corps liaison officer, returned by airplane at dusk to the island shortly after the bombing and reported that fires there were everywhere. Fifty men were killed and many more wounded.[17] "Everyone had begun to realize that there wasn't a great stock of food in reserve on Bataan so Stephenson sent the 17th Squadron on up to Limay to live off the Headquarters and 91st Squadron. They had built a fine, cool hide-away in a valley. Major Sewell at Headquarters felt that they would stay in their hide-away until Major Davies and the boys got back with their A-24s."[18]

The pandemonium of December 24–25 did not subside for the 27th Bombardment Group once they reached Bataan. In some ways it only increased. Once the more than one thousand men of the group was situated in the southeast corner of the peninsula near Bataan Airfield, the ramifications of having little food, fewer supplies, and no specific mission settled in. The week after Christmas the squadrons sent trucks back to Manila on a daily basis to pick up food and supplies. Even though MacArthur had declared the capital an open city, the Japanese still had not arrived. By about December 26 or 27, Homma was aware that MacArthur's forces were moving northward from Manila with the probable intention of retiring to Bataan and Corregidor. He decided, however, to adhere to the original operation plan, ordering the 48th Division to continue to advance on Manila. Nonetheless, within a day or two he began to dispatch units toward Bataan to attempt to block MacArthur's retreat.[19]

In his frustration McAfee observed: "It seems that the rout out of Manila wasn't necessary at all. The Japs aren't in Manila yet! What in hell was HQ thinking of. I can't understand all the confusion and mad rush. We left lots of supplies in Manila."

Fortunately, those last six days of December allowed the 27th and other units an opportunity to bring in as much canned goods and rice as they possibly could. Initially what the 27th hauled back stayed with them rather than being pooled and divided among the various units. Hoarding and caching were common, for no one knew for sure how long they would be on Bataan. Some still clung to the notion that the navy was on the way and would save them inside six months.

Lankford recalled when Lieutenant Stephenson took ten to fifteen airmen and a truck to Cabcaben after a barge full of equipment came in. The quartermaster called out organizations for someone to come and claim their items. If nobody answered, he would call out a second time. After the third call went out, if Stephenson wanted the equipment, he would yell out, "Ho," and send one of the men up to get whatever supplies or items that had gone unclaimed. The squadron needed a tug (a tractor to tow aircraft) at the airfield. One morning they spotted a Farmall tractor on the barge. The quartermaster called a second time for it and nobody claimed the tractor. When he called out a third time, Stephenson yelled, "Ho," and then said, "Lankford, go up and get that tractor and drive it back to the air field," even though the private had never driven one before.

Harrelson, who landed on Corregidor on December 24, remained there and worked as an assistant air officer for Reginald Vance. He recalled that during one of the frequent air raids, he went running for a shelter and accidentally hit MacArthur, who was also heading for a shelter, and knocked him down. That's the only "meeting" he ever had with the general.

Vance, the former commanding officer of the 27th, remembered that during one of the early bombings of Corregidor, he and another officer from headquarters arrived by jungle trail in front of MacArthur's house. The general was standing there defiantly with his arms crossed and said to his small audience, "This place will be a mass of rubble before I give in." Another time when he and MacArthur were out in the open during a bombing attack, he suggested to the general, "We should hurry that extra hundred feet and get out of the way." This was the wrong thing to say, because this stopped the general dead in his tracks. Hands on his hips, he said, "No Jap alive can make General MacArthur run!"

Harrelson kept telling Major Vance that he wanted to go over and join the 16th Squadron on Bataan. Eventually he received permission and met up with them at Bataan Field. Stephenson and McAfee went up to air-corps headquarters and got Harrelson officially transferred from the 2nd Observation Squadron to the 16th Squadron. His new duties included filling sandbags and pulling guard duty at night.

Major Davies's Trek to Australia and Frustration that Followed

Davies and the 27th airmen had left Nichols Field near Manila early on December 18 in a C-39 transport and two B-18 bombers. Halfway to Mindanao, the first leg of their four-thousand-mile journey, their plane flew into a tropical storm. Wind whistled through the many shrapnel holes in the planes, and after much bouncing and buffeting, at daybreak they finally landed at

Del Monte Plantation, five hundred miles south of Manila. But Davies and his airmen did not get to see much of the plantation on this trip, for they spent the daytime hours sleeping.[20] The three planes took off between 2:00 and 4:00 A.M. the next morning, December 19.

> Up from the Del Monte flat, the trusty old C-39 carried the boys and headed out for Tarakan, Borneo. The Dutch had a base here and they would service [the plane] on the way south. At dawn, the plane was following a string of islands to the south of Mindanao when, "Holy Hell," a Jap aircraft carrier was sighted. Time hung heavy and everyone craned his neck to see if dreaded Zeros would soon come after us. But they didn't and the crew within the plane breathed easier when the carrier was finally lost from sight. "Herman" Lowery and "Dick" Birnn were fast looking at their maps for an island in case the Nips did attack.
>
> Just outside of Tarakan, the weather became terrible again. Rain came down in sheets and the ship was helpless to get to Tarakan. It was decided to continue to Balikpapen, a Dutch base further south. So the sweat began. The C-39 had hardly enough gas to make the trip, so all mixture controls were set to maximum lean and the battle was on. Half way to Balikpapan, a huge mountain range was encountered with jungle so dense they could not see the ground. Climbing above was out of the question due to gas so soon a merry chase began between peaks and down canyons. There was a long interval of tenseness when the range dissolved and the lowlands were reached. At last Balikpapen came into sight and the C-39 sat down with but 28 gallons of gas. The flight was a thriller.
>
> That night everyone ate baloney and cheese and drank Dutch beer. The Dutch were quite good to the 27th and made the boys feel at home.[21]

Hubbard was in one of the B-18s. The bad weather during the last part of the trip to Tarakan forced his aircraft to fly below the clouds close to the ground. They landed in a violent rainstorm. After refueling, it was on to Balikpapan. He recalled that when they crossed the equator, Davies opened a bottle and all drank a toast, "Hooray for the wings of Mercury and to hell with Neptune." A couple of hours later they landed at Balikpapan and spent the night as guests of the Shell Oil Company. The next morning it was on to Macassar on the island of Celebes. The town looked like a South Seas movie set, with bearded, tattooed pirates lounging at tables drinking beer all day. After refueling, they left for Koepang on Timor. From there they flew to the Australian frontier outpost of Darwin, at the time only accessible by air or sea.

In Macassar the men of the 27th also saw machine-gun nests and barbed wire everywhere.[22] At Koepang, Timor, the pilots had their first encounter with Australians and their speech. To all it was queer to be called a Yank, especially for the southerners.[23] Those in the B-18s arrived in Darwin the day before the C-39. It is not certain whether Davies knew exactly where their dive bombers were in Australia before they arrived in Darwin. After repairs, their three airplanes were to return to the Philippines.

On December 21 Davies, while still in Darwin, received a message labeled "Secret Cypher Message" from Brereton in Manila telling him to send the two B-18s and the C-39 back at the earliest possible time with the maximum load of .50-caliber ammunition. Davies answered that message, apparently the same day, stating, "Two B-18s and one C-39 departing December 23 with 7,000 pounds .50-caliber ammunition." He also indicated in the message that Capt. Floyd Pell, one of the P-40 pilots, was available with another B-18 to ferry additional .50-caliber ammunition and then return to Australia with more pilots if Brereton so directed.

It is likely that if the three or four planes had returned to Luzon with the ammunition, many more pilots from the 27th would have been transported to Australia. But between the time Brereton sent his message and two days later, the situation had drastically changed on Luzon. The Japanese invasion had begun, and MacArthur's army was in full retreat. In fact, Savage recalled that he and some of the other 27th pilots still on Luzon were supposed to be picked up by a transport plane on December 24 and flown to Australia to retrieve more planes. Because of the deteriorating situation around Manila, though, that did not happen.

Meanwhile, Davies and his men boarded a four-engine flying boat, which had been impressed and militarized for use by the Royal Australian Air Force (RAAF), for the two-day trip to Brisbane, where they hoped their A-24s were ready to be flown back to the Philippines and ready to participate in combat. There were also three fighter pilots—Grant Mahony, Gerry Keenan, and Allison Strauss—from the 24th Pursuit Group who had come with them to lead back flights of the P-40s that had arrived with the A-24s.[24]

When their flying boat, the *Centaurus*, landed in Brisbane Harbor on the evening of December 24, the pilots were a disheveled, weary bunch. Because of the heavy load—twenty-six passengers and a crew of five—most of the seats were removed to lessen the weight.[25] The heat was oppressive. Most sat on the floor at the rear of the plane for the bumpy flight. At refueling stops along the way, the search for food often ended in failure. The first night, the group stayed at Townsville on the northeastern coast. According to Hubbard, they arrived late in the evening and were driven to a hotel where they enjoyed showers and good beds. All the bars and restaurants were closed that evening, but their hosts made sandwiches for them.

The next day they completed the last leg of the journey to Brisbane, landing at Hamilton Reach on the Brisbane River near the armed ships of the *Pensacola* convoy. A weary band of 27th pilots, many dressed in Aussie military outfits of shorts and short-sleeved shirts given them in Darwin, boarded cabs for a ride to Lennons, Brisbane's most modern hotel.

> A sadder looking bunch has never been seen walking up the side-
> walk to Lennon's. And they were stared at from every angle. Two
> days of living on the [airplane] floor traveling made what had been
> clean Aussie uniforms more like greasy, filthy rags. Unceremonially
> unloaded from six cabs onto the sidewalk, the boys piled everything
> into piles. Each had gas masks, tin helmets, and pistols that we either
> carried or wore and to the Brisbanites, who realized for the first time
> that the War was really on, they were quite shocked.[26]

Hubbard recalled that he was in a dirty, sweat-soaked flying suit and wore an Australian pith helmet picked up in Darwin. There they ran into a rather stuffy regular-army colonel who was appalled when he learned that they were U.S. troops. He proceeded to tell them they were a slovenly bunch and a disgrace to the U.S. Army: "His expression at seeing our U.S. insignias, our raunchy looking appearance, and our recently acquired Australian spirits [uniforms] was indescribable. He immediately demanded of Major Davies an explanation for our 'non-regulation' attire and was promptly set right by the diplomatic but forthright explanation. [We had been fighting in the Philippines and were down to pick up our planes and fly them back.]"[27]

It was Christmas Eve in Brisbane, and the men happily enjoyed the steaks and drinks that the bellboys rounded up for them.[28] This was the same evening their 27th comrades back in the Philippines were retreating by boat and truck to Bataan with nothing to eat. The next day the pilots found the planes still in crates and discovered that nobody in Australia worked on Christmas, despite the fact that a war was going on. Harry Mangan was told that "as soon as they could get them off the ship and on shore that they would be assembled and we would take those airplanes back to the Philippines." The crates were eventually moved to RAAF bases at nearby Amberley and Archerfield.

What seemed like a simple task proved almost insurmountable. Aussies were pressed into action putting the planes together, as were the remaining men of the 7th Bomb Group, who had come over with the convoy. Between them, the men set up an assembly line at Amberley, two shifts of twelve hours each, working twenty-four hours a day.

Initially the process was slow, but Hubbard remembered that the "Aussies went all out to help us but many small parts were missing. Nuts and bolts were easy to replace but on the armament side trigger motors, solenoids, and sights for the fixed guns firing through the prop and flexible mounts for the rear guns were more difficult and slow." Being able to improvise was an hourly occurrence. Hubbard recalled that a trigger motor was found, and an Australian machine shop then built more. Ring-and-post sights were made for the forward guns and mounts for flexible guns. The solenoids were replaced with a wire cable to manually fire the fixed guns. But problems continued.

> Zeke Summers cussed everybody and everything, because he couldn't get triggers, solenoids, practice bombs, gun mounts and ammunition. Doug Tubb ran around frantically in his jeep all day trying to collect spare parts, and wildly beat his head when none were available. . . .
> Instruments were bad, engines using oil, tires defective, and numerous other things were wrong. Packed carelessly, or in a hurry, the control cables were not anchored, making the job tougher still. Always at the last minute, we either had the part made locally or found it in the hodge podge of the Air Corps Supply. Sgt. Wesley knew more about what they had in Air Corps Supply than the men who were supposed to be running it. Everyone forgot about red tape. If we had to have something, we just signed our name to an order—or stole it.[29]

Mangan was just as perturbed by the situation of the A-24s multiple configurations. "Some came from Savannah, some still had mud from the Louisiana Maneuvers on the tires, and some from new production so there was no standard configuration. Some of them had self-sealing tanks and some didn't. Some had armor plates, some did not. None of them had workable guns." Later when they could not get airplane tires, they used truck tires instead.

The Army Air Corps had obtained seventy-eight A-24s, mostly from the U.S. Navy assembly line at the Douglas factory in Santa Monica, between June and October 1941. Some of the planes, however, were not new and came directly from the navy. Davies expected, or at least hoped, that seventy-seven of them would be with the convoy, which was about the number needed to adequately equip his four squadrons back in the Philippines. Yet only fifty-two A-24s had been shipped. The army had ordered model SBD-3As, but the navy substituted a number of older model SBD-2s, which did not have self-sealing fuel tanks or armor plating. Fifteen additional A-24s eventually arrived in Brisbane from the United States on February 25, 1942, for use by the 3rd Bombardment Group.[30]

The frustration felt by those pilots who finally received planes only to find them still needing work is shown in a letter Hubbard wrote to his wife during that first week in Brisbane. "I intend to shoot a few Depot officers back in the States. This has been a screwed up business from beginning to end. In spite of all our letters in the U.S. before we left about armament shortages, the bloody guns were still short vital parts. Not to mention such things as sights and bomb release units." In the *27th Reports* Davies states: "The persons in America responsible for sending our dive-bombers over without gun mounts, trigger motors, sights, etc. in my opinion are subject to trial for criminal negligence. Never send equipment into the combat zone unless it can be immediately used for combat."[31]

Despite the almost insurmountable problems, on December 29 Robert Ruegg flew the first A-24 from this makeshift production line. A week later more were in the air and needed only armament for combat. The P-40 pilots in Australia were equally frustrated in getting their aircraft ready for action by the lack of Prestone, a coolant that was essential for operating the liquid-cooled engines, little if any of which had been sent with the convoy. Although every effort was made to obtain Prestone locally, only enough was found for some of the aircraft. It was weeks before enough coolant was available to get the majority of P-40s in the air.[32] By mid-January 1942 the enemy had broken the ferry route of refueling stops to the Philippines, so it was no longer possible to fly these short-range single-engine aircraft to the islands.

Davies did send the C-39 and at least one B-18 back from Darwin. He said the planes got as far as Macassar before having to turn back because of Japanese advances. The *27th Reports* indicates that Floyd Rogers and Alexander Salvatore from the 27th, flying the C-39, made it as far as the Dutch East Indies, then returned with the plane to Darwin, joining up with the 27th pilots in Brisbane shortly afterward. Heiss and Timlin, two other 27th pilots who had flown one of the B-18s to Darwin, also attempted to go back to the Philippines. They flew to Timor and then to Macassar, from which they flew off across the Macassar Straits to Balikpapan on Borneo but, encountering a bad storm, turned back. They then learned that because of Japanese advances they would not be able to make it back to the Philippines. Heiss and Timlin then flew back to Timor, arriving on December 24, and helped the RAAF personnel there celebrate Christmas. Flying on to Brisbane, they rejoined their comrades in the 27th.[33]

Meanwhile, back on Bataan, Stephenson and the 16th Squadron worked feverishly during those first weeks getting Bataan Airfield ready for the A-24s that they felt sure would descend from the skies at any moment.

Life on Bataan

Before the army engineers destroyed the Calumpit Bridge, a truckload of 91st Squadron airmen went looking for aircraft parts. They passed through a burning village that had just been bombed. A Japanese twin-engine "Betty" bomber (Mitsubishi G4M1, with a crew of seven) kept flying low over the highway, machine gunning anything that moved. This prevented the Americans from leaving the cover of trees and continuing their mission. Sgt. Laurent "Larry" Martel of the 91st got all of the men together, rifles and machine guns ready, in the ditches on both sides of the road and waited for the plane to fly over again. At his command, they all leapt up and fired at once, hitting the plane about where the bomb bay was located. The Betty exploded and crashed in a nearby rice paddy. Many Filipinos who had been hiding in the fields under the trees came out and cheered. These 27th Bomb Group men believed that they were the first non-antiaircraft unit in the Philippines to shoot down a bomber from the ground.[34]

When MacArthur initiated his aggressive plan of meeting the Japanese on the beaches of Luzon, supplies were moved out of Bataan and stored closer to that supposed front. The original plan called for storage of food and supplies on the peninsula for 43,000 troops for a six-month period.[35] In reality, Bataan would fill up with more than double that number of people, as civilians also retreated there and needed to be fed. Much of the food supply before the retreat was stored in Manila and at Cabanatuan in central Luzon. In addition, Bataan was a rugged, mountainous peninsula that offered little area to grow crops. After January 1 no more supply trips were made: army engineers blew up the Calumpit Bridge spanning the wide Pampanga River at 6:15 A.M. to delay the Japanese entry into the peninsula. The tons of supplies left in Manila and Cabanatuan fell into enemy hands.[36]

Meanwhile, the quartermaster found it difficult if not impossible to get an accurate accounting of the food situation. His best guess was bleak. Almost immediately, MacArthur put the Bataan troops on half-rations, which meant a diet of two thousand calories, or thirty ounces of food a day, per man.[37] That is about enough for a healthy, inactive person. But the soldiers were actively fighting for their life. Later, even this amount was reduced.

The army established a supply depot at Little Baguio, ten miles south of Stephenson's camp. Every day the quartermaster would distribute supplies according to the number of men in a unit. An officer's responsibility is to look after his men, and from a supply standpoint, the 16th was better off than most other units on Bataan. There is an old military saying, "The officer in charge is responsible for getting his troops fed, paid, and promoted." At least for the moment, the men were not concerned about getting paid or promoted.

The *27th Reports* states: "Stephenson was in charge of the Squadron and the field. McAfee was the Field Operations officer. Bender the Engineering officer. Dillard took over the building of revetments. The other squadrons felt they had a laugh on the 16th since all they had to do was be comfortable and wait."

That waiting ended on January 2, when MacArthur ordered all air units, including the 27th Bombardment Group and most of the 24th Pursuit Group, to begin infantry training. Classes were held daily on using the old Enfield rifles. The men fired a few rounds into Manila Bay for practice, and some even drilled in hand-to-hand combat. But these were mechanics, technicians, and pilots, and few ever had basic infantry training, which normally takes months to complete. On Bataan this was compressed into a few weeks. The 16th's men, however, were merely issued rifles and did not have to drill, for they were too busy taking care of Bataan Field. That was the good news. The bad news was that the airfield was one of the usual targets for daily Japanese bombing runs.

Squadrons of the 27th Bombardment Group at the Front

The 27th Bombardment Group, trained to fly and maintain airplanes, spent three and a half agonizing months on Bataan as infantrymen before the surrender. Those at the front were like fish out of water. Over half of the enlisted men in the 27th had attended various Army Air Corps mechanic schools and other training programs to learn their craft. It would take months and years to train new men who had their skill levels. Wohlfeld, executive officer of the 27th, recalled: "The men with me were not professional infantrymen. They were Air Force mechanics, technicians, or communications men. Some of the officers were pilots. They didn't know what to expect. They were just remotely acquainted with the rifles they carried."[38]

After retreating to Bataan, General Wainwright's North Luzon Force became I Corps and General Parker's South Luzon Force became II Corps. I Corps defended the west half of Bataan, facing the South China Sea, and II Corps the east half, facing Manila Bay. Mountains divided their areas of responsibility. Wainwright's corps had three Philippine Army divisions (1st, 31st, and 91st) plus a portion of the 71st Division and the Philippine Scouts' 26th Cavalry. Parker had four Philippine Army divisions (11th, 21st, 41st, and 51st) and a Philippine Scout regiment, the 57th.[39]

The 27th Bombardment Group had about as many men as an infantry battalion, and each of its squadrons of about two hundred were the approximate size of an infantry company. In early January the 27th, combined with the 48th Materiel Squadron, became the 2nd Battalion, 2nd Provisional Air Corps Regiment. Col. H. H. C. Richards, an air-corps officer, first commanded this regiment of converted airmen, but later in January Col. Irwin E. Doane, an infantry officer, replaced him. The unit was assigned to Parker's II Corps. On January 5 the battalion moved north on the East Road to the village of Abucay next to Manila Bay. The Abucay-Mauban line, the principal American-Filipino defensive position, started about a mile or so north of town, stretching from Manila Bay westerly across the peninsula for about twenty miles toward the town of Mauban on the South China Sea. Mountains, the tallest of which is Mount Natib, 4,422 feet high, split the line perpendicularly in the middle, leaving a gap of about five miles between I Corps and II Corps. U.S. leaders thought Mount Natib was not only impossible to defend but also unnecessary since no military force could possibly come over the precipitous crags, ravines, and cliffs.[40] Leaving this gap in the front line has remained a controversial decision.

After the 27th arrived there as the 2nd Battalion, corps leadership determined that there were more troops on the front line than necessary, so the unit was sent south to the reserve line.

During December and January, Homma became a victim of his own success. His rapid advance to Manila and conquest of most of Luzon exceeded all expectations of his superiors, both in Tokyo and within the Southern Army, his next higher headquarters. This resulted in the transfer of one of his divisions, the 48th, from Luzon to fight elsewhere. Japanese commanders expected that capturing Bataan would be simple as the disorganized defending troops would retreat almost immediately to the village of Mariveles at the southern tip of the peninsula, make a brief stand there, and then withdraw to Corregidor.[41]

Homma began a major assault against the Abucay-Mauban line on January 9. The most intense fighting was on the eastern end, but there was also

5. Situation on Bataan, January 8, 1942. Until about January 26, H1 (Hospital 1) was located near Limay. *Courtesy U.S. Army*

Legend:

⊠ = Allied infantry unit

◁ = Allied horse cavalry unit

⊠ = Japanese unit

⊠ = brigade

⊠ = division

⊠ = regiment

–xxx– = corps boundaries

continuous fighting going on all along the front. The Japanese were able to penetrate the line in many areas, though sustaining significant loses. Hundreds of snipers infiltrated into Allied areas, some dressed as Filipinos, climbing trees and picking off American and Filipino soldiers.

The men of the 27th were back on the reserve line of defense, called the Orion-Bagac line (though also referred to as the Pilar-Bagac line). This sixteen-mile-long position stretched from just south of Orion on Manila Bay across the peninsula to near Bagac on the South China Sea, with 1,920-foot-high Mount Samat cutting through about midway between the villages.[42]

The eastern half of the Orion-Bagac line was a mountainous jungle area with rice paddies in the lowlands near the bay. The 2nd Battalion's location was about two miles from Manila Bay. The San Vicente River crossed the reserve line at a point that separated the battalion from the 32nd Philippine Army Regiment. Their area of defense was on the edge of high ground. Below to their front were rice paddies and canals with barbed wire strung defensively. The men used M1917 Enfield and M1903 Springfield rifles as well as some Browning automatic rifles. The squadrons on the front lines were said to have had a disproportionately large number of machine guns, for they had rounded up many of the .30-caliber air-cooled machine guns that had been meant for use in various types of aircraft, adding ground mounts to the weapons. They had also brought along some of the .50-caliber machine guns from aircraft that had been destroyed on the ground. These were used for antiaircraft defense as well as against enemy soldiers. All officers and many enlisted men carried .45-caliber Colt automatic pistols. Bayonets were scarce.

On January 5 the Hq., 91st, and the 17th Sq. moved to the 2nd reserve line [Orion-Bagac line] on the east side of the lines. They made anti-tank bombs out of beer bottles filled with gasoline, put up barbed wire, and generally dug in as if they were seasoned troops from the German Army. They kept this position for two weeks and never saw a Jap, but they got in much valuable training, which was to bear on their future.

Upon the reserve line, the other three squadrons got their first taste of the Nip dive bombers when the Japs put a bomb in the 17th Squadron's kitchen. For the second time on Bataan the 17th was kitchenless. The 27th was beginning to feel like a veteran outfit though. All night long the 155's [U.S. artillery pieces] pounded the Japs, and all day long the Japs pounded us.[43]

The uniforms worn by the men of the 2nd Battalion varied. Leather shoes deteriorated rapidly in the tropical humidity. Steel helmets were mainly worn only during attacks because of the heat, and also because they produced noise banging against things while going through the brush. Some wore the air-corps coveralls, but these were a nuisance for field duty, especially when one had to relieve oneself. Many coveralls were cut at the waist and made into two-piece uniforms, but the bare flesh in the middle was exposed to mosquitoes. Canvas leggings were worn by some, but they were time consuming to put on and take off since they had to be laced up. The uniform worn by most seemed to be no underwear, no socks, a shirt, trousers, field boots or oxfords, and a baseball-type cap. The pith helmet, or Philippine sun helmet, was considered a luxury because air could pass through the vents at the top, though this created a whistling noise; this also could prevent one from hearing attacking aircraft, which were common at the front.[44]

The 454th Ordnance Company had been attached to the 27th since Savannah. On Bataan they had two jobs. The men continued to function as a bomb-ordnance unit, though now their main responsibility was handling artillery shells, moving around to handle ordnance in various locations. Their other job was as an infantry unit responsible for part of Bataan's beach defenses. The area they defended was along Manila Bay about halfway between the front lines to the north and Mariveles to the south.

The Bataan Air Force

Stephenson's decision to find work for the 16th was important for a variety of reasons. It kept them busy and got them doing what they were trained for—flying-related business including maintaining aircraft. Secondly, it kept his men out of the infantry and the front line. The 2nd Observation Squadron eventually took the 16th Squadron's three-hundred-yard-wide spot in northern Bataan on what would soon become the front line next to Stirling's 17th Squadron. McAfee in his diary lamented his unit's fate, "If the 27th Bomb Group is sacrificed over here for nothing, I'm going to shoot a dozen of those low isolationist congressmen who wouldn't spend any money on an air force." He wrote this two days before being assigned to Bataan Field. At least now, he thought, he might be able to get checked out in a P-40 at Bataan Field and get some flying time against the Japanese.

Bataan Field lay between the villages of Lamao and Cabcaben, and by no stretch of the imagination was it a finished airfield. Civilian engineers began work on it before the war started, and it featured a narrow two-thousand-foot runway sloping down from the wooded hillside toward the Manila Bay shore-

9. Brig. Gen. Harold H. George at Bataan Field, early March 1942. *Courtesy Hugh H. Casey Papers, Historical Division, U.S. Army Corps of Engineers*

line.[45] An engineering unit was still grading the runway with a Caterpillar, trying to make it level, one hundred feet wide, and five thousand feet long, when the 16th took over. Large rocks from this excavation lined the runways. The airstrip eventually crossed the East Road, and each time airplanes landed or took off, traffic had to be halted. Some were told the extension was needed so large bombers could land there.

Fighter planes (or "pea shooters," as army pilots often called them) started to arrive at Bataan Field on or about December 29 and 30 as the other Luzon airfields were closed and remaining planes evacuated to Bataan. The peninsula had two other military airfields at the time. Both of these were farther north and closer to where the Japanese army would begin its assault on Bataan.[46]

After General Brereton left the Philippines with his staff on December 24, 1941, Col. Harold H. George, chief of staff of the 5th Interceptor Command, had assumed command of what was left of the Far East Air Force in the Philippines. This included about five thousand Army Air Corps personnel as well as a lot of trucks and another six hundred personnel from the Philippine Army Air Force and their archaic aircraft. He also inherited Brereton's new Packard automobile.[47] George was forty-nine years old and had grown up in

Lockport, New York. During World War I, he had scored five victories over German airplanes, qualifying him as an ace.

On December 30, 1941, it was officially announced from Corregidor that FEAF headquarters had been transferred to Australia—or wherever General Brereton finally pitched tent. George then was named commanding officer of the 5th Interceptor Command, which for the most part *was* the air-corps personnel and aircraft left in the Philippines.[48] The colonel's official headquarters was located near the southern tip of Bataan in an area nicknamed "Little Baguio." Army hospitals and other service troops were located there too. At the beginning of January 1942, George's air force consisted of about twenty aircraft, most of them P-40 fighters along with some older P-35 fighters and observation planes. Japanese air units in the area had them outnumbered many fold.

George set up a second but smaller headquarters on the side of a hill facing Manila Bay only a few miles from Bataan Airfield. The position gave him a good view of the bay and surrounding areas from which to direct the fighters. He had local Filipino workmen build a shack that looked similar to what many of the surrounding farmers lived in. He thought that even though it was out in the open, the place would not be bombed or strafed. Only a handful of his staff was located there with him.

Reginald Vance functioned both as an air officer for MacArthur's headquarters on Corregidor and as a liaison officer for George. In his latter role, he personally piloted an "ancient Philippine Army biplane" most days from the airfield on Corregidor to Bataan so that he could meet and exchange information with George. He carried his own 30-30 rifle for protection and a bolo knife, a long, heavy, single-edge machete, which he planned to use for survival if his plane was shot down or crashed for other reasons.[49]

Airstrips on Bataan were notoriously dusty. A mixture of water and molasses was sometimes sprayed on the runways to keep the telltale dust to a minimum.[50] On January 4 George sent all of his P-40 aircraft at Pilar Field in northeastern Bataan to Del Monte Airfield on Mindanao for safekeeping due to the advancing Japanese army. This effectively closed Pilar, and many of its personnel were then converted to infantrymen. Nine of the P-40s at Orani, another airfield farther north on Bataan, were transferred to Bataan Field that same day, leaving no operational aircraft at Orani. The airmen there were also converted to infantry. On the morning of January 7, the Japanese entered northern Bataan only three miles north of Orani. This left George only Bataan Field from which to conduct tactical operations. Most of the general's personnel by this time, including pilots (except those at Bataan Field), were assigned infantry duties.

Twelve revetments were built at Bataan Field under the trees about two hundred yards uphill from the landing strip to hide and protect the P-40s and the expected dive-bombers, though by mid-January only a hopeless optimist actually believed the A-24s were coming.[51] According to McAfee, to make matters worse, the Japanese on the other side of the bay could see what was happening at the field. Often the enemy knew when a P-40 was going to take off—there was some evidence that a spotter was located high on the hill behind the airfield.

On January 7 a Japanese fighter jumped a P-40 as it left the field. Leland Sims recently recalled about that take off: "The P-40 lined up on the landing strip, the throttle was moved forward, increasing the power of the engine. When the plane began to slide on the hard surface, the brakes were released. Increasing in speed as it went along the runway, the plane left the ground before the end of the runway." The enemy fighter spotted the P-40 immediately, and a brief dogfight was on.

Engaging Japanese fighters in extended dogfights, however, was not an everyday job for the P-40s. By this point the planes were not in the best of shape. If a pilot saw that he had a great advantage, he would attack the enemy. But the few remaining aircraft were used primarily for reconnaissance. On the afternoon of January 8, George had nine P-40s available, two P-35As, and one older A-27 (the combat version of the AT-6 trainer).

Some old-fashioned ingenuity converted the P-40s into makeshift dive bombers. Savage said they "rigged up a release with a lever to drop a bomb. The lever allowed the bomb to clear the propeller. They used that plane successfully to dive bomb Japanese troops. We did wonders with what we had. If our pilot could time it right and come back and land when the Japs were gone, then he'd live to do it again."

Some Japanese pilots tended to fly over at almost the same time every day, and after the Americans began to recognize their planes, they gave the pilots nicknames such as "Good Time Charlie." Bender added: "The few cars that became available had their tops cut off so that in the case of ambush, immediate action would be facilitated. There was no such thing as a warning, for the only equipment available for warning were the ears of the men on the ground."

Savage happened to be in the control tower when a P-40 took off. Right afterward, a Japanese dive bomber dropped a 500-pound bomb near the control tower. There were five people in the tower, and the bomb missed them by ten feet. It broke Doc's eardrums and unbuttoned his shirt to his waist.

One of the daily chores the men had was to go out and cut fresh brush and foliage to camouflage the revetments. If it were not fresh, the Japanese pilots might detect how it was different from the adjacent foliage and decide to bomb or strafe that location. Wrecked aircraft near the airstrip were sometimes partially camouflaged to fool the enemy into thinking they had found a hidden aircraft. They would attack these decoys.

Through the period of January 1 to January 25 the 16th Squadron on Bataan Field suffered 32 bombings with no casualties to themselves although four men from an engineer outfit were killed. Their record on Bataan Field was the best yet since through all that bombing, not a man was hurt, not one airplane was scratched, nor a single piece of equipment damaged. The 16th drew a big white circle in the middle of the runway so that the Japs would have a target to shoot at. They never hit it but they came too darn close for comfort.[52]

Bender recalled that he and Stephenson, after a good pasting by Japanese bombers, ran out to see if there was anyone who needed attention. Shouting that he was going down to the end of the field to look, Stephenson jumped into a car and sped down to the far end. A bomb landed pretty close to the car and stopped him. The enemy had come back, but because he was in a car, he did not hear the noise of the aircraft. When he got back to Bender, Stephenson got out of the car. He presented an odd appearance in that his beard, which at the time was a full growth, was covered with dirt and dust thrown up by the explosion. When he patted his beard, he looked like a powder puff. Bender's comment to him was, "Anything for a laugh."

By the middle of January, the 16th Squadron had established a fine camp. Their hideaway in the jungle was, according to McAfee, "cleaner, safer, and cooler" than other units' camps. They even built a dam to collect water for daily bathing. The P-40 pilots flying out of Bataan Field billeted near them. Jungle growth made the camp hard to spot form the air. The roads out to work places on the airfield were certainly not superhighways but at least were covered by trees. Men immediately began building some kind of covering near their stations. Some used shelter halves, which were made into lean-to coverings, and camouflaged them with branches or anything else they could find. Monkeys chattered overhead constantly, and wild pigs, snakes, and other animals were seen.

Drs. Mango, Schultz, and Marrocco, whose squadrons had become front-line infantry units, were also up there, as was Dr. Joseph Ginsberg of the 48th Squadron, 27th Group. Each manned a company clearing station or first-aid station somewhat to the rear of their respective squadrons. Dr. Hochman recently recalled that most of his sick-call visits to other nearby units were at dusk or during the night to avoid daytime bombings.

The morale of the 16th was a problem Stephenson faced daily. Keeping his men busy at the airfield and improving their living conditions helped immensely. But radio reports and rumor often worked against his efforts. Reports from San Francisco were often inaccurate, and Tokyo radio boasted that the men on Bataan would soon be driven into the sea. When McAfee heard that news, he wrote: "Not on their life! They're arrogant bastards now that they're winning. Wheeler, Nye, and Lindbergh [U.S. isolationists] sure sold us out. Wish people in the States would quit sending us their heartfelt wishes and praises of the work we're doing and instead start sending us things to fight with." Bender said the San Francisco broadcasts boasted of the "vast numbers of guns, tanks, planes etc. that were being manufactured. We were getting none of it in the spot we were in. That news from San Francisco might have been all right for local consumption in the U.S., but it didn't sound like much to us locked in the jungle by the enemy."

Things to fight with were precisely what most of the rumors were about. A sergeant from another outfit told McAfee that his commanding officer told him that so many U.S. planes were flying over to the Philippines that he could not count them. The most common rumor was that a never-ending convoy of ships from Pearl Harbor was about to enter Manila Bay and liberate Bataan and Corregidor. Gerrity said, "Major Montgomery invented a yardstick for measuring the terrific crop of rumors: one bomb equals 'many bombs,' 2 airplanes equals 'many airplanes,' one banca [a native outrigger boat] equals 'a fleet of transports,' a batch of Jap leaflets equals 'many parachutists.'"

Doc Savage, like Gerrity, McAfee, and Stephenson, was a pilot without a plane. While in the field on Bataan, he earned his nickname, "Doc." There was a comic book and movie hero at the time called Doc Savage, who was a bearded man of bronze and licked everybody he fought. On Bataan Columbus Savage got tired of shaving with a mess-kit knife and let his whiskers grow. Soon he had a nine- or ten-inch growth of beard, which was fire engine red. Because the magazine character was also a redheaded guy with red whiskers, the guys started calling him "Doc." He never lost that nickname.

Under Doc's guidance, the 16th had buried a good deal of the food that it had trucked in during the last week of December. Most of this was crackers and canned meat, which complemented the daily ration of rice they were getting from the quartermaster. But the squadron was also good at augmenting its food supply. Sometimes a carabao (water buffalo) would wander across the area, but it would not make it very far before becoming part of the 16th's mess. In addition, Savage had a sergeant who would go out with his Enfield rifle and shoot a wild pig so that the men could have wild boar for a couple of days.

There was plenty of evidence that wild pigs abounded near the squadron's campsite. The men organized pig hunts so that they would have pork. One time they decided the best way to hunt wild pigs was with a 30-06 military rifle at night and a flashlight. The idea was to find an area along the trail showing fresh pig activity, locate the animal with a flashlight by shining it in the eyes (which reflected the beam), then shoot it between the glowing eyes. Not all the hunting parties were successful. One safari consisted of five volunteers, including Bender: "Suddenly I heard a sound like the roar of a freight train, and this roar seemed to be coming down the path directly at me. This animal passed within what seemed about an inch snorting and grunting all the way. This experience ended the safari for that night and forever because the wild pigs apparently didn't know the rules of the game."

The 16th, according to McAfee, ate two meals a day—one at 8:00 A.M. and the other at 4:00 P.M. Both usually consisted of rice and hash, which according to the *27th Reports,* the troops called "slum gullion." There was little bread and canned tomatoes only occasionally. On January 24 a colonel visited trying to find out if the squadron had extra food buried. He found none.

The Japanese knew full well that forcing the refugees to Bataan would compel the Americans to feed them, a factor not considered in War Plan Orange. To ensure an equitable distribution, the quartermaster sometimes moved supplies to Corregidor, where they were stored and then disbursed evenly throughout Bataan. This, of course, raised the suspicion of the troops on Bataan who thought that while they were fighting and starving, their comrades on Corregidor were feasting. And since the maxim that "an army fights on its belly" is often accurate, the combat ability of the men of Bataan was compromised. Occasionally in January, ships broke through the Japanese blockade and brought in some rice, but it was never enough.

Farmers in the Philippines used carabaos the same way Stephenson had used horses back on the Arpin farm—for plowing and hauling. When the Japanese entered Bataan, many of the farmers abandoned their property and livestock, which roamed free across the peninsula, though not for long. The carabaos were rounded up, slaughtered, and shipped to Corregidor for cold storage. Many considered them so tough that surely one expended more calories trying to chew the meat than they gained by digesting it. Eventually, the army's horses and mules met the same fate. The 16th also hunted monkeys, iguanas, snakes, and various birds to augment their diet.

Food was not the only thing being rationed, for the men were limited to one cigarette a day. A few even traded one of their meals for an additional cigarette.[53] With the men in a weakened condition, they were more susceptible to infections and other diseases.

Despite the hardships, the 16th Squadron was settling in with its job at Bataan Field. Although they were not flying, the airmen were making a definite contribution to the defense of the peninsula by maintaining the airfield. Other elements like Stirling's 17th were up at the front stringing barbed wire, digging foxholes, and engaging the enemy as infantrymen. Stirling made a visit in January to see Stephenson and McAfee at the airstrip and to swap war stories. That was the last time he ever saw Stephenson.

The Reserve Line becomes the Front Line

On January 14–15 the Japanese achieved a breakthrough on the left flank of the II Corps sector of the Abucay-Mauban line. During the next ten days, this breech could not be contained. By the nineteenth, enemy troops were behind the main line of defense and advancing up the Abo-Abo River valley in the direction of the Orion-Bagac line.

The next day the 2nd Battalion (in whole or in part) was ordered up near the Abucay-Mauban line on the Guitol Ridge on the east side of Mount Natib, overlooking the confluence of the Abo-Abo and Modica rivers, where the men constructed fortifications.[54] Some limited action against the Japanese took place in this area. Fierce fighting continued in other areas, and some American and Filipino units at the front had already given way. Also, the Japanese had gotten into the rear area of a portion of I Corps and blocked the West Road, cutting off the main line of retreat for some I Corps units, which then began to withdraw along the beach. It was clear that this entire front was in jeopardy, so MacArthur ordered the I and II Corps to withdraw to the Orion-Bagac line (reserve line), about eight to twelve miles south. Most of the troops reached this position on January 24–26. During this time, the 2nd Battalion also returned to the Orion-Bagac line, now the main line of resistance.

The airmen-turned-infantry were responsible for the defense of approximately fifteen hundred yards of the Allied front on Bataan. Each squadron was responsible for about three hundred yards of this position. Facing north from left to right, the 48th Materiel Squadron had the first sub-sector, then the 91st Squadron, the Headquarters Squadron the 2nd Observation Squadron (occupying the position of the 16th Squadron, which remained at Bataan Airfield), finally Stirling's 17th Squadron (on the right). To the 2nd's right were five more squadrons, which made up the 1st Battalion, 2nd Provisional Air Corps Regiment. To the right of the 1st Battalion was the 31st Philippine Regiment, and to the left of the 2nd Battalion was the 32nd Philippine Army Regiment. The 2nd Battalion spent the next two and a half months defending this position, part of the II Corps area referred to as Sector B.

SSgt. Jesse Knowles of the Headquarters Squadron said this about the 27th becoming an infantry unit: "We knew as much about that job as a goat knows about riding a bicycle." The American and Filipino defenders dug a zigzagged trench, four feet deep and forty inches wide, along the entire Orion-Bagac line, extending the width of Bataan. About one-third to three-quarters of a mile beyond the front was another area called the Outpost Line of Resistance. Men there were positioned about two hundred feet apart so that the enemy could not attack the main line undetected. The pickets on the outpost line would rotate out about every four to eight hours.

> On the night of January 25, the American Forces were pushed back to the final defense line [Orion-Bagac line]—any point further would result in the collapse of our forces since the formation of the terrain permitted no further withdrawals. At this point, the 27th Group, part of the Air Corps Provisional Regiment, took up a front line position. On this same date a force of 700 Japs landed behind the lines on the west coast. The situation was critical. A major Jap effort on the front developed at the same time, and so January 25 was a black day for Bataan. Artillery duels kept on and patrol skirmishes were frequent, but outside of this, fighting was nil. Our Air Force at this time consisted of five P-40s. On the first of March, three more of these five were lost and our air strength was down to two ships.[55]

"Is the Pope Catholic?"

Near the end of January, Stephenson, McAfee, Bender, and Stafford were given a secret assignment. A January 25 notation in McAfee's diary tells the story: "Maybe we are going south but I don't know how in the hell we'd go. It doesn't look like we are going back to the Sq. [16th] We hated telling the boys goodbye. I love these enlisted men. They are the salt of the earth and the backbone of the Army. They're my boys and I promised I'd be back."

Stafford recalled this about the secret mission: "I was sleeping and Pete Bender woke me up and asked if I wanted to leave Bataan in a submarine. My reply was 'Is the Pope Catholic?'"

Bender remembered that Stephenson came into camp with the news that four of the pilots were going over to Corregidor. They were advised that they could bring only the clothing that they were wearing, which caused a laugh since that was about all the clothing they had anyway. The men thought they might be going to Australia to pick up the aircraft diverted there, imagining they would come back with a roar over the field and start operations against the Japanese. They broke open a bottle of whiskey and polished it off, drinking to the time when they would return with ample reinforcements to beat back the enemy.

As leader of the 16th, Stephenson likely felt the same way as McAfee about the loyal and hardworking men he had to leave behind. Lankford remembered that Stephenson was the type of guy who would think nothing of walking over and starting a friendly conversation with one of the privates. Sgt. Kenneth Farmer said that James Scruggs, the 16th Squadron's first sergeant, showed his respect by always referring to him as "Lt. Glenwood G. Stephenson." Farmer thought that both Stephenson and McAfee were different than other West Pointers, down to earth and not aloof. He also thought Stephenson really looked after his troops.

Stephenson recommended Savage as his replacement. Savage did not know until after the lieutenant was gone why he was selected. Colonel George told him later that Stephenson had said that Doc was the only man he would entrust with the squadron. "I was a mess officer at Savannah and that stayed with me until Bataan. The other job, squadron commander, I inherited from one of the Hudson High boys [a nickname for a West Pointer, the academy being located on the Hudson River]."

Harrelson drove Stephenson and the other pilots to Mariveles in a dark green 1935 Plymouth four door. After he dropped them off, he traded the car to some navy guys for a bag of rice. They then drove him back to Bataan Field.

That night Stephenson and the others slept on the ground. The next day they patiently waited at Mariveles until nightfall for a launch to take them over to Corregidor.

5

Escape to Java

THE LAUNCH TRIP FROM Mariveles to the docks at Corregidor was only about six miles, but it gave Stephenson plenty of time to contemplate the hazardous adventures of the past two months and wonder what the future held for him. Perhaps he thought about his wife, Ann, back in Savannah, worrying about the dismal war reports from the Philippines, and the irony of her reading and worrying about Bataan during the next few weeks, and he would not even be there. The last time he communicated with her was shortly before Christmas—maybe in his new destination he could contact her. He likely thought about the men of the 16th Squadron left at Bataan Field. They had been on half-rations for nearly a month, and all had lost weight. Their clothes were tattered, and many had long beards, but they did not complain and accepted their orders willingly. Their situation was bleak—either death or becoming a prisoner was what lay ahead for them unless help arrived soon.

His emotions that day would likely have been on a roller coaster. While he worried about his wife and his men, he could not help but be proud of the fact that on that day, January 26, he was promoted to captain along with other 27th Squadron leaders, Willie Eubank (commander of the 91st) and Warren Stirling (commander of the 17th). He might also have thought about his brief tenure as a squadron leader, how he had led his men at Lipa, on the Manila docks, and during the truck convoy to Bataan. The 16th had enjoyed somewhat better food and shelter than many of the other units during January. It is true that he and his pilots were not in the air, but Bataan Field proved effective as a base for P-40 reconnaissance flights and other missions. He and his fellow squadron officers had kept the airfield and planes operational and their men alive. At about this same time, his boss, Harold George, was promoted to brigadier general.

Stephenson and his colleagues also must have been pleased to think that they would soon have combat aircraft. That same day their 27th comrade, Tom Gerrity, attached to Wainwright's headquarters near Mariveles, expressed his frustration at being a pilot without an airplane: "[Japanese] airplanes fly over us most of the day. The whistle of their planes is driving me nuts. I have been trained to fight in that element, but haven't gotten an airplane to use against them. They roam around like cub planes at a municipal airport, machine gunning and bombing wherever they see fit, without opposition."

When their launch docked at Corregidor, the men did not see any submarine. Stephenson, McAfee, Stafford, and Bender were quickly whisked inside the rock fortress. Their minds left the past and focused on the future. Bender later wrote: "We were to board the first submarine that came in to take us away, the location being unknown even at that time. Secrecy appeared to be the word now for it seems that many others also sorely wanted a place on the voyage. They would have done anything to take our places."

Life on Corregidor was certainly different than on Bataan. It was the largest of the four fortified islands that protected the entrance to Manila Bay. Fort Mills was located on Corregidor. The other three islands also had forts: Fort Hughes on Caballo, Fort Drum on El Fraille, and Fort Frank on Carabao. Before December 8, there were about six thousand troops stationed on the islands, but after that the population swelled considerably. When the U.S. Navy base at Cavite was destroyed by air attacks, many of the navy and Marine Corps personnel and equipment were moved to Corregidor.

Corregidor is a tadpole-shaped island, with its head pointed west and its tail easterly toward Manila. It is almost four miles long, with the head portion, called Topside, rising to about 500 feet above sea level. A number of buildings were located there, including administrative buildings and the mile-long barracks. Back toward the tail, there is a lower plateau referred to as Middleside, and below that is a narrower neck about six hundred yards wide known as Bottomside. This latter is almost at sea level and had docks on both sides. Directly to the east of Bottomside is Malinta Hill, which contains a labyrinth of tunnels. The longest east-west tunnel stretches for 836 feet and has an entrance through volcanic rock. Another series of tunnels housed a hospital. Many of the soldiers, doctors, nurses, and even civilians stayed in the tunnels for protection once the heavy bombing and artillery barrages started. General MacArthur and his staff directed the war effort from underground.

The huge guns of Corregidor and the other three small islands denied access to the Japanese Navy and their merchant marine. As long as MacArthur held these, he was the gatekeeper for Manila Bay. The powerful guns at his disposal were still keeping Japanese artillery and navy at bay. The four pilots observed that, despite rumors to the contrary, the Rock (as Corregidor was called) was also suffering food shortages and, like Bataan Field, was getting its daily dose of bombing raids.

January 27 came and went, and still no sub appeared. Stephenson and McAfee spent the day visiting old West Point classmates Gus Cullen, Robert Wheat, Herb Pace, and Robert Cooper. McAfee recalled: "They're all trying to be optimistic but I know Corregidor will fall as soon as the food gives out on Bataan. Watched the Nips dive bomb Bataan Field this P.M. The poor 16th. I hate to leave the boys. But somehow I want a chance to fight in the air. That's why we're leaving." Bender writes in his memoir: "Corregidor, on Topside, was by this time a shambles. It had been the target for many days on the enemy calendar. None of the buildings was standing and the air smelled of char, now very familiar to us. There was a certain smell seemingly peculiar to a bombed out place. It was a burnt smell but another smell [dead bodies] too."

Down under to "Down Under"

January 28 came and went too, and still no sub. Stephenson and McAfee played bridge and looked over the island and the damage the Japanese bombers had inflicted. They were told that Corregidor's guns had already shot down 143 enemy planes. General MacArthur and his family lived next to them and ate in the same dining area. McAfee noted in his diary that the general appeared calm.

The following day came and went and still no submarine. The pilots started to doubt if there was going to be a secret mission after all. McAfee thought: "I guess we're not going. The sub hasn't come. Just as well. I feel as if we're running out on the boys. How in the hell are we going to get out of here? The Japs are just waiting for us to starve to death."

Later that night Stephenson and McAfee saw the overdue sub, the USS *Seawolf*, surface, and they were impressed by her size. The *Seawolf* was a Sargo-class submarine built in Portsmouth, New Hampshire, and commissioned in 1939. She was 311 feet long and displaced 1,500 tons.[1] Her skipper was F. B. "Fearless Freddy" Warder. The sub had patrolled the South China Sea off the coast of Luzon during December 1941. On the way to Corregidor, the vessel encountered Japanese aircraft and ships during the day.[2] One of the convoys she encountered was a Japanese invasion force headed for Balikpapan, Borneo. After diving and enduring occasional depth charges, the *Seawolf* thereafter spent most of the daylight hours submerged, using the cover of darkness to travel on the surface, which was faster. Running submerged with a heavy load accounted for the *Seawolf* being three days late.

Little did they know that they had two army generals to thank for sending the sub.[3] Brereton was now in Australia to command the U.S. Army Air Corps there and help MacArthur with the defense of the Philippines in any way he could. In attempting to follow that order, he found that few masters of merchant ships, even with the promise of a large financial reward, wanted to test the waters controlled by the Japanese military. Brig. Gen. Julian Barnes, who had commanded the army troops on the *Pensacola* convoy, was put in charge of the U.S. base facilities in Australia, which were meant to support the troops in the Philippines and Java. The best that Brereton and Barnes could do at this point was request that the navy send a submarine to the Philippines. On January 16 the *Seawolf,* loaded with 675 boxes of ammunition (thirty-seven tons) was sent.[4] To make room for this cargo, sixteen torpedoes were removed, leaving the sub with only the torpedoes in her tubes. Sailors literally crawled over the ammunition to get to their bunks.[5] What the *Seawolf* returned with from the Philippines was up to MacArthur and the navy.

While the much-needed ammunition was unloaded at the Mariveles dock, the wind shifted, and the sailors could smell the rotting corpses from the failed Japanese invasion of several nights before at Longoskawayan Point a few miles to the west.[6] The sub remained docked only at night, submerging during the daylight hours in Manila Bay.

Returning to Corregidor at dusk, the *Seawolf* was ready for its return load—twelve army pilots, a physician, six navy officer pilots, six navy enlisted pilots, one navy yeoman, one British intelligence officer, sixteen torpedoes, and spare parts.[7] J. M. Eckberg, a crewmember, remarked about the cargo, "out of it [a truck] came more than a score of the most disreputable human beings in Army uniform I had seen. They looked as if they might have stepped by magic right off New York's Bowery. They were gaunt, and their fatigue uniforms were dirty and tattered." The passengers were cautioned to keep quiet and to stay out of the sailors' way.[8]

The airmen still did not know where they were headed when the sub sailed at 1:00 A.M. on January 31. Again, they thought it odd that a bunch of young pilots (McAfee called them all punks except for the older Vance and Doc Marrocco) were selected to leave the embattled Philippines while MacArthur and other big shots stayed behind.

The pilots also did not know that it was something besides high-ranking military personnel that had been their competition for a place on the submarine—gold and silver bullion. Faced with impending defeat, MacArthur knew that the money could not fall into Japanese hands, but at the same time he realized that these young aviators could pilot the planes necessary to keep his supply lines open from Australia. MacArthur explained to Vance about the pilots being substituted for the gold, saying, "You're literally worth your weight in gold!"[9]

The intelligence officer onboard the sub was Maj. Gerald Wilkinson. The British had been trying to get him out for some time. In fact, at 3:30 A.M. on January 11, Vance had taken off from Bataan Field with Wilkinson to deliver him to Mindanao, but the engine seemed to lose oil pressure, and they had to turn around. The plane crashed while attempting to land in complete darkness; both men sustained minor injuries. Not only did the British want to get Wilkinson out but MacArthur was also hoping that when he met up with his chief, Gen. Sir Archibald Wavell, he would be able to persuade him to send help back to Bataan. The other Army Air Corps personnel leaving on the sub were specifically requested by Brereton and included Vance, who would again function as his intelligence officer. Dr. William Marrocco, the senior physician for the 27th, was a graduate of Georgetown Medical School in Washington, D.C. He was not only a flight surgeon but also a trained otolaryngologist (ears, nose, and throat specialist). Marrocco would become Brereton's senior flight surgeon on Java. Harold George was also among those requested, and when Vance informed him of this, George commented: "You tell Brereton I'll come when the time has come. In the meantime, I refuse to go."[10] General Sutherland had told Vance that there were still some extra places in the submarine and he should fill them. Vance thought that the fighter pilots (of the 24th Pursuit Group) and bomber pilots (of the 19th Bombardment Group) had all of the favors, and so he decided to add pilots from the 27th to the list.

Crew member Red Hanson said: "It seemed that every time you turned around you bumped into somebody. All the pilots had was the clothes on their back. We shared everything with them including our food and cigarettes. They were the nicest bunch of guys. We were all literally and figuratively in the same boat."

McAfee went first to the galley. He had forgotten what good food tasted like. "I'm waxing fat with this food," he later declared. "It's delicious. Plenty of it and always coffee at any hour. They promised us turkey too!" Willie Eubank, who had commanded the 91st Squadron of the 27th, was the other pilot besides the four from the 16th Squadron who Vance had selected to evacuate. He made note of the sleeping accommodations: "My bed was between two torpedoes. It was mine for 8 hours a day." Vance, being the senior American passenger onboard, got the deluxe accommodation—the skipper's wardroom table was his bed.

To pass the time, Stephenson and McAfee played bridge while the others checked out books from the *Seawolf* library. Captain Warder also gave them a tour of the sub. At night McAfee volunteered for watch duty as they ran on the surface. During the day, the *Seawolf* submerged, and the 27th pilots slept. Bender noted that the air in the submarine "got a little stuffy but not too uncomfortable even with the overload of passengers that were traveling on it at that time. A cigarette, for example, would not continue to burn unless puffed on almost continuously."

While listening to the San Francisco radio station, the men heard accounts of a naval battle that had been going on in Macassar Straits. Located between the islands of Borneo and Celebes, the six-hundred-mile-long straits were the site of a four-day struggle that resulted in five Japanese transports being sunk by Allied ships. It was the first significant loss at sea for the Japanese after two months of uninterrupted success. The *Seawolf* passed through those straits on the way to Java, and the crew hoped they could see some action. By the time the sub arrived on the scene, however, the battle was over. They also may have heard about a U.S. Navy action that made the headlines in the newspapers that day. On February 1 the Pacific Fleet went on the offensive a couple of thousand miles east. Rear Adm. William Halsey's *Enterprise* carrier task force made a raid on Kwajalein atoll in the Marshall Islands. The attack damaged several Japanese ships and killed the garrison's commander.[11]

The *Seawolf* passed the equator on February 6. In honor of the occasion, a big turkey dinner with all the trimmings was served. For the pilots who had been on half-rations, life did not get any better.

But the voyage for the American pilots ended sooner than expected. Bender recalled: "We did not know until the day before we landed that our destination was to be Surabaya, Java. We disembarked at that city and not Australia as we had believed up to that point, eight days after having left Corregidor." Hong Kong had already fallen and Singapore was about to fall. According to rumor, the Japanese were ready to move south toward Java, where Surabaya, the third most important Allied naval base in the Far East, was located.[12]

Surabaya

The *Seawolf* steamed on the surface of the Straits of Surabaya and into the shallow harbor channel. A modern travelogue describes Surabaya, Java's second-largest city, as "a humid, polluted urban sprawl housing over four million people. It is not a place to go on holiday. It is a city built for commerce and not one of great cultural and artistic wealth." This port city was not much different in 1942, when it had 350,000 inhabitants. But to the pilots who had not set foot on land in a week, it was heaven sent.

Surabaya had long been an important trading center on the northeastern Java coast. Four centuries earlier spices had attracted the Dutch to this island. Like many European countries, the Netherlands looked to these new lands for their economic potential rather than for colonization purposes. Dutch families sent to the island often stayed for decades, but they were there primarily for administration of commerce and not necessarily interested in either improving the quality of Javanese life or becoming a part of it. With its massive port, Surabaya became an important city in the Dutch economy. And it soon became important to Japan, which coveted the valuable harbor and naval installations as well as the region's rubber and, most importantly, inexhaustible oil supply.

By 1940, as the war in Europe escalated and Germany occupied the Netherlands, Dutch control over Java dwindled. By February 1942 the Japanese, who were making great strides in seizing countries for their Greater East Asia Co-Prosperity Sphere, were by far the greatest threat to continued Dutch control of the island. Oil was the key. Ninety percent of Japan's oil was imported. For eight months prior to Pearl Harbor, Japan had suffered from an embargo of oil and scrap iron from the United States, which had supplied over half of these resources essential to Japan's war machine. They then looked toward the East Indies to satisfy their oil needs, but the Dutch successfully stalled. So Japan finally chose the option of conquest to obtain these resources.

When Stephenson and his Army Air Corps colleagues stepped off the submarine, they were met at the dock by a familiar face, Capt. Frank Kurtz, one of the B-17 pilots who had been stationed at Clark Field in the Philippines when the war broke out. He was now assigned to Java with the 19th Bomb Group. Lt. Col. Eugene Eubank from the 5th Bomber Command had temporarily made Kurtz his liaison officer between group headquarters at Singosari (near Malang) and the U.S. Navy at Surabaya.

Interestingly, Kurtz was somewhat of a celebrity. Besides piloting one of the B-17s from the States to the Philippines in October 1941, he had represented the United States at the 1932 Olympics in Los Angeles and the 1936 Olympics in Berlin as a high diver. Before joining the Army Air Corps, he also held the Junior World Landplane speed record.[13]

For the pilots in the first day back on land, the crucial Far East political and economic concerns played second fiddle to more mundane issues. McAfee wrote: "It certainly is a pleasure to have a meal with all the trimmings. And, of course, it is so much better to be getting a full supply of oxygen in the morning. We went out to have a beer and ran right into an air raid. This is quite a place. The [native] men wear dresses and caps and everyone rides a bicycle. The Dutch just drink beer and sit."

Kurtz arranged for the army pilots to stay that first night at the Oranje, a big, luxurious hotel in Surabaya. It had long hallways, large rooms, and big windows to let the wind blow through at night. Guests pumped Stephenson's group for news about Bataan, and in return they learned about the war effort on Java and elsewhere. The men partied and danced the night away with any woman who would dance with them in the hotel's main ballroom. They deserved this little rest and relaxation that night. Except for the eight days they had just spent in the crowded submarine breathing fetid air, they had been bombed and strafed almost daily for two months. Bender said this about the Oranje: "We enjoyed ourselves as though in heaven. We ate ice cream, ate chocolate, drank beer and whiskey, and ate great food as served in the very best and most picturesque of hotels. I became enamored of draft Heinekens."

The air raid that Stephenson, McAfee, and their comrades experienced upon arrival in Surabaya was a sample of things to come. When they left Corregidor on January 31, the Japanese had not yet attacked Surabaya, but during the week they were at sea, the naval and air bases there had sustained bombings on February 3 and 5. The Japanese also targeted the hotels because they housed high-ranking Allied military leaders. Many of the large white buildings in the city were soon painted green to blend in with the landscape.

Little did the pilots know that after leaving the frying pan of Bataan so to speak, they were now entering the fire of Java, the 650-mile-long main island of the Dutch East Indies. The Allies had now chosen to hold a new line against the onslaught of the mighty Japanese military moving relentlessly south. Burma anchored this line to the west; Darwin, Australia, to the east; and at its center was the "impregnable bastion" of Singapore. This line also included the Netherlands East Indies, where the Allies' joint command in the region, the Australian, British, Dutch, American Command (ABDACOM), had established its headquarters on Java.[14] Created in early January 1942, ABDACOM territory included Burma, Malaya, Singapore, and the Netherlands East Indies, which comprised Borneo, Celebes, Sumatra, and Java as well as a number of other islands and the northwestern portion of New Guinea; later that month the Darwin area of Australia was added. The original directive in the creation of ABDACOM also included the Philippines, but there was confusion as to its exact relationship to forces there. It seemed that it was supposed to be supporting MacArthur's command in any way

6. Southwest Pacific, including areas in ABDACOM or ABDA command. *Courtesy Little, Brown, and Co.*

it could, yet MacArthur was not under its chain of command but rather reported to General Marshall in Washington.[15]

ABDACOM

Major General Brereton had left the Philippines and arrived at Batchelor Field late in December 1941 to meet with the remnants of the 19th Bombardment Group. They now had only ten flyable B-17s of the thirty-five they had arrived with in the Philippines two months earlier and the pilots and other personnel who had gotten out of the Philippines. He told them that the U.S. Army's Far East Air Force, of which he was the commander, was moving all of the bombers to Java at once. As the conversation continued, it soon became apparent that Brereton's air force consisted of only the ten B-17s. The general also told them that within three months, more than one thousand aircraft would be arriving on Java from America for use by the Allies. The 19th left for Java on December 30.[16]

They would become part of ABDACOM, commanded by Gen. Sir Archibald Wavell, a veteran British military leader. Lt. Gen. Sir Henry Pownall, who just days earlier had been appointed British commander in chief for the Far East, would become Wavell's chief of staff. Pownell's Far East forces, all the troops in Singapore and Malaya, became part of Wavell's command. Lt. Gen. Sir Arthur Percival, who was left in charge of those troops, would be left "holding the bag" in Singapore as the Japanese closed in.

The Japanese had invaded the Malay Peninsula along the Thailand-Malaya border on December 8, 1941, with the intent of capturing Malaya and the island of Singapore, about four hundred miles south. Both were governed by the British and contained assets that Japan wanted: Malaya was a leading producer of tin and rubber; Singapore was a major commerce center and had excellent port facilities and a large naval base that had been completed in 1938. During December 1941 and January 1942, the 25th Army, commanded by Lt. Gen. Tomoyuki Yamashita, made steady advances south through jungles and swamps in hot pursuit of the British defenders; some areas the Japanese traversed had previously been considered impassable by many British military leaders. By the end of January, Yamashita had progressed to the southern end of the Malay Peninsula and was poised for the assault on Singapore, in some areas less than a mile away. The British Army, with its Indian and Australian allies, had lost about 19,000 killed or captured during the fighting in Malaya. Most of the troops responsible for defending Singapore were battle-weary veterans of the Malayan campaign. But the Allied defenders now had no naval support and almost no air support.

Wavell's deputy commander in ABDACOM was George H. Brett, an air-corps officer who in late December 1941 had been appointed commander of U.S. Army forces in Australia. In early January 1942 Brett was promoted to lieutenant general so that his rank would be commensurate with his new responsibilities on Java. Admiral Hart led ABDACOM's naval command, ABDAFLOAT. (As it turned out, a better name would have been "ABDA Sunk.") By this time most of ABDACOM's high command, with the possible

10. British leaders in the Southwest Pacific, Air Chief Marshal Sir Robert Brooke-Popham and Gen. Sir Archibald Wavell. Brooke-Popham was commander in chief of the British Far East Forces until December 1941; Wavell would soon command ABDACOM forces. *Courtesy Australian War Memorial*

11. American military leaders, Batavia, Java, January 10, 1942. L to R: Rear Adm. William R. Purnell, chief of staff, U.S. Asiatic Fleet; Adm. Thomas C. Hart, commander, U.S. Asiatic Fleet; Lt. Gen. George A. Brett, deputy commander of Allied forces in the Southwest Pacific; Maj. Gen. Louis H. Brereton, commander, Far East Air Force. *Courtesy National Archives and Records Administration*

exception of Brereton, had effectively written-off reinforcing the Philippines as a wasted effort.[17] Even some of the American leaders, including Hart and Brett, seemed to agree.

Each of the other three parties of ABDACOM had their own interests regarding what should or should not be defended. The British had been interested in strengthening Singapore and preventing Japanese advances into the Indian Ocean toward Burma, India, and their assets in the Middle East. During January and February, Wavell made at least three visits to Singapore to consult with his generals there in an attempt to halt the enemy. The Dutch wanted the Dutch East Indies saved, and the Australians were mainly concerned for their own country. But the Australians also wanted Singapore secured because they thought it was important to the defense of the region, having committed their 8th Division as well as other military personnel to the island's defense.

By February, ABDACOM headquarters was at Lembang, high in the mountains of western Java near the city of Bandoeng. General Brereton had the dual task of being in charge of FEAF and deputy commander of the ABDACOM air force.[18] When in charge of FEAF, he saw his duties as primarily supporting the defense of the Philippines and not that of Singapore, Java, or Australia unless ordered to do so by Washington. This position was compromised by his duties in the Allied regional command.

ABDACOM land forces consisted of units from the four countries. Understandably, the 100,000-man Dutch army garrisoned throughout the islands was the largest group, with over a quarter of their troops on Java. Dutch officers commanded mostly native enlisted men. The Australians supplied two battalions that had just arrived from the Middle East. The British had some artillery units and a squadron of the 3rd Hussars, with twenty-five light tanks. Also on Java was the U.S. 2nd Battalion, 131st Artillery Regiment along with elements of the 26th Field Artillery Brigade and a contingent of U.S. Marines with the navy.[19]

The American artillery units had arrived in Brisbane with the *Pensacola* convoy. They were then loaded, along with naval supplies, on two of the fastest ships in the convoy, the *Holbrook* and the *Bloemfontein.* The two set sail on December 28 for Manila but because of the rapidly deteriorating conditions there and areas along their route, were diverted to Darwin. The *Bloemfontein* then transported the artillery units to Java.[20]

Since the onset of war in early December, the 27th had participated in the only major U.S. military action against the enemy anywhere in the world. Now Stephenson and his colleagues would get to be players in the Dutch East Indies, the only other area besides the Philippines where the U.S. Army and the Army Air Corps would be significantly involved in battle during February 1942. As was the case in the Philippines, the supplies and equipment necessary for combat would be inadequate in quantity and quality. The men could not count on supplies and reinforcements from the United States or Australia, as the Japanese Navy and its air forces controlled most of the supply routes.

Surabaya was not only the main naval base for the Dutch Navy in that area of the world, but since the Americans had lost Cavite in Manila Bay, it was now home to the U.S. Asiatic Fleet as well. The base was particularly valuable for the American submarines that were attempting to disrupt Japanese convoys. Surabaya had all the facilities and shops for repairing ships. Destroying and/or capturing Surabaya, as well as the airbases there, would be critical to the conquest of the East Indies. After Hong Kong fell, Singapore was the only other major Allied naval base in that area, and the Japanese had already neutralized it.

This was the last useable Allied naval base north of Australia, and in some respects it was better equipped than Singapore. Neither it nor the airbases in the Dutch East Indies had radar, which meant that Allied interceptors could not usually respond to air attacks in a timely fashion. Worse yet, because of the lack of warning, Allied aircraft were frequently destroyed on the ground by Japanese bombers and fighters.

The Dutch early warning system consisted of coastwatchers and was not very reliable. It depended on how far away the enemy was when sighted, how fast they were flying, and at what altitude (Japanese bombers usually flew above 20,000 feet). When the system worked, pilots typically had twenty to twenty-five minutes of advanced warning. Japanese spies in the East Indies were thought to be feeding back information on aircraft and ship movements, location of hidden airfields, and expected times of arrival and departure of Allied aircraft.

In October 1941 Air Chief Marshal Sir Robert Brooke-Popham, then British Far East commander, had arranged for the Dutch fighter aircraft to take part in the defense of Singapore and British fighter aircraft to come to Java's aid.[21] Neither group of war planners foresaw that American aircraft would play a greater role as the defending force on Java because the British force would mostly be destroyed in the defense of Singapore and Dutch fighters turned out to be no match against the Zero.

Besides the bewilderment produced by their new surroundings, the newly arrived Americans probably wondered where their planes were and just what they were supposed to do. Colonel Vance and Willie Eubank received orders to go to Batavia, local headquarters for U.S. forces.

West Point graduate and recently promoted Maj. Charles Sprague of the 17th Provisional Pursuit Squadron eventually came to meet the new arrivals. A damaged twin-engine Beechcraft had evacuated Sprague from Bataan on January 2. In eastern Java he commanded a gallant band of outnumbered P-40 pilots who, along with some Dutch pilots who were flying outdated aircraft, had the impossible task of defending the island.[22] On February 11 Sprague put the 27th pilots to work. McAfee, Stafford, and Bender received orders to go to a village called Ngoro to report to the headquarters for the 17th Pursuit Squadron for nonflying duties. Their airfield was a few miles away at Blimbing.

McAfee and the other two drove the forty miles southwest to Ngoro, arriving late at night. In his diary he wrote: "We routed a very pessimistic Dutch private out of bed and he in turn got some coolies up who fed us some very tough meat and vegetables. However, it was food and better than

7. Map of Java, with airfields, cities, and towns. *Courtesy Little, Brown, and Co.*

the hash and 'corned willy' we were used to normally [on Bataan]." McAfee was not happy with his new assignment. The 17th Provisional pilots under Sprague were doing all the flying in the relatively few P-40s at their disposal. McAfee wanted to fly too and not sit at a desk. He tried to offer suggestions on efficiency but was rebuffed. He soon came to the conclusion, "They'll learn like we did in the Philippines—the hard way." Like most grounded pilots, he felt bored about his mundane tasks but like a true pilot took pride in the job Sprague's outnumbered squadron was doing.

Stephenson, because of his brief experience in building the airfield at Lipa and more importantly his operation of Bataan Field for a month, was sent to Modjokerto, approximately twenty-five miles southwest of Surabaya, to help supervise the building of the airfield there. With the aid of two Dutch officers and twelve hundred Javanese, the airfield, formerly a rice paddy, was constructed with bamboo mats covered by four inches of dirt. The runway, three thousand feet long and one hundred feet wide, was finished in three days by the native laborers.[23]

Stephenson was puzzled as to what had happened to the 27th pilots who had left the Philippines for Australia in December and also what had happened to the A-24 dive bombers they were supposed to fly back. The bewilderment did not last long. On February 12, Zeke Summers and ten other pilots flying the A-24s landed at Modjokerto. After taxiing his aircraft to the revetment, Summers and Stephenson were very surprised to see each other. Stephenson was brought up to date on what happened to the 27th pilots and their A-24s.

The A-24s Are Finally Ready

The men talked long into that February 12 night. Each one's incredible tale of how they got from the Philippines to Modjokerto since the war broke out in early December was punctuated with "I can top that!" Stephenson filled in Summers on the details of the 27th's retreat to Bataan and his job at the Bataan Field. He told of how most of the men, including Warren Stirling, had been turned into infantry. He also told him about their West Point classmates he had talked to on Corregidor, whose future on Luzon held either death or capture. Summers had a laugh at Stephenson's harrowing escape with McAfee on the *Seawolf*—two West Pointers needing the navy to save their butts.

Summers in turn told Stephenson the story of his escape by plane to Australia and his frustration in trying to put together the A-24s. By the time the dive bombers were finally ready, the refueling route back to Bataan was held by the Japanese. He and the other 27th pilots, therefore, concentrated their efforts on training for what some thought might ultimately be the defense of Australia.

Their concerns were well founded. A large portion of the Australian Army and its equipment were off with the British fighting the war in the Middle East. Their 8th Division was about to be lost with Singapore, and as yet no American infantry units, with the exception of some troops from the *Pensacola* convoy, had landed on Australian soil.[24] To the citizens, about the only U.S. military presence in January and February 1942 had been the army airmen scurrying around their country trying to put an air force together. The Australians went out of their way to help. Harry Mangan recalled: "I can't say enough about the Australian people even if I tried. We looked like absolute saviors to them. Here comes this little group of pitiful Americans [the 27th] who were willing to risk their own fame and fortune for them in their most desperate hour. They looked upon us as gods. If they had something, you could have it."

The 27th needed Australian help desperately. After finally assembling the rest of the A-24s, Major Davies looked for opportunities to put the dive bombers to good use. Since many American pilots on hand had either few hours flying the A-24s (or in some cases none at all), training was essential.

Hubbard observed that they started to train casual (not assigned) pilots who had been on the *Pensacola* convoy. Volunteer gunners for the extra planes came from the 7th Bomb Group. Some of the A-24s were in a bad way—instruments were out and a number were written up for excessive oil consumption. There were no spare engines. One time Bob Ruegg and Hubbard went out to test the sights on a live bomb drop when they were diverted to check a reported submarine south of Rockhampton (north of Brisbane) as no friendly subs were in the area. After searching for some time, they sighted what might have been a periscope wake. They dived with satisfying accuracy and explosions but no results. They probably attacked a whale.

The training operations were conducted at Archerfield and Amberley outside of Brisbane. In a January progress report, Davies informed General Brereton on the attempt to reassemble the A-24s and P-40s. An average of three planes of each kind was finished each day. His report indicated that twenty pilots from the old 27th Group were with him. RAAF officers helped develop the training syllabus for the A-24s and the P-40s and also helped with instructing new pilots just arrived from the United States.

The first part of the training was a ground school and classroom study devoted to instruments, controls, and signals used for formation flying and dive bombing. Finally, the students were checked out in the aircraft. Some of the 27th pilots dubbed the training operation as "Little Randolph," a reference to Randolph Field in Texas where many of them had learned to fly. But not all of the training results were good:

> Harry Galusha gave daily lectures on low flying, acrobatics over the field and buzzing. Apparently his well-meant effort was expended to very little avail. Lt. Leo Alverson thought the Summer Resort of Southport should be given a proper first-class buzzing. He tried it, and ended up by hitting a wave with his prop and crash-landed on the beach. An island just south of Southport was used as a target and was riddled with Aussie practice bombs. On another occasion, Patrick Armstrong made an emergency landing and in the excitement neglected to lower his wheels. The powder charge in the practice bomb was set off, and this had the bystanders in a sweat until they realized that the ship wasn't on fire. The days passed rapidly by, the boys became better and better until finally it was decided that they were ready to be placed into individual squadrons.[25]

12. Pilots Dick Launder, William Beck, Fred Klatt, and Finley MacGillivray at Charters Towers. *Courtesy Richard Launder and William Beck*

By January 23 Davies had formed the 16th, 17th, and 91st Provisional Squadrons. The 91st was led by Edward M. Backus of Vernon, Texas, one of Stephenson's roommates onboard the *Coolidge*. During the 1930s, he had been a pilot for both American Airlines and Pan American Airways. Like many others in the 27th, at one time he had served with the 3rd Attack (Bomb) Group. Lowery, the former commander of the 17th Squadron from Hattiesburg, Mississippi, took over the 17th Provisional Squadron. Floyd "Buck" Rogers of Sheridan, Arkansas, became the leader of the 16th Provisional Squadron. He had commanded the Headquarters Squadron back in the Philippines. Pilots from the *Pensacola* convoy were added to these units to bring them to strength.

A number of those pilots were fresh from West Coast training schools when assigned to the group at Amberley. They were eager to get into combat aircraft, and most proved very capable. Second Lt. William Beck had finished flight school the previous October. Upon arrival in Australia as a casual pilot, he was assigned to be a motor-transportation officer. When his superiors found out that he was a pilot, they shipped him to the 27th instead.

Second Lt. Richard Launder was another pilot who had arrived with the *Pensacola* convoy and was assigned to the 91st Provisional Squadron. He was raised in California and attended college at the University of Southern California. He then joined the Army Air Corps and, like Beck, had just completed his pilot training at schools in California a few months earlier.

Because of the anticipated Japanese invasion of Java, Summer's 91st Provisional Squadron was ordered there in early February. "The 91st under Captain Backus, with 15 A-24s, flew first to Darwin by way of Charleville, Cloncurry, and Daly Waters. One thing amazed the whole flight across Australia. The Australian grapevine told the people that the planes were coming long before they arrived. At each place they landed, all the natives knew of the arrival and where the flights were headed. Summers' plane was out [of action] because of excessive use of oil [a nightmare problem of the A-24s]."[26] Launder remembered that when they hit Daly Waters about lunchtime the next day, the flies attacked almost immediately. "It was unbelievable! After the first bunch hit you, if another wanted to land, he would have to double park. The lunch was served on a hot tin plate and consisted of Bully-beef stew with topping. Honest to God, it was so encrusted with flies, you couldn't tell what it was until you waved your hand over the plate."[27]

On February 9th Captain Backus and two other A-24 pilots left for Koepang [on the island of Timor near Java, the next stop in the journey]. He was scheduled to follow a LB-30 [a modified B-24 four-engine bomber] and 8 P-40s. Being unable to keep up, he followed his own course and reached Timor all right. The LB-30, however, got lost and the 8 P-40s were forced down in the wilds of the island. Of course, Backus, only having flown for the airlines for seven years, couldn't miss the island. Arriving without any announcement at Koepang, the three A-24s received a warm reception. The Australian ack-ack [antiaircraft guns] cut down the flight and succeeded in puncturing the gasoline tank on Backus' plane. On February 11, Galusha with 11 planes [including Summers] left Darwin for Koepang. All planes arrived safely over the 530 miles of open sea with a ceiling of 50 feet which at times was not conducive to peace of mind. The 11 ships were refueled [at Koepang] and the crews spent the night in some barracks about one mile from the field.[28]

Launder observed this about the English in Koepang. "They were immaculate in their all-white uniforms laced with gold braid. Never would you suspect they knew they were to end the war in a matter of days at most." The dinner was an unforgettable experience. The commanding officer at the head of the table rose, wine glass in hand, and toasted, "Gentlemen, [all rise], the King." Launder said, "This wasn't some God-forsaken island somewhere at the end of the earth; this was a Hollywood movie set!" The next morning, the A-24s were off to Java.[29]

Summers also left at daybreak for Denpasar, Bali. Arriving at a deserted airfield, he thought the Japanese had already taken over the area. The Dutch, however, were hiding in the bushes when he landed. After a few anxious minutes, they came out to refuel his plane. An hour later Summers was back over open water heading for Java. Along the way, he got his first glimpse of the Japanese Navy—four destroyers—but did not attack because none of the A-24s was carrying bombs. That night the 91st stayed at Pasirian.[30] Early the next morning, they headed for Modjokerto.

With the 91st safely at their new base on February 12, Davies planned on bringing the 17th Provisional Squadron to Java. The reconstituted 16th was based at Lowood Field near Brisbane and on February 12 received orders to head to Batchelor Field near Darwin, then fly to Java with the 17th.[31]

There is an apocryphal story about one of the 27th pilots who lost his way across northern Australia and had to perform a belly landing in the desert. The A-24's lower pan was scraped off and the propeller bent. In his telegram back to headquarters, the pilot said: "Forced landing. Please send ground crew." He received no reply and sent a second message: "Washed out belly pan and prop. Please send spares." Apparently, there were no spares and no reply. A few days later the American asked the Australian homesteader he was staying with to send a third telegram. "Still grounded here. What shall eye [*sic*] do?" Finally, headquarters replied, "Why don't you marry and settle down." At that point the lieutenant used the corrugated iron from the farmer's shed to make a belly pan and took his propeller into town, where a local blacksmith hammered it roughly into shape. The pilot was able to fly his plane back.[32]

The 17th had a monumental task in getting the dive bombers ready for Java:

> The A-24s they [the 17th] were flying had truck tires on the wheels, hand triggers on the guns, armored seats that restricted control stick movement to a few inches, no self-sealing tanks, oil burning engines, and unreliable guns. Java was in danger and the planes were needed if the Dutch were to survive. Everyone painted his name on the

cowling and attempted to make their respective ship as fit as possible. You could see "Texas Tornado," "Wild West," "Your Ol' Uncle Harry," and what not. Yes, if nothing else, the gang had guts and spirit. They knew what their chances were against a pack of Zeros.

Davies also knew what those "chances" were. Earlier, in a letter to higher headquarters, he had stated: "If possible, I would like P-40 squadron to depart Darwin at same time as A-24s for necessary protection. A-24s practically helpless if encountered enemy opposition, which I understand can be expected en route north of Darwin."[33]

On February 17 the squadron followed the same route across Australia the 91st had: Charleville, Cloncurry, and then to Daly Waters, 310 miles south of Darwin. It was a flying adventure to say the least. Hubbard noted that "maps were scarce and landmarks even scarcer. We were told to watch for the road through Daly Waters to Katherine where the railroad from Darwin ended."

The pilots soon realized that they must have missed the road to Katherine but eventually found the railroad tracks and a nearby grass landing strip. The planes were low on fuel. Davies found an old-fashioned crank phone in a shack. He spoke with Batchelor Field and ordered fuel to be delivered on the next train through. The following day after refueling, the 17th flew to Batchelor, outside Darwin, and met the 16th. About this time the Japanese began bombing the Darwin area, prompting Davies to move the A-24s back to Daly Waters for safety. But Daly Waters was no picnic. Hubbard thought the place was the fly capital of the world. When they stopped work to drink tea, one had to blow the flies off the cup and sip quickly.

Soon the 17th returned to Batchelor, and Davies received the bad news. Koepang, a refueling base and airfield on Timor, had fallen to the Japanese, as had the island. A vital staging field between Darwin and Java, Koepang was 530 miles from Darwin, and the A-24s limited range made refueling there an absolute necessity. But now the Japanese held the airfield and could use it for offensive operations.[34] The disappointed pilots of both the 17th and the 16th Provisional Squadrons consolidated and remained in northern Australia to defend the Darwin area. The 91st would have all the adventure on Java.

Meanwhile, Back on Java

After the 91st's arrival on Java at Modjokerto on February 12, Stephenson provided some Allied hospitality for the pilots as they awaited the expected arrival of the 16th and 17th Provisional Squadrons. He arranged for the pilots to be housed at Bangersol, a nearby Dutch sugar plantation.

The welcome they [the 91st] received was beyond any expectation. These Dutch people took the boys right into their homes and hearts. Good baths, good food, good whiskey, good beds, had became rarities to the boys. At Bangersol, they had all and more too. Just imagine the luxury of having someone to look after every need after the hardships at Daly Waters and Batchelor Field. Each household had at least five servants and all were eager to serve. Glen was hobnobbing with the Javanese princess and Dutch Army bigwigs, and he did a magnificent job of getting needed things done. He got American cheese, ham, and eggs from Surabaya.[35]

The 16th and 17th Provisional Squadrons never came, and the 91st's Java "vacation" lasted only four days. On February 15 Stephenson and Captain Backus, flew to Bandoeng, about three hundred miles west of Modjokerto, to attend an ABDACOM conference. There they learned that the British had surrendered Singapore.

The Impregnable Citadel Topples

Although the fall of Singapore had been expected for at least a week, the actual surrender on February 15 was a devastating blow for the Allies. General Percival surrendered 85,000 troops to General Yamashita, who had used approximately 30,000 highly motivated men to capture the island. In the years since, relatively few leaders involved with the defense of Singapore and Malaya, including Churchill and Wavell, have escaped blame for this military catastrophe. Many had been led to believe that Singapore was truly an impregnable citadel of the Pacific. Ships of the Royal Navy, which were elsewhere or sunk, were supposed to operate from the island and keep the Japanese Navy in check. In theory, if Australia were attacked, British warships stationed there would come to her rescue. Percival not only surrendered precious troops but also a major naval base and air fields. Losing them was bad enough, but now those installations were in Japanese hands and could be used against the Allies. Worse yet, the Japanese military could now focus its might against Java, New Guinea, and the northern coast of Australia.

Singapore's surrender was doubly bad for the almost defenseless Aussies. Not only had they lost the 8th Division's first-line troops there but most elements of the 6th, 7th, and 9th Divisions were still overseas with the British fighting in the Middle East. The remaining militia at home was for the most part poorly equipped, poorly trained, and lacked significant leadership.

Australia had supplied the RAF with nine thousand airmen, which included the personnel of five squadrons, but like their army counterparts, some were lost with Singapore while others were in Europe and elsewhere. The RAAF also lost some squadrons at Singapore.

Although Australia seemed ill-prepared for a possible invasion, it was her responsibility to supply Britain with troops for a war in Europe, the Middle East, or elsewhere, while in turn Mother England would defend Australia if invaded. The problem was that Britain was fully engaged trying to save itself and its many possessions in the Middle East, India, and elsewhere, its military spread too thin. It is highly unlikely that the British could have also mounted a major defense in Australia at that time. Australia's position had now changed from that of a contributor to Britain's war effort in distant theaters to that of a nation that might have to fight for her own survival.[36]

If there was any good news for the island continent in all of this, it was that when the air bridge with Timor closed, it stranded the 16th and 17th Provisional Squadrons of the 27th Bombardment Group in Darwin, making these units immediately available for air combat in that part of Australia.

Singosari

After hearing of the disastrous news about Singapore, Backus telephoned the 91st at Modjokerto and ordered them to pack up and fly to Batavia (now Jakarta), Java's capital. Located in the northwest corner of the island, Batavia had about twice the population of Surabaya and was much more cosmopolitan. But the 91st did not get to enjoy the city's amenities. After staying there overnight, the squadron was on the move again, this time to the airbase at Singosari. This was seventy miles due south of Surabaya and six miles from the city of Malang. American Bomber Command headquarters would soon move to Malang.

U.S. air units on Java consisted of squadrons from four air groups. The 17th Provisional Squadron of P-40 fighters had been formed around a dozen veteran pilots from the 24th Pursuit Group who had gotten out of the Philippines.[37] The 91st Provisional Squadron of A-24 dive bombers was led by senior pilots from the 27th Bombardment Group. There were also portions of two heavy-bomber groups, including what was left of the 19th Bombardment Group from the Philippines. The other was the 7th Bombardment Group, one squadron of which had left the United States and arrived in Hawaii (on their way to the Philippines) during the Japanese attack on Pearl Harbor. (That squadron of B-17s never made it to the Philippines and only some to Java.) The 7th's ground personnel had been part of the *Pensacola* convoy diverted to Brisbane; many were then sent on to Java. The first planes from the 7th arrived on Java on January 10, flown from the United States. The heavy-bomber squadrons at Java received additional aircraft via the ferrying routes from the United States, but as the Japanese offensive intensified, their attrition rate was about equal to the number of replacements arriving. The 7th's three squadrons flew both B-17s and B-24s.

The heavy bombers' airbases were at Singosari, Madioen, and Jogjakarta. None of the Americans seemed to be able to pronounce the name of the latter airfield and therefore nicknamed it "Jockstrap."[38] Airfields, missions, the Allied chain of command, and the exact position of the Japanese invasion forces seemed to be changing on a daily basis.

The B-17s and B-24s were kept quite busy during the Java campaign. Early on they were sent on a couple of missions over the Philippines to bomb ships at Davao in support of MacArthur's troops and on two missions to Malaya to bomb an airfield in support of the troops defending Singapore. Most of their missions, however, were against shipping as the Japanese moved south, invading Borneo, Celebes, and other islands.

The Netherlands East Indies Air Force at that time had about two hundred planes, all leftovers, outmoded, and obsolete. Some of their bombers were B-10s, which the U.S. Army Air Corps had discarded long before. Their fighters were mainly Brewster Buffaloes, which the Zeros far surpassed, being about 100 mph faster and having a rate of climb three to five times faster.[39] Bender remarked about the Dutch and their slow, outdated Martin B-10 bombers, "Sometimes seven or eight would go out, and perhaps on a good day, two or three would come back." In early February, however, the Dutch obtained fourteen modern Hurricane fighters from the British.

On February 19 the 91st was ready for its first mission. Down to seven planes from the fifteen with which it left Brisbane (some crashed and then were cannibalized), the A-24s were fueled and hand loaded with bombs at Singosari, ready to head east to Denpassar, on the island of Bali, to look for the Japanese invasion force, which consisted of two transports, a light cruiser, and seven or eight destroyers. Eight B-17s and B-24s had sortied from Singosari earlier and bombed the convoy without success.[40] As the dive bombers left their revetments, an air-raid signal caught everyone's attention. The five A-24s on the east side of the field were rolled back to their protective revetments. The two on the west side, piloted by Harry Galusha from Little Rock, Arkansas, and Summers, soared off into 27th Bomb Group history:

Due to a mix up in orders, Harry L. Galusha and Zeke Summers were ordered to take off and fly around for an hour to the south of the field. Someone yelled, "Take off, you're on your own!"

The planes took off and flew south. Galusha called to Summers and asked, "Shall we go over Bali way and see what we can see?"

Summers knowing full well what Galusha was thinking about replied, "You're the man with a wife and kid. Let's go!"

So they headed for Bali [about 150 miles away]. It was known that 30 Zeros were in the vicinity so Galusha and Summers tried to stay just under some clouds. Luckily, there were two layers of stratus clouds at 10,000 feet and the other at 12,000 feet. They stayed between these two layers all the way over.

Their luck still holding, the lower clouds thinned out just over Bali [where Summers had safely refueled only five days before]. There, nestling in the harbor were two ships, a cruiser and a transport. With fear in their hearts and those same hearts held in only by their teeth, the pilots dived on the two boats. Galusha picked the transport and Summers the cruiser. Lady Luck still being with them, their makeshift sights were just enough off the line to make the 660-lb. bombs drop short of the 110-lb. ones. Both pilots recorded direct hits with the 110-pounders but near misses, so they thought, with the 660-lb. jobs.[41]

Summers recalled: "We both dived at the same instant. We went straight down as we liked to do. We dropped the loads at 3,000 feet I pulled out at 600 feet and noted that the troop ship was smoking and appeared to be burning. I didn't get a good look at my cruiser, but from what I could see the ship was smoking with no visible flames."

The surprise was evidently complete. The Japs had never seen any Army dive bombers before because those two were the first ones to ever make a dive in actual combat. The lack of ack-ack showed that [surprise]. The Jap's only hit was a small shrapnel hole in the fuselage of Galusha's ship.[42]

The two planes returned safely to Singosari and an anxious Backus. He had not been fooled for a minute as to the pilots' intentions when the two ships took off. He was really worried about what Eubank at bomber command would say.

Two hours later navy PBYs reported that both the transport and the cruiser had sunk; the airmen hypothesized that by hitting the water, the bombs had penetrated below the line of armor plating before exploding, therefore having a terrific concussion effect and breaking the bulkheads of the boats. McAfee noted in his diary: "Heard that Summers and Galusha got a hit on a cruiser and a transport all by themselves. They were told to fly around until the air raid was over and come back, but no, they went on down to Bali and laid their eggs. They ought to be decorated." Summers proudly remarked: "We were on the deck for going on a mission without orders, but when reconnaissance planes flew over, they gave us a clean bill and awarded us the Distinguished Flying Cross. I was the first Army pilot who made the first dive in WW II in a Navy airplane using Dutch bombs and Javanese gasoline." He later added, "It was a good thing we sank those ships, or I guess both of us would have been court-martialed."[43]

The Dutch were impressed with this early American air success. As Franz Bax, a young lieutenant in the Dutch Navy stationed in Surabaya, remembered, "We didn't see how we could lose the war with these guys." That night the 91st Squadron and their two new heroes celebrated with a big dinner and drinks in downtown Malang.

Japanese records from the war, which were not always totally accurate, indicate that neither ship was sunk. According to one source, two B-17s arrived over the target earlier, but their bombs missed the ships. A bomb dropped by a dive-bomber, however, struck the transport *Sugami Maru*.[44] The hit destroyed an engine, but the ship was able to get underway with assistance from an escort. Another source claims that a bomb from a B-17 struck the transport, which was towed away by a destroyer escort.[45] If the Japanese records are correct, the cruiser and transport may have left by the time the U.S. Navy surveillance planes arrived, and seeing no ships, the PBY crews assumed that they had sunk.

The day after their feast, the airmen were in the skies on another mission. The A-24s were loaded with bombs at Singosari, but the mechanics again experienced difficulty fitting the bombs to the attachments since they were navy planes converted for army use. Not counting the unplanned bombing by Galusha and Summers the day before, the A-24s were about to make the first official Army Air Corps dive-bombing raid of World War II.[46] Edward M. Backus, James A. Ferguson, Richard H. Launder, Harry L. Galusha, Douglas B. Tubb, Robert F. Hambaugh, and Julius B. Summers Jr. piloted the A-24s on the mission.

According to the *27th Reports,* seven A-24s led by Backus and sixteen

P-40s led by Sprague returned to the Straits of Lombok to attack Japanese ships.[47] The P-40s were intercepted by thirty Zeros, and the dogfighting that ensued kept the Zeros off the slow A-24s, which needed the fighter cover in order to do their work.

Second Lieutenant Tubb's plane seemed to have been hit by antiaircraft fire as he started his dive, according to fellow pilots. There was no attempt to pull out of the dive and he did not release his bombs.[48] Tubb and his rear gunner were the only fatalities among the A-24s. Tubb was a 27th pilot from Smithville, Mississippi, who had come out of the Philippines.

Of the five A-24s that returned, one was so badly damaged that it never flew again. Two Japanese ships were claimed sunk—a cruiser credited to Backus and a destroyer—but Japanese official records indicate no such losses, rather that ABDACOM warships damaged two destroyers.[49] Regardless, the A-24 pilots were awarded the Silver Star for gallantry in action for this attack.

There were few P-40s left, however, to provide the much-needed cover for the dive bombers. Although only one Zero was claimed to have been shot down, five P-40s did not return after the dogfight, including Major Sprague's ship. The squadron commander parachuted after being hit, and his chute was supposedly spotted by "Fearless Freddy" Warder, whose submarine, the *Seawolf,* was patrolling the waters off Bali. Sprague died, however, before he could be rescued.[50] Grant Mahony, took over the fighter squadron. He had left the Philippines on December 18 for Australia with Davies's group of pilots. The two other members of the 91st shot down during that raid were luckier:

Launder had an oil line shot away and his engine started cutting out. He wasn't sure as to his whereabouts and when he saw a field he was confident it was a Dutch airport. However, when he saw rising suns painted on the airplanes, he realized his error. He had almost landed on the airport at Denpassar just taken over by the Japs. He was forced down in the sea, however, about 8 miles north of the Japs. He and his gunner, Sgt. Lovenichen [sic, Irving W. Lnenicka] walked 58 miles around the west coast of Bali keeping away from the Japs and just ahead of them. At each town the Balinese Burgermeisters would come out to greet them. They were also given tea and bread. At one place, Launder asked for beer. Nodding okay, the burgermeister snapped out an order. Thirty minutes later a tired dusty native entered with a bottle of hot beer under each arm. After 58 miles of walking, the two men finally procured bicycles. However, they were both so worn out that they couldn't pedal up the hills. They could only coast down.

After three days of walking, Launder and Sgt. [Lnenicka] reached a fisherman's village on northwestern Bali. There they were given an outrigger canoe with two natives to paddle for them. For thirteen hours they paddled across [the] water separating Bali and Java. One native paddler was Mohammedan and kept wailing to the heavens to give them good weather. Finally, after nearly four days of hardship, the men were put ashore near a Dutch outpost. After convincing the Dutch officers in charge of their identity, they were given money and clothes and sent back to Surabaya.[51]

The twenty-one-year-old Launder's casual comment about the adventure was, "I guess we were the last American tourists to leave Bali."[52]

The Dutch sent the duo on a local train, which Launder described as the "Toonerville Trolley," to Dutch headquarters in Surabaya for interrogation and notified the 91st Squadron Headquarters that the two had been rescued. The men got off the train in Surabaya but headed directly for the Oranje Hotel, which seemed to be a watering hole for many of the 27th pilots. Summers, who had learned that the two were headed for Surabaya, anticipated that they would stop first at the Oranje and met them there. Between bottles of Heineken, he anxiously explained to them about the results of the air raid they had participated in a few days before, also telling them the sad news about Tubb and his gunner. They decided to skip the Dutch debriefing and got in their squadron staff car (a Buick), which had the headlights painted out, and headed back to Malang, where Backus, to celebrate their return, took them to a restaurant for dinner. When they returned to the airbase at Singosari, the rest of their colleagues met them with much backslapping and howling. Launder found out, however, that the 19th Bombardment Group had already evacuated the airbase a few days before and the 91st had only three A-24s that were flyable. He learned that the rest of their comrades were very pessimistic about their chances of remaining on Java.

The Japanese had taken Bali, east of Java, so the airbase could be used for their final assault on the main island. Both Allied aircraft and warships had attempted to stop the invasion but had little effect. To the Allied Air Command, the fall of Bali spelled the end of the air defense of Java because no place on the island would be out of reach of enemy aircraft and getting reinforcements in would be much more difficult.[53] ABDACOM headquarters put the machinery of evacuation into motion.[54]

During this time, the Japanese also invaded Sumatra, the large, oil-rich island northwest of Java. Their objective was to capture the city of Palembang, site of two large oil refineries and production of 100-octane aviation gasoline. Earlier in January, the British, with permission from the Dutch, had sent Hurricane fighter squadrons and somewhat outdated bombers to Palembang for defensive purposes and to help patrol the shipping lanes and supply routes to Singapore. In late January Wavell approved a plan to move most of the military aircraft from Singapore to Sumatra. Although he knew that the troops in Malaya needed air support, he was fearful that the planes would all be lost in the near future if he did not relocate them. Operational control of the RAF and RAAF units moved to Sumatra was then transferred from British command in Singapore to ABDACOM in Java.[55] Also during this period, thousands fled from Singapore in small boats. Many of them, including women and children, were killed or captured en route to Sumatra and Java.

The Japanese conquest of Sumatra took place between February 14 and 18. Some units parachuted in to quickly seize the airfields and oil refineries. Dutch, American, and other refinery workers did their best to destroy manufacturing facilities before evacuating their plants. RAF units on Sumatra fought hard and sustained significant losses. The last of their remaining eighty flyable aircraft there retreated to Java on February 16, where they regrouped and joined that island's defenders, while RAF ground-support personnel followed in boats. Allied air units on Java flew many missions to Sumatra in an attempt to disrupt the invading forces. These attacks continued after the RAF withdrew.[56]

McAfee, who had not had any flight time as yet, knew the end was near: "I have an awful feeling about Java. The Japs will certainly take a crack at it and I know it'll fall flatter than a cake and twice as quick. I understand from G-2 [Intelligence Section] that the Japs have a large convoy coming down this way from two directions."

On February 16 Wavell informed London and Washington that the Allied position on Java appeared doomed unless there was a rapidly increased naval and air presence, which was next to impossible. Capt. William Hipps, a planning-staff officer with ABDACOM, later recalled Wavell's talk: "We listened to Sir Archibald give this briefing on what was happening in the Far East [Java] with the war. After two days of listening to him, I thought to myself, I know what I am going to plan—I'm planning how to get the hell out of here!"

That is exactly what happened. Brett and Brereton both advised their superiors in Washington that the Allies' days on Java were numbered and that evacuation plans had to be made. Between February 23 and 25, ABDACOM was dissolved, and the defense of Java fell to the Dutch, their governor general, and other Allied ground troops. Brereton left for India on the twenty-fourth and turned over command of U.S. air operations on Java to Eubank. Wavell and his staff also flew to India courtesy of the U.S. Army Air Corps. Brett, who was now safely back in Australia, was in charge of what was left of American land and air forces in Java and Australia.

On February 24 Winston Churchill supported a plan by the British Admiralty for British and Dutch naval units to leave Java. That same day he warned the king of England that "Burma, Ceylon, Calcutta, and Madras in India, and part of Australia may also fall into enemy hands."[57]

About the only thing going well for McAfee was finding enough Heinekens. "When we hit the hills, I'll have to take a couple of bottles along." He was still doing liaison work for the fighter squadron, and as finance officer, he was handling the money issues. Stephenson was working for Bomber Command at Malang. Occasionally the two friends would meet in Surabaya while on business and have dinner. A peaceful meal was out of the question since the Japanese were bombing the city with everything they had. So far the two pilots were fighting the war on the ground in Java. Their compatriots, the pilots of the 91st, were getting all the air action. In late February those airmen were waiting for orders to attack the expected Japanese invasion convoy.

The 27th and the Battle of the Java Sea

The costly Battle of the Java Sea prefaced the landings of two large Japanese invasion forces at multiple sites in eastern and western Java on February 28 and March 1. Forty-three troop transports were seventy miles out at sea north of Surabaya protected by battleships, cruisers, aircraft carriers, and destroyers. On February 27 the four remaining A-24s, piloted by Galusha, Summers, Ferguson, and Hambaugh, prepared to take off and join the naval battle, but Hambaugh's hydraulic system failed, forcing him from continuing the mission. The other three, led by Galusha, headed north and met up with about ten P-40s that would provide fighter protection. About a half-dozen B-17s and some Dutch and British aircraft also participated in the battle. Although the A-24 pilots had volunteered for this mission, Galusha stated that their aircraft were in very poor condition and should never have left the ground.

Galusha, Summers, and Ferguson had been ordered to attack transports. When they arrived on the scene, the naval engagement had already been going on for much of the day. According to Galusha, the pilots had been given no intelligence as to friendly activities, making it very difficult to determine which ships were hostile. Eventually, they located the troop transports, considerably farther north and well protected by other warships. At 4:57 P.M. the dive bombers finally went into action, breaking through intense antiaircraft fire from the escorting vessels. They claimed six direct hits and three close misses, sinking three transports. Accompanying P-40 pilots witnessed one ship sinking, but Japanese officials denied that any transports were lost at that time.[58]

Allied forces were outnumbered both in the air and on the sea. On the water ABDACOM forces led by Dutch rear admiral Karel Doorman put up a valiant but futile fight. The Japanese invasion was only delayed briefly, but most of the larger ABDACOM ships were sunk. Hundreds of Allied sailors were killed, including Doorman.[59]

That same day twenty-seven crated and much-needed P-40s were delivered to Java by sea and probably assembled later by the Dutch. Out at sea south of Java, the USS *Langley,* one of the old American aircraft carriers, which had another thirty-two P-40 fighters, army pilots, and other air-corps personnel, had been headed to Ceylon but was called back.[60] Japanese bombers sunk the old ship as it steamed from Australia to Java.

There was no airfield at Tjilatjap, but this port had been chosen for delivery of the *Langley*'s cargo because it was less likely to be bombed. The "ready-to-fly" P-40s could not be flown off the old carrier, so to get them to the cleared fields that would have acted as airstrips, the approach roads had to be widened—trees cut back or removed and native huts demolished—to make way for the P-40s' wingspan.[61]

When the three A-24 pilots returned to Singosari from their strike, they looked at the almost deserted airfield, except for a few officers and men from their own outfit, and knew they were not going to stay long. Their orders were to report to Jogjakarta two hundred miles away and to bring any flyable airplanes with them. Summers's dive bomber was so badly damaged from the raid that it was no longer airworthy. Summers and Launder flew the only two planes remaining out of the fifteen that they had almost a month earlier to Jogjakarta the next morning. The rest of the pilots piled into a large Buick sedan and drove.[62]

Summers flew Galusha's ship and Launder flew Ferguson's ship over. Galusha led the motor convoy. This flight, by the way, cleared up a big mystery for Summers. He had been wondering why his ship was slower than Galusha's. Upon getting into Galusha's ship, Summers saw that Galusha had only three flight instruments remaining: a compass, the manifold pressure gauge, and the air speed indicator. Galusha had removed his altimeter, flight container equipment, his oil temperature and pressure gauges, and lots of other equipment to make his plane lighter. Small wonder it was faster.[63]

Yet Another Evacuation-Escape

The airbase at Jogjakarta was a beehive of activity. Some air-corps personnel flew in, some arrived by car, and others took the train. Located near the Indian Ocean, Jogjakarta was one hundred miles south of the large Japanese invasion occurring at Kragon on the Java Sea. Stephenson, McAfee, and the rest of the 91st Squadron as well as the pursuit pilots had only a brief window of time to find a way off of Java. With a relatively short range, the A-24s and the P-40s could not make Australia and were abandoned. Besides the airmen, there were also civilians who needed to be evacuated, many of whom were families of oil-company workers. There were few large planes available that had the range to make Australia—five B-17s and three LB-30s were shuttling men out of Jogjakarta. One of the B-17s used for evacuating troops was functioning on only three engines.

McAfee, Stafford, and Bender were afraid that they were going to be left behind, so the three decided to stick together and find their own way out. There was a damaged Army Air Corps C-52 (the military version of the DC-3 airliner) at the airfield. They decided to repair its left and right elevators in the tail section, damaged from hitting a barricade a month before. They drove hundreds of miles almost across Java to a machine shop at Bandoeng to get the elevator bar fixed. Even after this, they did not have all the necessary parts to repair the other damage but decided, after working feverishly for days, that the plane was flyable. The Dutch officer in charge of the field begged them to take along his wife, who was pregnant, and one of her friends with a baby.

McAfee wrote in his diary: "Tried to take off last night [February 26] but the right engine quit on take off so we didn't make it. The Japs got on [Java] yesterday afternoon. Pete [Bender] and I have been working harder than hell trying to get the ship ready. There are so many Japs over the island we're scared to take off in daylight."

The next night their takeoff was successful. They started for Australia with no navigation charts but carrying a large atlas. Since Australia is such a large landmass, they thought that they could hardly miss it. The flight southeast was relatively uneventful, though flying just over the wave tops during the last portion of the trip to avoid enemy aircraft that were usually in the area. When they made landfall, McAfee and Bender were able to pinpoint features from their atlas and locate Batchelor Field, where they refueled before continuing on to Daly Waters. McAfee wrote about the harrowing trip: "We made it. Brought with us two women—one pregnant and one with a baby. Landed at Daly Waters at 2:00 P.M. [about a six-hour trip] Wired Col. Davies at Batchelor that we were in Australia. We feel fine and are again safely out of the way of the Japs. But for how long?"

The *27th Reports* relates: "On the night of February 28, all the remaining men of the outfit were evacuated to Broome, Australia in LB-30s and B-17s. From there they went to Perth and so on around the coast of southern Australia. They were reassigned in Melbourne and sent to the 3rd Bombardment Group in Charters Towers."

Earlier Brereton had been given authority to commandeer all airplanes in the Dutch East Indies, including commercial airliners from the Dutch, Australian, and British, as the situation continued to deteriorate. These planes were to be used to evacuate civilians who were not citizens of the islands as well as some Dutch dependents.

Hipps, who was working for Brereton, was assigned the additional duty on Java of evacuating these civilians, including oil-field workers and their families, by air back to Australia and elsewhere. Many of them had just fled from Sumatra. He contacted the Dutch airline officials whose planes had all been grounded and hidden, setting up an evacuation program. Hipps had to personally sign for each ticket with the promise that the U.S. government would reimburse the airline. As a result of running this evacuation for several days plus his other duties, he barely made it out of Java himself. Hipps flew out from Jogjakarta with Lt. Col. Eugene Eubank in one of the last B-17s to leave.

Some American personnel, realizing that there were too many evacuees and too few planes at Jogjakarta, took the train to the port city of Tjilatjap. There they boarded the Dutch freighter *Abbekerk,* which originally had been reserved for the transport of Army Air Corps units. Almost fifteen hundred Dutch, British, and American military personnel were crowded onboard the vessel; there were not enough lifeboats or life vests for them all. Nevertheless, the *Abbekerk* finally set sail on the evening of February 28. The food onboard was terrible, most of the passengers slept on the deck, and the ship's armament was weak.

About this same time, two Allied warships, which had just participated in the Battle of the Java Sea—the heavy cruiser USS *Houston* and the Australian light cruiser HMAS *Perth*—were just leaving the Java Sea and entering Sunda Strait for the Indian Ocean. They met up with major elements of the Japanese

Combined Fleet and decided to fight it out. Although they may have sunk as many as four Japanese troop transports, the *Perth* was sunk shortly after midnight and the *Houston* less than an hour later.

Leaving Java afterward and heading south into the Indian Ocean toward Australia was particularly precarious because the Japanese had decided to close this route to the Allies. Four of their fleet aircraft carriers along with their escorts were operating in the area. The Japanese also had two battleships and two heavy cruisers placed between Java and Australia as well as many submarines. A day before the *Abbekerk* sailed, Japanese bombers had sunk the USS *Langley* along the same route.

Japanese carrier-based planes also sank the USS *Pecos* just off the south coast of Java. The *Pecos* was a fleet tanker equipped to fuel vessels at sea and was carrying survivors from the *Langley* as well as survivors from three other U.S. warships that had been sunk recently. That same evening the U.S. destroyer *Edsall,* which was headed to Tjilatjap with U.S. Army pilots and other air-corps personnel rescued from the *Langley,* was attacked and sunk by Japanese warships and carrier-based aircraft, all within earshot of *Pecos* survivors clinging to flotsam. The *Edsall* had no known survivors. The sinking of the *Langley* underscored the confusion during the evacuation of the Allies from Java and raised grave concerns about coordination of multinational commands such as ABDACOM. The carrier was bringing Army Air Corps personnel to Java at a time when the Americans and their Allies were evacuating. The British also lost the cruiser *Exeter* and two destroyers on March 1 while attempting to escape around Java's western tip.

Two hundred and sixty officers and men still waited to depart on March 1. The three LB-30s took thirty-five passengers each and the five B-17s thirty-one each. Just after midnight on March 2, the final LB-30 flight left Jogjakarta. The Japanese, just eighteen miles away, were closing in. After the plane was airborne, the Dutch cratered the runways.[64] Relatively few American airmen were left behind. Four were in the hospital and too injured to be moved, while others had not made it to the airfield in time.[65]

The 2nd Battalion, 131st Artillery Regiment, a National Guard unit from Texas, was not as lucky. They had been with the *Pensacola* convoy and arrived on Java on January 13. The 538 men of the unit were ordered to stay behind and fight with the Dutch and other Allied ground forces even though the situation was clearly hopeless.[66] Many RAF pilots and ground crews were evacuated, but a couple of RAF squadrons were also ordered to stay behind and fight. By the time the American airmen were evacuated in early March, the RAF had perhaps a dozen flyable combat aircraft left on Java.[67]

After the Japanese conquest of the Philippines, Filipinos often hid Americans and looked after them. Americans and Filipinos jointly carried out guerrilla operations there. The two nationalities had worked well together in peacetime, tended to trust each other, and were fighting for a common cause. This would not be the case in Java, however, where the Indonesians were hostile to the Dutch after the invasion and believed that the Japanese were giving them a chance to be rid of their European masters.[68]

None of the A-24s that went to Java returned, and some of the 27th's pilots were killed. But much was learned about the dive bomber's effectiveness during their two weeks of action. The aircraft showed promise of being successful against shipping, but their short range and reliance on fighter cover were weaknesses that needed to be overcome.[69]

None of the P-40s would return from Java. Eighty-three fighters had set off for Java, but only thirty-nine arrived and saw action. According to Edmonds, another fifty-nine were shipped on the *Langley* and *Sea Witch,* all of which were lost. B-17 and LB-30 loss rates were also high. Forty-nine B-17s and twelve LB-30s made it to Java. During their forty-five days there, these bombers had flown forty-four missions, many of them against enemy shipping and bases on other islands. Twenty B-17s and three LB-30s were evacuated from Java in late February and early March—the rest were lost to enemy action, accidents, or deliberately destroyed.[70] By the time of the evacuation, the U.S. Navy had only three remaining PBY Catalina flying boats of the twenty-four they had started with at Cavite in the Philippines less than three months earlier.[71]

In the early morning hours of March 2, Stephenson's overloaded plane reached Broome, Australia. He was hungry and tired but thankful to be out of harm's way for the present.

6

March and Command Changes

TODAY BROOME, AUSTRALIA, is a tropical paradise lying between the white sand beaches of the Indian Ocean to the west and the Great Sandy Desert to the southeast. Its reputation for beautiful pearls made the town a melting pot before World War II as adventurers from many countries sought their fortune. But in February 1942, residents were interested in only one thing—getting out of town. Most of the inhabitants had already left by the end of the month.

Broome Disaster

When Allied fortunes for Java turned sour in February, plans were made for the evacuation of military personnel. Broome was hurriedly chosen as the receiving port because of its protective bay suitable for flying-boat landings. Receding tides, however, occasionally stranded planes, and passengers often had to walk a half mile through mud just to board the aircraft for the next leg to Perth, sixteen hundred miles away. Many flights arrived at night, and passengers often spent a hungry night onboard rather than risking a walk to shore.[1]

Inland, the Broome Aerodrome was expanded to accommodate the huge B-17s and B-24s. Often after one landed, a local crew of unemployed laborers ran out and repaired the grass runway before the next Flying Fortress or Liberator set down. On the morning of February 24, U.S. Army Air Corps personnel arrived to set up and coordinate the receiving end of the air evacuation of Java. The following day evacuees began arriving aboard Empire flying boats and DC-3s. The next evening B-17s landed. The three local hotels soon ran out of food. Refugees arrived faster than they could be dispersed to other parts of the country.

As planes poured in, Broome seemingly became the busiest airport in Australia, with as many as fifty-seven aircraft arriving in one day.[2] The key, however, was to get these planes out as quickly as they emptied and refueled. About 3:00 P.M. on March 2, a Japanese reconnaissance plane appeared, made three circles over the port at nine thousand feet, and then disappeared. As a result, captains of all aircraft were warned to take off as soon as possible after daybreak the following morning.[3]

Despite this warning, there were still six planes loading on the airfield and fifteen flying boats in the bay when nine Japanese Zeros arrived about 9:20 A.M. There was no warning of their approach. Broome was defenseless—no radar, no antiaircraft guns, and no fighter planes. Two of the flying boats had just come in from Java filled with passengers, and an American B-24 had just taken off, filled with sick and wounded soldiers, headed for Melbourne. Three of the Zeros went after the B-24 and quickly shot it down before rejoining the other six Japanese fighters, which flew leisurely over the area strafing targets in Brook Bay and at the Broome Airdrome. Almost every airplane was destroyed, including the B-24 that General Brett had used to escape from Java on the night of February 23. The Zeros destroyed two B-17s, two Dutch twin-engine Lockheed airliners, and as many as fourteen or fifteen flying boats in the bay.[4] An estimated eighty people were killed, including forty-five Dutch refugee wives and children. One Zero was shot down by a Dutch pilot on the ground with a machine gun he had removed from an aircraft under repair. Another Japanese pilot had to crash land in the sea on his way back.[5] Stephenson, however, was lucky again. His B-17 had left Broome earlier that morning and proceeded on to Melbourne in the far southeastern corner of Australia.

Actually, his was not the last B-17 to leave Java. At Bandoeng an Army Air Corps sergeant, Harry Hayes, who was in charge of the inspection and repair depot there, realized on March 2 that no airplane would be sent back for him. He looked over the three B-17s that had been shot up and bomb-damaged and repaired one with help from native laborers who worked at the local railroad shop. He was ready to fly on March 4. An American civilian pilot, Gerald L. Cherymisin, who had flown a B-17 before the war, agreed to fly the plane. A Dutch air officer, 1st Lt. Siblot J. Kok, volunteered to be the copilot. They took on twenty passengers, including 2nd Lt. J. B. Criswell, one of the A-24 dive bomber pilots from the 27th. While they were preparing to take off, Zeros came over and strafed the plane, causing further damage. It had to be rolled back under the trees for more repairs but took off that night with only three engines running; the instrument panel was lit with a flashlight. The plane made it safely to Australia, probably on the morning of March 5. Elsewhere, Dutch airmen subsequently made it to Australia with another

B-17 they had repaired. There were many other attempts to leave Java by air early in March and even after the surrender. Some made it, others did not.[6]

On March 5 the *Abbekerk,* much to the relief of its beleaguered and desperate passengers, docked at Fremantle on the western coast of Australia.[7] In late February and early March, many other merchant vessels packed with civilians and military evacuees left Java's harbors for Australia and elsewhere. Most were sunk by the Japanese as were other smaller Allied navy vessels fleeing the island.

In Melbourne Stephenson was finally free of the Japanese bombers that plagued him for the past three months. In that short span Japan had captured Hong Kong, Singapore, Timor, Bali, and many other islands, including the U.S. possessions of Guam and Wake. Burma, another country that had been under ABDACOM protection, during March was also in the process of falling to the Japanese, who wanted its oil and rice supplies as well as to deny its use by the Allies as a back door for military supplies to the Chinese. Java surrendered unconditionally on March 8. Thousands of Dutch troops became POWs as well as many British and Australian soldiers and airmen. The Americans of the 2nd Battalion, 131st Artillery Regiment who were left behind to fight also became prisoners.[8]

The brief respite that the 27th airmen enjoyed in Australia was comparable to a badly beaten football team using halftime to regroup. Not only the 27th but also the entire Allied war effort in the Pacific had struggled futilely so far. In those early months badly needed equipment and reinforcements were out on the high seas steaming to Australia. And in Melbourne in March 1942, there was a collection of defeated and demoralized Allied units. But they would soon be welcoming newly arriving men and equipment.

The Philippines Hang On

Congratulatory messages were received weekly on Bataan and Corregidor telling the beleaguered forces how much the United States admired their fighting courage. As far as a delivery date for their requests for food, ammunition, and replacements, the replies were vague. The following message from President Roosevelt to President Quezon is typical: "While I cannot now indicate the time at which succor and assistance can reach the Philippines, I do know that every ship at our disposal is bringing to the southwest Pacific the forces that will ultimately smash the invader and free your country. Every day gained for building up the forces is of incalculable value and it is in the gaining of time that the defenders of Bataan are assisting us so effectively."[9] The "Battling Bastards of Bataan," as the men on the front line were known, then extended their bitterness to MacArthur, who visited the peninsula and his commanders there only once, on January 10. In their minds he had retired to the relative safety of Corregidor. They labeled him "Dugout Doug."

MacArthur was fighting a war within a war without being fully appreciative of it. While his struggle against the Japanese in the Philippines was a piece of the wartime puzzle, the conflict in Europe was a much greater piece. MacArthur speculated that a stronger bond existed between Washington and the Allies fighting in Europe than between Washington and Corregidor. He was right. At the time, England and America's first priority was defeating Germany and Italy. Other competition for resources came from the Soviet Union, which the Allies needed to keep engaged with Hitler's armies on the Eastern Front and also prevent from negotiating a truce with the Germans. To accomplish this, the United States had promised and was about to implement a plan whereby a significant number of American merchant ships would be dedicated to supplying the Russians with millions of tons of food, oil, and war materials.[10] Nonetheless, some attempts to help the troops in the Philippines were made.

Ten Million Bucks and Whatever It Takes

American efforts to aid the Philippines were also hampered by merchant captains who refused to venture into waters controlled by Japanese surface ships and submarines. Relatively few vessels arrived in Manila Bay; most were submarines. The air-transport route to Del Monte, except for long-range B-17s and B-24s, also dried up as the Japanese captured important airfields and refueling stops along the way.

In January and February, before Java fell, General Marshall desperately tried to get supplies and food to the troops on Bataan and Corregidor. He had sent Brig. Gen. Julian Barnes in Melbourne the first blockade-running message on January 18. Barnes had replied, but his answer did not satisfy Marshall. On January 19 he sent Barnes another message, which indicated the necessity of immediate action:

> Report on blockade indicates urgency my instructions not fully
> appreciated. . . . Time does not permit exclusive dependence upon
> dispatch of food supplies to NEI [Netherlands East Indies] for trans-
> shipment. Imperative that local resources in every port be exploited
> to maximum through purchase and immediate dispatch. Vigorous
> execution necessary. Agents with cash must be placed on NEI and
> British Islands by plane. Actions and results are imperative.

MacArthur reports food situation PI [Philippine Islands] becoming most serious. States blockade light, may easily be run by bold action. Imperative organize comprehensive efforts, run blockade, and deliver supplies MacArthur. Use funds without stint $10,000,000 now available. May be spent whatever manner deemed advisable. Arrange advance payments, partial payments for unsuccessful efforts, and large bonus for actual delivery. Determine method, procedure, payments, but must get results.

Organize groups of bold and resourceful men. Dispatch them with funds by air to NEI, there to buy food and charter vessels. Rewards for actual delivery to Bataan or Corregidor must be fixed at level to insure utmost energy and daring on part of masters. At same time dispatch blockade runners from Australia with standard rations and small amounts of ammunition each. Make movement on broad front. Use many routes, great numbers of small or medium size boats. Continue incessantly until satisfactory level supplies secured. Only indomitable determination will succeed. Success must be attained. Risk will be great. Reward will be proportionate.[11]

Barnes put Col. John Robenson in charge of this task, who at the time was commanding U.S. troops at Darwin. Barnes directed: "You and six other officers will proceed by commercial or army plane on special mission to Java, NEI. Officers selected will be of junior grade, athletic, resourceful, and of sound judgment. Further detailed instructions follow by letter."[12]

Robenson was a capable officer who would have large amounts of cash readily available to help expedite his task. After he and his men arrived on Java, they received little sympathy or cooperation from most ABDACOM leaders, especially the non-Americans, who had pretty much written off the Philippines. Robenson sent two Philippine cargo ships loaded with supplies back to the islands. The Japanese sunk both on the way. He purchased 3,000 live pigs on Bali, which he intended to have delivered by small native cargo ships to Surabaya, where they would be slaughtered and then shipped to the troops on Luzon. The shipments to Java, however, were halted after the arrival of Japanese planes patrolling the waters between the islands. The last boat to leave Bali had 150 pigs aboard and a native crew of eight. The boat arrived at Java after Japanese strafing attacks with only one crew member and six pigs still alive.[13] Eventually, Dutch vice admiral Conrad E. L. Helfrich made available four old cargo ships, but Robenson had to find the crews. He succeeded in obtaining men for one ship and provisioning it.

That freighter left Java shortly before the invasion there and was also sunk by the Japanese.

Although Robenson and his men worked diligently to carry out their mission, they never did get food or supplies to the Philippines. Only a handful of other vessels made it through during that period.

The Battling Bastards of Bataan

The Japanese launched an offensive against the Orion-Bagac line on January 27, having landed troops a few days earlier at various beachheads to the south, behind I Corps lines, on the South China Sea side of Bataan. The fighting was intense for about a week and a half, after which the enemy withdrew after sustaining significant losses.

After February 8 there were sporadic Japanese attacks against the front lines. There were also regular dive-bomber attacks and artillery bombardments. During February there were constant rumors that help was on the way. Although the men had their backs to Manila Bay, many were optimistic at this time. "The Japanese artillery would fire a barrage every evening about chow time as the mess truck came in, stirring up the dust. You didn't have to be much of an [artillery] spotter to indicate where the truck stopped."[14] Trucks were parked between large bamboo thickets, which usually provided excellent protection from the shells.

Another landing strip was made ready by army engineers a couple of miles south at Cabcaben by the end of January, and a few planes were transferred there from Bataan Field in early February. On February 23 a third airfield was opened at Mariveles, and a few pursuit aircraft went there.

Bataan Airfield continued to function, as craters along the runway from daily bombings were usually repaired at night. The 16th Squadron, now commanded by Doc Savage, maintained the airfield and helped service the dwindling number of fighters. Besides the P-40s, the field was used by other aircraft to shuttle personnel and other items to Corregidor and various airfields farther south still under Allied control. When pilots returned from Del Monte, they usually brought back medicine, cigarettes, relatively small quantities of food, and sometimes liquor for the men in various units. The latter helped morale. In late March and early April, shuttle traffic increased as certain people were evacuated to Del Monte. Some of them would eventually leave the Philippines on American bombers flown in and out of Del Monte.

Harrelson flew a two-winged Stearman trainer at night over to San Jose on

Mindoro three or four times to pick up sugar and alcohol from the members of the Mindoro Detachment of the 48th Materiel Squadron. Some of the men would mix this almost pure alcohol with pineapple juice and drink it. According to Harrelson, one time the squadron leader, Savage, made the comment to some of those drinking the pineapple juice–alcohol mixture, "You grown men are acting like a bunch of children."

On the front, the 27th was having a time. Rocky Gause was the Communications Officer. He was trying to get a radio going to send cables home. Warren Stirling had a long beard and was doing a good job with the 17th. Gilbo, Patterson, and Whipple were the backbone of the 17th—they were always out on patrols. Once, during an artillery barrage, "Whip" fixed hot cakes for everyone regardless of the shells.

During most of March, everything was fairly peaceful—food was scarce and the boys were gathering the remains of the already harvested rice crop and shooting monkeys and anything else they could find to eat. Mel Swenson was over on Corregidor helping an AA outfit, and often he sent tidbits of food that helped out a great deal.[15]

Food continued to be the top priority. There was never enough. The men were fed twice a day. Rations, cut back as the days passed, usually included a few ounces of soupy boiled rice and canned food such as salmon or tomatoes. Animals increasingly were fair game, including snakes, iguanas, wild pigs, monkeys, dogs, horses, and pack mules as well as the occasional water buffalo. As the food situation got worse, a new duty was added to the squadrons of the 2nd Battalion—food detail. The men on that detail would go out and find additional food to supplement the rations for the squadron. Each member was allowed to find food any way he could as long as he did not tell his commanding officer how or where he got whatever he brought back.

There were numerous types of military medical facilities on Bataan, ranging from first-aid stations up to hospitals staffed by Americans, Filipinos, and on the other side of the front lines, Japanese. Most if not all had insufficient quantities of medicine and other supplies. Almost all of them were makeshift. The U.S. Army had two large hospitals on Bataan. Initially, Hospital No. 1 was located near Limay and had some wood-framed open structures with roofs. Tents were added as needed. In late January, however, when the reserve line became the front line, that hospital was moved back to within a few miles of the U.S. Army Hospital No. 2 between Cabcaben and Mariveles. They were both located off the East Coast Road in the jungle. Although they had some tents and small framed buildings, most of the wards were out in the open, with no roofs or other covering overhead for the patients. As time went on, the patient population grew, with Hospital No. 1 having an estimated eighteen hundred American, Filipino, and some Japanese POW patients. Hospital No. 2 had about seven thousand patients.[16]

The Philippine Army had a hospital in the rear area that cared for their soldiers as well as Filipino civilians from the refugee camps that sprang up nearby. The U.S. Navy had medical facilities at Mariveles. Their more seriously sick and wounded, many of them marines, were usually taken to the U.S. Army hospitals on Bataan or Corregidor.

Hochman, who was the 16th Squadron's physician at Bataan Field, eventually became a patient at Hospital No. 2 and then a member of staff. He had tremendous ulcers on his leg, so severe that he could not walk. It took quite a while for them to heal. But when he was able to walk again, he was assigned to work in a ward and did not return to the 16th Squadron.

Tropical diseases and other conditions afflicted nearly all of the Bataan defenders at one time or another. Approximately 80 percent of the men eventually had malaria; if the symptoms were not severe, the soldier was kept in the front lines. By early April, 75 percent had diarrhea from intestinal disorders.[17] Skin fungus, heat prostration, tropical ulcers, dengue fever, beriberi, hookworm, and pellagra were also common.

First Lt. George Kane, adjutant for the 27th Bombardment Group, was required to advise II Corps headquarters as to the number of effective troops on frontline duty. This was never as many as 50 percent. "I cannot adequately describe the gaunt physical condition our men were in due to the lack of food and quinine and the increased tension. Barely a day went by without the Japanese overhead."

Men were frequently sent out on patrols into enemy-controlled territory and behind enemy lines. Some, including those from the 2nd Battalion, were killed or wounded while on these missions. Those who volunteered were usually given extra food. Enterprising Filipinos were bringing in food and cigarettes near Pilar by boat, and both Japanese and American patrols patronized them. Before going on patrol, the men would take orders and collect money for items the Filipinos were selling.[18] Members of the 27th assumed that there was an unofficial truce between the American and Japanese there. One night, however, the Japanese ambushed some of the American customers near the store.[19]

Who's in Charge?

When Stephenson reached Australia, he had to wonder if anyone was in charge. Three months earlier, the first day of the war in the Philippines, Capt. William Hipps commanded the 16th Squadron (now led by Stephenson), 1st Lt. Herman Lowery led the 17th, 1st Lt. William Eubank the 91st, and Lt. Floyd Rogers, the Headquarters Squadron. They all reported to Major Davies, the 27th's commanding officer, who in turn reported to Col. Eugene Eubank, commanding officer of the 5th Bomber Command. Eubank reported to Maj. Gen. Lewis H. Brereton, the commander of the Far Eastern Air Force, whose boss was Lt. Gen. Douglas MacArthur, who commanded the U.S. Army Forces in the Far East. That simple chain of command, however, was to change rapidly in the weeks to come as many 27th officers left for Australia.

The constant change in leadership put the 27th in a vulnerable situation that became worse on December 24, 1941, when MacArthur ordered General Brereton, with his FEAF headquarters, to establish a new base of operations in either Java or Australia. Hipps, Stephenson's old boss, also went with Brereton. That day Stephenson and the 16th Squadron were stationed at Lipa when the puzzling orders came to retreat to Bataan and leave all equipment behind.

Once on Bataan, Stephenson wanted to know who was going to give orders now that Brereton was gone. That honor fell to Col. Harold George, who set up headquarters for the air corps on the peninsula. On December 28 Stephenson and McAfee approached the colonel about getting a job for the 16th—maintaining Bataan Field and its aircraft.

That was the start of a strong bond between Stephenson and George that would later continue in Melbourne. During January 1942, the air-corps chain of command for the 16th was relatively simple—Stephenson reported to George, who in turn reported to MacArthur, or at least on paper that is how it should have worked. But on Java just about everything, including command and control, seemed to be in an constant state of flux. When Stephenson arrived in Melbourne, the chaos continued. Brereton, who had commanded FEAF, was not there but in India. Stephenson watched American, Australian, and even Dutch senior officers jockey for leadership positions in what was to become the Allied Air Forces.

MacArthur, Boats, Planes, and Trains

Unknown to Stephenson, Brett, Brereton, Wavell, and even MacArthur, in March the chain of command in Australia was to embark in an entirely new direction. When the situation on Java appeared doomed, Prime Minister Churchill and President Roosevelt made an agreement: England would defend the Burma-India war theater and the United States would defend the Pacific Ocean, including Australia. That country would be placated if an American was named supreme commander of the war effort in their area, especially with the promise of more U.S. troops and equipment. They agreed that one man had the military knowledge for defeating the Japanese and the charisma not only to lead his own troops but Allied forces as well. That man was on Corregidor.

As early as December, after the Philippines defenders retreated to Corregidor and Bataan, George Marshall strongly recommended to Roosevelt that MacArthur be ordered to Australia as commander of all Allied forces there. Marshall thought the MacArthur was too valuable a soldier to lose.[20] At the same time, Australian prime minister John Curtin had cabled a warning that Singapore was only weeks from falling and asked for immediate aid. Churchill happened to be in Washington meeting with Roosevelt. They both realized that the situation in the Far East had deteriorated so rapidly and seriously that despite their "Germany First" policy, the dispatch of fresh forces to check the Japanese had to be given top priority.[21] Curtin was pleased when he learned that MacArthur might lead the Allied effort there because he desperately wanted an American commander to symbolize the U.S. commitment to Australia.[22] On March 2 MacArthur received orders from Washington to get to Melbourne for the purpose of commanding all the U.S. forces there. While Allied troops were escaping Java by flying to Australia, plans were also being made to get the general on the continent too.

Earlier, on February 23, MacArthur had been encouraged by Washington to leave Corregidor for Mindanao and organize a base of operations there. The general delayed his decision. Commanders, he asserted, do not leave troops in the middle of a battle. He fully expected to die with his men on Corregidor and Bataan and continued to delay into March. Meanwhile, American newspapers and broadcasters speculated on MacArthur's escape, which the Japanese military picked up on. Japan's response was to increase air and sea patrols around Manila Bay.[23] His leaving would not be so secret after all.

Roosevelt could wait no longer. He ordered the general to Australia so he could lead the army that soon would be assembling there. The method of departure was up to MacArthur. His choice was the PT (patrol-torpedo) boat.

PT boats were near and dear to MacArthur's heart. These boats varied somewhat in size, though PTs in the Philippines were seventy-seven-foot-long wooden vessels armed with four torpedo tubes, two twin .50-caliber machine guns and two .30-caliber machine guns.[24] Their purpose was to destroy enemy ships by arriving quickly at the scene of action, delivering a lethal blow with their torpedoes, and then rapidly withdrawing. MacArthur, in his 1930s plan for the defense of the Philippines, surmised that one hundred of these boats could repel a Japanese invasion.[25] Subsequently, six PT boats arrived in Manila two months before the outbreak of the war and fought in the defense of both Bataan and Corregidor. By March, however, only four were operational, and all were in need of repair and engine overhauls. The commander of this flotilla was Lt. John D. Bulkeley.

On March 10, the day before MacArthur left for Australia, he summoned Wainwright to Corregidor to inform him that he was leaving, though he would still be in charge. He also explained that he was dividing his army into four subcommands: Wainwright would command the troops on Luzon, which basically meant the forces on Bataan; General Moore would continue to be in charge of the harbor defenses, which included Corregidor and the other three fortified islands in Manila Bay; Gen. Bradford Chynoweth would command the troops on the Visayan Islands, which lay between Luzon and Mindanao; and Gen. William Sharp would command the troops on Mindanao. Separating his forces thus gave MacArthur a tighter reign over his army from Australia, and if one of his subcommanders had to surrender, it would not apply to the other three.

Then, as a last parting shot, he promoted Col. Lewis Beebe on Corregidor to brigadier general and deputy chief of staff, putting him in charge of all of the supplies, which included the food. As deputy chief of staff of USAFFE and MacArthur's representative on Corregidor, Beebe functioned as Wainwright's superior.[26] MacArthur planned to run things remotely like a puppeteer. After all, as grand field marshal of the Philippines, this had been his army. He spent six years building it. Perhaps he thought that he had the right to dictate the terms for its Armageddon. To further assure success in directing his army from Australia, MacArthur took the key members of his general staff with him and left their subordinates behind.

MacArthur's escape plan was for the four PT boats to slip out of Manila Bay on Wednesday, March 11, after dark. Besides the crew, each boat would have additional passengers, mostly MacArthur's trusted advisors, later known as the "Bataan Gang," even though many of them had rarely if ever set foot on Bataan. General George, the air force chief on Bataan, also was among the passengers. MacArthur, his wife Jean, their young son Arthur, his Chinese nurse, and Brig. Gen. Richard Sutherland, his chief of staff, rode in Bulkeley's boat.

Although the Japanese Navy had a blockade near the entrance to Manila Bay, MacArthur had done his homework. The Americans already had information on enemy ship locations and air patrols throughout the Philippines from coastwatchers and other sources, but they needed the most current ship movements. At 3:00 A.M. on March 11, an army plane left Bataan and was instructed to fly a patrol over water to Mindanao, looking for Japanese vessels. This would be basically the route that MacArthur's party would take by PT boat.

Also that day, one or possibly two P-40s equipped with belly tanks for long-distance flight were used to fly south to about the limit of their fuel range and return. The pilot who left at 3:00 P.M. saw a destroyer off the northwest coast of Mindoro and a destroyer or cruiser heading north off the southwest tip of Mindoro.[27] Finally, the U.S. submarine *Permit* would be shadowing MacArthur's flotilla for about the second half of their voyage and could be called upon, if needed, to rescue personnel if one of the PT boats should fail (as one boat would). The sub could also attack any Japanese warship that might become troublesome to the escape party.

Around 8:00 P.M. that rainy evening, MacArthur boarded one of the PTs from a pier on Corregidor. Everyone waited onboard the boats until the report finally came in from the P-40 reconnaissance flight with the location and estimated course of enemy ships. The planned escaped route was altered once it arrived. U.S. artillery opened up with diversionary fire. MacArthur's PT boat left Corregidor and was joined by the other three that put out from various obscure inlets. About 9:15 P.M. the four vessels, each powered by triple Packard engines, left Manila Bay. Although each engine was capable of producing 1,200 hp, the overworked, under-maintained engines could only propel the PT boats to a speed of about 25 mph, a far cry from their over 40 mph when new. The sea was rough that night, which worked to their advantage. The rolling surface and white caps prevented Japanese destroyers from spotting the low, squat boats and their wakes.

The plan, fortunately, was not to ride the PT boats all the way to Australia but only to Mindanao, 560 miles from Manila Bay. On the morning of Friday, March 13, three of the four boats, but all of the passengers, arrived at Cagayan, Mindanao.[28] One of the boats was scuttled en route and the crew rescued by submarine.

MacArthur had previously ordered Lt. Gen. George Brett, who was in Australia, to send three or four B-17s with experienced crews to Del Monte to evacuate himself, his family, and his staff. Brett, unfortunately, had difficulty finding three airworthy B-17s, but he chose three among the handful that had survived the Japanese assaults against the Philippines and Java. Only one arrived on time and, without brakes, had to make a sharp U-turn to avoid going off the end of the runway. MacArthur was seething when he saw these battle-weary planes and then muttered that 1st Lt. Harl Pease, the pilot, was "only a boy."[29] He rejected the airplanes as unsafe. (Interestingly, Pease would later become a Medal of Honor recipient.) Information about MacArthur's highly secret arrival at Del Monte spread far and wide among the Filipinos. The Japanese at Davao supposedly knew too.[30]

Four days after the general left for Australia, rations on Bataan and Corregidor were further reduced by a third.[31] In Washington the War Department was completely ignorant of MacArthur's new command arrangements and that he had taken so many members of the senior staff there with him. They thought that Wainwright, in fact, was now in charge of all American and Filipino troops in the Philippines.

On March 14, B-17s stationed at Townsville, Australia, were officially transferred from the U.S. Navy. Brett sent three of these "newest model low-mileage aircraft" to pick up MacArthur and his group. One ditched off the coast of Mindanao. The other two arrived during MacArthur's fourth day on the island.[32]

Shortly after midnight on March 17, the remaining two planes soared into the air for the five-hour trip to Australia. The ride was turbulent, several of the passengers became airsick, and all of them held their collective breath when the planes crossed over Japanese-held islands. Shortly after the rising of the morning sun, the pilots spotted Darwin but could not land because Japanese planes were in the area. Instead, they headed for Batchelor Field forty miles away.[33] For the moment, they were safe but not happy.

Brett, anticipating MacArthur's bad temperament, sent only two emissaries—Brig. Gen. Ralph Royce and William Hipps—and two DC-3s, borrowed from the Australian National Air Ways, to meet the general's party. He figured the fewer the messengers, the fewer to blame. They were waiting at Batchelor for MacArthur's arrival. Hipps recalled: "When MacArthur stepped off the plane, he looked much older than he really was. He was wearing his long johns. The underwear came all the way down to his ankles. He made disparaging remarks about the airplane accommodations when he should have been glad he had made it safely out of the Philippines."[34]

At first, after spotting railroad tracks in the distance, the general insisted on making the thousand-mile trip to Alice Springs by rail. But Alice Springs was in the middle of nowhere and in the middle of the continent. When told that the tracks only went another twenty miles out to where the cultivated land ended, he then demanded to make the trip by motorcade. At Alice Springs, MacArthur suggested, they could board a train for the rest of the journey to Melbourne. His wife wanted nothing more to do with airplanes anyway. Dr. Charles H. Morhouse, the physician who accompanied the group, cautioned the general that the motor trip across a hot, dusty desert interior would not bode well for his son's health. Arthur was already being given fluids intravenously, and Morhouse was concerned that the boy might not live through the proposed overland trip. With that information, MacArthur ordered everyone to get in the DC-3s.

As they reluctantly moved to the planes, the air-raid sirens screamed. Hipps remembered: "One of our Air Corps pilots was listening to chatter on his airplane radio which was coming from the U.S. Air Corps people in the Darwin area. He called me over and said it sounds like there are some Zeros headed our way. I immediately went over and told the pilots of MacArthur's two planes." The planes took off at once. After landing at Alice Springs, the bedraggled travelers found out that the once-a-week train to Melbourne had left the day before. MacArthur insisted that they were done flying and asked Brett to send up a special train to take them the rest of the way. Most of the staff, the Bataan Gang, continued to Melbourne by plane.

MacArthur and his family boarded a small train—an engine, two cars, and a caboose—for the 1,028-mile trip to the southern port city of Adelaide. One of their stops was at Terowie, a town about 140 miles north of Adelaide, on March 20. He thought his arrival there was supposed to be secret, but when he stepped off the train, a huge cheer went up from the locals who had gathered there. When asked whether he was headed to the United States, he told the gathered crowd: "The President of the United States ordered me to break through the Japanese lines and proceed from Corregidor to Australia for the purpose, as I understand it, of organizing an American offensive against Japan, the primary purpose of which is the relief of the Philippines. I came through, and I shall return." His party changed trains and continued their journey.[35]

The general arrived in Adelaide on March 21. Knowing that a speech had to be made to the large crowd that had gathered, he scrawled a few lines on the back of an envelope, which were almost identical to those he had used in Terowie. At the time few, including MacArthur himself, realized the enormity of his "I Shall Return" line. In the months to come, the three words would seem to gain a life of their own, especially for those in the Philippines.[36] MacArthur continued on to Melbourne. His eleven-day odyssey was over, he was ready to go to work.

On March 20 it had finally been made clear to Wainwright that he was in charge of all of the troops in the Philippines, gaining promotion to lieutenant general. The War Department informed MacArthur in Melbourne two days later of Wainwright's status.[37] Brig. Gen. Albert M. Jones then took over I Corps. When Wainwright left for his new headquarters on Corregidor, he put Maj. Gen. Edward P. King, the artillery commander, in charge of all troops on Bataan.

MacArthur established his headquarters in Melbourne and instructed his telephone operators to answer incoming phone calls with, "Hello, this is Bataan."[38] With the surrender of Java on March 8, practically all of the Dutch East Indies was now under Japanese control. Bataan and Corregidor were barely holding on. The general immediately wanted reports on how many troops, ships, and planes he had at his disposal to mount a counteroffensive against Japan and learned that they were not enough. Fortunately, his appearance in Australia coincided with the March arrival from the United States of fresh troops, much-needed tanks, artillery, and most importantly pilots with new planes. Also at that time major elements of two Australian divisions that had been fighting in the Middle East returned to bolster their homeland's defenses.

MacArthur's title was still the same as it had been since the previous July, when he had been called back to active duty in the U.S. Army, commander of USAFFE. Although notified on April 3 that the Australian and Dutch representatives in Washington had informally approved a directive outlining the scope of his proposed new command, it was not until April 18, once the various governments and other parties were in agreement, that he was officially appointed supreme commander of the Southwest Pacific Area (SWPA), which included Australia and all territory west of Latitude 159 East, which included the Dutch East Indies and New Guinea.[39] The Pacific Ocean area and everything east of that longitude, which included New Zealand and the Solomon Islands, was placed under the command of Adm. Chester W. Nimitz.[40]

Stephenson and Hipps were both working in Melbourne at the headquarters of FEAF and the Allied Air Forces, which was a hybrid of American and Australian air personnel. General Brett was in charge, and Air Vice Marshal W. B. Bostock of Australia was chief of staff. Brig. Gen. Ralph Royce, U.S.

Army Air Corps, was the senior air-staff officer. When Gen. Harold George arrived in mid-March as part of MacArthur's entourage, he was appointed chief of air operations, with his office next to Royce's. Vance, the former commanding officer of the 27th, became assistant director of intelligence.[41] Stephenson worked for George.

FEAF headquarters in March was vitally concerned with accurately and efficiently distributing the enormous amount of supplies and personnel that were pouring in from the United States. Much of it was arriving in Melbourne. By the end the month, 80,000 U.S. Army troops had been specifically sent or were being diverted to Australia, and hundreds of Army Air Corps planes were arriving there.[42] It was considered an extremely gutsy and controversial personal decision by Roosevelt to deploy precious infantry divisions and air assets to Australia at a time when the Allied strategy was to defeat Germany first. And the navy badly wanted reinforcements to build up its command in Hawaii.

The 27th Regroups and Merges with the 3rd Bomb Group

While Stephenson's route out of Java in early March took him to Broome and then to his desk job in Melbourne, other 27th pilots were scattered throughout Australia.

The 16th Provisional Squadron had arrived at Batchelor Field with seven A-24s on February 17 or 18. Another eight planes of the 17th Provisional Squadron was about a day or two behind them. The two squadrons had intended to leave Batchelor or the RAAF airfield at Darwin for Java on about February 19, first stopping to refuel at Koepang on Timor. They had to wait at least a day or two at Batchelor until it could be determined if it was safe to land in Koepang because of the rapidly advancing Japanese forces.

Since mid-January American pilots had been flying P-40s from Brisbane to Java using the same route as the A-24s intended to take. In February two P-40s were left behind in Darwin with engine trouble. These were the only two modern Allied fighters in northern Australia at the time.[43] In fact, Australia had only one modern fighter of its own, a Hurricane, which the British had reluctantly loaned out in August 1941. It had been shipped without guns and was used for exhibition flights to raise money for the empire-wide Spitfire Fund.[44] On February 15 a squadron of around ten more American P-40s arrived in Darwin, commanded by Maj. Floyd "Slugger" Pell, for patrol duty. Three days later their orders changed, and they were to fly to Java the next day. Ten of them left on the following morning behind a B-17. About ten minutes after departure, Pell received a report that the weather was deteriorating, so all of the fighters returned to Darwin. When they arrived at about 10:00 A.M., five landed and five stayed in the air on patrol—Darwin had no radar. Just then a large group of Japanese fighters and bombers appeared overhead. A couple of P-40s, including Pell, who had just landed, took off to join the fight. Nine of the ten P-40s were shot down, and two others were destroyed on the ground undergoing repair. Pell and other pilots were killed. One fighter made it to Batchelor Field about forty miles away and crashed. Hubbard recalled: "During the air raid on Darwin, one P-40 escaped, but was so badly damaged it crashed at Batchelor. I was there at the time and it was certainly destroyed, which probably accounts for it being considered [by others] destroyed at Darwin, since it was in the Darwin landing pattern when it was hit." The members of the 16th Provisional Squadron learned about the air raid in Darwin from that plane.

The city of Darwin was heavily damaged, and more than two hundred people, including those on ships in the harbor, were killed. The port had forty-seven vessels at anchor. Ten were sunk, including the *Meigs,* which had delivered the 27th's A-24s to Brisbane. Many other vessels were significantly damaged. About 190 fighters and bombers from four aircraft carriers carried out the initial attack. Just before noon a second strike occurred at the RAAF airbase, conducted by fifty-four land-based bombers from airfields on Celebes and Ambon, which had been in Allied hands until a few weeks earlier.[45] The RAAF facilities and runways were badly damaged as were many aircraft. Terrified survivors fled Darwin in a massive exodus, which was described as a "panic-stricken flight." These people feared that an invasion would soon follow. Darwin soon became a ghost town. Many buildings were destroyed and fires burned that evening in the darkness, shrouding the coastal areas in smoke from burning fuel dumps.[46] After these raids, the 16th and 17th Provisional Squadrons were about the only air force remaining in that part of Australia.[47]

Hubbard remembered Darwin as being in total chaos. Bob Ruegg and Sonny Walker borrowed a land rover–type vehicle and made a night trip to the city, locating the burned-out shop that had made adapter bands to fit the army 500-pound bombs into the yoke that swung them clear of the propeller blades when released during a steep dive. They found enough scorched bands to equip each of their planes. They also reported that the airbase was almost totally destroyed and half the town was burning.

No orders came in for a day or so, Hubbard recalled, and the first, supposedly from the new U.S. command (in Melbourne), showed a typical lack of understanding of airplanes: "All A-24s at Batchelor, unload bombs. Take off and intercept hostile planes approaching Darwin." Brian "Black Jack" Walker, the Australian squadron commander at Batchelor, delivered it to Davies and watched him read it, then took it from his hand and slowly tore it up saying, "You never received this."

> The 16th settled at Batchelor with dysentery, poor food, and the heat. The 17th joined us shortly and Colonel Jim [Davies, who had just been promoted to lieutenant colonel] got his boys out and we found beer, gin, iceboxes, and a few other things to make life easier. In between times, we bombed up, evacuated, dropped our bombs, bombed up again, flew patrols, wrecked a few ships and generally kept busy. Taking off one morning early to hit a Nip carrier, Schmidt rolled his ship over taking off with a 500-lb. egg. Smitty and his gunner lit rolling [exiting a plane rolling on the ground] and never stopped till they were in the dive trench. No explosion! Then there was the classic day the A-24s went out to protect Darwin from the Jap Zeros.[48]

The 16th and 17th Squadrons saw action as the Darwin area continued to endure bombing raids. The A-24s were unsuited to intercept enemy aircraft, but both squadrons had plenty of opportunity to do just that. Their main function was flying patrol in the Darwin area. Some remained on standby with 500-pound bombs to be used against enemy shipping. An invasion was expected soon.[49]

These orders came from Area Combined Headquarters (A.C.H.), which was the joint air force and navy defense-area headquarters. Examples of the type of orders the 27th pilots received at Batchelor Field follow:

> A)   TO: BATCHELOR REPEATED C.W.R. [Central War Room]
> FROM: A.C.H. DARWIN   3/3 [March 3]
> A-24 TO PATROL COAST TEN MILES EACH SIDE OF DARWIN IN FLIGHTS OF SIX EACH
> PERIOD UNTIL 0900Z/3/3[.] OBJECT COAST FAMILIARISATION AND PROTECTION DARWIN FROM ENEMY BOMBERS[.]
> OPS [operation] IMPORTANT
> B)   TO BATCHELOR
> FROM A.C.H. DARWIN
> ALL A-24 AND WIRRAWAYS TO TAKE OFF AND PATROL AREA FROM BATCHELOR TO DARWIN UNTIL DUSK 4/3 [March 4.] OBJECT PREVENTION OF DESTRUCTION ON GROUND[.]

TABLE 1

Airplane	Top Speed	Armament
Douglas Dauntless A-24 Dive bomber	250 mph	2 .50-caliber machine guns in nose and twin .30-caliber machine guns used by rear gunner
Commonwealth Wirraway Fighter-bomber	220 mph	2 or 3 .30-caliber machine guns forward 1 or 2 .30-caliber machine guns used by rear gunner
Lockheed Hudson twin-engine Attack bomber	222–246 mph	2 .30-caliber machine guns in nose 2 .30-caliber machine guns used by rear gunner
Mitsubishi Zero (A6M1-3) Fighter	333 mph	2 20-mm cannons mounted in the wings 2 7.7-mm (approximately .30-caliber) machine guns in nose
Curtiss Kittyhawk P-40E Fighter	345 mph	6 wing-mounted .50-caliber Browning machine guns

The *27th Reports* states: "March, dust, and heat and the [27th] HQs settled in the combined 16th and 17th. There were a series of [higher] HQs in the Darwin Area and in the event of excitement [expected Japanese bombing raids] they all gave varied orders. Unfortunately the 17th proved to be the goat for the majority of the excursions. For a while, the 16th and 17th made a run between Daly Waters and Batchelor regularly for some false alerts."

During this time in the Darwin area, the Aussies had a handful of their own planes that they were flying called "Wirraways" and some older two-engine Hudson bombers. Hubbard said, "Although our A-24 dive bombers were no match for the nimble Zeros, the Wirraways and Hudsons were even less so." A few weeks after the Darwin raid, American P-40s began to show up at Batchelor. The P-40 was the only plane available at that time that could go up against the Zero.

Batchelor Field, being closer to Darwin, had more amenities than Daly Waters, which made the daily routine somewhat comfortable. Hubbard recalled that "Batchelor seemed like paradise in comparison, having trees and shade." In contrast, Daly Waters, according the *27th Reports*, "Had flies, no water, no beer, no food, and hot as Hades. A good place to avoid!" Australians have a terse description for the area: "Mile after f—king mile of f—k all [absolutely nothing]." During March, enemy reconnaissance aircraft were sighted as far south as Daly Waters.[50] At one point Hubbard's squadron was sent to Katherine, fifty miles south of the rail line from Darwin. He recalled: "Katherine had a beautiful stream running alongside the field and we soon joined Aussies cooling in the water near the beach. I noticed a uniformed Australian sitting up on the bank with a rifle cradled in his lap and asked what the guard was there for. The reply, 'Oh, that's the croc watcher. If he shoots, get out quick!'"

The 27th airmen were convinced that they did not want to spend the rest of the war at either Daly Waters or Katherine. They were also certain that command and control had to improve and that the A-24s were not very reliable. Flight orders came from many different commands, two levels in Darwin, Brisbane, and even air-corps headquarters in Melbourne. Hubbard believed that some orders were impossible, while others conflicted with each other. After one two-hour flight, he and his gunner were adding oil to the A-24 engine. It took thirty-two quarts to fill it. Neither remembered how much the oil tank was supposed to hold, but looking in the tech manual, they learned that it was thirty-six quarts. That was enough for Hubbard. He decided not to fly the plane again unless it was on an actual mission.

The excessive-oil-consumption problem in the overused aircraft was because many of their engines had been in need of overhaul before the planes were ever shipped to Australia. Unfortunately, it would be weeks before the 27th could find better bombers to fly. Summers said, "We laughingly had a saying that the old planes [A-24s] would run out of oil before they would run out of gasoline." The *27th Reports* states: "There are more A-24s in Brisbane so the Colonel, Hub, Ruegg, Sonny and Ed headed south to get them. Ruegg, Sonny and Ed by QANTAS Flying Boat again with a shipful of wounded Yanks from a boat that tried to make the Philippines. To Brisbane March 10 and we take over 15 A-24s from the 3rd Group."

It would be in Brisbane where McAfee, Bender, and Stafford, who had escaped from Java, rejoined the 27th. Their return, however, would be different from Stephenson's reunion with the unit. Instead of Broome, their flight out of Java landed at Daly Waters. The three were given the okay to head to Brisbane for two weeks of rest. There were, unfortunately, no rides out of Daly Waters that day. Two days later they left on a Dutch airliner filled with women and children from Java. The plane stopped at Charleville, approximately five hundred miles west of Brisbane, and then continued to Melbourne. The airmen were on their own for transit to Brisbane. They were broke but arranged to live on credit at a local hotel. Then they decided to go by train, which consisted of two sheep cars and McAfee, Bender, and Stafford. It made about twenty mph. Finally on March 9, they entered Brisbane and checked into Lennons Hotel. They were eager to get back to work and fly an airplane.

American fighter squadrons began to arrive in the Darwin area, and by mid-March the 16th and 17th Provisional Squadrons were relieved and ordered back to Brisbane. On March 22 McAfee and his colleagues joined up with Colonel Davies at Amberley Field and were reassigned to the portion of the 27th in Australia.

As the situation started becoming more tense in New Guinea, Davies and his men received orders to go to there. On March 25 they went to Townsville, which was the jumping-off point from the northeastern coast of Australia. At this time they were still the 27th Bomb Group, but the unit did not have any mechanics, only pilots and gunners. The men did not even have typewriters or clerks, nor any other means of keeping records.

While in Townsville, Davies heard that the 3rd Bombardment Group was about seventy miles inland. He flew over to Charters Towers for some maintenance work. Davies claimed that "It was such a delightful situation" there that he and his men attached themselves to the 3rd Bombardment Group.[51]

The 3rd Bombardment Group, the 27th's sister unit in Savannah, was in Australia but lacked airplanes and had junior pilots, with only a first lieutenant in charge. On January 31 the unit had left Oakland, California, for Australia on the transport *Ancon*. Their A-20s, however, were deployed elsewhere for submarine patrol as were their senior officers.[52] The remaining men were promised A-20s for Australia, but the unit arrived on February 25 with only fifteen A-24s, of which Davies had already taken possession.

In March, after ten days of unloading their equipment and placing it on a train, the 3rd moved from its temporary quarters on a Brisbane racetrack to Charters Towers about seven hundred miles north. It was not a pleasant trip. Pfc. Jack Heyn recalled that it took three days to get to Charters Towers, the weather was hot, windows were open, and they had a pretty steady barrage of soot and cinders. The cars consisted of compartments that accommodated six people on benches on either side. Luggage racks were on either side above them, and they kept barracks bags there during the day. At night they put the bags on the floor between the benches so that two men could sleep on them, one on each bench, and one up on each luggage rack.

Davies, who had served with the 3rd Attack (Bomb) Group in the mid-1930s, knew the officer in charge, 1st Lt. Robert F. Strickland, and he knew the A-20s and the A-24s the 3rd had flown in Savannah. But most importantly, he also knew how to pull strings as well as the chain of command in Australia—Eubank from Bomber Command as well as Harold George. After a few meetings in Brisbane, Davies and members of the 27th there were ordered to report to Charters Towers to become part of the 3rd Bomb Group, the same unit the 27th had been cloned from at Barksdale in 1940.[53]

In late March the officers and enlisted men of the 27th arrived at the new base with their mostly worn-out dive bombers.[54] The 3rd had pilots and support staff, but the 27th had some planes, leadership, and most importantly, pilots with wartime experience. It was time to go on the offensive. Maybe now they could do something to help their comrades still on Bataan. Mangan wrote in his diary: "I feel as though the U.S. has let us down over here. Wonder how the rest of our gang on Bataan feels. We all think of them a lot here—more than we say or write."

Charters Towers

Charters Towers was then considered one of the prettiest inland towns in Australia. Located eighty-five miles from the coast and approximately seven hundred miles north of Brisbane, this community of just fewer than ten thousand was a testimony to its nineteenth-century gold-mining success. Wealthy citizens from those days had constructed elegant buildings that even today are a fixture on its main thoroughfare.

Heyn recalled that Charters Towers sort of reminded one of the Old West towns in the cowboy movies. A lot of the buildings had wooden structures hanging over the sidewalks. It had its share of pubs and restaurants and two movie houses—using the term "house" loosely. The cinemas were roofless with canvas lawn chairs for seats. In the event of rain, the movie was canceled.

For several weeks before the Americans arrived, according to Mangan, the Aussies had been working on this airfield, which consisted of two fairly long dirt-and-gravel runways. The airfield was finished in six weeks by as many as six hundred men working day and night using trucks and bulldozers. Most of the "mullock heaps" (refuse or rubbish sites left over from mining) were used for paving the runways. Allegedly, many of them contained low-grade gold, which gave the runway a touch of elegance. According to Ralph Harrell, during certain parts of the day, depending on which direction the sun was shining, you could see the gold dust sparkling on the runway. Davies piloted an A-24 as the first plane to land on the golden runway on March 25. Other 27th pilots with their planes soon followed.[55]

By this time, forty-two officers and sixty-two enlisted men of the 27th were in Australia, but most were not from the original group still in the Philippines. They included rear gunners and others who were assigned to the 16th, 17th, and 91st Provisional Squadrons in Melbourne and along the way as well as pilots and enlisted men who had escaped from Java. A number of the officers had been casual pilots from the *Pensacola* convoy. In late March or early April, Stephenson was reassigned to the 27th or assigned to the 3rd Bombardment Group. He hitched a ride from Melbourne to Brisbane in a military plane and joined up with the pilots and enlisted men there. Those who did not fly to Charters Towers in A-24s were put on a train along with supplies and equipment and sent to their new airbase. According to Summers, Davies put Stephenson in charge of the Army Air Corps personnel traveling on that train, and Stephenson put a lieutenant in charge of each car to prevent any pilfering of supplies. They arrived in Charters Towers sometime in early April.

In the meantime the men of the 3rd Bomb Group, who were living in tents, were kept busy at the new airfield and camp on the outskirts of town. The group composed five flying squadrons: the 8th, 13th, 89th, and 90th, and Headquarters (which later functioned only as an administrative unit).[56] After Davies was officially put in charge, he called the officers together and told them that he did not want to hurt anybody's feelings but was placing two squadrons under the leadership of his more experienced pilots from the 27th. Capt. Herman Lowery took over the 13th and Capt. Floyd "Buck" Rogers the 8th. Lts. Don Hall and Bennett Wilson, who had come over with the 3rd, remained in charge of the 89th and 90th respectively, though Capt. Ron Hubbard from the 27th would soon take over the 90th.[57] Because the 8th Squadron had flown the A-24s in Savannah, they received the dive bombers. The other squadrons were still without planes. Mangan wondered about the merger, "How is the 3rd going to like the old 27th. They used to be big rivals back in Savannah."

Several hundred miles to the north, RAAF personnel at Port Moresby, New Guinea, were begging Allied headquarters in Melbourne to send help. The only aircraft they had were a few twin-engine Hudson bombers and PBY Catalina flying boats for bombing and reconnaissance missions over enemy positions in New Guinea and elsewhere. The Japanese had captured the twin ports of Lae and Salamaua, New Guinea, on March 8 and were using them as bases from which to bomb Port Moresby. On March 10 two U.S. aircraft carriers, the *Lexington* and *Yorktown,* arrived near Port Moresby and launched raids over the rugged Owen Stanley Mountains on Lea and Salamaua in conjunction with Australian aircraft out of Port Moresby.[58] Although several ships were claimed to be sunk or damaged in the harbors, the Japanese continued their strikes against Port Moresby. On March 31 the 8th Squadron, 3rd Bomb Group, equipped with the A-24 dive bombers, left for Port Moresby to help take the pressure off the Australians. The original 27th men led the flight from Charters Towers to New Guinea. Rogers was in charge but had to drop out in Port Moresby because of dengue fever. Ruegg, who was raised in Oregon and Idaho and had been a pilot with the 27th since completing flying school in May 1940, led the squadron in his place.

> The A-24s were ordered north. Buck Rogers leading with thirteen planes. The number was unlucky because five were left at Cooktown [Australia] due to one reason or another. Due to a wrong report from Cooktown as to sundown in Port Moresby, we got in after dark and lost two more ships due to bomb craters on the runway. Off the next morning, April 1, 1942, with five planes and escort [six P-40s]. Weather bad at Lae so dropped our bombs at Salamaua.[59]

That attack was the 3rd Bomb Group's first combat mission of the war but resulted in little damage. In the following weeks the 8th Squadron received more of what was left of the A-24s and replacement parts from Charters Towers. They continued to fly missions out of Port Moresby and, with fighter escort, bombed airfields and destroyed planes at Lae and other Japanese-held positions in New Guinea. About those raids Mangan later observed, "We would head up to Lae and Salamaua with four or five planes, which we thought was a pretty good size task force but today would be laughable."

Earlier, on March 21, the RAAF 75th Fighter Squadron had arrived with newly issued P-40s, the first modern pursuit aircraft to be stationed there. Some of the planes, however, did not yet have the gunnery sights fitted. Three others were damaged by friendly fire when they initially attempted to land.[60] The Yanks' dive bombers and Aussies' fighters worked closely on missions out of Port Moresby. The attrition rate was high for both squadrons in the early days. It would be another forty-four days before Army Air Corps fighter squadrons began to be stationed there.[61]

Reverse Lend-Lease and Pappy Gunn

In an inversion of the U.S. government's Lend-Lease program, Davies succeeded in "borrowing" American-made B-25s from the Dutch with the intent of possibly returning them sometime down the road. Although he may have lacked legal authorization, the 3rd Bomb Group desperately needed the planes. Besides, Davies rationalized, everything is supposed to be fair in time of war. Certainly at this point, the 27th had little going its way. Davies did not act alone in pulling off this B-25 coup. He had the legendary Paul Irving "Pappy" Gunn whispering in his ear.

Pappy Gunn was indelibly etched in the minds of many who served in the Philippines and the Southwest Pacific Theater. Gunn had dropped out of school at age thirteen, then at age seventeen, he was given the choice by a judge of either going to prison or joining the military after he had been apprehended running moonshine. He chose the navy and served during World War I. He reenlisted in 1923 and later became one of the best naval aviator instructors in the United States. He spent twenty years in the navy and served in the dual role of aircraft mechanic and fighter pilot off aircraft carriers. He attained the rank of chief petty officer.

Just before World War II, Gunn lived in Manila with his family and was operations manager for an unscheduled three-plane airline based in the capital called Philippines Airlines. When war broke out, he quickly joined the U.S. Army Air Corps and was made a captain, with instructions to take over and operate PAL's three twin-engine Beechcrafts for ferrying military personnel and delivering official mail, dispatches, drugs, food, and other critical material as directed.[62] On Christmas Eve, 1941, Gunn was ordered to fly some of Brereton's staff to Australia and remained there to help the new command by shuttling men and supplies to Java and elsewhere. But his sympathies were with the Philippines, where his wife and children remained in Manila and soon became prisoners of war. Pappy's war with Japan then became very personal.

According to Davies, Gunn was assigned to the 27th, probably after the group of pilots arrived in Australia in December.[63] He was very helpful in getting the A-24s reassembled in Brisbane. Pappy (or Papa) at age forty-two was three years older than Big Jim Davies; the two became close friends. In late March Gunn too became a member of the 3rd Bomb Group at their new field at Charters Towers. While only the 8th Squadron had planes—the A-24 dive bombers—the rest of the group was still waiting for their promised A-20 attack bombers.

There are many official and unofficial versions of what happened after this, the truth probably being somewhere in between. Supposedly during a March flight to Brisbane, Gunn saw a dozen or so brand new Mitchell B-25s built by North American Aviation Company sitting idle on the flightline at Archerfield. These bombers were assigned to the Dutch. Both Americans thought their men could use them better.

One source indicates that Gunn convinced Davies to steal the bombers. He allegedly told Davies: "All I know—those Aussies could sure use aerial help up in New Guinea. We could give them plenty with 24 Mitchells." Davies flew immediately to FEAF ADVON (Advance) headquarters in Brisbane to see Colonel Eubank, who had been acquainted with Davies in the Philippines. Eubank welcomed the visit until he learned of Davies's intentions.[64] The colonel was hesitant to approve the proposal but was realistic enough to know that the Americans needed the new bombers and the Dutch could not use them. He signed the authorization papers, and Davies rounded up Gunn and twenty-two other pilots and caught a mail plane to Brisbane.[65] The duty captain knew little of high-level decisions concerning allotments, strategies, or operations when Davies and his group showed up to claim the bombers. "I wondered who the hell owned these planes," the officer said. "They've been sitting here a couple of weeks."[66]

The above account of the heist contains some exaggeration. Other versions of flying the planes out of Brisbane, though, do not differ dramatically from it. Hubbard wrote in his memoir that since the Dutch "were not under the Allied Command and not flying missions, it was requested that they let the 3rd Bomb Group have the planes, which would be replaced by the next new B-25s en route from the States. They refused, but did agree to give the 3rd pilots some transition time." After practicing takeoffs and landings one afternoon, Davies and his crews walked out to the planes, took off, and never came back.

Pilot Dick Birnn remarked in his diary on March 31, 1942: "Our B-25s really belong to the Dutch. They bought them and are mad as hornets—but we are better equipped to fly them—and I guess that's war."[67]

The *27th Reports* states: "Davies was ordered on the 2nd of April to pick up 15 B-25s from the Dutch in Brisbane, so he sent 30 pilots and 15 enlisted men right down to Archerfield to get some. Numerous troubles ensued—the Dutch were not informed of the exchange—when they did find out the straight dope, they hid most of the spare parts. Eventually the ships were ferried to Charters Towers and two of the ships were torn up on landing though no one was hurt."

Whichever method Davies and Gunn used, by the end of the day, the Mitchells were safely in the air and on their way north.[68]

Allegedly, when someone higher up realized that Davies had stolen the Dutch B-25s, FEAF Headquarters ordered the planes returned immediately. The 3rd Bomb Group's history indicates that when the bombers landed to refuel, Davies and Gunn faced another confrontation. Upon FEAF orders from Melbourne, the major at the field wanted the planes detained.

"Major," Davies said, "I have a written authorization and you know that under Army regulations, a signed order supersedes an oral one."

"Are you questioning General Eubank, Major?" Pappy Gunn suddenly blurted. "We'll have them hitting Lae and Salamaua within a couple of days."[69]

Supposedly, Gunn also threatened the base commander with a court-martial. The officer looked at Davies and said, "I guess a written order does supersede an oral one." With that, the B-25s once more took to the air. By midnight they were landing at Charters Towers. By 1:00 A.M. the Mitchells were safely placed in the previously unused revetments. By 2:00 A.M. the pilots were sleeping soundly.

The next day all hell again broke loose. The Dutch wanted the planes immediately flown back to Brisbane by Davies and his pirates. Davies told them they could have the bombers back but had to fly them out of Charters Towers themselves. With a diminished pilot corps, there was little the Dutch could do. As consolation, FEAF Headquarters informed them a board of inquiry would look into the matter. A day later they determined that Davies had merely picked up the wrong planes and would return them shortly. Big Jim, however, said he could not do that. Something BIG was in the wind.

The theft was said to have caused a diplomatic uproar, with loud screams and notes of protestation from both the Dutch and American ambassadors. Both the official Dutch version and Dutch military historian Peter C. Boer indicate that the B-25s were handed over to the Americans and were not really stolen. The 3rd Bomb Group initially obtained twelve from the Dutch and seven from the Army Air Force. One crashed on landing at Charters Towers and was lost. Another returned after takeoff to Archerfield, where it sustained damage when its landing gear collapsed. This aircraft was given back to the Dutch two months later after repairs.[70]

Before attempting a secret mission, Gunn quickly determined that the B-25s were not combat ready. After discovering that the Dutch had removed some of the state-of-the-art Norden bombsights, Gunn retuned to get them and was told that he could have D8 bombsights (which were less sophisticated) instead; the Dutch said they wanted to keep the Nordens for training. But one way or another, Gunn was able to obtain the Nordens and return with them later that night. Different versions exist as to how he did this. One alleges that Gunn barged into the warehouse with a machine gun and demanded the needed equipment, or else.[71] Regardless, the next day he was busy with the mechanics installing the Nordens and getting the B-25s ready for their mission.[72]

Billy Mitchell Bombers

The B-25s at Charters Towers were C-model bombers. Lee Atwood, North American's chief engineer, hit upon the name "Mitchell" for the aircraft. Brig. Gen. William C. Mitchell's blunt, controversial views about the future of air power earned him a court-martial in 1926, and he was suspended from active duty for five years without pay. Mitchell decided instead to resign his commission and spent his remaining years preaching the wisdom of developing air power.

A B-25C's crew size varied but typically included a pilot, copilot, navigator, bombardier, and a gunner or two. The plane achieved a maximum speed of 272 mph, a service ceiling of 24,000 feet, and a range of up to 1,500 miles depending on bomb loads, fuel loads, and other factors. Two Wright Cyclone 14-cylinder engines powered it, each developing 1,700 hp.

Pappy Gunn was a no-nonsense visionary of what an airplane's fighting capabilities could be. What he needed was more information on the B-25's engineering. Fortunately, with the Dutch B-25s North American had sent one of their field-service representatives, Jack Fox.

Fox was working with the Dutch pilots and mechanics in Australia when Davies acquired the B-25s. Knowing that something important was in the wind, he easily made the transition to Charters Towers and working with the 3rd Bomb Group. His first meeting with Gunn, however, supposedly did not go well. After watching an American crew emerge from a just-landed B-25, Fox demanded of the pilot how much experience he had flying the bomber. Gunn replied testily: "Who needs checking out? Besides, it has a stick and throttle doesn't it?"[73] Mangan recalled that changing from the A-20 to the A-24 to the B-25 was not as difficult as it might seem: "A pilot was a pilot. You were expected to fly anything they had. The configuration of the airplanes and engines and the speed was so much easier then."

It took time to get the B-25s ready, and Davies was anxious to get them into combat as soon as possible. Modifications were being completed and Gunn guaranteed the bombers would be ready in a few days. The pilots were eager to get checked out in the new planes, as the *27th Reports* explains: "The 27th pilots along with the 3rd Group boys spent the first few days familiarizing themselves with the B-25Cs with which the group was being equipped. After bouncing around the skies for months in the A-24s, the B-25s felt like a ball of fire to the fellows for the first few hours, until they became accustomed to the extra speed and power."

The 13th and the 90th Squadrons received the bombers on their return to Charters Towers on April 3. The 89th Squadron provided support for both squadrons while waiting for their A-20s to arrive. Davies already had orders for a mission.

7

Royce's Raid—Overshadowed by Doolittle

THE JAPANESE CAPTURED the airfield at Gasmata on the southern coast of New Britain on February 8. Their carrier-based planes in the Solomon Sea then used the field to launch attacks on Allied positions and to soften up the defenses for their planned invasion of New Guinea.

Gasmata

On April 5 Davies and his B-25s flew to Port Moresby. There he met with Group Captain (colonel in the U.S. military) James Hewett, the commander of the Australian 9th Operation Group, who requested that Davies's B-25s bomb the Japanese airbase at Gasmata. He told Davies that the B-17s' high-altitude bombing had been ineffective, and his own Australian twin-engine bombers could not make the eight-hundred-mile round trip with a full load of bombs.[1]

The six Mitchells, led by Herman Lowery with Davies on his wing, took off for Gasmata on April 6.[2] Because of the distance necessitating an extra fuel load, only four 300-pound bombs were carried by each plane rather than the usual eight. Nevertheless, the raid caught the Japanese by surprise, with thirty enemy bombers claimed to have been destroyed on the ground. This was the very first American mission with the B-25. They worked flawlessly, and all returned safely.[3]

Mangan recalled those first months flying out of Port Moresby in 1942: "We never had fighter escorts with our B-25s. On the Gasmata raid, we saw no Jap fighters on the ground or in the air. We encountered none and had little damage. The one thing we learned was that Gasmata was too far away from Port Moresby. We had little fuel left upon return."

The Mitchells headed back to Charters Towers on April 7. When they landed, the returning pilots described the action over Gasmata to an attentive crowd. But the mission pilots themselves were more interested in the latest

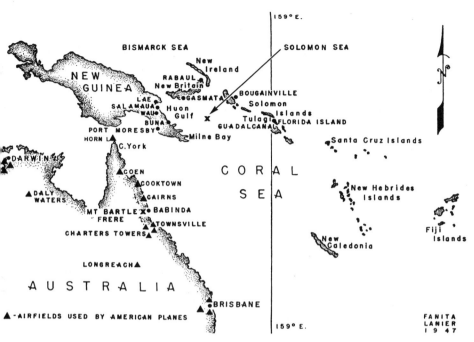

8. Northeast Australia, New Guinea, and surrounding islands with airfields used by U.S. Army Air Corps, 1941–42. *Courtesy University of Chicago Press*

hot rumors. They were told a really big secret mission—a long haul over water—was in the works. Their curiosity grew moments later when Davies, Gunn, and McAfee rushed out of headquarters and jumped in another plane to fly to FEAF Headquarters in Melbourne. The *27th Reports* states, "The next day it became a certainty that something was in the wind when the 13th along with some 90th squadron ships took off for Brisbane to pick up bomb bay [fuel] tanks."

Bataan Gang—Grasping for Straws

Onboard the evening flight to Melbourne were Davies, McAfee, and Pappy Gunn. Davies and Gunn thought they might be disciplined for their brazen theft of the Dutch B-25s.[4] They spent the night in Sydney and then took off before dawn for Melbourne. Once there, they had a four-hour meeting with Brig. Gens. Harold George and Ralph Royce.

The topic of this top-secret conference, attended by other high-ranking officers and Capt. Frank Bostrom, a B-17 pilot from the 19th Bomb Group, was when and where to strike Japanese positions in the Philippines. Earlier, on March 29, Brig. Gen. Richard Sutherland had informed General Brett that MacArthur wanted an offensive air mission to the Philippines. After MacArthur arrived in Melbourne to assume his new command, Wainwright contacted him in late March requesting that a squadron of bombers be sent north to help get supply ships loaded with food, gas, and oil through. Those vessels were already in Philippine waters several hundred miles south of Corregidor at Cebu City and Iliolo, but their captains would not attempt to run the Japanese naval blockade without significant military support. This request was likely the initial motivation for the proposed raid.[5]

MacArthur wanted both his troops on Bataan and Corregidor and the Philippine citizens to know that they were not forgotten—his "I Shall Return" speech was not just momentary political appeasement. Then again, the general felt additional pressure to pull off such an air raid, for his old employer, President Quezon of the Philippine Commonwealth, had just arrived in Melbourne. Quezon too was adamant that something more be done regarding military air operations in the Philippines.[6]

Sutherland told Brett that it was up to him as to who would lead the mission. Brett chose Royce, but it took Royce at least a couple of days to reluctantly agree to volunteer for the mission.[7] In those early days of the war, squadrons of eighteen bombers or fighters were often led by a first lieutenant and sometimes a lowly second lieutenant. Having a general lead the mission of thirteen airplanes would have been as much for show as anything would. During the American Civil War, when Abraham Lincoln was informed of a Confederate raid resulting in the loss of Union Army generals as well as horses and cattle, he is alleged to have remarked: "It's too bad about losing the horses and cattle. At least I can make new generals." Maybe some of that logic was used in determining to send Royce on this highly risky mission.

Initially, MacArthur thought the planes that could reach the Philippines—the B-17s and the B-25s—could actually land at Bataan and Cabcaben fields. Air corps leaders let him know that the runways were not adequate for the big planes. He also thought that ships laden with supplies could break the Japanese naval blockade and reach Corregidor if they had proper bomber cover. MacArthur next considered that a possible bombing raid over Bataan might allow many troops to escape through holes in the Japanese lines and move into central Luzon to begin guerrilla activities. In many ways he and his military advisors—the Bataan Gang—were grasping for straws. According to Hipps, who at the time worked in FEAF Operations, plans for the raid continued despite objections from Brett, the Allied air commander. The raid would be "carried off despite all the advice from experienced combat pilots."[8]

In early April some of the fighter pilots were transferred from Bataan Field to Del Monte. On the evening of April 6, the P-40 pilots at Del Monte were all called to a secret meeting by Orrin Grover, who commanded the 24th Pursuit Group on Luzon. After he locked the door and pulled down the window shade, he told them that a formation of B-17s was expected in from Australia at any moment and that the men would be involved in a very important mission. He explained that in the southern Philippine waters there were seven ships loaded with food, which were going to attempt to get through to Bataan. But three Japanese cruisers and seven destroyers were blockading the peninsula and other points along the way, plus a number of fighters and bombers that could be called on in support. Grover further explained that the B-17s would bomb Japanese airfields in the morning and then hit the Japanese ships in the afternoon. The P-40s would fly reconnaissance, and on the second day, if there were any warships left, the P-40 pilots would strafe them and notify Del Monte so the B-17s could return to bomb them. And if they could get some fragmentation bombs from Bataan, the P-40s would attack the warships too. After that, the relief ships would start their three-day voyage to Corregidor, with the P-40s flying cover. Two of the PT boats that had evacuated MacArthur and his party would also escort the cargo ships. After that, the four Mindanao-based P-40s involved with escorting the ships would join the two remaining P-40s at Bataan Field and resume normal operations there. After listening to this briefing, the P-40 pilots thought their chances of surviving the mission were about zero.[9]

With the shift of the B-25s from the Dutch to the Americans and with the success of the Mitchells at Gasmata, air-corps leaders saw an opportunity to satisfy MacArthur's desire for an air strike in the Philippines.[10] Davies, who lead the Gasmata raid, agreed to this provided that an adequate fuel supply could be placed onboard allowing them to fly nonstop to Mindanao.[11] George and Royce wanted to send a squadron of B-25s and a squadron of B-17s on the raid, but there were just six B-17s in commission, only three of those could be spared for the operation.[12] On April 8 MacArthur radioed Wainwright, whose army on Bataan was in its final day of collapse, to inform him that the bombers were now identified that would come to their rescue: two B-17s and nine B-25s (there would actually be three B-17s and ten B-25s). They would not be leaving Australia until either April 9 or 10, depending on when the installation of the extra fuel tanks in the B-25s was completed.[13]

After wiring Herm Lowery at Charters Towers on April 9 to bring nine other ships to Brisbane for gas-tank refitting, Davies, McAfee, and Gunn headed there also. The B-25s were already being worked on when the trio arrived. By noon the planes with bomb-bay fuel tanks were back at Charters Towers being loaded with food, medicine, and other supplies.

Del Monte Bound

Although considered a suicide mission by many and accepting only volunteers, Hubbard remembered that everyone volunteered. The *27th Reports* states that the pilots "begged" to be included on the mission. Those selected left Charters Towers about 1:00 A.M. on April 11. Pilot versatility was an asset in Hubbard's case. He pointed out to Davies, "I'm qualified as a bombardier and navigator as well as a pilot and it might be handy to have an extra pilot along." The lieutenant colonel agreed. After climbing into the plane, Hubbard checked the compartment, the switches, and the Norden bombsight. Shortly after takeoff, Davies wanted to get some rest, so Hubbard and McAfee flew the bomber to Darwin.

Because a dusty dark runway prevented the aircraft from taking off at the planned one-minute intervals, the B-25s did not fly in formation to Darwin, some 1,150 miles to the northwest. Pilot Howard West later recalled that after they were airborne, their navigator, Bill Culp, told him and Harold Maull, the other pilot, that he had forgotten the maps that were necessary to navigate from Charters Towers to Darwin. Someone on board hurriedly found a *National Geographic* map of Australia. After looking over it, West told them that he thought he could find his way to Darwin, especially since the month before he had been flying A-24s with the 17th Provisional Squadron out of the Darwin area. He decided that if he flew a certain northwest course, he would get to the recognizable point on the *Geographic* map from where he would head due west, which would take them to Darwin. West said, "In other words, we used 'true pilotage' to find Darwin, and it worked."[14]

Once in the area, the bombers circled while waiting to land at dawn since the field was without lights. All safely touched down. Davies had gotten lost and arrived two hours after everyone else. At Darwin a message from MacArthur's headquarters awaited the task force, stating that Bataan had just surrendered and directing the flight to proceed to Del Monte Airbase on Mindanao and carry out combat operations against the Japanese.

Scarcely a day went by that the 27th's officers in Australia did not think about their comrades back on Bataan. They read accounts and heard the rumors on how bad the situation was there. MacArthur's departure from Corregidor on March 11 dampened whatever optimism they had for the beleaguered forces remaining behind. Still, when Bataan fell, it was a shock.

Besides the men of the 27th, Stephenson knew that several of his West

Point classmates were part of the Bataan surrender. What he did not know, however, and what worried him, was how many men from his squadron and other acquaintances were already dead by that time. The Japanese military was already well known for its brutality and atrocities in China and Manchuria, but it was hoped that captured Americans and Filipinos would be treated better. Like others around the world, the 27th in Darwin did not anticipate the infamous Death March out of Bataan. When MacArthur received the grim word about the surrender, he issued the following announcement: "The Bataan Force went out as it would have wished. Fighting to the end [of] its flickering forlorn hope. No army has ever done so much with so little and nothing became it more than its last hour of trial and agony. To the weeping mothers of its dead, I can only say that the sacrifice and halo of Jesus of Nazareth has descended upon their sons and that God will take them unto himself."[15]

Royce and Davies again briefed the crews on the weather over the Philippines. This update, however, was only a guess. Hubbard remembered that "if Del Monte was closed in [by weather] the only possibility was to let down over water and come in on the wave tops and find the airport or crash." When the briefing was over, the men went out to the planes.

Eleven B-25s left Charters Towers as part of the raid. Of the crews that made it to Darwin, sixteen of the pilots and copilots (counting Hubbard) were 27th pilots who had gotten out of the Philippines. Twelve other former 27th pilots from the Philippines remained behind in Australia or were flying A-24s out of Port Moresby. Pilot Henry Rose said decades later that he did not know about the mission until they had all left and that he may have been on an assignment elsewhere.

Stephenson did not go on this mission, and one can only speculate why. By this time he probably was checked out in the Mitchell, but Davies probably wanted pilots with the most experience flying the bombers. Because he was not on the Gasmata mission and had not flown while on Bataan or Java, he might not have been chosen for that reason. In his last letter to his wife, dated April 10, only hours before the mission, Stephenson mentions that he expected to be off again somewhere else the next day. Maybe, like Rose, he was sent elsewhere. But the letter indicates he probably intended to be on that mission. After having all the adventure on Bataan and Java, he may have decided to give other, more gung-ho members of the 27th a chance to seek their revenge. Stephenson had been bombed and strafed for four of the past five months, but he may have thought that he would have plenty of other opportunities to even the score.

The flight left the RAAF field at Darwin for the Philippines at about

10:30 A.M. and included ten B-25Cs and three B-17s; the eleventh B-25 remained at Darwin because of a bad cut in one tire. According to the *27th Reports*, the pilots, Ralph Schmidt and Dick Birnn, both former 27th pilots, wanted to go, but Davies persuaded them not to. They made no effort to hide their disappointment at being left behind. On Pappy Gunn's B-25 roster was an engineer with only the suspicious name of "Midgett," no other first or last name. But "Midgett" may have been Jack Fox, the North American representative who wanted a firsthand look at the B-25s in action.

The seven-hour, fifteen-hundred-mile flight was a mixture of anxiousness and boredom. Most of the crews were still tired from their flight from Charters Towers to Darwin. Royce was a passenger in the lead B-17; Davies led the first flight of five B-25s; and Strickland led the second group of five.

> Discreetly detouring around Jap-held islands along the route, the B-25s flew high and around the southern coast of Mindanao late in the afternoon. The weather had been remarkably good but over the islands formidable black cumulus rain clouds towering up to 20,000 feet barred the way. The formation was forced to spread out and more or less fly independently.[16]

The flight was accomplished mostly over water to avoid enemy spotters. By the time the bombers reached the Mindanao coast, they encountered violent thunderstorms as darkness was closing in. Huge mountains were in front of them. Without navigation aids, they thought they were lost. Then, according to Bender, "all at once, as if by magic, there was a hole in the cloud cover below us, and we were able to see a portion of the airstrip at Cagayan, just a few miles from Del Monte." Most of the B-25s landed safely within minutes of each other just as the sun was setting. Many on Mindanao had never seen a B-25 before and thought that the first planes to appear were Japanese until they saw the white star on the underside of the wing.[17]

One of the B-25s got lost momentarily, and the pilot let down below the clouds to see where they were. They quickly spotted Davao in southern Mindanao, which had recently become a Japanese air and navy base, off in the distance. He did a quick turn and then dropped to treetop level until arriving at Del Monte. Startled natives on the ground, accustomed to Japanese Zeros, ran for cover. This B-25, piloted by Heiss and Townsend, landed after dark. Earlier in the day, when the B-17s arrived, Brigadier General Sharp, who commanded the troops there, was on hand to greet Royce as he climbed out of his plane.

All thirteen bombers initially landed at Del Monte No. 1 strip, which was the main U.S. Army airfield on Mindanao. The plan that day was to quickly send the planes to the other well-camouflaged dispersal fields before Japanese reconnaissance planes sighted them. Some were to go to Valencia, about forty miles away, while others, including the three B-17s, were to go to the newly constructed field at Maramag, which was about fifty miles away and had a four-thousand-foot grass landing strip. Camouflaged revetments had just been completed there for the B-17s and other aircraft. This new airfield was manned mainly by personnel from the 19th Bombardment Group. Although Royce was strongly encouraged to send the aircraft to these dispersal fields that afternoon, for some reason he chose to keep the B-17s at Del Monte No. 1.[18]

That evening there was a long meeting held with Royce, the pilots, and key people from Sharp's staff to plan the bombing raids based on intelligence gathered and other factors. Bender recalled that they were "to attack targets in and around the Philippines until the available bomb stockpile and/or the fuel supply was depleted."

Hubbard's plane and four others flew to Valencia, landing in a big meadow and towed to dispersal areas. Davies recalled that when they rolled in, "Before we could get out of our airplanes, out of the jungle came natives, each with a great big piece of brush, and covered them up completely."[19]

The other flight of five, led by Strickland, remained at Del Monte for the night. Under the cover of darkness, the ships taxied down a dirt road and were dispersed under coconut palms. The bomb-bay tanks were removed and bombs loaded. The combat crews were briefed on the mission for dawn the next day and then rolled up in blankets under the planes for a much-needed rest.

Things at Valencia, however, were not going as smoothly. Hubbard stated: "We started downloading the bomb bay fuel tanks in order to load 500-pound bombs for tomorrow's mission. All of this was accomplished by good old manpower and straining muscles. It was dark by the time the tanks were down and moved to a safe spot, and we started loading bombs." A technical problem with the bomb release, however, kept the pilots up most of the night looking for a solution. It was dawn when they finished.

Missions Originate behind Enemy Lines

The last five U.S. Army fighters on Mindanao included four P-40s and one P-35, which had recently arrived from Bataan Field. These planes had been out flying reconnaissance and looking for suitable targets for a couple of days before the bombers arrived from Australia. One of the pilots had been ordered to fly his P-40 from an airfield on the island of Panay north to Luzon to scout out Nichols Airfield. There he reported seeing more than one hundred Japanese aircraft of all sizes parked wingtip to wingtip in neat rows.[20] Bender, who was too excited to get much sleep, said about the forthcoming mission: "Here we were surprising the enemy for the first time. What a pleasure going over the target after having taken so much grief [on Bataan] without having anything with which to hit back."

As the sun came up on the morning of April 12, Strickland's flight was assembling out over the water for an attack on the shipping in Cebu Harbor; Lowery's flight was assembling over Valencia. One flight consisted of "Strick" [Strickland] and Major Hipps in the lead, Maull and Howie West, Smitty and Pete Talley, Peterson and Harry Mangan, Feltham and Linn; Captain Lowery's flight had "Snake" Lowery and Sonny Walker in the lead, Col. Davies and McAfee with Hubbard, Gus Heiss and Ed Townsend, Pappy Gunn and Pete Bender, and Wilson and Keeter.[21]

Three of the P-40 pilots who were stationed at Maramag were ordered to fly to Davao and strafe the enemy airfield there. The mission was to commence at dawn, but it was foggy, and they did not get airborne until 8:00 A.M. Just after they took off, they saw five twin-engine bombers flying right at them. At first they thought they were Japanese but soon realized that these were five B-25s that had just taken off from another airfield for their mission.[22]

Hubbard's group assembled in a loose V formation on the way to Cebu, an island north of Mindanao. About halfway to the target, a Japanese transport appeared ahead, and Davies decided to drop one bomb from each plane but save the rest for Cebu. Later reports claimed that the ship sank just offshore. By the time Davies and his B-25s arrived over Cebu City Harbor, Strickland's group had already hit the airfield. Hubbard recalled the scene: "There were two big ships in the harbor so three of the planes were directed at the ships. I lined up on the warehouses and docks on the right, and the last B-25 took the left side. I watched my string of five 500 pounders walk thru the dockside warehouses setting off several fires and dockside explosions." When the bombers left, both ships were burning. The Japanese never expected to be hit.

13. "Lounge-Lizard," a B-25 flown on Royce's Raid. Shown in this photograph, taken at Charters Towers, are the crew. Standing, L to R: Sergeant Newman (upper gunner), Sergeant Young (crew chief), Sergeant Dudos (lower gunner and radio operator). Kneeling, L to R: J. Harrison Mangan (pilot), Oates (from RAAF; copilot), and Sergeant Land (bombardier). *Courtesy Ronald Hubbard*

The raid on Cebu was not without danger. According to Mangan, "a piece of shrapnel about six inches long came through the window behind my right shoulder and hit the armor plate in my seat just behind my head and made a loud clank and fell on the floor. That's as close as I ever came to being killed."

The planes returned to their dispersal fields at Valencia and Maramag, and ground crews immediately sheltered them under the camouflage of the dense jungle growth. Royce called the initial surprise raids a success: "It was a picnic. The planes came back to dispersed positions, which were never located by the Japanese, loaded up again and sent out, half to bomb Davao and half to bomb Cebu again."[23]

After a slow, laborious refueling by hand from fifty-five-gallon drums, the B-25s were bombed up and headed north to Cebu and south to the former U.S. Naval Base at Davao Harbor. This time the Japanese were waiting, their antiaircraft fire much heavier.

On the Cebu mission, McAfee saw a Japanese seaplane circling in the clouds. "I remember wondering why they always picked the lead plane, but this took all the prizes. He dived down, overshot, turned in the middle of a dive right on us, pulled out again, half rolled, climbed, and did an Immelmann [a half-loop and half-roll to turn in the opposite direction] right down on our tail—all this in a seaplane and not a pursuit mind you."[24] The bombers concentrated their drops on the undamaged areas of the harbor and returned to Del Monte.

At 7:30 A.M. that same day, two of the three B-17s had taken off from Del Monte No. 1 to bomb targets on Luzon. Royce declared: "I sent one [B-17] to Batangas and it sank a tanker. I ordered the other to look for cruisers and other warships in Manila Bay, but none was seen so the plane bombed Nichols Field."[25] Capt. Frank Bostrom said about the Nichols bombing, "We started one big fire and banged up the runway, hit hangars and other buildings—some warehouses and some gasoline stores."[26] On his way back Bostrom flew just east of Corregidor and waggled his wings in greeting to the men on the Rock. They were reported to have been "dazzled by what they saw."[27] The third B-17, which had limped in the afternoon before on three engines, stayed behind for repairs.

Soon after the raids, Japanese planes began to appear over Del Monte No. 1.[28] Royce recounted the events: "While the 3rd bomber was being repaired, a Japanese scout plane, which we called Photo Joe, came around and spotted her. When the two other Flying Fortresses came back, Japanese bombers then had several targets to shoot at and finally destroyed one with a direct hit and damaged the two others somewhat."[29] Additional enemy planes arrived and dropped bombs, which again hit the already destroyed B-17 and also tore up the main landing strip. The men there were furious at Royce for refusing to disperse the B-17s to the other fields. Especially upset were many of the P-40 pilots, who no longer had planes to fly and thought that they would be evacuated to Australia in the three heavy bombers (now down to two).[30]

At Del Monte No. 1, ground crews worked feverishly on the two B-17s that were salvageable and repaired the damaged runway. Just before dawn on April 13, those two planes left for Australia with some of the crew of the destroyed B-17 and additional passengers. One bomber barely cleared the fence at the end of the runway.[31] Royce stayed behind to direct further B-25 raids.

The next morning, flush with the success of the previous day's bombing, the B-25s headed back to Cebu and Davao. Orders that day were to attack Davao Airdrome with 100-pound bombs. As they approached the target, the pilots noticed a large ship in the harbor and that a floatplane had just taken off. Davies decided to take on the floatplane and the ship while the others hit the airport. Davies recalled, "I called the bombardier over the telephone. 'Hub' [Hubbard], see that baby? I'm going to give you a crack at him.' I put our big ship into a dive. We were doing some 300 mph when we came level with the Jap to let the bomber shoot."[32]

Hubbard waited until the floatplane was close and then opened up, causing minor damage. While maneuvering to get another shot, he excitedly took the gun out of the ball socket, jammed it against his shoulder, and continued firing. Eventually the top turret gunner finished the job on the floatplane. Hubbard's shoulder was black and blue for a week. Davies later laughed at the injury: "On landing, we found the bombardier's hands had been skinned and covered with blood as he had poked his gun from one slot to another in attempting to get proper aim."[33]

The B-25s continued to hit other targets in and around Davao and Cebu the rest of the day. Runways, planes, ships, docks, warehouses, barracks, and headquarters buildings were all victims on the second day. The Mitchells even strafed enemy troops.[34] The new B-25s proved effective on any target. Although designed for medium-level bombing, the planes were also adept at attacking at low levels. Hubbard tried this on the large Japanese ship in Davao Harbor. "One thousand feet was too low to set up a normal tracking sight so I set in a fixed angle just short of the ship and let the stick of bombs walk through it. One hundred-pound bombs with instantaneous fuses throw out a hail of shrapnel. There was a lot of surface damage but the bombs were too small to sink a ship of that size."

McAfee, the copilot on Hubbard's plane, had fun with the bombing run. He wrote the names "Mother," "Daddy," "Julia," "Stanley," and "Sally" on the bombs. Neither "Julia" nor "Stanley," however, hit the vessel. Another B-25 added a touch of irony to the damage at the airdrome. Pappy Gunn bombed the airfield his company had built three years earlier, noting, "I was there when the hangar was built, and I was there when it was destroyed!"[35]

On the afternoon of April 13, the second day of raiding, the B-25 flown by Gunn and Bender was ordered to Santa Barbara, near Iloilo on the island of Panay, about 220 miles from Del Monte, to pick up four men who had been evacuated from Corregidor in two small planes. They were supposed to have arrived at Del Monte, but both planes had mechanical difficulties and could not continue. The four were United Press correspondent Frank Hewlett, China liaison officer Col. Chih Wang, and two Hawaiian-born Nisei who worked for U.S Army intelligence, SSgt. Arthur Komori and Clarence Yamagata. What the latter two were carrying likely rated them very high on MacArthur's priority list of those who would be allowed to board the B-25s returning to Australia. The Hawaiians were carrying the USAFFE G-2 (intelligence) and G-3 (operations) journals.[36]

Clearly, MacArthur wanted those journals out of the Philippines so they would not fall into Japanese hands. Komori had been sent from Hawaii to Manila in April 1941 as an undercover agent to work with the Japanese Cultural Bureau and also to monitor Japanese neighborhood groups. He subsequently worked for army intelligence on Bataan and Corregidor before being evacuated. Yamagata, a graduate of UCLA's law school, practiced law in Manila and was a part-time legal advisor to the Japanese consulate while working undercover for U.S. Army intelligence. His wife and children were living in Japan at the time.[37]

As successful as the missions were, all realized that they could not continue for long more than one thousand miles behind the enemy lines. Things were getting hot. Del Monte had been heavily attacked, and planes landing there had to be careful to miss the numerous bomb craters. It was only a matter of time before the enemy caught up with the B-25s. Everyone was happy to get orders on the evening of April 13 to load up and return to Darwin.

Priority List

Exiting Mindanao was possibly the most challenging part of the mission. Bomb-bay fuel tanks had to be reinstalled and gasoline again pumped by hand into the bombers. Then, to further increase the risk on the return trip over enemy territory with bombers that had been converted to flying gas cans, the planes were also loaded with approximately thirty additional personnel, both civilian and military, plus some of the crew of the B-17 lost on the ground. The additional weight taxed the limits of the airplanes. To circumvent the priority list, Lt. Tom Gerrity, Lt. David M. Conley, and Lt. Jack Wienert (three pilots from the 27th left behind on Bataan), who had made their escape to Mindanao, were added to the crew list. Gerrity and Wienert had been evacuated from Bataan at 3:30 A.M. on April 3 in an old single-engine flying boat that got airborne on its third attempt. The *27th*

Reports relates: "Gerrity and Wienert showed the strain of four months on beleaguered Bataan. They could give no information about the men of the 27th that remained on Bataan to the last, except that all the officers were still alive up to the last day and that casualties among the men had been small."

The thousands of troops under General Sharp's command on Mindanao knew the end was near. They were surrounded by the Japanese and had little hope for resupply or reinforcement. Their next higher headquarters on Corregidor was under siege, and because Bataan had just fallen, General Homma now could direct more troops to the Mindanao campaign. Most soldiers desperately wanted to leave the island, particularly the Americans, but only those at the top of the priority list would be passengers on the B-25s.[38]

Brett's headquarters in Melbourne prepared the list and wanted to get as many of the most trained and experienced Army Air Corps people out as possible, particularly pilots. General George, working for Brett, was adamant that the fighter pilots from his previous Philippines command be given high priority on the list, particularly those with the most combat experience since they could lead the squadrons of men and planes pouring into Australia from the United States. But MacArthur's headquarters had the final say, which is probably why two civilian reporters on Corregidor were ranked higher than most pursuit pilots on the final list. Another reporter who had left Corregidor for evacuation from Mindanao did not make the flight because his plane had mechanical problems along the way. Fortunately, for many of the pilots and some others who didn't get out with those B-25s, two LB-30s were sent to Del Monte later in the month and took out around sixty more passengers. There were still thousands who wanted to leave. Some eventually took to the hills and became guerrillas, but most would become POWs.

Among those civilians who made it out were reporters Nat Floyd of the *New York Times* and Frank Hewlett, bureau chief for United Press. Floyd was on one of the four PT boats that took MacArthur and the Bataan Gang from Corregidor to Mindanao in March. Hewlett had already made a name for himself when he coined the second-most famous slogan (after MacArthur's "I Shall Return") of the Pacific War.

> We are the battling bastards of Bataan
> No Mama, no Papa, no Uncle Sam
> No aunts, no uncles, no nephews, no nieces
> No rifles, no guns, or artillery pieces
> And nobody gives a damn.

Also onboard was Filipino flying ace Jesus Villamor, who had won the Distinguished Service Cross for his early war exploits. Col. Charles A. Backes, who was chief of staff of the Philippines Army Air Corps, was on one of the B-17s that had left twenty hours earlier, as was Lt. John D. Bulkeley, who a month previously had commanded the four PT-boats that had extricated MacArthur. In addition, the B-25s carried a quinine expert, several men from the Signal Corps, and even a stowaway, listed as a Sergeant Jefferies.[39] (See Appendix 2 for list of crew and passengers.)

About midnight, nine of the ten B-25s started taking off in a drizzling rain for Australia. Even with the extra weight, the planes got off nicely. The tenth, flown by Pappy Gunn and Bender, had its extra fuel tank destroyed on the ground during one of the bombing attacks on Del Monte Field and had to remain behind.

Mission Accomplished

Once in the air, the weary group settled in for the long flight back to Darwin. Most slept. Jack Wienert, a passenger on James Smith's plane, got a chance to copilot the Mitchell when symptoms of dengue fever hit Pete Talley. Bombardier Ron Hubbard also had the opportunity to act as a pilot, though he desperately wanted to sleep, because Davies kept dozing off and copilot McAfee was asleep in his seat. Hubbard recalled: "I soon dozed off. The changes in the engines' sound as we fell off and began to pick up speed woke me up, and I got on the flight instruments and eased back up to 9,000 feet, retrimmed the plane to hands-off flight. The rest of the night continued in the same pattern. I would fall asleep, wake up, and retrim the plane time and again."

Fatigue also affected Malcolm Peterson, who was at the controls of Harry Mangan's B-25. About two hours out of Del Monte, one of the engines started to act up. Peterson fell asleep at the wheel, and the plane suddenly started turning and diving. Mangan and the crew chief, however, got control of the airplane from Peterson and leveled out.

The rest of the fifteen-hundred-mile flight was fortunately uneventful. The planes landed at Batchelor Field after the sun came up on Tuesday, April 14. The weary crews crawled out of the bombers while the B-25s were refueled. For the moment, most had little appreciation of the historic nature of their flight. They had just completed the longest aerial assault at that point in history. The mission was accomplished against almost insurmountable odds. Newspapers across the United States were about to make the "Royce Raid" a household name. But at that moment fame mattered little. Most were just happy to be alive back in Australia. Hubbard recalled that even though Darwin

14. Davies and four of his crew of seven with their B-25 that participated in Royce's Raid shortly after returning to Charters Towers. L to R: Jim McAfee (copilot), Robert Newman (gunner), "Big Jim" Davies (pilot), Ron Hubbard (bombardier), and Tech Sergeant Young (crew chief). *Courtesy Ronald Hubbard*

had been heavily bombed, "It still looked wonderful to me, as I hadn't really expected to see it again. The realization finally sank in, 'We had survived!'"

Within the hour, the B-25s, at least those that did not need mechanical attention, were in the air again for the eleven-hundred-mile trip to Charters Towers. That night the airmen were back on the ground, giving members of the 3rd the details of their dangerous missions. The B-25s had performed superbly. The crews had stories to tell, but they could wait. After fifty hours of grueling flying over four days, the only thing the weary crews were looking for was a soft bed for uninterrupted sleep.

Meet the Press

McAfee, Davies, and Royce, however, were not as fortunate. Their B-25 left Batchelor Field for Melbourne to report to Brett and MacArthur about the raid. Word had already reached Melbourne about their success before they landed. According to McAfee's diary, a large group of reporters was on hand to greet them; he finally got to bed, exhausted but relieved, at midnight.

The press and military leaders had a field day with the mission that week. U.S. citizens were looking for heroes, for success in the Pacific, and for the U.S. military to take the offensive. The Philippines raids accomplished that. Davies, however, talked about getting a measure of retribution for his fellow 27th Bomb Group comrades left on Bataan, boasting, "We smacked the hell out of them [the Japanese] and gained at least a little revenge for members of my squadron who fought in the front trenches of Bataan."[40]

The *New York Times* also reported that the raid bolstered Australians' view concerning the U.S. commitment to the Southwest Pacific: "The rank-and-file Australian takes the raid as proof of the striking power of the United Nations air arm in the Southwest Pacific and regards the bombings as a harbinger of further damaging offensive actions against the Japanese in the future."[41]

The strikes also affected the status of the Philippines in the eyes of the world after the fall of Bataan. "One thing the raid would do would be to impress the world with the fact that the Philippines were not lost but were still resisting the enemy. It is believed the raids will greatly encourage fighters on Corregidor, Cebu, and Mindanao and let them know they have not been forgotten."[42]

And perhaps most importantly, General Royce proclaimed the effect the raid had on the Japanese military. "The raids obviously threw the Japanese into a terrific panic. You can imagine their bewilderment when suddenly out of the sky appeared a bunch of bombers that let loose everything on them. They didn't know where the bombers came from."[43] A reporter also remarked: "In actual damage done, the raid was tactically small potatoes. But it proved that Australia is more than a rear area for attack on the near-by [Dutch East] Indies, that it is actually a first-class springboard for slashes into Japan's flank up into the South China Sea."[44] According to Japanese records, no ships were sunk during the raid.[45]

Davies, though, complimented the performance of the Mitchell B-25. "Full credit should be given the designers and workers, the North American Company and everybody who contributed in any way to the manufacture of the plane. We thank them from the bottom of our hearts, as do the men fighting in the Philippines."[46]

McAfee, however, did not join in the optimistic hoopla of the mission. Being junior to Royce and Davies, he kept his appraisal confined to his daily diary. In it he reveals his feelings about the political nature of their dangerous journey behind enemy lines: "We left only because there was no more gas. The news was given to the press that we were safely out. If the news had been withheld, the Japs would still be guessing. The wrong guy got credit for the flight."

In this last point McAfee was obviously referring to Royce, who did not fly during the mission but was merely a passenger to and from Del Monte. Supposedly, his plane developed engine trouble before the actual strikes. Royce, Colonel Davies, and Captain Bostrom, who piloted the B-17 destroyed at Del Monte, all received the Distinguished Service Cross for the mission. Some of the participants wondered whether the actual results justified the extraordinary effort required.[47] Harry Mangan questioned the wisdom of the mission: "To send the 3rd Bomb Group on this mission was to risk losing almost everything MacArthur had for an air force. The public relations realized from the raid was good, but it lasted only a few days. The risk was awfully big, and the real gain very little. Even money, they [the Japanese on Cebu and Davao] hardly knew we were there."

The fact that most of the 27th—comrades of McAfee and Mangan—were now POWs because MacArthur made them frontline infantry likely influenced opinions, especially after the airmen heard the following comment. MacArthur was lavish in his praise for the mission leader. "General Royce took the flight into enemy territory, created dismay and destruction at a time most important to our forces and has returned. I cannot too highly emphasize my pride in the work accomplished by American air forces participating."[48] McAfee and Mangan probably wanted Davies, who actually dropped the bombs, to get most of the credit. McAfee observed: "We won our spurs. We can do a job no matter how much politics there is to it."

Hipps stated that Bataan's surrender did not change the plans for the mission that much. "Our plan was to get to Del Monte and then rely on intelligence reports from there as to where to focus our air attacks. Much of the information as to where the Japs were and what they were doing came from the Filipinos and it was usually quite accurate." Mangan agreed with Hipps, adding: "Maybe there would have been more emphasis on attacking Japanese warships that were blockading Manila Bay. We would have had difficulty getting to Luzon from a fuel standpoint and also carry a load of bombs." The Japanese at that point controlled most of the refueling airfields. Mangan continued: "I don't know where else we could have refueled, possibly Iloilo on the island of Panay? There might have been a few crazy pilots who would have attempted to land on Bataan and then try to get out again."

Gunn and Bender's Ordeal

When Gunn and Bender returned to Del Monte on the afternoon of April 13, they discovered that their auxiliary bomb-bay fuel tank, which had been left there, was destroyed during one of the bombings. They immediately went on a scavenger hunt for something they could use instead. By dawn they had found two fuel containers that would hold just enough additional gas to get them back to Australia. But installing them was another matter. As soon as daylight approached, they had to fly the B-25 to Valencia, where it was hidden from enemy aircraft that day. The next evening they flew it back and worked all night. They took off again the next dawn because the fuel tanks were not yet fitted and ran into tremendous thunderstorms. Because of poor visibility, they flew out over the sea to avoid the mountains. They ran low on fuel and had to land at a small airstrip at Cagayan, which was totally covered in mud. That evening when they were taking off for the trip back to Del Monte, they barely made it off as the wheels brushed the top of the palm trees at the end of the strip. Eventually, they were able to get the extra tanks in the bomb bay but could not close the bay door. In addition, the fuel tanks themselves had leaky holes in them from previous bombings.

Finally, just before dawn on about the third morning, they took off for Australia. The ship smelled like a gasoline refinery, leaking fuel through the bomb-bay doors all the way back to Australia. Among Gunn's passengers was Capt. Henry Thorne, who had commanded one of the pursuit squadrons.[49] The B-25 landed at Batchelor Field without mishap, refueled, and headed for Cloncurry. They touched down in total darkness, due to misinformation about when sundown occurred there. Local cars had to go out and turn on their headlights so the pilots could see the airfield, just missing some of the hilltops as they landed. The following morning they took off for Charters Towers. Mangan later said this about Gunn: "He spent a lot of the war trying to figure a way to get his family out of Santo Tomas POW Camp in Manila. I have always thought Pappy somehow thought he could use the Royce's Raid mission to evacuate his family from Luzon. Military rules and regulations bothered him not. Rules be damned. He was fighting a private war."

Doolittle

The four months following Pearl Harbor produced nothing but discouraging report after discouraging report of Allied military setbacks. Bataan had fallen, and the war in Europe was going badly. What Americans needed was some good news. At the start of that mid-April week, Royce's Raid was making

15. Two American air-raid commanders after the war, Alaska, 1956 or 1957. L to R: James H. Douglas, secretary of the air force; Maj. Gen. John "Big Jim" Davies; Lt. Gen. James H. Doolittle. Davies and Doolittle led two of the first U.S. Army Air Forces offensive bombing raids of World War II. In April 1942 Davies bombed targets in the Philippines, while Doolittle led the famous raid on Tokyo. In 1945 Davies too led bombing raids against Tokyo. *Courtesy Henry Gundling Sr.*

front-page headlines in U.S. newspapers. By the end of that week, Lt. Col. James H. Doolittle's courageous mission striking at Japan's very homeland, not just some Japanese-held islands like Mindanao, thrust Royce's Raid into obscurity.

The American plan was to launch Doolittle's sixteen B-25Bs from Vice Adm. William Halsey's aircraft carriers about four hundred miles from the coast of Japan. But crewmembers of a Japanese picket (surveillance) ship, the *Nitto Maru,* spotted some of the warships from the task force, including the aircraft carriers, at dawn on April 18 and sent a radio message to the Japanese Navy.[50]

Halsey knew the *Nitto Maru* had gotten off a message but was not sure initially whether it had been received.[51] When the radio operators on the admiral's flagship, the *Enterprise,* heard the sudden increase in Japanese Navy signal traffic, they knew that the enemy fleet was on the move and likely headed for them.[52] The B-25s immediately took off at four-minute intervals from the *Hornet,* which was plowing through storm-swept seas more than six hundred miles from the Japanese coast. When the last of them was safely in the air, Halsey ordered his task force to head due east and out of harm's way.[53] Their radar picked up enemy aircraft coming after them.

Doolittle's raiders found only scattered resistance as they released their bombs over Tokyo, Kobe, Osaka, Yokohama, and Nagoya. They dropped a total of sixty-four 500-pound bombs and incendiaries on rail and dockyards, a fuel refinery, utility plants, and ships in port. Relatively minor damage was inflicted. The planes continued on to China, where they either crash landed or their crews bailed out because of fuel depletion due to the early launch. One ship landed in Russian territory. Doolittle initially thought the raid a failure, for all sixteen of his B-25s were lost. The War Department would later come to believe that if the planes had been launched from four hundred miles out as planned, Halsey's ships might have sustained significant damage from enemy aircraft.[54]

Shadow of a Doubt

What Doolittle did not anticipate was that the American public, hungry for success, heroes, and revenge, would take his raiders to their collective hearts. While Royce's Raid captured the imagination of the American people, the Doolittle Raid overwhelmed it. A week after it happened, Royce's Raid was relegated to a footnote in history, even though its participants had flown much longer distances than Doolittle's raiders, repeatedly attacked the enemy, probably inflicted more damage, and lost none of their ten B-25s and only one of three B-17s. But both raids accomplished something that had been missing from the war thus far. They were offensive actions deep into enemy territory that for once knocked the Japanese on their heels. The raids produced that shadow of a doubt in the minds of the Japanese military and citizens that things were perhaps not going as well as they thought.

Harry Mangan thought that the Doolittle Raid had two components the man on the street sorely needed in 1942. "First, Doolittle was already on his way to becoming a hero for setting many aviation records and the American public needed a war hero. Second, he bombed Tokyo, Japan's capital. The timing couldn't have been better. This was exactly what the American public needed after hearing bad news coming from the war front day after day."

Back at Charters Towers, the 3rd Bomb Group only heard bits and pieces about the Doolittle Raid. The squadrons were so preoccupied with their own problems and missions that neither McAfee's or Hubbard's diaries nor the *27th Reports* even mention the raid on Tokyo. The Japanese had designs on New Guinea, and the Battle of the Coral Sea was on the horizon. Although the men of the 3rd were too concerned about their future to give their past much thought, the pilots from the 27th continued to wonder about the fate of their comrades left on Bataan.

8

"No Mama, No Papa, No Uncle Sam"

For the men of the 27th who made it out of the Philippines, uncertainty about the fate of comrades left behind lingered with them for the rest of the war. Their sentiments are reflected in the *27th Reports:* "What happened to the 27th we don't know until Tokyo gives up. We do know this though, it would be a cruel and insane enemy, who, after victory, could not treat such brave and honorable foe as gentleman and brave soldiers."

But what actually did happened to the majority of the 27th who remained behind on Bataan? Why did those forces surrender, and what happened afterward?

March was a relatively quiet month on the Bataan front lines. General Homma's superiors in Tokyo had originally given him a deadline of February 8 for the conquest of the Philippines. Subsequently, he had a lot of pressure on him to speed up the capture of Bataan and Corregidor. With Singapore, the Malayan Peninsula, and the Dutch East Indies now under their control, the Japanese Imperial General Headquarters in Tokyo could devote more attention to the pesky army holding out on Bataan and Corregidor. They had considered replacing Homma but instead replaced his chief of staff with Maj. Gen. Takaji Wachi, over whom they had better control. In addition, Tokyo considered Homma too soft on the enemy and so also assigned the infamous Col. Masanobu Tsuji, who had just come from Singapore, to Homma's staff. Tsuji was to ensure that Homma got the job done quickly on Luzon. The colonel also served as the General Staff's "eyes and ears" in Homma's headquarters; when he was present, his fellow officers knew they were under scrutiny.[1] Some thought Tsuji was a spy who worked directly for Gen. Hideki Tojo, Japan's premier, minister of war, and dictator generally.

Tsuji was somewhat of a legend within the Japanese Army and was detested by many. He was well known for cruelty and barbarous acts toward the enemy and had repeatedly committed atrocities in China and Malaya. He had also been instrumental in mass murders in China and in Singapore, following the British surrender. The colonel often argued openly with generals and gave orders in the name of his superiors without their knowledge or authority.[2] Tsuji preached, to those who would listen, that the Philippines campaign was a racial war. He believed that all enemy soldiers captured on Bataan should be executed: the Americans for being colonialists, and the Filipinos because they betrayed their fellow Asians and fought on the side of the Westerners.

Although Homma's troops were susceptible to the same tropical diseases and battle injuries as the Americans and Filipinos, he was able to replace them with fresh soldiers. American commanders on Bataan did not have that option. By early April General King's force on Bataan, at least on paper, had an estimated 11,796 American troops, 8,270 Philippine Scouts, and about 59,000 members of the Philippine Army. But about 24,000 of these troops were either hospitalized or too sick to be combat effective. There were also 6,000 civilian employees and about 20,000 refugees.[3] The men defending at the front were totally exhausted from lack of sleep. The lack of food, which put them at almost starvation level, only compounded the problem. Almost all of the men had lost significant weight, and frequently their ankles were swollen, a complication of malnutrition.

The Filipino soldiers, who had entered Bataan as raw, frightened recruits, were now tough, battle hardened, and dependable.[4] Their patrols roved deep into Japanese-held territory, some of the men dressed in native clothing. Wainwright's headquarters concluded from these and other sources that the II Corps area would be where the Japanese would focus their main attack, the terrain there being more suitable for infantry and armor assaults.

The April Japanese Offensive

People around the world were following the Bataan/Corregidor stalemate, which was becoming a major embarrassment for the powerful Japanese war machine and demoralizing to Homma and his 14th Army. In Tokyo Prime Minister Tojo became progressively more impatient and encouraged the Army Operations Section of the Imperial General Headquarters to devise a plan to solve the problem. The entire operations staff worked on a solution for a week, concluding that the most unexpected place of attack was Mount

Samat, the rugged hill 1,920 feet high sitting just behind the center of the American front line. The plan was relatively simple, calling for a concentrated air and artillery bombardment on a two-and-a-half-mile sector in front of Mount Samat, followed by a full-scale infantry drive. (This area was occupied by the left flank of the II Corps.) According to their calculations, resistance would be crushed, and the Americans would surrender.[5]

The Japanese General Staff sent reinforcements, including the 4th Division from China, a 4,000-man detachment of the 21st Division, and the powerful 1st Artillery Corps.[6] Aerial reinforcements also arrived in mid-March to help finish off the resistance on Bataan and Corregidor, including sixty army heavy bombers and a contingent of navy fighters and dive bombers.[7] In late March, attacks began to increase on the front lines. Homma's main offensive began on April 3, Good Friday, with a massive two-day artillery barrage against American and Filipino units at the front. That same day the newly arrived heavy bombers flew 150 sorties against the frontline positions.

The Japanese began their major infantry assaults against the II Corps sector on April 4. They won breakthroughs all along the main line of defense, and by Easter Sunday, April 5, they were consolidating these major gains. The next day a counterattack was attempted but was met by a fresh Japanese offensive, which ended in disaster for the defenders.

At 6:00 A.M. on April 7, one area of the Japanese attack focused on the 32nd Philippine Army Regiment, which was located just to the west of the 2nd Battalion (27th Bombardment Group). At about 7:00 A.M. mortar and machine-gun fire tore into the 48th Materiel Squadron's area, located at the extreme west of the 2nd Battalion's sector. At 10:00 A.M. regimental headquarters issued orders to withdraw the entire battalion to the regimental reserve line about three miles back. The former airmen retreated and established their new position by noon. About 1:30 P.M. the enemy was sighted by battalion scouts. Thirty minutes later, though, orders came for the battalion to withdraw to another area. Meanwhile, the unit was taking heavy fire from Japanese small arms and mortars. Return fire stopped the advance temporarily, but most of the front line disintegrated in confusion that day as the troops retreated. Some units manned the regimental reserve line as a delaying action, while others continued to retreat toward the southern tip of Bataan; some soldiers even thought they were leaving the peninsula. Pfc. Elbert Hampton of the 48th Materiel Squadron recalled: "When the front lines gave way, the Japs were pushing us hard, and we were scrambling to get out of there. We thought we would wind up on Corregidor, but that never happened."

A group of Filipinos holding Japanese propaganda pamphlets came by the 48th Materiel Squadron headed for the Japanese lines to surrender. A captain convinced them to stay with the 48th overnight in hopes that they would not surrender, but by morning they had disappeared.

First Lt. George Kane, the adjutant of the 27th, was sent by Maj. John Sewell, the commanding officer of the 2nd Battalion, to inform the 32nd Philippine Army Regiment to move back from their position to a river junction near the East Road. But they had already left. Kane returned through the jungle to where he had left the 2nd Battalion, but no one was there. Gunfire was heavy and the Japanese close. Eventually, he came to the 16th Squadron's bivouac area, but they had already left too. Kane spent the night there. That night the ordnance people were destroying an ammunition dump nearby. "I had the 27th's American flag and the 27th's colors [unit flag]. I burned them both so the Japanese couldn't get them."

Sgt. William LaFitte of the 17th Squadron was posted on the outpost line of resistance, which was about a mile in front of the main line. After the replacements did not come, he said to his partner, Private Kern, "You stay here, and I'll go back and find out why our replacements haven't arrived." He went back to the front lines and found nobody there. On his way back, he saw Japanese tanks coming out of the woods and about one hundred infantrymen charging in his direction. He knew he could not get to Kern, so he headed in the opposite direction. LaFitte never saw him again.

The Americans and Filipinos retreated toward the southern tip of Bataan. The retreat took place over a couple of days as the Japanese relentlessly pushed on. A series of defensive lines were set up but eventually abandoned. Men became separated from their units. Confusion, sickness, and hunger continued to plague them. Units would merge with other units as new lines of resistance were temporarily formed and then abandoned. Orders were often conflicting. At various times during the retreat, different personnel from the 2nd Battalion were assigned to rear-guard delaying actions when tactically practical. Along the way, the men would periodically stop to eat when they could and when rations were available. Some of the terrain they had to travel over was rugged, with little or no tree cover. There were deep ravines to traverse and streams or small rivers to ford. When the retreating men crossed open areas, Japanese aircraft dropped incendiary bombs on them. In some areas, however, troops held key positions up until the time of surrender.[8]

A severe earthquake occurred on the night of April 8, which rocked the entire peninsula, adding further confusion. Pvt. Michael Tussing Jr. of the 91st

Squadron recalled the earthquake: "The trees were bending over and the old recon four-wheel truck I was lying next to rolled over me. It seemed it lasted for five minutes, but I'm sure it couldn't have lasted more than one."[9]

Brilliant lights also could be seen as ammunition dumps were set off and boats filled with bombs were destroyed so they would not fall into enemy hands.

Surrender

At 10:30 P.M. on April 8, General Wainwright, on Corregidor, ordered General King to have I Corps launch a counterattack to protect their right flank because the II Corps defensive lines had collapsed. King ignored the order. He knew it could not be executed and thought there was no possibility of halting the Japanese advance. In his view the campaign was over. At midnight he called his staff together to tell them of his decision to surrender the troops on Bataan. Col. Jim Collier, who was on King's staff, recalled: "Like the notification of the death of someone who had been terminally ill for some time, to everyone in the room, it was no surprise. Yet, it hit us with an awful bang and a terrible wallop."[10] All of the units were notified and given instructions on how to carry out the surrender. This included the destruction of all materiel of military value. About two thousand men were able to escape to Corregidor by small boats and barges that evening, including some members of the 27th. During Wainwright's last conversation with him at 3:00 A.M., King did not mention his plans for surrender.

The 17th Squadron's commanding officer, Warren Stirling, recalled that word of the coming capitulation got around very quickly. He was exhausted and laid down on the ground, soon falling asleep. He did not wake up until the next morning, even though there was an earthquake that night, and soon afterward threw his pistol into Manila Bay.

Cpl. John Connor of the 454th Ordnance Company heard of the imminent surrender and received orders to disable the trucks so that the enemy could not use them. "We shot rifles at the engine blocks and did other things to make sure that our trucks were unusable." The night of April 8, Captain Blakeslee, his company commander, ordered the men to climb to the top of Mount Mariveles. He wanted to follow the supposed high ground between the mountaintops north and escape through enemy lines. When they got to the top of the mountain, however, they could see that there were no such connecting ridges. Blakeslee then told his men that they could either try to escape or individually surrender to the Japanese—the choice was up to them. That night Connor slept in the jungle near the main road. "We could hear the Jap units marching by. Many were on horseback. They were singing Japanese war songs as they passed by. There were also many tanks going by. The next morning, some of us found Jap units that we surrendered to."

On the morning of April 9, some of the men of the 27th met up with elements of the Philippine Scouts and learned that the surrender would take place at 11:00 A.M. They were also told that Japanese units were in front of and behind them, so the best thing to do would be to pull off the trails and let the enemy forces go by until the surrender went into effect. About an hour later Japanese tanks came through, spraying the jungle ahead of them with machine-gun fire. Most of the men destroyed or otherwise got rid of their weapons. They were disappointed about the surrender but at the same time relieved to have the fighting end. Many had believed that there would be no surrender, that they would fight to the last man. Roosevelt, MacArthur, and Wainwright had made statements to this effect repeatedly. Some of the men went to sleep.

Paul Lankford of the 16th Squadron was on duty at the airfield when he was told that the front lines had just given way and trucks would soon arrive to take his unit to Mariveles. He trucked out that night, taking catnaps along the way, and arrived at the port in the early morning. That is when he learned of the surrender.

Sgt. Kenneth Farmer of the 16th Squadron was also at Bataan Field. There was no electricity, so the men used battery-powered lamps and red-and-green flashers to signal the few airplanes that remained when each could take off or land. Before he left the airfield, Farmer buried some of his personal belongings, a watch and a ring or two. He also had a very valuable set of air mechanic tools, which he buried.

When Harrelson at Bataan Field heard of the rumored surrender, he remembered that Doc Savage called the men together. He got all the food out that they had remaining, had his men eat it, and then they all started walking south toward Mariveles. Sgt. John Wood, also of the 16th Squadron, recalled that the officers called them together and told the men to take some of the remaining rations and fill their canteens. Then they said, "You're on your own from now on."

Wood and three others decided to follow trails to Mariveles instead of walking on the main road. They got lost. Soon they came across three Japanese soldiers, whom they surprised. Taking their rifles, the Americans then had to decide what to do with them. Under the circumstances, they could not take them as prisoners and could not let them go. They finally decided that their only choice was to kill them. Afterward the four wandered around in the jungle for about four or five days. Finally, they turned themselves in to the Japanese. Even though he spent over three long years as a starving POW, Wood later recalled: "I'm not proud of what we did to those three Japanese soldiers we captured and killed, but we were young 20-year olds at the time, and we didn't see any other real option. I'm 83 now, and every time I think about what we did, it still bothers me."

Not too far from where Wood had encountered the enemy soldiers, the Japanese used wire to bind together as many as four hundred Filipino soldiers who had just surrendered and then slaughtered them using swords and bayonets.[11]

King's decision to surrender the troops on Bataan was unilateral. He said at the time, "If I do not surrender to the Japanese, Bataan will be known as the greatest slaughter in history." He further argued: "Already our hospital, which is filled to capacity and directly in line of hostile approach, is within range of enemy light artillery. We have no further means of organized resistance."[12] His quartermaster reported that he only had one-half ration of food left for each soldier. King had not received approval from anyone in the high command to surrender, and if he had attempted to do so, his request probably would have been denied. The general thought he probably would be court-martialed for his action after the war. When Wainwright, who was on Corregidor, learned of King's decision to surrender that morning, he tried to contact him and countermand the move. Also, MacArthur, who was safe in Australia at this time, cabled General Marshall in Washington to tell him that he was opposed to the surrender of troops on Bataan: "If it [the army] is to be destroyed it should be upon the actual field of battle taking full toll from the enemy."[13]

Earlier on the morning of April 9, King sent Col. Everett Williams under a flag of truce to arrange a surrender meeting between himself and General Homma. The Japanese held Williams and instructed his driver to return with King, promising safe passage. As King proceeded toward the enemy lines with two Jeeps and four other members of his staff displaying white flags, they were attacked a number of times by Japanese aircraft, forcing them to pull off the road each time. Eventually, King, wearing his last clean uniform to look dignified, met at a farmhouse with Col. Motoo Nakayama, Homma's senior operations officer, to discuss terms; Homma would not attend the meeting unless General Wainwright was present.

When the Japanese learned that King was only surrendering Bataan and not Corregidor too, they were quite upset and initially would not discuss the surrender unless Wainwright showed up and also agreed to surrender

Corregidor. Eventually, Nakayama did hear him out and informally agreed to end the fighting on Bataan. King raised concerns about the condition of his men and requested that the American and Filipino troops be treated in accordance with the Geneva Convention. He also requested that the vehicles under his command be used to transfer his men, under supervision of the Japanese, to wherever Homma desired them. Nakayama categorically turned down these requests. When the general repeated his concerns about the safety of his troops, Nakayama cut him off by saying, "The Imperial Japanese Army are not barbarians." King knew he had no leverage and no choice but to surrender unconditionally. Since he did not have an officer's sword, he removed his .45 pistol and set it on the table at approximately 12:30 P.M.[14]

The American officers were instructed to assemble their men at the Mariveles airport, where the Japanese soon arrived. Hampton said, "they [the Japanese] started taking watches and rings from our men." Farmer recalled the fun the guards had harassing the prisoners: "A group of guys stripped me down. They were real experts. They got my military Ray Ban sunglasses, a ring and a fountain pen. They got what they wanted real quick." Sgt. Frank Corbi of the 48th Materiel Squadron noticed that the Japanese soldiers started looking for anything with gold. They took his watch because they thought it was gold, then noticed a ring—the wedding ring from his deceased mother—on a string around his neck. A sympathetic Japanese officer watching told the guards to stop.

Corporal Connor of the 454th saw some nearby Filipino POWs starting a fire to cook rice. The Japanese came over and stomped the fire out, telling them, "No Fires!" After they left, the Filipinos started the fire again, a very bold act. Soon the Japanese came back and started chasing them. The Filipinos yelled for the Americans to help them, but without any weapons, they could do nothing. They caught one of the Filipinos and hit him in the back of the head. He was repeatedly bayoneted and then dragged away by his feet with his head flopping from side to side. Nearby, another twenty-five Filipino soldiers had been rounded up and were being used for bayonet practice.[15]

Although there were a number of reasons why MacArthur and Wainwright did not want their troops to surrender, one was likely the incredible brutality and atrocities for which the Japanese Army was already well known. About 300,000 (some Chinese estimates are higher, some Japanese estimates lower) Chinese soldiers and civilians were murdered in the capital city of Nanking after the city had fallen to the Japanese in December 1937. In many cases captured or surrendered Chinese soldiers were executed by machine guns; any who survived were bayoneted.[16] In some cases the Japanese poured gasoline on their captives and burned them alive, in others they used poisonous gas. An estimated 20,000 women were raped by Japanese soldiers after the city's capture. These brutalities and atrocities took place over a six-week period, and much about the Nanking massacre and rape was then known around the world.

Edward King surrendered his army to Homma and his soldiers, veterans of the war in China.

The Bataan Death March

Probably no term emanating from the war in the Pacific has aroused more emotion than "Death March." The Japanese Bushido fighting code—"The Way of the Warrior"—which emphasizes fighting to the death, made those soldiers look upon the surrendering American and Filipino troops as the lowest form of humanity. Their code forbade showing chivalry, compassion, or mercy to the weak, which in one sense accounts for their barbaric treatment of the prisoners. The lack of adequate organization for moving the POWs out of Bataan also led to unspeakable results. Homma expected that there were 50,000 Filipino and American troops at most on Bataan at the time of surrender. Instead, there were more than 70,000. His haste to move his forces to Mariveles to begin the siege on Corregidor while moving 70,000 prisoners north out of the peninsula contributed to the horrendous, inhumane acts inflicted on their captives.

After the Japanese got to Mariveles, they lined up the men in rows of four across, one hundred to a group, and started them marching. Personal items like watches, coins, and rings were stripped from the prisoners during the march. Seldom during this time were they allowed food or water. After a mile or two, a Japanese soldier hit Stirling in the back of the head with his hand and grabbed his musette bag and canteen. Stirling started to go after him, but Mel Rosen, a West Point classmate, grabbed him. Without a canteen, he was in a lot of trouble. But a Filipino sympathizer along the way handed him a bamboo section that had a hole in it on one end and was filled with water. Stirling used it from then on as his canteen.

Having a full canteen was vital to the POWs. Sometimes the Japanese used a tantalizing form of water torture. Cletis Overton of the 16th Squadron recalled that "all along the road were artesian wells with water just flowing out of a pipe. Occasionally we were allowed to stop by the side of the road near one of these gushing wells. They'd make us sit there looking and listening to it for an hour or two. Then they'd move us along without any water."[17]

Those too weak to walk in the scorching heat were bayoneted, shot, or otherwise struck and left for dead along the dusty roadside. Some who were still alive but could not stand up were thrown into holes their fellow POWs were forced to dig and then covered with dirt. One American tallied twenty-seven headless corpses before he stopped counting.[18] Sgt. James Gautier Jr. of the Headquarters Squadron recalled Japanese guards with clubs hitting the POWs as they walked single file into a barbed-wire compound where they would spend the night. He said that behind the guards was a pile of men evidently bludgeoned to death. He also stated that Japanese soldiers walked into the compound with the heads of American soldiers stuck to their bayonets. "The Japs paraded their trophies around taunting us and trying to terrorize us."[19]

Survivors of this phase of the Death March stayed alive by just concentrating on putting one foot in front of the other until they reached the railroad station at San Fernando. But the anticipated relief of riding a train after marching approximately sixty miles was short lived. Groups of one hundred or more prisoners were packed like sardines into sweltering boxcars measuring thirty-three feet by eight feet that had little or no ventilation.[20] Kane recalled about the crammed boxcars: "They had us loaded in like toothpicks in a toothpick holder. They closed the door. Nobody could lie down." Lankford added, "We were in those steel boxcars for about four hours before they opened the door again when we arrived at Capas." Harrelson recalled that the heat and humidity: "When they closed the door to the boxcar, you had trouble catching your breath. A number of men passed out. Since we were packed in so closely, they could only slump over slightly. We were able to pry the boxcar door open a little bit, so some of us did get some air."

By the time the doors were finally opened at Capas fifteen miles and four hours later, hundreds of men were dead. The weary prisoners then staggered several miles to Camp O'Donnell. William Dyess described the ride as "like being in an oven." When the doors finally opened, "prisoners tumbled out into the glaring sunlight, and the wretchedness of their condition brought cries of compassion from Filipino civilians who lined the tracks. The ground was almost too hot to touch. The heat dried our filth into our pores."[21]

The average length of time to complete the journey to O'Donnell was four to five days. Not all POWs started at Mariveles. Some joined the march along the way, while many from I Corps on the west side of Bataan crossed over the peninsula farther north and joined the others at Balanga. General King's headquarters had actually spared a significant number of trucks from destruction so they could be used to transport his men after the surrender, but the Japanese chose to use most of them for other purposes. One author has claimed, however, that about half of the Bataan prisoners rode to San Fernando in trucks from Balanga, a distance of about thirty miles.[22]

Occasionally POWs were treated more humanely by their captors and even offered cigarettes. From time to time during the march, the Americans were turned over to Japanese soldiers from different units assigned to guard them—one group might give the POWs very little trouble, while another could be very cruel and brutal. Cpl. John Connor from the 454th remembered being fed a bowl of rice a couple of times during the march. Each time, while in line, Filipinos who were serving the rice would also fill his canteen from a water barrel. He did not recall the lack of water being as much of a problem as many of the others—either his group just happened to be luckier than some or was one of the last to join the march, by which time it was better organized. Some men escaped into the hills during the Death March. The vast majority who never reached Camp O'Donnell, however, died on the way, either in the boxcars or alongside the road, executed by Japanese guards. The U.S. Army Center for Military History estimates that up to 650 Americans and between 5,000 and 10,000 Filipinos died on the march.[23]

But not everyone suffered. Drolan Chandler and his friend James Dyer, both privates from the 27th's Headquarters Squadron, had grown up together in Detroit, Alabama. They decided to escape at the time of the surrender with about four others. They got ammunition, guns, and canteens and headed into the jungle. But the men did not get very far before everyone became thirsty. Drolan volunteered to climb down the mountain to a stream and fill all of the canteens. "I went down to the bank of the stream. I laid my gun down and slid down the bank, and I slid right down in front of a Jap officer, but I didn't see him to start with. I started dipping up water out of the creek into the canteen. This Jap officer said, 'That water is contaminated. Get water out of that barrel. It's been boiled.'"

Chandler filled the canteens and started up the bank but the officer, who spoke fluent English called him back. He asked Chandler where he was from (Detroit) and then asked him how far it was from Sulligent, Alabama. The officer had attended college at the University of Alabama and told the American that he wanted him to drive his car. As it turned out, Chandler and the officer had some mutual friends in Alabama. While Chandler chauffeured the Japanese officer in his little Ford along the route of the Death March, they both observed a guard walking around an American officer and poking him with a bayonet. The Japanese officer told Chandler to stop. Turning around and taking out his pistol, and without ordering the guard to stop, he shot the Japanese soldier, then drove on.

Chandler spent four weeks working for this officer, who was then transferred farther south in the Philippines. He offered the American an opportunity to go with him, but Chandler, very sick with malaria, told him he wanted to join his fellow POWs. He was taken to Manila and put in Bilibid Prison Hospital, where he almost died.

Buck Prewett, also from the 27th's Headquarters Squadron, got a ride in a railroad car during part of the Death March, though to a different location. On about the day of the surrender, he headed over to one of the hospital areas to get some more Atabrine, a medicine for the treatment of malaria. While there, the Japanese showed up with trucks. It was his impression that they were going to transport some of the non-ambulatory patients in these vehicles. The soldiers rounded up those who could walk, including Prewett, and marched them off as a group. On about the second or third day, the Americans were packed into a cattle car with a dung-covered floor. The group of approximately two hundred POWs was taken to Cabanatuan, where they worked for several weeks preparing existing buildings to become a POW camp.

Dr. Hochman was at Hospital No. 2 on Bataan at the time of the surrender. The noise and the confusion there were terrible. The next day Japanese soldiers with fixed bayonets overran the hospital. "We just stood still," Hochman recalled. "We were scared. We didn't know what the hell was going to happen." He was ordered to stay there and continue caring for the thousands of hospitalized soldiers, American and Filipino, all of whom were either too sick to make the march or did not leave for various other reasons. The more than eighty female U.S. Army nurses, who had been caring for patients at two army hospitals, had been evacuated to Corregidor just before the surrender.

The Japanese thought that the Americans on Corregidor would not dare fire on their own wounded, so they placed twenty-three artillery pieces around Hospital No. 2 and used them to bombard the island.[24] Corregidor, however, did fire back, and although they tried to avoid hitting the hospital, several soldiers there were killed. Hochman recalled: "For thirty days from the time of our surrender on Bataan until Corregidor's surrender, we were subjected to the most intensive artillery bombardment and noise. . . . I thought I would go out of my mind."

Camp O'Donnell

If the journey to O'Donnell was a Death March, the destination itself was a death camp. It has been estimated that in the seven weeks that O'Donnell existed, sixteen hundred Americans and sixteen thousand Filipino soldiers

16. Burial detail at Camp O'Donnell. POWs carry dead comrades in blankets tied to poles. *Courtesy Gen. Douglas MacArthur Foundation*

perished there. After arrival, the men would be addressed and berated by the camp commandant through an interpreter. He would also tell them that they had to bow to any Japanese guard they encountered or be severely punished. A hungry Private Hampton saw a potato peel lying in the dirt as he staggered into Camp O'Donnell, quickly snatching it up and eating it.

Ken Farmer said the worst things about O'Donnell were "hunger, thirst, and continued harassment by the Japanese. They had only one water spigot at Camp O'Donnell for us, so we had to wait hours to fill our canteens." The Japanese also gave speeches on how much they despised the Americans. The lack of food and water and the guards' physical brutality led to many deaths. Kane said: "We buried as many as 50 of our soldiers some days, maybe twice that many. We put the bodies in trenches. We stacked one body on top of another." He also recalled that the death rate among the 16th Squadron on the Death March and in the early days of the prison camps was only about half of what it was among the 17th, 91st, Headquarters, and 48th Materiel Squadrons. This was because the 16th had been working at the airfield in the rear area and were in better condition and better able to supplement their increasingly meager rations during the siege.

The Japanese guards, just to be sadistic, would intermittently turn off the water spigots, sometimes for up to an hour or more while there were long lines of men waiting to fill their canteens. While they waited, the POWs had to wonder whether they would survive this ordeal and where MacArthur was with the army he was supposed to lead back. The POWs from the 27th also had to wonder where their comrades were who had gone south to retrieve their dive bombers.

9

Air Missions over the Coral Sea and Beyond

THE MOOD AROUND the Charters Towers airfield in April 1942 was vastly different for the pilots than the previous four months of the war. For the most part, the 27th Bombardment Group men spent the first 113 days of the war fighting a losing battle with the Japanese. When they merged with the 3rd Bomb Group, they were going on the offensive. The success of the air missions over Gasmata, Lae, and Mindanao made the pilots all stand a bit taller. There was a swaggering bounce to their step for the first time in months. General MacArthur, in Melbourne, now knew who they were, and he had plans for them. After the success of Royce's Raid, the Japanese knew who they were too.

Queensland and the War

In March and early April, there were ominous signs that Japan had designs on landing troops on Australian shores. In early April several unidentified aircraft were spotted over the Babinda area of Queensland and elsewhere. Many believed them to be Japanese reconnaissance aircraft. The most logical invasion spot appeared to be in northeastern Australia on the beaches just east of Babinda, approximately forty miles south of Cairns, where there is an opening in the Great Barrier Reef, which runs parallel to Queensland's coast. To do that, the Japanese first wanted to control Port Moresby in southeastern New Guinea and the Coral Sea.

The Royal Navy's Eastern Fleet commander, Adm. Sir James Somerville, was told on March 8 by his deputy, Vice Adm. Sir Algernon Willis, that a Japanese invasion of Australia "must be expected" after Java and New Guinea have been mopped up. Likewise, the Australian military chiefs of staff expected Port Moresby to be invaded in mid-March, Darwin in early April, and the island of New Caledonia soon after. Then they expected an invasion in May on the more heavily populated east coast of Australia.[1]

There were not many American or Australian troops in Queensland north of Brisbane in April 1942, though there was an American military presence at Townsville. The only U.S. troops of any significance in or near Charters Towers were the 3rd Bomb Group. With their men gone away to war, many Australian women took over the family businesses—shops, restaurants, and farms—in addition to raising the kids. Some families in northeast Queensland, fearing a Japanese invasion, even sent their children west away from the coast or south to Sydney or Melbourne to live. Allan Wakeham, who was nine at the time, remembered that of the seventy students in his grade school, only forty remained behind that April. Local governments even brushed open some of the old aboriginal trails leading west and lined them with supplies because of the expected evacuation.

Most of the families in the Charters Towers area experienced shortages of food, medicine, and gasoline. Fortunately, they were too busy to notice or complain much about the situation. Although threatened by the expected invasion, their biggest worry in 1942 was still whether or not their own men would return safely from their overseas war.

The townspeople gradually got used to the 3rd Bomb Group being around. They were glad to have at least a small contingent of soldiers in the area, though many also worried that the new airstrip might attract Japanese bombers. The civilians, however, went about their daily business as best they could, even though they did take notice of the area's increased military preparations, including the concrete bomb shelters being built in the middle of downtown streets.

Everywhere you looked in Queensland in April 1942, there was every indication that the war with Japan just might be coming to them soon. At the Charters Towers airbase too, this notion was taken very seriously.

Upon Glen Stephenson's return from Melbourne, he was temporarily assigned to Capt. Ron Hubbard's 90th Squadron.[2] Although a West Pointer and a captain, which made him one of the two highest-ranking officers in the squadron, Stephenson faced stiff competition for flight-line status with the throttle jockeys because, unlike some of the other original 27th pilots, he probably had not piloted a plane for at least three months. The first thing he likely wanted to do when he joined his new squadron was to get some flight time.

Harry Mangan recalled that when Stephenson came to Charters Towers, he was encouraged to fly the A-24s and the B-25s. The A-24 was a single-engine dive bomber that he flew back in Savannah. The twin-engine B-25s were unfamiliar to him but fairly similar to the planes he flew while with the Ferrying Command. Stephenson acted as a copilot on a B-25 flight around the area to learn the landmarks, to experience how the plane felt, and to get used to the noise. He probably did not have more than five to ten hours of flight time in April before his first mission.

Because it was built on a ridge, landing on the two gold-speckled runways at Charters Towers was occasionally challenging. The east-west runway had a ten- to fifteen-foot slope to it. Mangan believed that it was not that difficult to take off and land at Charters Towers. But there were worse problems than that. "Maps? They were unreliable. Landing at night? We used flare pots [emitting flames] to outline the runways. Food? We damn near starved to death. We always used to laugh at the Australian Camp Pie. It was something like mutton and curry sauce in a can. I don't think anybody could eat it. At least the Americans couldn't."

Supplying Charters Towers in the early days of the war was a difficult matter. Militarily, there were few barracks, harbors, railroad tracks, and airfields north of Brisbane vital for the eventual staging of offensive operations through New Guinea. And Charters Towers was north of Brisbane. The rail system was inefficient. Each state government ran its own railroad, resulting in no standard rail gauge. Often when supplies reached a state border, they had to be transshipped on another train in order to reach their destination. The supply and maintenance system ran as if it were still peacetime.

Another problem at the time was getting supply ships unloaded because of labor problems.[3] According to Lex McAulay, who was in the Australian Army, the Communist-controlled longshoremen came to work late, stopped frequently for breaks, enjoyed long lunches, and left early despite the fact there was a war going on so close to the country. They did not work on weekends or public holidays, and "all activity stopped completely at the first drop of rain."[4]

Active fighting units like the 3rd needed things yesterday and found themselves bogged down in needless paperwork that almost ensured that badly needed aircraft parts arrived weeks late. This so infuriated Davies, who was sending his men into the line of fire over New Guinea, that he wrote a memo to headquarters about the unit's frustration: "Instead of being all out to keep us supplied with everything we need, the supply organization makes obvious efforts to obstruct our getting anything." Pappy Gunn fumed with frustration when dealing with the quartermasters. He commented that they thought the way to win the war was to keep the supplies locked up in warehouses.[5]

Weather was a significant factor at Charters Towers for pilots. Being below the equator, the Australian summer has weather equivalent to the U.S. winter—April is like the Northern Hemisphere's September. Their summer temperatures averaged in the 80s, and by April the rainy season was just about ending. Often when returning from a flight over the Coral Sea in bad weather, the bomber pilots trying to find the field would look for a landmark like the Burdekin River. The Burdekin originated one hundred miles north of Charters Towers and eighty-five miles south of Mount Bartle Frere in the Seaview Range and Gorges Range and flowed south through the town. One hundred miles south of Charters Towers the river made a 180-degree turn and flowed north and then east before emptying into Upstart Bay and the Coral Sea. Because modern navigational maps were scarce in 1942, in bad weather aircrews coming in low below the clouds would often hedgehop looking for the Burdekin as an indication that they were closing in on Charters Towers.

Any time off afforded the pilots a chance to write home. Howard West remembered pilot Gus Heiss writing love letters to his girlfriend back in the States while playing "Clair de Lune" over and over again on the phonograph he had lugged all the way from Savannah. Stephenson sent two letters from Australia. One was sent to his father in Milwaukee on April 2 and arrived five and a half weeks later. "Haven't written many letters, in fact none except to Ann, and don't know whether they got back. Arrived in Australia about 3 weeks ago and have been moving around ever since. Am O. K. Regards to all." In his April 10 letter to his wife, he indicated that sending mail to him now would be easier as he had an APO (Air Post Office) number—APO 922, San Francisco. "Seem ages since I left you," he told her. "Hope you've been getting my letters as I've mailed them from the Philippines, Java, and all over Australia. Haven't been in one place over a couple of weeks since this war began. Haven't much left of what I started from home with—your pictures, a raincoat, and a pair of wings."

After Davies and the rest of the crews returned to Charters Towers from the Philippines, plans were being made in Melbourne to take advantage of this adventurous band of pilots and their new B-25s. MacArthur needed to know Japanese ship movements in the Coral and Solomon seas. Most of those vessels carried enemy troops and supplies headed for New Guinea, the Solomon Islands, and possibly Australia. By knowing where they were, MacArthur hoped to predict what islands would soon be attacked.

By March 1942 the Japanese High Command had given the green light for the invasion of Port Moresby, already a main target of their bombing and strafing attacks.[6]

Rabaul

Rabaul is a town located on New Britain about five hundred miles east of Port Moresby. Before the war, several thousand citizens lived there, and it was the administrative center of Australia's mandated island territories to the northeast, including a portion of New Guinea. There were active volcanoes in the harbor area, and the crater from one poured black volcanic ash over the town from mid-1941 through October of that year. Nevertheless, Australia began basing troops there in April 1941 because of fears of Japanese aggression.

Japanese war planners realized that the southeastern area centering around Australia seemed a probable starting point for an Allied counteroffensive. To strengthen their perimeter in this sector, they decided to effect the "seizure of strategic points in the Bismarck Archipelago." Rabaul, they determined, had great potential value to the Allies as a naval base for protection of air- and sea-transportation lines to Australia and also thought it could serve as a base for bombing attacks against the key Japanese naval stronghold of Truk. Conversely, if the Japanese controlled Rabaul, it would secure Truk's southern flank and give the navy an advance airbase to control the seas northeast of Australia.[7]

In early January 1942 the bombing of New Britain began, and most citizens of European descent evacuated. On January 22 the Japanese landed up to six thousand troops there; organized resistance ended the next day. Twenty-eight Aussies were killed in the fighting, and the rest of the defenders, estimated at 1,370 men, split into small groups and withdrew into the mountainous jungle terrain. During a roundup by the Japanese in early February, many Australians surrendered or were captured around the Tol Plantation. On February 4, separate groups of POWs were taken into the jungle, 158 of whom were executed by bayoneting or shooting. The Tol Massacre was unprovoked. Subsequently, another 400 Aussies escaped from New Britain or were evacuated by boat or airplane. Those who remained either surrendered or were captured over time. Relatively few of them survived the war.[8]

Shortly after the Japanese took control of Rabaul, the U.S. Navy planned a raid against the harbor with the aircraft carrier *Lexington*'s task force. The units were detected, however, 460 miles out on February 19. Aircraft from the *Lexington* shot down several land-based Japanese bombers that had come out to attack the task force, but with the element of surprise lost, the raid was aborted.[9] The Japanese used their bombers at Rabaul to interfere with Allied shipping and to bomb other targets in the Coral Sea area. Over time, Rabaul became Japan's most important base in the Southwest Pacific, with its excellent deep-water harbor and the five airfields that would eventually be built.

Australia had a highly organized coastwatcher network, with individuals located on the southeastern New Guinea coast as well as other islands bordering the Bismarck, Solomon, and Coral seas. Many were recruited from among the postmasters, policemen, harbormasters, schoolteachers, and other coastal residents, and some were members of the military. They sent coded messages by radio to Australian military intelligence regarding ship, air, and troop movements. They also helped rescue downed Allied flyers.[10] In April coastwatchers on the islands of the Bismarck Sea reported a large Japanese naval flotilla gathering at Rabaul. Enemy troops and ships were also gathering at the islands of Palau and Truk. Allied headquarters learned from code breaking and other sources that the enemy would soon make a move against the Solomons and Port Moresby. During this time, the Japanese also moved the powerful Genza Air Group, with three hundred bombers and fighters, to Rabaul.[11] The task of finding the enemy and where the ships were headed fell to the 3rd Bomb Group.

New Guinea

New Guinea is the second-largest island on earth, extending from its southern tip 1,500 miles in a northwesterly direction. Mountain ranges run down the middle of the island, with some peaks over 16,000 feet high. Its widest portion in the middle is about 430 miles across. Its closest point to Australia's mainland is about 100 miles away. The Owen Stanley Mountain Range divides the southeastern part of the island, with some peaks over 13,000 feet. Most of the island is covered with dense jungle and rain forest, but there are also extensive areas of grasslands and swamps. Over the centuries, many European countries had claimed portions of New Guinea. The southeastern half is known as Papua and was taken over by Great Britain in 1884 and transferred to Australia in 1906. A mandate after World War I also gave Australia control of the northeastern portion of New Guinea.

An estimated 1.8 million natives lived in Papua and the other Australian mandated islands to the northeast during the 1940s. This included some cannibals, headhunters, and some tribes retaining a stone-age culture. Port Moresby is located on the southwest side of the island and is about three hundred miles from the closest point of the Australian mainland. After Rabaul and Lae fell to the enemy, it became the Allied administrative capital of the Australian territory of Papua. By March 1942 most of the two thousand Australian civilians living in the area had been evacuated because of the expected invasion. Much of the native population had disappeared into the interior, and many of the native militiamen had been sent back into the hills to work on airfield construction. They cut down high grass and trees and helped level land for runways.

Although several military airfields were being built around Port Moresby, only two were functioning at that time. The civilian airport, which had opened in 1933, was also being used by the military, referred to as "Three Mile," "Kila," or "Kila Kila." The 3rd's A-24s flew out of there. The Seven-Mile Airdrome, which would later also be referred to as "Jackson," was built for the military and had just opened. It had longer runways, which were needed for the larger bombers.

Port Moresby had a harbor with wharves on one side and about a hundred native huts on stilts bordering the water's edge on the other. The Australian Army had one brigade there, which consisted of about two thousand militiamen who were poorly trained (when compared to the regular army) and lacked adequate equipment and supplies.

Major land battles had not yet begun in New Guinea. This was due to a combination of reasons. The mountain range served as a barrier between the northeast and southwest sides of the island, and the Japanese Army had other fights to finish. The long siege of Bataan and Corregidor caused significant military assets to be diverted, which also contributed to the delay of the Port Moresby invasion.

Reconnaissance

The long reconnaissance missions the 3rd Bomb Group was about to begin did not have the excitement or adventure of the bombing missions over Gasmata, Lae, and Mindanao. In fact, the scouting B-25s could not sink a Japanese ship if they wished. According to Mangan, their bomb bays were filled with the extra fuel needed to extend their range beyond two thousand miles.

The 3rd started flying its long-distance scouts on or about April 19. They were likely selected for the mission because many of their B-25s had just had the auxiliary fuel tanks reinstalled for their return from the Philippines. Some of the B-17s from the 19th Bomb Group out of Townsville were also assigned to reconnaissance missions, as were some of the RAAF Hudsons and PBY Catalinas out of Port Moresby. The 22nd Bomb Group, headquartered in Townsville, flew scouting missions at that time, but theirs were often coupled with bombing raids.

A typical B-25 mission from Charters Towers to Port Moresby started with the pilots and navigators meeting in a small briefing room to get the latest weather information. They also received their radio codes and final instructions. Since they typically left in the early hours of the morning, the preflight inspection and performance briefing with the crew chiefs were conducted in the dark.

Rumbling down the runway and reaching the takeoff speed of 115 mph, the craft nosed up into the air. The copilots would pull the landing-gear handle, hollering "Gear up!" Once the airplanes were on course for the three-and-a-half-hour, 740-mile flight to Port Moresby, the pilot would often turn over the controls to the copilot to allow as much flying time as possible to aviators who would soon be piloting their own B-25s.

Ninety percent of the route was over open water: the Great Barrier Reef and the Coral Sea. When daylight was sufficient, the crews looked for Osprey Reef, three hundred miles south of Port Moresby, as a navigational aid. When visible, the formation appeared as a halo of pink water against the blue sea.

Landing at Port Moresby, even in daylight, was no picnic. Wrecked airplanes were strewn along the edges of the runway, and Japanese fighters and bombers frequently flew in from the east over the mountains and paid unpleasant and unannounced calls on the airfields. The bomb craters they left on the dirt-and-gravel runways had to be filled and tamped as quickly as possible, but often the repaired hole was of a different density than the surrounding material. Mangan recalled that having a tire roll through such a soft spot felt as though something had grabbed the plane. Many of the dispersal fields for aircraft coming to Port Moresby were not completed by April 1942. Upon landing, crews seldom found anyone to meet them or direct them to dispersal areas, so pilots simply parked their planes where they judged best.

The 8th Squadron of the 3rd Bomb Group, with almost two dozen A-24s, had already been operating out of the Port Moresby area for three weeks. West Pointers Zeke Summers and Virgil Schwab were there, facing Japanese Zeros almost daily. Launder remarked about the enemy fighters: "They would come in off the ocean, fly down the runway thirty feet in the air, do a slow roll or two, and all this amid a hail of machine-gun fire, and climb out of there—as if to laugh at us. These guys were good!"[12]

Refueling was completed as quickly as possible, since most pilots wanted to spend the minimum possible time on the ground with the enemy so near. At this early stage, Seven-Mile Airdrome had a single gasoline truck that was not always available, so the pilots and their crews would often have to roll 55-gallon drums of gasoline up to their planes and refuel themselves. Afterward, the B-25s on reconnaissance duty ventured out on the most dangerous part of their missions, over land and sea controlled by the Japanese.

The flights could take the planes north toward Kavieng on New Ireland, north of Rabaul; south toward DeBoyne Island of Southern New Guinea; or somewhere in between. Sometimes they flew over or around the dangerous, cloud-shrouded Owen Stanley Mountains. They might also fly over the Coral Sea or the Solomon and Bismarck seas.

When the gas tanks had just enough fuel remaining to safely get back, the plane returned to Port Moresby, refueled, and headed back to Charters Towers. Occasionally, the crews stayed overnight at Port Moresby and headed back early the next morning. Most, however, did not want to leave their planes on the ground for very long. Some of the missions from Charters Towers flew northeast over the Coral Sea and back without refueling, using the special fuel tanks from Royce's Raid. Mangan described reconnaissance as "sticking a whole bunch of fingers over the Coral Sea. We'd fly out for a couple of hundred miles, make a right turn, fly back towards the land then start the whole thing over again. We made sort of a grid arrangement looking for these surface vessels. We had no intention of engaging the ships, just find out where they were." The Japanese, however, were very clever about moving their fleets, often using bad weather as cover.

Sometimes during these flights, Japanese airplanes could not be avoided, but in most cases the reconnaissance aircraft managed to evade enemy fighters. Finding the Japanese ships was sometimes easy. Mangan stated, "We had no navy to speak of in the area, so the general attitude was 'If you see a boat, it ain't ours.'" Sometimes it was harder. "Ship identification? Oh, Lord I don't think many intelligence people even knew what a Japanese fighting ship looked like at that time. And we sure didn't have silhouettes or models to look at either!"[13]

The flight back to Charters Towers could also be challenging. Mangan said they had no navigational aids of any kind, like a radio beacon or an electronic homing device, at that time. "What we had was called 'true pilotage.' You'd looked at some kind of map and ground references and then tried to figure out where you were. We didn't dare want to get caught above an overcast on the way back. We went down and down, and down until we were practically on top of the water until we got to a land mass."

Missions, April 19–21

In the early hours of April 19, 1942, the 91st Squadron was called upon to furnish two B-25s to perform reconnaissance in the New Guinea–New Britain area. Lt. Ralph L. L. Schmidt was the pilot of one of these planes, with Lt. Richard R. Birnn as copilot, Technical Sergeant Barlow as bombardier, and

Lt. J. A. Riola as navigator. The second B-25 was flown by Lt. John Jefferson Keeter as pilot, with Capt. Glen Stephenson as copilot. Birnn's diary indicates the plane flown by Schmidt flew reconnaissance missions on April 19, 20, and 21. The aircraft flown by Keeter flew one on April 21 and is assumed to have also flown another with Schmidt on April 19 and 20. The missions between the two planes were coordinated so that they could presumably cover as broad an area as possible without overlapping. Since Schmidt, Birnn, Keeter, and Stephenson did not survive the war, the only remaining eyewitness accounts of the missions flown on those three days come from the diary of Lt. Richard Birnn. The routes flown by Keeter and Stephenson would not have been identical to those flown by Schmidt and Birnn; nonetheless, they would have been similar except for the return flight from Port Moresby to the Australian mainland by Keeter and Stephenson on April 21. Birnn recorded the following observations in his diary for April 19–21:

> 19 April 1942—Charters Towers
> Returned here yesterday. Was alerted at 0100 (19 April) to fly to New Guinea to fly a recon mission, gassed at Port Moresby and took off at 0900 to reconnoiter the NE coast of New Guinea.
> Saw lots of beautiful island with native building and white beaches—just like you see in the movies. Couldn't go back to Moresby until after 1500, as the Japs raid the field almost daily. Landed at Moresby, gassed and took off for Townsville. Lucky to get in at Townsville—all other fields were closed and it was after dark. Townsville just happened to be open. Had 17 hours of almost continuous flying except time out for gassing.
> 20 April 1942—Townsville
> Headed back for Moresby today. Arrived and spent the night under the wing of my plane. Took off at dawn to patrol. They briefed me that there were no mountains in New Guinea higher than 14,000 feet. I flew by one with my altimeter reading 16,500. New Guinea is just a mass of mountains—90% of country is wild. Lots of gold and lots of mining camps—some above 13,000 feet.
> Covered the NW corner of New Britain, then New Hanover and part of New Ireland. Saw two large Jap transports in the harbor. Flew around them but got no AA fire. Went across the channel to Kavieng. Saw nothing at the airport but some Jap activity in town.
> On the way home, flew off the Solomons and took pictures. Then turned out to sea and flew over Lae, which was heavily infested with

Japs. Just as we got over the field, I saw five Zeros climbing up to meet us—never seen planes climb so steeply. Some nearby clouds offered me some cover, and I got into them as fast as I could. No fun being caught out alone by Zeros. Pictures turned out okay. We saw 21 Jap planes on the field. After gassing at Moresby we returned to Townsville with an overall flying time of 27 hours out of 60. Moresby was considered too dangerous to remain overnight.

On the morning of April 20, B-25s from the 13th Squadron also flew to Moresby from Charters Towers. Harry Mangan's diary mentions that they left at 3:00 A.M. in a driving rain. While the two B-25s of the 90th Squadron were out on reconnaissance, the B-25s of the 13th Squadron flew to Salamaua on a bombing raid. Mangan wrote: "We did well. Stayed at Moresby, but a few minutes on our return as the Nips were on their way to Moresby and we had to service on the run. Tore out of Moresby and made it over to Horn Island." Horn Island had an RAAF airfield, frequently used by American aircraft and just off the northern tip of Australia's mainland, about three hundred miles from Port Moresby. Mangan may have headed there instead of Charters Towers because he did not have time to take on enough fuel to make it all the way back or possibly because the weather south of Horn Island was deteriorating—perhaps both.

Two days later Birnn wrote in his diary:

> Returned to Moresby. Took off the next morning (April 21) to patrol the Rabaul area. This is the strongest Jap base in this part of the world—located on the NE corner of New Britain. B-26s bombed the docks just before we arrived—which helped to warm things up for us.
>
> As we approached, we saw three B-26s pass under us, being chased by four Zeros. There were plenty of clouds, so we were not seen. A few minutes later, we saw more Zeros, but gave them the slip in the clouds. We picked up three transports off Rabaul Harbor, took pictures from low altitude of York Island, just off the mouth of the harbor. On our last trip over we got some AA fire, which put a small hole in our tail and then saw a Zero closing in. We took to the clouds and headed for home. While passing over St. George Channel, we picked up a surfaced submarine. We strafed it and it immediately disappeared beneath the surface. Hope we sank it or at least did some major damage. Had a lot of fun this day.[14]

The other B-25, flown by Keeter and Stephenson, also returned to Port Moresby to refuel for the trip home. Their reconnaissance that day had included photographing Japanese installations at ports along the Bismarck Sea, including Madang northwest of Lae, Lorengau on the island of Manus, and Cape Cloucester on the northwestern tip of New Britain. They reported their findings to the intelligence officer at Seven-Mile Airdrome, and if they were lucky, obtained an estimate of the weather conditions for the trip back.[15]

Although Stephenson was a captain, control of the plane was assigned to 2nd Lt. John Jefferson Keeter from Throckmorton, Texas. Raised on a ranch where he was the oldest of eight children, Keeter developed an interest in flight at an early age. One year at the Throckmorton County Fair, a barnstormer pilot flew into town and landed in a nearby airfield. He flew people over Throckmorton for the princely sum of three dollars. The youngster scraped together the money, took his first airplane ride, and was hooked on flying. He got his pilot's license while a student at Texas A&M. Although Keeter had just arrived in Australia from the States in late February with the 3rd Bomb Group, he was a B-25 veteran compared to Stephenson because of his recent participation in Royce's Raid—he simply had more hours in the Mitchell. Keeter was a flying-school classmate with Harry Mangan in 1940 and was considered an excellent flyer. Second Lt. Wesley E. Dickinson, another pilot with the 3rd, thought Keeter the best of the new young pilots. In the skies over Savannah, they had mock dogfights in the PT-17 two-wing primary trainers. Keeter, Dickinson recalled, always won.

The other second lieutenant on the flight, Eugene Tisonyai from Coshockton, Ohio, held the all-important position of navigator. Tisonyai attended Ohio State on a baseball scholarship and graduated in 1939. He then trained at Maxwell Air Base in Montgomery, Alabama, before leaving for the Southwest Pacific. Like Keeter, Tisonyai was a Royce's Raid veteran.

The bombardier was TSgt. William Lancaster from Nashville, Tennessee. Although the flight was not technically carrying bombs, Lancaster provided another set of eyes to spot Japanese ships. James English from New Orleans was the engineer. The two gunners were Sgt. Jimmy Morris, also a Royce's Raid veteran, and SSgt. George DeArmond, both from Louisiana. DeArmond, twenty-six, doubled as the radio man and had married a Savannah girl just weeks before the 3rd left Hunter Field for Australia in February 1942. He and Stephenson were the only married men on the flight.

The plane took off and the pilots set a south-southwest course for Australia. The return flight could often be just as dangerous as the flight over

17. Crewmembers of B-25 #41-12455 during its fateful reconnaissance mission of April 21, 1942. Seated in cockpit is the pilot, 2nd Lt. John Keeter. Wearing dress uniform and hat is the navigator, 2nd Lt. Eugene Tisonyai. In uniform without a hat is the gunner and radio operator, SSgt. George DeArmond. *Courtesy the Keeter, Tisonyai, and DeArmond families*

Japanese-held areas. There was always the weather. Cyclones occasionally hit Queensland at this time of year, and rainsqualls were a daily occurrence. Flying around or through these storms presented challenges. Fierce winds, accompanied by lightning and hail, could also blow a B-25 off course.

For the first portion of the approximately 740-mile flight back to base, they probably set the plane on light cruise, which used approximately 120 gallons of fuel per hour. By the time they hit the Australian coast, they would have more than enough fuel to make Charters Towers. There was likely idle chatter throughout the plane as the Mitchell headed south. In the nose Tisonyai was busy plotting the return trip and calling intermittently on the interphone system with new course headings. As the plane neared the coast north of Cairns, Stephenson and Keeter could see bad weather. Radioman George DeArmond sent Charters Towers a message in Morse code letting them know the bomber's position, which was still over water. It was now 6:10 P.M.

The pilots checked the compass heading and talked over the interphone system to Tisonyai. With the mass of ominous dark clouds ahead, they slowly lowered the plane because they did not want to be caught above the overcast when they reached land. Pilots returning from Port Moresby would try to approach the coast near Cairns and follow the coastline south until they saw a landmark—a point, an island, a river, a mountain, a road—which would be used as a reference by the navigator to plot a new course to Charters Towers. It was 6:15.

Keeter probably spoke over the interphone system and ordered the other six sets of eyes to scan in all directions and let him know when a landmark was spotted. Maps in April 1942 were often misleading. For instance, the Survey Branch, Department of Interior, located at Canberra, most likely compiled the map used by the crew of B-25 #41-12455, and it usually indicated only the highest peak in a mountain range.[16] In this case that peak would be the 5,284-foot South Peak of Mount Bartle Frere. If the crew, in fact, knew that they were on a correct heading from the Cairns area back to Charters Towers, then according to that map, they would safely pass just to the east of South Peak. The height of the nearby peaks, like North Peak, was not shown.

Darkness was rapidly descending on Queensland. Storm clouds partially blocked the sun. It was hard enough to spot objects thousands of feet below the bomber, let alone look at a map in a dimly lit cockpit. Pilots sometimes aborted their landing attempt at Charters Towers in bad weather and went back to Cairns. Was the crew considering that option? Also, pilots attempting to land in the dark usually used the lighted runways of the Garbutt Airfield in Townsville, forty miles east of Charters Towers and along the coast. Were they contemplating that alternative?

The pilots kept an eye on the fuel gauge. If enemy aircraft were not in the area, they would have had time to take on 670 gallons, which filled the wing tanks, before leaving Port Moresby. That would have been more than enough to reach Charters Towers, Cairns, or Townsville. Tisonyai gave his best guess as to the location based on the compass heading and other factors. It was now 6:30. They hoped to beat the clock on the rapidly descending darkness. Depending on weather conditions, in the distance the coast could have been sighted.

As Keeter guided the plane through the turbulence and toward the coastline, a few faint lights might have been seen from towns and villages along the coast. But what towns were they? After three weeks at the base, crews on the ground still had difficulty traveling the streets of Charters Towers in broad daylight, let alone recognizing Queensland's landmarks from the darkening evening sky. Although the government initiated limited war-related evening blackouts, it was still possible to see lights below. Tisonyai again checked his calculations. He tried to compute the wind speed to see if maybe they had drifted off course. Were they lost, as a few believed? If they mistakenly thought they were on an accurate course to the airbase from east of the Bellender Ker Range, then the only obstacle ahead was Mount Halifax, northeast of Charters Towers, which rose to only 3,486 feet. It was now 6:49.

Some, however, believe that they knew their exact location and were following Highway 1 from Cairns, that they were about to fly right down the middle of the mountain range through the Mulgrave River valley. At 6:50 they passed above the small town of Edmonton on Highway 1. A minute later they were over Gordonvale, which was seven miles north of Babinda, and were about to enter the Bellenden Ker Range. Gordonvale generally had less cloud cover than the Babinda area, but this evening was an exception. It is possible that in the approaching darkness and low storm clouds, the crew never saw that their landmark, Highway 1, curved to the southeast after Gordonvale toward the Coral Sea in order to go east around the mountains and then continue on to Townsville. Seventeen-year-old George Perkins heard the plane flying over the Mulgrave River as he was felling scrub in the Goldsborough Valley. Although he could not actually see the plane, it seemed to be flying low. Flying over his farm, the bomber frightened his cattle in the corral. Perkins thought the plane might have been lost as it seemingly started to climb and turn west to avoid Walsh's Pyramid.

By 6:53, B-25 #41-12455 had passed the Pyramid but was dangerously close to Mount Massey and Mount Harold, all nearly 4,000 feet tall. If the crew saw the peaks off to the left, they might have thought they were safely flying down a valley that had an exit to Charters Towers or Townsville at the far end. Maybe they thought they could save some valuable time in the approaching darkness by flying between the mountains instead of around them. They probably did not know that there was a dead end to the Mulgrave River valley. They were six minutes away from the 5,000-foot North Peak of Mount Bartle Frere, a peak whose altitude was probably not on their map.

Down below, on Stager Road two miles southwest of Babinda, Lido Poppi and his family were just sitting down for supper. It was 6:57. Just then Lido heard the engines of a large plane overhead. Something did not seem right to him. Large planes usually did not fly over Babinda. (Even today, planes flying from the south to Cairns, just north of Babinda, go out over the sea on their eastern path into Cairns or fly well to the west of the mountain when approaching from the west.) Worse yet, Lido thought, this one also seemed too low to be flying near Mount Bartle Frere.

In Happy Valley, also southwest of Babinda and near the eastern base of Mount Bartle Frere, the time was 6:58, and thirty-three-year-old Karl Stager was changing stations on his wireless. He too thought it strange that what sounded like a large airplane would be passing overhead at this time of night, in this kind of weather, with Mount Bartle Frere nearby. He turned down his radio and walked outside.

Back at Charters Towers, a worried Davies ordered men to be ready to light the flare pots that lined the runway for ship #41-12455. He was hoping the bomber would land at any minute.

In the cockpit there was almost certainly confusion. It was very difficult to see anything in the rainsquall. The layer of clouds and fog surrounding Mount Bartle Frere reduced visibility to near zero.

Karl Stager remembered: "It was fairly dark and cloudy. I could hear the plane from my verandah. When I first heard the engines they appeared to be running all right, but I could not see the plane or any navigation lights. After a few seconds, I heard the engines of the plane stop and the sky was lit like a half moon in a westerly direction."

Lido Poppi was about to go back into his house "when suddenly the sound of the engines cut out, and at the same instance, there was a bright flash. It lit the clouds as plain as can be. Then there was a bright glow that lasted for a minute or so, and then it slowly died down, and that was it."

It was 6:59. Karl Stager went inside to call the police station. The theme music for the 7:00 P.M. ABC News was just beginning. B-25 #41-12455 sliced through the trees and jungle in a straight line. Lido Poppi, who days later was with the search team, described the bomber's contact with the vegetation this way: "Dead level, straight as a die, pruned like a hedge, like you would with a whipper snipper." It probably had not deviated off the course it had set minutes before.[17]

The plane first contacted the thirty- to fifty-foot tops of the trees lining Mount Bartle Frere's slopes. They barely slowed the plane. In a split second the bomber hit the face of the North Peak at approximately 150 mph. The impact disintegrated the plexiglass nose and pushed back the pilot's compartment. The engines too were forced back from the front edge of the wing. The portions of the wing beyond the engines that were riveted to the inboard wing broke off. Fuel lines running to the engines were severed and fuel tanks ruptured. An estimated two hundred gallons of high-test gasoline sprayed out from the aircraft, dousing the vegetation in all directions.

The volatile fuel too had been moving at 150 mph. It hit engine hot spots and immediately ignited, and instantaneously the gas-coated foliage burst into flames. The heat set off a barrage of machine-gun bullets that exited through the metal ammunition boxes stored in the plane. Flares ignited. The sky around Mount Bartle Frere was filled with the bright glow from the raging flames. Rain and the thick, damp vegetation, however, quickly extinguished the inferno.

The plane creaked, groaned, hissed, and slowly, almost as in slow motion, slumped into the gully under the North Peak. Another three hundred feet of altitude, and B-25 #41-12455 would have missed the North Peak and made the gold-speckled runways of Charters Towers or the lighted runways of Townsville.

Shortly after hearing the bomber fly over and presumably smash into the mountain, the Babinda townspeople conducted their own search, without success. They were anxious to find out exactly what kind of plane it was. There was a rumor circulating that it was Japanese and sent to bomb the Babinda Sugar Mill. Also, a Guinea Airways plane had gone missing that day with twelve people aboard, and some in Babinda thought that it was wrecked on the mountain.[18] A small single-engine Wirraway from Cairns was called in a day or so later to search the mountain. After finally spotting the crash site, the pilot flew low over Babinda and dropped the following message on the local football field: "Have located burnt patch approximately 4300 ft. up southwest in dead line with plantation. Will circle town and fly as near as possible. Endeavor [to] get bearings."

A Babinda official, Mr. J. C. Williams, a member of the local detachment of the Volunteer Defence Corps, grabbed a compass and watched as the plane, piloted by Tommy McDonald, a Cairns aviator, flew twice over the village to indicate the direction of the crash. Other aircraft also took part in the search. A plane piloted by Colonel Davies may have been among them.[19]

Mount Bartle Frere is Queensland's highest mountain and is 180 miles to the north of Charters Towers. Its tallest peak is 5,284 feet. Its slopes are covered by rain forest. The average monthly rainfall from January to mid-April is 30 inches. The yearly rainfall average is 150 inches. Locals say that when you cannot see the mountain, it is raining; when you can, it is about to rain. Roads, paths, and some of the caves were remnants of the area's gold-mining era many years earlier. Aussie Garth Gray described Mount Bartle Frere's slopes this way: "Very rough, steep and covered with impenetrable jungle. Lots of mud and leeches, and the rocks are covered with mould [*sic*] which if wet is slipperyer [*sic*] than greased glass. The forest is laced with stinging trees and wait-a-while [also called the lawyer vine, for once one gets into its clutches, it is very hard to get away]. Most of the snakes are harmless."

Keeter's fellow pilots from the 3rd had trouble accepting that his plane was missing. Second Lieutenant Dickinson exclaimed: "Jesus, Keeter of all people. I can't believe it. He was a hell of a good pilot." Another second lieutenant, Leo Baker, remarked: "I couldn't believe it. He could fly rings around the rest of us."[20]

The accident scene was horrific. By the time searchers arrived on April 29, the stench of decaying flesh was overwhelming. Those in the nose, the navigator and the bombardier, received the worst of the impact. Bill Wakeham, one of those first to arrive on the scene days later, recalled, "Intestines were strung up in trees, no bodies were whole, heads were off, feet were in boots, and everything was burnt." The remains were buried in seven side-by-side shallow graves. After this task was completed, some of the local searchers grabbed a souvenir—a propeller, a machine-gun bullet, a box of tools—and descended the mountain.

On May 1, ten days after the crash, the "official" search party of the local police, volunteers, and U.S. Army representatives Davies, medical officer 1st Lt. Edward G. Jeruss, Chaplain Joseph W. James, and 1st Sgt. Clarence E. McCain, finally arrived. They unearthed the graves and set about the grisly task of identifying the bodies. Some, most likely those at the rear of the B-25, were not as badly mutilated and still had their dog tags on. Identification for those in the front was more difficult. For instance, Tisonyai's dog tags were found alone on the ground. On the left hand of one body was a shiny ring etched with the words "West Point" and "Duty, Honor, Country." Those remains were placed in a body bag and marked "Captain Glenwood Gordon Stephenson."

Davies located the Norden bombsight, which was top secret, and according to the locals, used a tomahawk to destroy it. The officials then marked the graves individually with seven crudely made crosses, each bearing the name of one of the seven men.

Aftermath of the Crash of Bomber #41-12455

On his return to Charters Towers, Davies turned over all personal effects to 1st Lt. Phillip A. Kulin. He gathered the few other items from Stephenson's locker at Charters Towers, placed everything in a box, and shipped it all to 412 E. Duffy Street, Savannah, Georgia. A month later Stephenson's widow, Ann, opened a package that contained a few items of clothing, a raincoat, some pictures of her, a pair of wings, and a West Point ring.

Later that year another party ascended Mount Bartle Frere to retrieve the bodies. The graves were unearthed, and new body bags were placed around the old. The remains were removed from the mountain and placed in lead-lined caskets. Briefly, the coffins sat on the verandah of the Babinda Courthouse. Days later they were taken to a cemetery, some reports state in Ipswich in southern Queensland, for burial. Another source indicates they were interred on December 14, 1942, at the U.S. Military Cemetery in Townsville.[21]

Why were the bodies taken off the mountain during this phase of the war? Some say the U.S. military, true to the idea of "Leave No One Behind," decided to retrieve the remains. Many Australian sources, however, hold to the myth that one of the pilots' fathers was a powerful American millionaire who subsequently placed pressure on the U.S. government to return the bodies. Some Australian sources even identified this man as being Stephenson's father. Nothing, however, could have been further from the truth. At the time of the crash, Gordon Stephenson, who had financially barely survived the Depression, was unemployed and living in Milwaukee.

After the war the bodies were exhumed from the cemetery. Four were returned to the United States for burial. Stephenson and two others were reburied in the National Military Cemetery in Hawaii, known as the Punchbowl. The cemetery overlooks Pearl Harbor, where on December 7, 1941, the lives of Glenwood Stephenson; his wife, Ann; his family in Wisconsin; and all American citizens were changed forever.

The exact cause of the crash has never been determined. One theory is that someone in the plane spotted the Mulgrave River through a break in the clouds over Gordonvale and thought it was the Burdekin River, which was just north and east of their Charters Towers base. With darkness fast approaching, Keeter would have eased back on the throttle to slow the plane and get a better look. He might have thought, "Other crews had successfully hedgehopped the Burdekin in bad weather to return safely to base, why can't we?" Just south of Gordonvale, the Mulgrave bends to the west, makes a half circle back to the southeast, continues south toward Mount Bartle Frere like a reverse question mark, and then branches in two directions and stops only a few miles (a minute by B-25) short of the North Peak. Interestingly, when pilots flying from Cairns to Charters Towers first spot the Burdekin, it also has the aerial appearance of a reversed question mark. In the approaching darkness, could the men have mistaken the two rivers?

Some other theories are founded on what was known about the weather conditions in Queensland at the time. The weather at the time was described as overcast with low clouds and light showers squalling across from the southeast.[22] A logical explanation could be that the plane was blown off course by a storm, got lost, and the crew did not realize how dangerously close they were to the cloud-and-fog-shrouded Mount Bartle Frere. Winds generally come out of the southeast off the ocean and blow toward the mountain. After finding a landmark, like Highway 1, near Cairns and then plotting a course back to Charters or Townsville, the bomber hit the strong winds, and the crew perhaps did not realize how rapidly they were being pushed inland.

It is also possible that the B-25's compass went haywire. Some believe that the magnetism in the mountain might have affected the compass and sent the crew on a tragic heading over the Bellenden Ker Range rather than around it. Others speculate that the bomber simply ran out of fuel, but the plane was flying dead level when it hit Mount Bartle Frere. If they filled the wing tanks, they should have had enough. Ralph Schmidt's diary entry of April 14 (after No. 41-12455 had returned from Royce's Raid) suggests another potential cause when he mentions that the airplane "was full of bullet holes."

Others hypothesize that the legendary gung-ho attitude of American flyers might have been a contributing factor. Many Australians were both amazed and alarmed during the war by Yank pilots' disregard for things like thick cloud cover and high mountains. One Aussie veteran observed: "To an

Aussie or a British pilot, a safe distance to clear a mountain was somewhere around 1,000 feet. To a Yank, an inch was as good as a mile!"[23] Were Keeter and Stephenson between a rock and a hard place—too low to fly over the mountain's North Peak but too high to see vital landmarks because they were engulfed by clouds and rain squalls? Before they could decide what to do, they hit Mount Bartle Frere. (For commentary on the crash by two former 27th/3rd Bomb Group pilots, see appendix 3.)

10

The Changing Tides of War

FLUSH WITH QUICK, easy victories, except of course for Bataan and Corregidor, the Japanese Navy that spring considered the possible conquest of Australia as the next logical step in denying the Americans a staging area in the Southwest Pacific. Although Australia had a population of only seven million and many of its combat units were off fighting elsewhere, the Japanese Army thought the country was too vast a land to adequately invade and manage. Their proposal to counter the expected U.S. buildup was to capture island groups like Fiji, Samoa, and the Solomons to the east and northeast of Australia as well as New Caledonia. From these islands, the Japanese could then dispatch waves of bombers to cover the intended U.S. supply route and send the anticipated convoys to the bottom of the Coral Sea. Australia would then be isolated and effectively out of the war.

Japanese intentions were twofold. First, they wanted to establish a base in the Solomons, six hundred miles to the east of Port Moresby, New Guinea. Second, they wanted to capture Port Moresby itself, considered essential to their perimeter defense in the region.[1] If they had this harbor, they could deny the Americans a staging and refueling base from which to attack Japanese-held islands. Allied planes flying from Charters Towers then would have a difficult time reaching the occupied islands and returning to base afterward. MacArthur's plan, which called for moving troops up the island chain toward the Philippines, also required Port Moresby as a vital stepping stone. To go on the offensive, the Americans unquestionably wanted to retain the town. If the Japanese captured it, they, in turn, could attack targets along Australia's northeastern coast, including Queensland's ports and Charters Towers airfield.

Port Moresby

While search and recovery operations were still underway on Mount Bartle Frere, the 3rd Bombardment Group continued bombing runs over New Guinea and reconnaissance operations over the Coral and Solomon seas, looking for Japanese naval activity. On April 24 Hubbard led a mission of six well-armed B-25s from Charters Towers and headed to Port Moresby as their staging point. They were to attack the Japanese airdrome at Lae the next day. Hubbard was in the lead plane in the loose formation, which ran into a series of severe thunderstorms shortly after takeoff. He had all he could handle maintaining control of the bomber when he considered the possibility of lightning setting off the bomb fuses. He wished he never thought about it. As the bomber neared Port Moresby, the cloud buildup seemed to indicate the presence of the rugged Owen Stanley Mountains. After descending to five hundred feet to get a better view, Hubbard guided the plane through the mountains to a safe landing. His B-25 and another piloted by Harold Maull were the only ones that made it to Port Moresby—one stayed behind at Charters Towers with mechanical problems and three had to ditch in the Coral Sea. The mission was scrubbed.

The next morning a large force of Japanese bombers and fighters were sighted headed his way, and Hubbard was ordered to evacuate the airdrome immediately. Once safely in the air, he announced over the intercom: "I hate to carry this load of bombs all the way back to Charters Towers. We might as well go to Horn Island [off the north coast of Queensland] by way of Lae." He turned toward Lae and dropped his bombs, catching the Japanese completely by surprise. The B-25 made it back to Australia, where the crew was awarded the Silver Star for their effort.

According to Frank Bender, who had to ditch his B-25, the flight left Charters Towers so they would arrive at Port Moresby just before dark to avoid Japanese detection of the bombers on the ground. At one point, as Bender's plane neared New Guinea, the clouds opened and they saw enemy aircraft, which also might have spotted them. Then, according to Bender, they ran into a "granddaddy" of a thunderstorm. By the time the bomber approached the New Guinea coast, it was already fairly dark. The pilots could recognize the coastline by the white breaking waves below, but they had lost their orientation in the thunderstorm and were not sure on which side of Port Moresby they were. They flew up and down the coast in both directions. By this time it was dark, and the B-25 was almost out of fuel. Bender discussed the situation with the crew. They decided they would rather ditch the airplane in the water as a group than to bail out individually in the shark-infested waters. Bender stayed out from the shore for fear of hitting one of the rocky ledges that jetted out into the sea and difficult to see in the darkness. After crash landing in the sea, everyone got out of the plane and made it ashore. Bender had fractured bones in his left hand.

The following day natives took the Americans to a primitive plantation, about an eight-hour walk through the jungle. They met an Australian plantation owner whose wife and family had already been evacuated to the continent. They spent about a week there, afterward traveling to a mission and then eventually by boat to Port Moresby. Another boat took them to Townsville, where Bender was hospitalized with malaria and treated for his hand injuries. All of his crew survived. W. R. Johnson's B-25 crew also survived their ditching and made it back separately. William Barker and his crew, except for the top gunner, were all killed when their bomber crashed.

Besides bombing runs, the other 3rd Bomb Group task in late April and early May was to try and determine where the Japanese fleet was in this vast area so that Allied planes and ships could counter their moves. One day Launder was on a mission of B-25s flying single file over the Coral Sea. About halfway to Port Moresby they hit a squall line. Launder remarked: "Let me tell you about squall lines in the southwest Pacific. They are hairballs of the first magnitude." His ship was positioned several miles behind Deke Emerson, flying at about five hundred feet above the water when both planes entered dark clouds. Suddenly, the other B-25 came straight at Launder out of the mist. Emerson, who had entered the squall, did not like it and decided to turn around. To avoid colliding with Launder's ship, he yanked back on the yoke, sending his bomber into a stall from which it could not recover before hitting the water.[2]

By the end of April, two U.S. fighter units were stationed at Port Moresby: the 35th and the 36th U.S. Army Pursuit Squadrons. Both flew single-engine Bell P-39 Airacobras. Unfortunately, the pilots soon learned that the early version of the Airacobra was a turkey, even when Buzz Wagner of the 5th Fighter Command led the squadrons in some of the outings.[3] Mangan recalled: "The P-39s were no match for the Zero. The pilots were told not to engage them because they would be 'dead meat.'" The P-39s soon were assigned to attacking ground targets. Launder felt the same way as Mangan about the aircraft in a dogfight. "The P-39 was a flying coffin if you happened to find yourself in one facing a Zero or two."[4]

During this time, General Royce vented his frustrations in trying to help support the U.S. Navy South Pacific Command. He was not told where naval vessels were or what they were doing. All he knew was that, with only a few hours notice, he was asked to cooperate in some faraway naval action. With his strike force in Queensland, the bombers had to fly about six hundred miles to Port Moresby and refuel before even heading out on a mission. Because of this, it was frequently impossible to comply with navy requests for bombing support.[5]

The Battle of the Coral Sea

The Americans knew the Japanese operational intentions in the region. Intelligence had broken the top-secret Japanese naval code and learned that a contingent of cruisers, destroyers, battleships, and aircraft carriers—the *Zuikaku* and *Shokaku*—were in the Coral Sea to prevent U.S. ships and planes from harassing the landing of troops and equipment in the Solomons around May 3. They also knew that a week later the Japanese intended to invade Port Moresby. Up to this point in history, naval battles were usually fought with ships in visual contact firing at each other from relatively short distances. The Battle of the Coral Sea was contested in a different manner.

Both navies knew that land- and carrier-based planes sinking each other's ships would probably determine the outcome. Pearl Harbor had already demonstrated what air power could do against a battleship. Both sides deployed their battleships, cruisers, and destroyers around their carriers to form a protective screen, concentrating their antiaircraft fire so that low-flying planes trying to drop bombs and torpedoes against the carriers would never survive the run to the target. Spotting the enemy first would be important in determining the winner.

The atmosphere with the U.S. Navy forces approaching the Coral Sea was described as "watchful, tense." They knew that "strong Jap forces were on the prowl, defeating Allied forces wherever encountered."[6]

The Battle of the Coral Sea was fought over a five-day period in early May 1942 and proved to be a giant chess game played out by ships and planes.

On the first day of May, the Third Group started running patrols from Charters Towers east over the Great Barrier Reef and out over the Pacific towards New Caledonia. Three or four planes went out each morning. The crews would get up at two-o'clock for a cup of coffee and would then be briefed by Captain [1st Lieutenant] McAfee. Take-off was usually at four-thirty. Then a long eight or nine hours of searching for enemy shipping. These patrols were sent out until the end of the Battle of the Coral Sea.[7]

Former 27th pilot Henry Rose flew a reconnaissance mission on May 2 to Bougainville Island in the Solomons, about six hundred miles northeast of Port Moresby.

His ship was some 2½ hours out of Moresby when the right engine objected strenuously with three loud barks. Slightly repulsed at the idea of swimming home, Rose started his return to Moresby. Dodging through thunderstorms, he was suddenly surprised at the beautiful but ugly sight of a Japanese sea-going submarine fully surfaced about a mile ahead. Without bombs, probably as surprised as the Jap lookout on deck, he attempted to sink a sub with machine gunfire—his success remaining a master of complete speculation except that the answer could only be a loud NO!

Engine repaired, the morning of the 3rd of May, he was ordered to fly a cross-course search with J. R. Smith. Lost, slightly bewildered already, Rose was first finding himself by buzzing Buka Passage [a channel between Buka and Bougainville] when a four-engine flying boat came cruising by. Having identified it as a Jap, not a U.S. Navy ship [airplane], Rose proceeded to try to use a B-25 as a P-shooter [fighter], makes one pass and then is joined by J. R. Smith. Together they made pass after pass at the Jap, but after 35 minutes running fight during which some 3,000 rounds were fired by both, the flying boat remained airborne and they were forced due to lack of gas and some very large holes in Smith's ship to return to Moresby—sadder than wiser.[8]

Hubbard described that episode as comparable to an old-time naval engagement with ships sailing along, side-by-side, blasting away at each other.

Birnn, having returned to Moresby with another ship, asked to be sent to a quiet area on his mission for the 4th because his lower turret was out. On the mission he was suddenly startled to see three uncharted islands ahead. Which on closer investigation, turned out to be the Jap's largest aircraft carrier and two very heavy, heavy cruisers. Returning to Port Moresby, he flew over a sub tender, alongside of which two subs. Both crashed dived before he could strafe them.

The morning of the fifth, Rose was ordered to locate the carrier *Shokaku* and report the position of the carrier Birnn had seen. Then he was to circle, sending a steady signal so that the B-17s could home on him and bomb the Jap ships. These orders were carried out and he remained in the immediate vicinity for slightly over an hour dodging Jap Zero fighters by hide and seek tactics through the clouds. Forced to return to Port Moresby, Rose found that the B-17s had never taken off.[9]

Another source indicates that Lee Walker, a former 27th pilot then with the 3rd and flying a B-25, sighted a carrier with two destroyers as escorts on May 5, shadowing the enemy vessels for an hour while reporting their location. A swarm of Zeros eventually drove him off. After he called in the location, a ground dispatcher in turn called the 19th Bomb Group, whose B-17s were on patrol in the same area but were unable to locate the enemy ships.[10] It may well be that Rose and Walker were pilot and copilot in the same B-25.

By May 5 all three active squadrons of the 3rd were either at Port Moresby or brought up to the town, anticipating engagement with the Japanese invasion force. On May 6 Gus Heiss from the 3rd located a big ship and two destroyer escorts and reported their position.[11] A few days later Heiss was about to take off from Port Moresby when his B-25 was strafed by Zeros. A bullet smashed through a window, grazed Heiss in the back, and then went through the head of the copilot, Vernon Heidinger, who was killed instantly. Their crew chief was killed by machine-gun fire while running from the plane.

The Japanese drew first blood on May 7, when planes from the *Zuikaku* and *Shokaku* attacked the American tanker USS *Neosho* and its destroyer escort, the USS *Sims,* disabling both. The Japanese at first erroneously thought the *Neosho* was a carrier. Mistaking ship types was one problem both sides encountered during the battle. Likewise, there were numerous instances of both sides thinking "friendlies" were enemies and vice versa. On May 7 an American reconnaissance pilot reported what he thought was the main Japanese fleet. About forty carrier-based planes were launched only to find that the "Japanese Fleet" consisted of two old cruisers and three converted gunboats. The American planes faced only nine Japanese fighters in that brief encounter.

During this time, ships under MacArthur's command also cooperated with the U.S. task force. This group consisted of three cruisers, two Australian and one American, and a few destroyers, searching for the Japanese invasion force. On May 7 these Allied ships successfully warded off attacks by both Japanese and Americans aircraft, land-based bombers from Rabaul and B-17s from Townsville.[12]

Finally, on May 8, reconnaissance flights from the two opposing carrier groups almost simultaneously found the other's main fleet. The U.S. carriers, the *Yorktown* and the *Lexington*, launched almost ninety planes that morning to attack the Japanese fleet 175 miles away. Simultaneously, the *Shokaku* and the *Zuikaku* did likewise. Many of the Japanese pilots were cagey Pearl Harbor veterans. The *Yorktown* pilots severely damaged the *Shokaku* but could not sink her. Meanwhile, Japanese fighters and bombers persistently attacked the *Lexington*. By the end of the afternoon, the carrier was on fire, and its remaining airborne planes had to land on the *Yorktown*. By early evening the order was given to abandon the *Lexington*, and by nightfall American torpedoes sent her to the bottom; U.S. naval leaders did not want the carrier to become a floating propaganda prize for the enemy.

During the Battle of the Coral Sea, the 8th Squadron of the 3rd Bomb Group, with its A-24 dive bombers, was standing by at Port Moresby. Launder recalled that Buck Rogers gave the pilots a pep talk about them being the only ones to stop the Japanese fleet when it came within range. "It sounded more like a death sentence," he said. The pilots got their parachutes and went to the operation shack to await the orders to take off. Minutes ticked by slowly. Finally, one of the pilots strolled over to the Aussie radio room, and the operator was exchanging messages with the ships in the Coral Sea already engaging the enemy. The A-24s were not needed.[13]

Adm. Chester Nimitz, commander of the U.S. Pacific Fleet, ordered the American fleet to retreat from the Coral Sea. The Japanese fleet pressed forward, looking to finish the *Yorktown*, but fortunately turned in the wrong direction. By the end of the battle, two of Japan's large fleet carriers were out of action. Experts estimated that it would take up to three months to repair the *Shokaku*. The number of pilots and airplanes on the *Zuikaku* were so depleted that the Japanese Navy calculated it would take at least a couple of months to bring the fresh pilots just out of training up to combat readiness.[14]

In addition to these losses, a smaller Japanese aircraft carrier, a destroyer, and some other vessels had been sunk. The Americans lost the carrier *Lexington* (along with the *Neosho* and *Sims* earlier), and the *Yorktown* was badly damaged. The Japanese erroneously thought the *Yorktown* was sunk too. In addition, sixty-six U.S. planes were lost, and 543 men died. The Battle of the Coral Sea appeared to be a Japanese victory, but strategically, the Americans won. Japanese plans to expand to the south were foiled, and Port Moresby remained in Allied hands. After assessing their loss of planes and combat crews in the Coral Sea, planners decided to suspend the invasion of Port Moresby until early July. The Japanese thus were denied the base they needed to knock out air power from Australia.[15]

Perhaps, most importantly, the Combined Fleet was deprived of two of its large aircraft carriers for the next operation—but the Japanese high command was so overconfident of success, they thought they did not need these carriers anyway.[16] The next encounter was the decisive Battle of Midway the following month, when the Japanese fleet was soundly defeated and lost four aircraft carriers, all veterans of Pearl Harbor. Two more carriers might have made the difference in that battle. The *Yorktown*, in contrast, was rapidly repaired at Pearl Harbor and returned to fight at Midway (though finally destroyed in that battle).[17]

Noteworthy military observations were made during the Coral Sea action. The U.S. Navy's confidence was given a boost when sailors realized that the Japanese "fight to the death" mentality was not unbeatable. Naval leaders realized that future major battles in the Pacific would soon be fought without ship-to-ship interface. Many surface battles were yet to be fought, including the Battle of the Leyte Gulf, the biggest naval engagement in history in terms of naval tonnage, however carrier-based planes and submarines would replace the battleship as the naval weapons of choice by the end of the war. The Americans as yet did not have a fighter to match the Zero's maneuverability, but they realized that the Zeros had neither adequate armor nor self-sealing gas tanks. A well-placed burst by an American pilot usually resulted in a dead Japanese pilot in a burning Zero.

The Americans also learned that there was inadequate sharing of Allied reconnaissance information with the U.S. Navy, which might have been an important contribution to the battle. Apparently, the sighting of enemy aircraft carriers and other warships on May 4 and 5 by the 3rd Bombardment Group and others from MacArthur's command were not received by Rear Adm. Frank Fletcher, the task-force commander. The exact location of these enemy ships was not known by the navy until May 7. But it also seems that information was not flowing in the other direction. A B-25 crew returning to Port Moresby from a strike on an enemy ship sighted "other aircraft" attacking the same Japanese vessel. This was their first clue that the U.S. Navy was in the neighborhood.[18] During that crucial month, the 3rd's B-25s flew more than 120 over-water reconnaissance missions.[19]

Corregidor Surrenders

The rise in confidence and the initial successes in the Coral Sea were tempered somewhat by the news on May 6 that the Stars and Stripes was lowered on Corregidor. MacArthur issued the following statement: "Corregidor needs no comment from me. It has sounded its own story at the mouth of its guns. It has scrolled its own epitaph on enemy tablets. But through the bloody haze of its last reverberating shot, I shall always seem to see a vision of grim, gaunt, ghastly men, still unafraid."

Among those "grim, gaunt, ghastly men" were some from the 27th and several West Point classmates of McAfee, Stephenson, Stirling, and Summers. The actual surrender, which was not simple, occurred after weeks of massive artillery and aerial bombardment and while Japanese infantry and armor were overrunning portions on the island. Wainwright began sending radio messages to Homma at 10:30 A.M. on the sixth, but the Japanese land assault, artillery barrages, and air attacks continued. The radio station, The Voice of Freedom, continued to send surrender messages in English and Japanese. At noon the U.S. flag was taken down and a white bedsheet raised.

Around 1:00 P.M. a Japanese officer on the island was made aware of these intentions, and soon word came down that Wainwright would be taken over to Bataan at 4:00 P.M. While he waited to meet Homma there, Japanese reporters and photographers spent about a half hour photographing and filming him and his accompanying staff officers. When Homma arrived and learned from Wainwright that he was only willing to surrender Corregidor and the three fortified islands in Manila Bay, not the rest of the Philippines, he went into a rage and refused to accept the American's surrender offer. Wainwright was taken back to Corregidor. His troops had already surrendered, but Japanese artillery continued to pound parts of the island as the terms of surrender were worked out. By threatening to massacre all of the men on Corregidor, Homma compelled Wainwright to broadcast on a Manila radio station late the following night that all other troops under his command in the Philippines must surrender.

MacArthur sent General Sharp on Mindanao a message to the effect that orders emanating from Wainwright had no validity. "If possible, separate your force into small elements and initiate guerilla operations. You, of course, have authority to make any decision that [the] immediate emergency demands." Nevertheless, Sharp surrendered his troops on May 10 for fear that his comrades on Corregidor would be executed if he did otherwise. General Chynoweth on Cebu reluctantly surrendered his troops on May 16, and Col. Albert F. Christie, commanding the garrison on Panay, surrendered on May 18. The last subordinate unit did not surrender until June 9. Some Filipino battalions and other guerrilla groups never capitulated.

POWs from the other three fortified islands were brought to Corregidor,

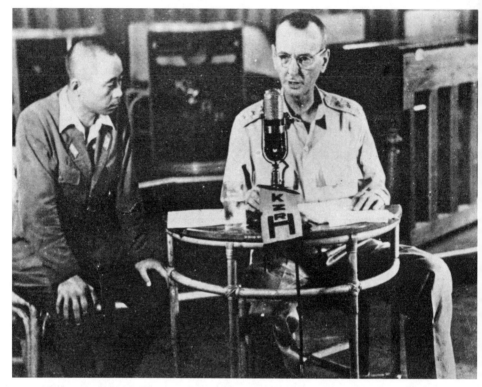

18. Maj. Gen. Jonathan Wainwright at a Manila radio station, where he began broadcasting surrender instructions just before midnight, May 7, 1942. *Courtesy Gen. Douglas MacArthur Foundation*

where the total number of men swelled to more than 12,000. They were kept there under threat of annihilation for two additional weeks while terms of the surrender were being fulfilled.

The army hospital in Malinta Tunnel was allowed to function, but otherwise American and Filipino prisoners were herded into an area only fifteen hundred feet long by five hundred feet wide, where they would remain until removed to POW camps. The conditions were reported to be appalling. Thousands of biting blue-black flies swarmed everywhere. Many corpses lay nearby and were horribly swollen. Sanitation was totally inadequate. Soon POWs were assigned the task of collecting and disposing of the dead soldiers.

The food and water situation remained critical. The Japanese took what they wanted of the food supplies on the island and rationed what was left. Cpl. Calvin Swanson of the 91st Squadron recalled about the water problems: "The pressure from the water system wasn't very good. You'd have to wait all day to get a canteen full of water." About the food situation he said: "The flies were so bad that any time you had any food, they just totally cover it. Many died of dehydration due to lack of water and their diarrhea. My belief is that if they had kept us another week, there wouldn't have been many left to be taken to prison camps." Swanson and the other POWs were later moved to Manila, marched down Dewey Boulevard, and put on exhibition for the Filipinos, then placed in Bilibid Prison.

Twenty-seventh Bombardment Group Pilots in the 3rd

The 27th pilots who did escape the Philippines, however, were rapidly making a name for themselves with the 3rd Bomb Group. Both the 13th Squadron and the 90th Squadron now were flying B-25s. Port Moresby continued to be a vital airdrome for the Allies, and it was known that the Japanese were not going to give up in their effort to seize it.

On May 12 Ed Townsend of Brookings, South Dakota, who was another former 27th pilot at Charters Towers, crashed his B-25 at the end of the runway while taking off. Most believe he lost an engine during his run. His plane, carrying a full fuel load, reached an altitude of about one hundred feet when it suddenly started to veer to the left and crashed, bursting into flames. Townsend, who was badly burned, died a few days later.

On May 20 "Buck" Rogers got lost in bad weather on his way to Wau, about fifty miles south of Lae. He spotted a crashed B-25 at a small airstrip in the jungle and landed there to check on the condition of the crew members, who were from the 3rd Bomb Group. After talking with them, he flew on to Wau and subsequently returned to Port Moresby, where he was ordered to go back with two other pilots and their A-24s to retrieve some of the downed airmen. Two of those three pilots crashed while attempting to land—one because his engine cut out and the other because his plane hit a soft spot on the field. The pilot of the third A-24, who landed safely, was killed the next morning while trying to take off. Rogers, who sustained a broken nose, made it back to Port Moresby in about a month. It took Oliver "Ollie" Doan, the other former 27th pilot who had crashed on landing, about two months to return.[20]

Daily reconnaissance and bombing missions continued on the northeast coast of New Guinea, and the air over New Guinea and other nearby islands saw numerous dogfights. Not all turned out favorably for the 3rd. On May 25 the group suffered a terrible loss when five of the six B-25s that Capt. Herman Lowery, a former 27th pilot, was leading were shot down by Japanese fighters over Lae. McAfee recorded in his diary: "This is the worst day we

19. Third Bomb Group pilots who had previously served with the 27th Bomb Group in the Philippines (except Rubenstein and Strickland). This photograph was taken on the steps of the 3rd Bomb Group's officers' club, referred to variously as "The 3rd Slug House" and "The Last Slug," Charters Towers, October 1942. Top row, L to R: Sam Rubenstein, "Big Jim" Davies, James R. Smith, Henry Rose. 2nd row, L to R: Alex Salvatore, John C. Wienert, Zeke Summers. 3rd row, L to R: Ron Hubbard, Oliver Doan. 4th row, L to R: Harry Mangan, Howie West, Thomas "Pete" Talley. 5th row: Harry Galusha. 6th row, L to R: Robert "Fort" Hambaugh, Bob Ruegg, Pappy Gunn, Bob Strickland. Front row, L to R: Leland Walker, Francis Timlin, Jim McAfee. *Courtesy Maj. Gen. John H. Henebry and Mrs. Oliver Doan*

have ever had. Herman Lowery, Slim Wilson, Arlen Rulison, Shearer [who survived the war and died in 1989], [and] John Keel all shot down over Lae. Everyone is feeling terrible." Mangan wrote in diary about the losses: "Most of our trusty enlisted bombardiers and gunners, as well as the C.O. and the operation officer went down in one day. How the 13th [Squadron] will run without Herman remains to be seen. Well, guess we've all got to buck up and carry on."

The 3rd Bomb Group lost twelve B-25s in two weeks. An awards and promotions ceremony was held at Charters Towers a few days later, which was hastily arranged to help boost the low morale.

> From: 3rd Bomb Gp (L), Charters Towers, Qd.
> To: General Brett
> 3GB___5–26–42 NEED YOU BADLY NOW WITH PROMOTIONS COMMA MEDALS COMMA AND CITATIONS FOR 3RD BOMB GROUP STOP THEY GOT LOWERY YESTERDAY STOP AM SENDING AUSTRALIAN CO PILOTS TO BRISBANE IN EXCHANGE FOR AMERICAN CO PILOTS FROM THE AIR TRANSPORT COMMAND STOP JAPS NOW ATTACKING B-25S FROM FRONT KILLING PILOTS STOP THEY GOT FIVE B-25S OUT OF EIGHT YESTERDAY STOP UNTIL PROTECTION AFFORDED CAN EXPECT SAME RATIO OF LOSSES STOP THEY ARE STILL HITTING THE BALL [flying missions against the enemy], BUT NEED A LITTLE BOOST FROM THE SOUTH [FEAF Headquarters]
>
> DAVIES

General Brett attended, and almost all of the surviving pilots from the 27th were promised "battlefield" (temporary) promotions, which they would get a few days later. The three squadron leaders, who were all 27th veterans, were promoted to major: Floyd Rogers, Ron Hubbard, and Herman Lowery, though Lowery had been shot down and killed on the twenty-fifth. (The typewritten promotion order dated May 28 states that the rank is effective on "28 May, 1942.") Jim McAfee, Zeke Summers, Bob Ruegg, Gus Heiss, Tom Gerrity, Harry Galusha, and Jim Smith were promoted to captain. Henry Rose, Oliver Doan, Bob Hambaugh, Ralph Schmidt, Dick Birnn, Francis Timlin, Leland Walker, Harry Mangan, Tom Talley, Pete Bender, and Howard West were promoted to first lieutenant. Many others from the 3rd were also promoted. Brett also decorated many who had participated in Royce's Raid with the Silver Star for distinguishing themselves by gallantry in action against the enemy.

Two weeks later Birnn's diary recorded some good news: "Shearer came back tonight. After his other engine failed, he hit the water [May 25th raid]. A Zero strafed them [the crew] a few times while they were swimming in the water. After that, they swam to shore, and some natives took them to a New

20. Sgt. Ralph Harrell, a bombardier of the 3rd Bomb Group, with two natives, Port Moresby, New Guinea, Christmas Day 1942. *Courtesy Ralph Harrell*

Guinea Volunteer Riflemen Camp at Wau. Twelve days later a plane came and picked them up."

Later in June Birnn, from Washington, D.C., was test flying an A-20 when he crashed in Moreton Bay near Brisbane and died. After fourteen successful missions without a problem, Birnn was away from the combat zone for some deserved "R&R" when he crashed.[21] Some wondered at the time why experienced combat pilots from the 3rd were also being used as test pilots.

The group cross-trained cooks, truck drivers, aircraft mechanics, and others due to the high attrition rate among the flight crews at Charters Towers. Pfc. Ralph Harrell was an aircraft mechanic but volunteered to become a bombardier after several were killed, causing a shortage. The training was supposed to last three months, but after the first month, when one of the remaining bombardiers injured his thumb firing a .50-caliber machine gun and could not go on a mission, Harrell officially became a bombardier on a B-25. Aussies from the RAAF supplemented the aircrews as copilots, navigators, and gunners.

Harrell was flying with a group of six B-25s when Zeros attacked them. One of the armor-piercing rounds went through the cooling jacket of his .30-caliber machine gun, damaging the barrel and jamming his gun. But he had two other .30-caliber machine guns to use in the nose of the plane for backup.

During this same attack, debris from another shell went through the escape hatch and knocked the pilot unconscious. The copilot took over. A cannon slug damaged one of their engines. When they got to Port Moresby, the crew surveyed the engine damage and discussed whether they should stay in Port Moresby overnight or try to make it the 740 miles over the Coral Sea and across the mountain range back to Charters Towers. The B-25s were rugged old birds, according to Harrell, and they all voted to head back that night since they were vulnerable to air attacks at Port Moresby.

Lt. Leland A. Walker, another former 27th pilot, crashed his B-25 around Fisherman's Island near Port Moresby and was able to return to duty. Two members of his crew were killed.

The Japanese Navy fighter group the 3rd had to contend with was the elite Tainan Kokutai. This group had flown together since China and strafed Clark Field in the Philippines on the opening day of the war. They were transferred to the Dutch East Indies when that campaign heated up and then to Rabaul after Java fell. Many members were forward deployed to Lae. In August 1942, squadrons returned to Rabaul to deal with the U.S. Marines on Guadalcanal. The 3rd would be attacked frequently by this group in New Guinea, particularly on raids to Lae, which was a real hot spot in 1942. Harrell recalled that sometimes when the Japanese fighter pilots were low on fuel or out of ammunition, they would put on a brief aerial show for the U.S. bomber crews before returning to base. They were hot pilots who liked to flaunt their abilities in front of the Americans. Sometimes they would stage mock combat with each other, do barrel rolls, or swing in close to the bombers and raise a middle finger at the crews. A number of high-scoring aces were members of the Tainan Kokutai, including Saburo Sakai, the leading surviving Japanese ace of World War II, credited with sixty-four kills.

Army Air Corps records indicate in July the existing American strength in the Southwest Pacific was insufficient for carrying out offensive operations and barely sufficient to prevent the Japanese from expanding into the Solomon Islands.[22] MacArthur's command submitted a plan for expediting delivery of some B-17s that had been promised as replacements. On July 20 General Arnold stated his objections:

In the first place, he reiterated that the South and Southwest Pacific did not comprise a major theater of operations. In the second place, by sending the B-17s to General MacArthur's forces as suggested in the plan, a group would have to be delayed in reaching England. In the third place, it was General Arnold's opinion that the ten planes would be far better employed against targets in Germany than against objectives in the South and Southwest Pacific.[23]

Trouble Brewing, Buna, Gona, and Guadalcanal

On July 21 the Japanese landed troops only one hundred miles away on the northeast coast of New Guinea, directly across the Owen Stanley Mountains from Port Moresby, and captured the coastal villages of Buna and Gona. The primary purpose of this invasion was to conquer Port Moresby by a land route. There were no roads across the unmapped Owen Stanley Mountains, only one main footpath, the Kokoda Trail (or Track). The trail in places skirted ledges along cliffs that dropped thousands of feet. The village of Kokoda was located on the other side of the mountains from Port Moresby in the foothills, about fifty miles inland from Buna and Gona, and had been used as an administrative post by the Australians. An airfield was nearby that if captured could be used for fighters and would be only ten minutes flying time from Port Moresby. Australian militia troops were sent to defend Kokoda and the airstrip.

During July, the Japanese, who had also been moving south from Rabaul into the Solomon Islands, were building an airfield on the island of Guadalcanal, another step toward the island of New Caledonia, controlled by the Free French. Predictions were that soon their long-range bombers would be able to interfere with shipping between the United States and Australia as well as the air-ferrying route from Hawaii through various islands to Australia.

Mangan's July 24 diary entry records that he and his crew made a beautiful run on two cruisers, four destroyers, and four transports that were apparently landing troops and supplies at Buna. One of the transports was already burning from a previous B-17 attack. The bombers bracketed a destroyer, which they later learned sank. Ten specks were closing in fast on the B-25, and they looked like Zeros. "I blew kisses when I saw they were wonderful P-39s of ours—the first pursuit of ours I have seen in the war [that is, pursuit aircraft flying fighter support for the 3rd Bomb Group)." Japanese records do not indicate any transports lost on this date in New Guinea waters.[24]

On the night of July 25–26, Townsville, then the most important airbase in Australia, suffered its first in a series of bombing raids. Intelligence reports

21. Alex Evanoff, commander of the 13th Squadron, standing on car hood to photograph his unit's B-25s at Charters Towers. *Courtesy Jack Heyn*

indicated that the flying boats probably came from the seaplane base at Gasmata on New Britain.[25] Therefore, a mission of five B-25s was planned for that day to hit the Japanese base. Pilots did not like flying missions to Gasmata because they had to fly over the Owen Stanley Mountains near enemy-held airbases on the other side; in addition, the round trip from Port Moresby was long enough, and they barely had enough fuel to make it back after carrying a load of bombs. The B-25s refueled at Port Moresby, but when they got as far as Buna, they were attacked by a group of Zeros, perhaps as many as twenty. The bomber formation tightened to better defend itself. Ralph Schmidt, a former 27th pilot, was leading the mission when he was shot down and killed along with his crew. The *27th Reports* noted the event: "Ever willing, capable, conscientious Schmidt was shot down in flames near Buna, New Guinea. His supposed death came after he had voluntarily assumed leadership of a very hazardous mission through three hot beds of Japanese pursuit planes to bomb Gasmata."

After about fifteen minutes into the fight, Bender's plane was hit by machine-gun fire, and he was wounded in the ankle. About two minutes later his plane was hit by cannon fire from one of the Zeros, and a fire broke out in the midsection. Part of the steering mechanism in the tail was damaged, and Bender knew he could not get the plane back to Port Moresby. Since he was over Japanese-held territory and the B-25 was flying on an even keel, he wanted to make a few more minutes toward Port Moresby before the crew bailed out. As the fire got worse, he rang the alarm and over the interphone system told the crew to jump. The copilot (an Australian sergeant named Hawter) could not get the hatch open above them, so he headed back to the main escape hatch. Suddenly, the plane began a violent spin, throwing Bender against the roof by centrifugal force. While the bomber was spinning toward earth, it exploded, and when Bender regained consciousness he estimated that he was about 3,000 feet from the ground; they had been flying at about 12,000 feet. He pulled the ring on his parachute, it opened, and he floated down and landed in some small trees. Before landing, Bender could see the smoldering fuselage of his plane nearby, so when natives found him, he insisted that they take him to it. He found his dead crew members. It was a gruesome sight. He buried them with their parachutes on. Only two of the gunners were not among the dead.

Because of the gunshot wound he had sustained, injuries suffered when the airplane blew up, and the effects of his parachute landing, Bender was no longer able to walk. Natives carried him on a stretcher to a missionary camp about a day's journey away. There he met an Australian doctor, Harry Bitmead, who treated his wounds. One of his two gunners, Sergeant Thompson, who had bailed out was there and in pretty good shape. They assumed the nearby Japanese had captured the other gunner, Cpl. Walter N. Cook. Bender was carried to a second missionary camp. His wounds became badly infected. Eventually, with the help of natives carrying him again on a stretcher, Bender, Thompson, and Bitmead crossed the Owen Stanley Mountains, and on the eighteenth day, they arrived at another mission on the southwestern coast of New Guinea. This was the same place where Bender and his crew had been treated during his crash in April. Bender was transported by canoe down a river to a sailboat. For two days he lay in a filthy hold infested with huge roaches while being taken to Port Moresby. He was flown in a B-25 to Townsville three days later and then taken to a hospital in Brisbane.

That so many would be injured or killed so early in the war was not without cause. Once the 27th pilots had planes, it was tough to keep them out of the sky. The point that too many of them who were in the thick of the war since December 1941 were losing their lives had been brought home in July

22. Third Bomb Group senior officers with visiting generals, Charters Towers, late July 1942. L to R: Capt. Sam Rubenstein, adjutant; Capt. James McAfee; Maj. Ron Hubbard; Capt. Tom Gerrity, commander, 90th Squadron; Capt. Donn Young; Maj. Floyd Rogers, commander, 8th Squadron; unidentified (with briefcase); Capt. Robert Strickland, executive officer; Brig. Gen. Kenneth Walker; Lt. Col. "Big Jim" Davies, commander, 3rd Bomb Group; Maj. Gen. Ralph Royce, commander, North-Eastern Area, Allied Air Forces (headquarters at Townsville); unidentified; Capt. Donald Hall, commander, 89th Squadron. Walker would soon replace Royce as North-Eastern Area commander and would be killed during a raid on Rabaul in January 1943. *Courtesy Ronald Hubbard*

1942 with the death of Maj. Floyd "Buck" Rogers, who led the dive-bomber squadron.

Blue Rock Clay Pigeon

Ron Hubbard recalled how dissatisfied he was with the A-24 dive bomber: "It was a disappointment, slow and heavy at the controls, its one good point was a very accurate bomb deliver from a near vertical dive. Without fighter cover they were nearly defenseless. Since we seldom had fighter cover in the early days of the War in the Far East, they soon had the nickname 'Blue Rock Clay Pigeons.'"

Mangan described the significance of the nickname. Pilots, he explained, were expected to shoot clay pigeons to learn aerial gunnery by leading targets. The pigeon was a round clay disk fired by a hand-held device. These disks, made by a company called Blue Rock, were used as targets for skeet shooting. "We figured that the A-24 was such a clunk and such a wonderful target for the enemy that the A-24s would be just like Blue Rock Clay Pigeons."

In a letter dated May 7, 1942, to higher headquarters, Davies critiqued the A-24: "Flying Qualities—too slow and obsolete for this war. Combat worth—all missions necessitate such large pursuit protection. Undersize wheels for weight of airplane—will stick anywhere except for hard, smooth surface. Types of mission—unable to get sufficient altitude with full bomb load to cross mountain ranges encountered on most missions. Partial and complete engine failures after an average of only 100 hours of operation. Insufficient parts and engines available."

Major Rogers was shot down on July 29 near Gona. With six other A-24s, Rogers crossed the Owen Stanleys to strike a convoy close to shore. But the enemy ships had strong fighter coverage. The dive bombers' own fighter coverage had difficulty staying with their much slower charges and had become separated from them at a crucial time. Five planes, including Rogers's bomber, were shot down; another A-24, riddled by gunfire, made it to Milne Bay, and only one made it back to Port Moresby unharmed.[26] In May Rogers had refused to go on further missions with the dive bombers operating out of Port Moresby without adequate fighter escort.[27]

The 3rd lost fourteen A-24s in two months of combat over New Guinea. They were significantly handicapped without adequate fighter cover against the faster, more nimble Zeros, and at that point in the war—the summer of 1942—there still were not enough Allied fighters in the theater to fly adequate escort missions. After losing five of seven dive bombers in an air mission over Buna that day, Davies, who had recently been promoted to colonel, got permission to pull the plug on the A-24's combat role. The army relegated the dive bomber to noncombat roles in New Guinea and Australia.[28]

William Beck, who flew A-24s with the 27th in the Darwin area and with the 3rd out of Port Moresby, commented: "One time, I flew a U.S. Army infantry type general in my A-24 dive bomber from Townsville to Charters Towers. The general sat in the rear gunner's seat. This was one time I didn't have to worry about being shot down or how good of a marksman he was with the .30 caliber machine guns because it was dark, and I don't think Jap Zeros had ever been between those two air bases."[29]

New Leadership

Back in Brisbane, MacArthur and George Brett did not get along for multiple reasons. MacArthur asked Washington to send him a replacement for Brett, who was commanding the FEAF and Allied Air Forces, including the RAAF and what was left of the Dutch East Indies Air Force. Hap Arnold wanted to send Lt. Gen. Frank Andrews, who was then commanding the Caribbean Defense Command, but Andrews, who detested MacArthur, turned down the job. George Marshall then gave MacArthur two choices: Jimmy Doolittle or Maj. Gen. George C. Kenney. MacArthur replied, "It would be difficult to convince the Australians of Doolittle's acceptability."[30] Perhaps the general, who was responsible for Royce's Raid, or members of the RAAF, which Doolittle would lead, had interpreted the success of the Tokyo raid quite differently than the American press and public. MacArthur chose Kenney. Arnold thought the blunt-talking Kenney probably would not last long in Australia. His outspoken and sometimes biting verbal manner had caused him to run afoul of the War Department General Staff previously.[31] He stood five feet, five inches tall and had attended college at the Massachusetts Institute of Technology prior to World War I. During the war, he flew seventy-five missions and shot down two German airplanes. By 1942 he was commanding the Fourth Air Force, which was responsible for the air defense of the U.S. West Coast and for training fighter and bomber crews.

Kenney arrived in Brisbane on July 28. That evening he spent a couple of hours talking to General Sutherland, MacArthur's chief of staff. Sutherland told him that the Army Air Corps was in a poor state there, that none of Brett's staff or senior commanders were any good, and that the pilots did not know much about flying. Kenney later stated, "In fact, I heard just about everyone hauled over the coals except for Douglas MacArthur and Richard Sutherland." The following morning Kenney met with Brett to hear his version of the state of affairs of the air corps in Australia. After that, he met with MacArthur, and according to Kenney:

For the next half hour, as he talked while pacing back and forth across the room, I really heard about the shortcomings of the Air Force. As he warmed up to his subject, the shortcomings became more and more serious, until finally there was nothing left but an inefficient rabble of boulevard shock troops whose contribution to the war effort was practically nil. . . . He had no use for anyone in the whole organization from Brett down to and including the rank of colonel. . . . Finally he expressed the opinion that the air personnel had gone beyond just being antagonistic to his headquarters, to the point of disloyalty."[32]

"General, I Didn't Ask to Come Out Here!"

MacArthur liked to pontificate to his subordinates, and loyalty seemed to be a favorite subject. He would say a soldier's loyalty was the most important quality in his character—"loyalty up and down," referring to the chain of command.[33]

When MacArthur paused, Kenney decided it was time for him to lay his cards on the table. According to Jimmy Doolittle's version, he responded by saying: "General, I didn't ask to come out here. You asked me. I think it was one of the smartest things you ever did, because I am the best goddamned air force commander in the world today." Kenney then told MacArthur that "his men would be loyal to MacArthur because they are always loyal to me and, through me, they will be loyal to you. You be loyal to me and my gang, and make this 50/50."[34] Kenney went on to tell him that if loyalty could not be maintained among his men, he would be packed up and ready for orders sending him back home. Kenney later recalled: "He [MacArthur] walked over to me and put his arm around my shoulder. 'George,' he said, 'I think we are going to get along together all right.'"[35]

After this meeting, Kenney left on an inspection tour of his troops around Australia and up in Port Moresby but did not assume command until August 4, the day Brett left Australia for home.

Soon after, the story goes, Kenney was upset because Sutherland, who supposedly was qualified as a private pilot, continued to interfere with air missions. He stormed into Sutherland's office, grabbed a sheet of paper, and put a pencil dot in the middle of it. He told him that the dot represented Sutherland's knowledge of aircraft use and the rest of the paper represented Kenney's knowledge. He further suggested that if he did not like it, they should go in and see MacArthur. Sutherland backed down.

Ralph Harrell recalled a reconnaissance mission from Charters Towers with two other B-25s. The clouds suddenly parted and below he could see two "big, fat Jap transports and two destroyers." The three bombers went after one of the transports, and Harrell zeroed in on a lettuce-green Studebaker on the deck that the Japanese may have obtained from the Philippines and were probably delivering to one of their commanders in New Guinea. The deck was laden with other equipment and supplies.

The first pass was at eight thousand feet, and Harrell dropped his bomb with the other two bombers behind cueing on him. They all missed. They came back again at five thousand feet, which was almost an ideal bombing altitude. Harrell missed the ship by twenty-five feet, but the bomb buckled the ship's plates below the waterline, which caused the transport to stop dead in the water. According to Harrell, Kenney had a standing offer for any enemy ship sunk over a certain tonnage: the crew sinking the ship would get a case of scotch, a seven-day leave in Sydney, and the Silver Star. Unfortunately, Harrell's plane was out of bombs and had to head back to Charters Towers. On the way home they saw a B-17 coming out to finish off the transport. The B-17 sunk the ship, and its crew got all the prizes.

The Saga of the A-20s

The 27th and 3rd pilots liked the A-20 they had flown back in Savannah for its superior speed and ruggedness. It was a splendid ground-support plane, but thanks to Lend-Lease, U.S. forces never got as many A-20s as they wanted. The 3rd Bomb Group had only one A-20 in early April, though by mid-May they had several. In most cases, however, parts were missing.

> The next two weeks [in May] were spent trying to get the necessary parts to put guns and [fuel] tanks on the A-20s. Pappy Gunn gets things done regardless. Delays, lack of authority, no parts, no men, no supplies, and other things and for three months trying to get the A-20s going, shortage of parts again, and more planes. We have 39 finally. No guns and finally guns, but no solenoids, solenoids, and no brackets, brackets, and no chargers, and so on.[36]

Davies observed, "These A-20s have been through four maneuvers in the States and, consequently, the maintenance problem is acute." Mangan added, "Why in the hell don't they keep that junk home and send us new stuff."

Two 450-gallon fuel tanks had to be added in the bomb bay of the A-20s because without them, the men quickly learned, its range was inadequate to operate from Port Moresby against targets on the other side of the Owen Stanley Mountains. Occasionally, Gunn, who by this time was functioning as sort of the engineering and maintenance officer for the 3rd, would get banned from the A-20 project by senior air-depot officers for his "unreasonable demands for action and general disregard for protocol." In those situations Bob Ruegg would take over supervising the project until Gunn was allowed back.[37]

> Along about the middle of May, the group armament officer with the assistance of the 89th Sq armament officer [one of the two may have been Gunn], had a brainstorm, and conceived the idea of putting four [.50]-caliber machine guns in the nose of the A-20s. This meant that space in the pilot's compartment had to be found to put the bomb control levers and bomb release switches. Work was started on an experimental ship. But before it could be totally completed, shops were set up at Amberley Field near Brisbane to make the installations. It took all of June to get the first ships ready. When enough ships with nose guns came back to Charters Towers, the 89th started to teach their pilots in the use of the guns, as well as to teach them how to drop bombs.
>
> The headaches of trying to keep the guns working soon began. On each flight difficulties arose with the guns not operating properly. In two cases, the broken hydraulic lines caused crash landings. Finally, the troubles were ironed out and the squadron did a lot of practice firing and bombing at the gunnery range![38]

Pappy Gunn had taken charge of installing the four .50-caliber machine guns in the nose of these planes. There were an additional two machine guns on each side in the front. These .50-caliber machine guns were probably easier to obtain than the .30-caliber variety because they were salvaged from wrecked fighter planes at the airbase. During Kenney's first visit to Charters Towers on August 5, he found the 3rd a "snappy good-looking" outfit and clearly understood the significance of Gunn's .50-caliber installment upgrade package. During the later 1920s, Kenney, who had been an instructor at the Air Corps Tactical School, rewrote and updated the manual for attack-aircraft pilots.[39] He asked Gunn to devise a special bomb rack so that these planes could also carry "parafrag" bombs.[40]

Launder learned to fly the A-20 very quickly. For an hour he sat in the single-seat cockpit with the tech manual, checking out everything. Then Harry Galusha, who had flown the A-20s back in Savannah, gave him his indoctrination ride. Launder sat below in the bombardier's seat as Galusha flew around the countryside at treetop level. Launder recalled: "I turned around and looked up there [cockpit] once. Harry had his head down, tun-

23. Douglas A-20 attack bomber in western Pacific area. Note the nose guns in this model.
Courtesy Jack Heyn

ing a radio for some good music. I'll never forget the song he tuned in; Paul Robeson singing 'Old Man River.' The guy was the coolest pilot in the whole Air Force, possibly second only to Jimmy Doolittle." By the end of the day, Launder was considered a full-fledged A-20 combat pilot. "It was 'on the job training' in a big way."[41]

Kokoda and Guadalcanal Campaigns

On August 7 the 1st Marine Division landed on Guadalcanal and nearby smaller islands, including Tulagi, with its fine harbor. This was part of a larger strategy by U.S. planners to capture the Solomon Islands, which begin about 180 miles south of Rabaul and run in a southeasterly direction for about 600 miles. Guadalcanal is one of the southernmost islands. The American high command planned to move north up the chain toward Rabaul. They also intended to capture the Santa Cruz Islands, about 200 miles east of the Solomons. Simultaneously they would secure the northeastern coast of New Guinea under MacArthur's command, and then move on to capture Rabaul.[42]

The marines were supported by a U.S. Navy carrier fleet comprising the *Saratoga, Wasp,* and *Enterprise* with a strong force of escorts. The leathernecks quickly captured the airfield on Guadalcanal, which was nearing completion, and renamed it Henderson Field; in fact, Japanese Army planes had been scheduled to occupy the base that very day. The marines recovered a large quantity of enemy supplies and undamaged equipment, which were useful in completing the airfield. Soon, however, an epic slugfest ensued for the possession of Guadalcanal as both sides pumped in reinforcements and a series of significant naval battles were fought in the waters surrounding the contested island.

As the struggle raged on Guadalcanal for months, military leaders questioned if the marines could hold the island. Sorely needed air units and most of the ships from MacArthur's command were lent to the navy to support the operation.[43] In addition, Pacific naval commanders almost continuously begged for air attacks against Rabaul, whose airfields, harbor, and the town itself were supporting the Japanese effort to retain Guadalcanal, by heavy bombers of Kenney's command.[44] The old, shot-up 19th Bombardment Group, veterans of the Philippines and Java, flew many bombing missions against the enemy base. The B-17s first flew up to Port Moresby for refueling before their trip to Rabaul and back. The bombing raids not only supported the marines on Guadalcanal but also interfered with the supply and air support the Japanese were providing to their troops in New Guinea.

During August, the Allies were finally holding their own in the skies over New Guinea but were continuing to give ground on the Kokoda Trail. Mangan, who had been flying missions out of Port Moresby since April, made a seemingly overly optimistic entry in his diary on August 14 but followed it with a cynical remark: "The New Guinea situation is well in hand—we have air superiority. And my friends die for that." His optimism, in part, reflected the significant drop off in daylight raids on airfields around Port Moresby by enemy bombers and fighters.

The "diggers," as the Australian soldiers referred to themselves, fought bravely at Kokoda but were overwhelmed by superior enemy forces. On August 16 the airfield there was lost. The Japanese, with the help of combat engineers, committed six battalions of infantry and about two thousand pack animals to carry their supplies and equipment during the campaign. Allied leaders in Australia rushed veteran troops from their 7th Division, which had recently returned from the Middle East, to Port Moresby.[45]

The 89th Squadron, 3rd Bomb Group finally flew thirteen of the Gunn-modified A-20s to Port Moresby on August 29. The next day eight of them followed twin-engine B-26 Marauder bombers to the airfield at Lae. After the B-26s bombed the field, the A-20s came in at treetop level and strafed the entire area with their eight forward-firing machine guns. During the days to come, the 89th flew many strafing and bombing missions along the Kokoda Trail and elsewhere.

Howard West, a pilot with the 89th, said that when they flew missions out of Port Moresby to Lae and other targets, there were almost always clouds around the Owen Stanley Mountains, thus forcing them to climb so that they could see the mountaintops and then fly either around or over them. A resulting problem he and fellow pilot Bill Beck recalled was that since the A-20s did not have high-pressure fuel pumps, sometimes the rear gunner would have to operate the manual pumps so that the engines would get the fuel they needed at the higher altitudes required to traverse the mountains.

In late August the Japanese landed about 2,200 troops on the north side of Milne Bay, two hundred miles southeast of Port Moresby at the eastern tip of New Guinea, the second part of a two-pronged attack. The Japanese wanted the use of the Milne Bay airfields, which were defended by two Australian brigades and two fighter squadrons at two airfields along with more than 1,300 U.S. engineering troops constructing a third airfield. Although the enemy troops had air support and some naval support, they were defeated during a nearly week-long battle. This hard-fought Allied victory was significantly aided by aircraft from the two squadrons at Milne Bay and those back at Port Moresby. This was probably the first significant defeat for Japanese land forces since their Pacific islands' conquest began in December 1941.[46]

Most of the enemy pilots the 3rd was facing at this time were experienced, talented aviators. But the Japanese did not shoot down all of the former 27th pilots who died in air crashes. Some met their fates otherwise.

Fatigue was another serious problem for the pilots of the 3rd, for there were still not enough flight crews in Australia. As soon as replacements arrived, they were trained on the bombers, which usually took weeks, not days. Many of the veteran pilots, especially those from the original 27th, worked very long hours during the early months.

Gus Heiss, a former 27th pilot who flew with Ed Townsend during Royce's Raid, mysteriously crashed into the Coral Sea during bad weather on September 4, 1942.[47] Sgt. Howard MacDonald was the top turret gunner in a nearby B-25 returning from the same mission to Milne Bay when he saw

24. Parafrag bombs exploding on a Japanese airfield in New Guinea. Note the parachutes near the ground, attached to bombs. *Courtesy Jack Heyn*

Heiss's plane turn on its landing lights, peel off to the right a bit, start losing altitude, and then go into a sharp decline toward the water. MacDonald recalled: "I saw the ship hit the water and then some flames on top of the water but not much. I didn't think that they ran out of fuel or they would have called on the radio. Our radios between planes were still working. I really never understood what happened. We had been climbing but I don't believe they stalled out."

By September 8 the Japanese had worked around the Aussie defenses in Kokoda Gap and were now in the downgrade on the Kokoda Trail, headed for Port Moresby. Allied air support continued to pound the enemy along the trail all the way back to Buna and Gona.

September 12 was a big day for the 89th when Capt. Don Hall led the 89th on the first raid using parafrag bombs in the SWPA. Nine A-20s, each carrying forty parafrag clusters, attacked the airfield at Buna. They were credited with destroying seventeen Japanese planes on the ground with a combination of strafing and parafrags.[48] Howard West later recalled flying at an altitude of a couple of hundred feet during the strafing-parafrag bombing runs and watching the Japanese scatter on airfields, wharves, docks, or barges as he let loose with his eight machine guns.

The Japanese soon advanced to the Ioribaiwa Ridge, which was about thirty miles from Port Moresby. On September 17, Japanese forward patrols reached the Imita Ridge, eighteen miles from an Allied airfield being built at Laloki, which in turn was only about eight miles from Port Moresby. During this time, the U.S. 32nd Infantry Division was sent to Port Moresby from Australia. To speed up their arrival, about 4,500 members were airlifted in.

The mood among the Allies in Port Moresby was somber despite the recent victory at Milne Bay. Since the past December, the Japanese Army had been uniformly successful in its many major campaigns, and Port Moresby was their next main objective. But on September 25 the Aussies attacked and drove the Japanese out of their advance positions on Imita Ridge. Three days later, with close and significant Allied air support, they recaptured Ioribaiwa Ridge and were now taking the offensive in the Kokoda campaign.

"General, There Is One Situation I Would Like to Bring before You"

Of his relatively small band of 27th Bomb Group pilots who made it out of the Philippines, Davies had lost about a third of them by the end of July. At the end of a letter to Kenney two days after the death of Major Rogers, Davies broached the issue of this high mortality rate. The first part of his letter discussed A-20s, their combat modifications, and pilot training. Near the end he turned to the 27th:

> General, there is one situation I would like to bring before you while I have the opportunity. Since our arrival in Australia they [the 27th pilots] have participated in almost every air battle. They sank surface craft in the Java Sea battle and have been continuously participating in the New Guinea air operations. The remaining members of the 27th Bombardment Group [nineteen men] are now members of the 3rd Bombardment Group. Although none of them have approached me on the subject, I would like to recommend they be replaced and returned to the United States. They are the very highest type of officers and men and should be returned with the understanding that their combat experience is to be used to train units in the United States to better further the war effort.[49]

Davies himself began using the former 27th pilots to train the new B-25 crews just out of flight school, reducing their opportunities to lead missions.

Finally, in early September a wire came from Washington stating that the 27th survivors would be rotated back home. McAfee wrote in his dairy: "The old 27th is going home! Replacements are being sent to us by air and we're to go home by air. Tonight is certainly a night to celebrate. The Colonel says we won't have to go on any more combat missions."

William Hipps recalled it this way: "Hap Arnold contacted General Kenney. He said, 'George, if you have any of those 27th pilots who got out of the Philippines who are still alive, for Christ sakes send them home'!" Hap Arnold visited MacArthur and Kenney in Brisbane during a fact-finding tour to the Southwest Pacific in late September 1942. He also traveled to Townsville and Port Moresby, where he had meetings with Army Air Corps and other military leaders.[50] During this visit, Kenney and Arnold discussed sending the Philippines-Java veterans back home for a rest. Arnold replied that he needed combat veterans to help train his aircrews in the States.[51]

As the pilots prepared to return home in October, Mangan recorded a miracle in his diary—Rocky Gause showed up in Brisbane from Darwin after 158 days in a boat from the Philippines: "I can hardly believe it. From present meager reports, he and another Joe made it in a banca all the way."

The Gause-Osborne Odyssey

Damon "Rocky" Gause was a pilot with the 27th in Savannah and, like Stephenson, was married there just before he left for the Philippines. He was part of Stirling's 17th Squadron and commanded a group of machine gunners after the unit was converted into infantry on Bataan. He also served as the group's communications officer. At the time of the Bataan surrender, he killed one of his Japanese guards with a knife and escaped by swimming to Corregidor. When the troops there surrendered, he escaped to the mainland and spent about two months moving around and being hidden by friendly Filipinos. During this time, he had a number of close calls with Japanese soldiers.

Gause met up with Capt. William Osborne, an infantry officer who had escaped from Bataan. The two of them killed in self-defense a German who they believed was a spy for the Japanese, and as a result of this, they decided to leave the Philippines. They purchased a leaky, twenty-foot, native-built motor-skiff sailboat from a Filipino, though the Japanese had already confiscated it. Taking the skiff anyway, they used it for their escape to Australia, a 3,200-mile journey through Japanese-controlled waters, not only in the Philippines but also Borneo, Celebes, and then down through Java and on to northern Australia. To provision their boat for the trip, they captured a

25. William Lloyd Osborne and "Rocky" Gause with their escape boat, renamed *Ruth-Lee* after their wives. *Courtesy Hyperion Books*

Japanese soldier who was guarding various necessary supplies on a nearby island. During their three-month odyssey, they met American soldiers who had escaped and were now guerrilla fighters. They also came upon friendly and hostile natives along the way.

The day after arriving in Australia in October 1942, the pair were flown to MacArthur's headquarters in Brisbane. They were then driven by staff car to meet the general. When they entered his office, Gause was not wearing shoes because his feet were too blistered, and although they had already been given clean uniforms by the Australians the day before, Gause and Osborne were clad in the filthy clothes in which they had traveled. MacArthur, who was well known as quite a dramatist himself, must have loved the scene. According to Gause, after they arrived in MacArthur's office and were announced, he walked to the general's desk, saluted him, and said, "Sir, Lt. Gause reports for duty from Corregidor!" The general returned his salute, peered intently at the two of them, slowly rose, and exclaimed, "Well, I'll be damned!"

During their debriefing, they likely told him about the last days of the men left behind on Bataan, including those of the 27th. They related what they knew of the horrors of the Bataan Death March and the torture and mistreatment of the prisoners, which they had learned of from Filipinos during their time on Luzon and also from escaped American soldiers they had met along the way.[52] Gause, along with Osborne, knew after their ordeal that they would be headed home soon. By this time too, Gause's 27th comrades in the 3rd also knew they were returning to the States.

Homeward Bound

On November 6, 1942, Davies, McAfee, and Hubbard boarded an LB-30 transport to San Francisco via Brisbane, New Caledonia, Fiji, Christmas Island, and Hawaii. Mangan recalled that he had a set of orders saying, "Get back to the United States any way you can!" While sitting at the Lennons Hotel bar in Brisbane, he ran into the flight crew that had just flown in Maj. Gen. Leroy Lutes. Mangan showed his orders and asked if there was a chance of flying back to the States with the general. He arrived in San Francisco on November 1, 1942.

Ironically, this was exactly one year to the day since he and his comrades had left San Francisco for the Philippines. To put it another way, of the 1,209 members of the 27th Bombardment Group and its two attached units that left on the *Coolidge* for Operation PLUM, about 20 returned to the United States a year later. Of the ten B-25s, including ship #41-12455, that participated in Royce's Raid and returned safely, nine were lost during the subsequent six and a half months.[53]

Kokoda Post Script

What follows are excerpts from Davies's debriefing conducted by U.S. Army intelligence in November 1942 after returning to the United States:

> Shortly before I left, we were close-supporting the Australian ground forces when the Japs were coming over the Owen Stanley Range. The commander of the Australians told me himself that if it hadn't been for our A-20s, the Japs would have taken Port Moresby. We hit them every morning and every evening with [the A-20s'] forward guns and fragmentation bombs [parafrags]. We didn't have very good targets. That is all jungle country in there and you couldn't see what you were doing; but we had an Australian liaison officer who worked right with the ground forces, and he always let us know where the forward lines were—where the concentration of Japs were most likely to be.

We couldn't see much of what we were doing, but our forces moved back in there and found a great many dead Japs that had been killed by .50 caliber ammunition and also by fragmentation bombs.

Their lines of communication were rather difficult, also because of the terrain and the jungle. We caught a lot of mules moving up there—though most of the supplies were carried by natives. We received information from Australian intelligence and we caught quite a few Jap boats bringing up supplies and back over the other side of the island we did also find other concentrations of supplies that we destroyed. Whatever bridges we could find, we destroyed. Those were the tactics that we used. It kept the Japs out of Port Moresby. The Australian ground forces couldn't praise the A-20s enough. It was kind of a morale builder for them; and a kind of moral scourge for the Japs.[54] We did keep a scoreboard out in front of Operations. One of them "Nips Nipped" was something like 37 Zeros when I left. The other one "Bottoms Up" was surface craft we had sunk. It wasn't so high. Most of our bombing was against airdromes.[55]

The flyability of the Jap Zero pilots definitely fell off in the period we were there. In our first encounter with the Japs, they were very, very aggressive. They would fly right through a formation—and stay right in there as long as they could with complete disregard of their own safety. [Whenever we hit one, it fell apart.] It was beautiful flying. But I can't say we are discouraging them by having hit so many. It looks to me that the Japs are not sending out as good a grade of pilot now—and they don't have the aggressiveness they did. I don't know the reason for it.

Just to show the climbing capabilities of the Zero—we took some pictures of a bomb run over Lae [altitude 15,000–16,000 feet]. The first pictures shows the bomb leaving the plane and the Lae airdrome underneath it. You can see the Zeros disperse. The next picture shows the bombs getting smaller, and you can see movement of the Zeros at take-off. Then the bombs are on the airdrome and all the Zeros are in the air and attacking the bombing formation. That is how quickly they can get up there.

They just about came straight up when they left the airdrome; but any time we hit them with .50 caliber guns, it would just about finish them.[56]

The village of Kokoda was retaken on November 2, and soon the Allies were using the airfield again. By the middle of the month, the Australian 7th Division was ready to begin a coordinated attack against Japanese-held positions in the Buna and Gona area. The U.S. 32nd Division had been flown across the Owen-Stanley Mountains and developed a base at Dobodura, about ten miles from Buna. They too were ready to begin the offensive in mid-November. The Japanese reorganized their command structure at that time to better handle the Allied advances in New Guinea and the Solomons. There was much competition for Rabaul's limited resources, which were needed in both places. Reinforcements from there poured into New Guinea. Lt. Gen. Hatazo Adachi, newly appointed to manage the Buna-Gona campaign, was told by Tojo to stop the Allied advance in New Guinea at all costs.[57] The battles for Buna and Gona were intense and bloody as the Allies fought their way across malaria-infested swamps and other terrain barriers against an entrenched and determined enemy.

During the Kokoda campaign, "friendly fire" by Allied aircraft was a potential and constant hazard and did occur, particularly when battles raged under rainforest canopies or when an infantry unit broke through enemy lines ahead of schedule. Also, friendly ground fire was a hazard to Allied aircraft during the campaign.

The Australians captured Gona on December 9. Buna fell about three weeks later with the aid of artillery, mortars, flamethrowers, grenades, and many Australian tanks brought in on barges from Milne Bay. Fighting, however, continued on for several more weeks as the Allies encountered strong pockets of resistance in the area. One of these was on the coast between Gona and Buna at Sanananda Point, where about two thousand enemy troops were ensconced on high ground with almost impassable swamps between them and the Allied troops. The few trails that crossed the swamps were well covered by mortar, machine guns, and snipers in the trees. A brigade from the U.S. 41st Infantry was brought in to help with mopping up.

Ralph Harrell had many bouts with malaria and dengue fever in New Guinea. One time he was in a hospital with some 32nd Division men from Michigan and Wisconsin who had just helped defeat the Japanese at Buna-Sanananda, and they had many stories to tell. According to the soldiers, they were not pulled out of combat until their body temperature was 105 degrees for several days. That was the campaign when MacArthur told Lt. Gen. Robert Eichelberger either to take Buna or die trying. Harrell remarked, "Don't ever ask a 32nd Division guy if he liked MacArthur."

11

POW Camps and Hell Ships

WHILE THE AMERICANS and their Allies fought a determined enemy in the Pacific and elsewhere, the nightmare continued for the POWs in the Philippines. In June 1942 Camp O'Donnell was closed, and the surviving prisoners were moved to a prison camp near Cabanatuan, about thirty-five miles east of O'Donnell. Actually, there were three camps nearby. Cabanatuan Camp No. 3 received the group of POWs from Corregidor, who had briefly stayed at Bilibid, on May 27, 1942. On May 31 another group of prisoners arrived at nearby Camp No. 2, however, the water supply there proved inadequate and the men were moved about a week later to Camp No. 3. Meanwhile, the prisoners from Camp O'Donnell staggered into Camp No. 1, pushing its population to seven thousand. Many thought at the time that the POWs from Bataan looked to be in much worse shape than those from Corregidor. The difference was probably because of the Death March, the conditions at Camp O'Donnell, and other factors. By October 1942 most of the prisoners in Camp No. 3 had been sent elsewhere, and the remaining men marched into Camp No. 1, which thereafter was the only facility operating at Cabanatuan.[1] Dr. David Hochman, along with many others who had worked at the hospital on Bataan, were taken to Bilibid Prison in Manila but eventually ended up at Camp No. 1.

Zero Ward

According to Dr. Hochman, the Cabanatuan camp was one of the most frightening places. "The death rate every day was so high, so alarming, and so scary, it was just unbelievable. It was a hellish experience. It was lousy." There was a ward called the Zero Ward, or death ward, where sick POWs were taken to die. "We had zero medicine and supplies to work with. Because of their dysentery, when I worked in that ward, I would sometimes be up to my ankles in liquid stool."

Japanese Prison, American Hospital, Cabanatuan, Philippine Islands, Known as Ward "O", you go in but never come out alive. 1944.

26. Prisoner in Zero Ward, Cabanatuan. *Courtesy Gen. Douglas MacArthur Foundation*

Paul Lankford said about Zero Ward, "If they took you there, your chances of survival were zero or close to it." Others said that two of the huts among the hospital buildings at the camp were called Zero Ward because when the buildings were counted and numbered, these two huts were overlooked and subsequently assigned the number "0." About ninety patients were kept in these two huts at any one time and were the most critically ill.[2]

The Japanese issued g-strings or loincloths to POWs whose clothing had worn out or was so badly soiled that they could no longer wear it. Many of the sicker patients in the hospital wards wore these as they lay in their own excretions. Some did not even have g-strings. Sgt. Emil Russ May from Washington County, Florida, a twenty-five-year-old former public-school teacher before the war, was typical of the patients lying in one of these hospital wards. He had been with the Headquarters Squadron of the 27th and was suffering from diarrhea and many other ailments, which might have included beriberi, jaundice, and malaria. He was too weak to even get out of bed. Some of his comrades from the 27th took him outside on January 6, 1943, and tried to wash him, then left him out in the sun to dry. He was dead when they went out to get him about thirty minutes later.[3]

Diphtheria Outbreak

In July 1942 a diphtheria epidemic broke out at Cabanatuan. An American Army physician, Capt. Harold Keschner, who was a pathologist, identified the bacteria by making a smear from open sores on a patient. The problem was treatment and isolation. Since airborne droplets spread the disease when coughing, men were ordered to sleep alternating head to foot in the crowded barracks, and the diphtheria patients were put in a separate building. The physician in charge of the diphtheria ward and treating those patients was Capt. Elack Schultz, a graduate of the University of Lausanne in Switzerland and the 91st Squadron's medical officer. The doctors convinced the Japanese that they had to have antitoxin not only to save the men but also to prevent the guards from becoming infected. Ten weeks later they finally received the antitoxin. About one hundred men died out of the 400–450 cases of diphtheria.[4]

Once the food and medical situation at Cabanatuan was somewhat stabilized, the Japanese started moving some of the healthier prisoners to other camps as slave laborers.[5] Brutality, however, continued to be a major problem for American POWs wherever they were.

27th Teamsters

Some from the 27th were among the POWs assigned to drive and maintain American trucks for the Japanese. Pvt. James Fred Dyer from Detroit, Alabama, was one of them. He escaped on July 4, 1943, with six others while on this detail and joined up with Filipino guerrillas. He was rescued by a U.S. submarine ten months later.

Sgts. James "Cajun" Gautier and Gradie Inzer had also been from the 27th's Headquarters Squadron. They were assigned to a truck detail elsewhere. Gautier, a Death March and Camp O'Donnell survivor, was driving a truck loaded with Japanese soldiers in the mountains when a tire blew out. He was told it was his fault and beaten. A short time later he intentionally drove the truck off a cliff in retaliation. He jumped out in time, but most of the soldiers were killed or seriously injured. A Japanese investigation concluded that the brakes were at fault.[6]

Dyess Shocks the Nation

In October 1942 Capt. William Dyess was sent with a large group of POWs by ship to the Davao Penal Colony, basically a work camp, on Mindanao. In April 1943 he and nine others made a daring escape. Dyess eventually was taken to Australia by submarine and then sent back to the United States. While he was recovering in an army hospital in the States, his story about his time in the Japanese POW camps and the Death March became known to the news media. The *Chicago Tribune* bought it and initially obtained permission from the War Department to publish. The secretary of war, however, changed his mind. After a four-and-a-half-month battle, the War Department allowed publication in January 1944. The story was serialized and syndicated to one hundred associated newspapers with a combined daily circulation of 10 million copies and an estimated daily audience of 40 million readers. Although other stories had appeared in the newspapers about atrocities in POW camps and on the Death March, most of the information had come secondhand. The Dyess story shocked the nation and precipitated public pressure on Washington to accelerate the war against Japan.

Bank Rescued

As the war progressed, many more prisoners got moved out of Cabanatuan and sent elsewhere; Capt. Bert Bank of the 17th Squadron, however, was one of maybe five hundred who were left behind, including some others from the 27th. Most of those left behind were sick and could not do much work. The Japanese, according to Bank, had murdered his doctor, Carl Mango, who was well liked by all of the 17th Squadron. Mango was sent to Palawan on a work detail and executed there with other POWs by the Japanese in December 1944. The POWs learned about this massacre on Palawan shortly afterward from Filipinos while they were on work details outside Cabanatuan. As a result of that, Bank and the other POWs expected to be killed too, but U.S. Army Rangers rescued them all in late January 1945 during a daring raid behind enemy lines.

Dr. Mango at Palawan

American POWs working as slave laborers had been building an airfield on Palawan, an island in the Sulu Sea approximately five hundred miles southwest of Manila. MacArthur started his invasion of the Philippines in October 1944. On December 14 the 150-man detail at Palawan was herded into three four-foot-deep bomb-shelter trenches with overhead cover. Then the Japanese guards poured gasoline on the shelters and set them on fire. POWs who tried to escape were shot or bayoneted as they dashed from the burning trenches. Only 11 of the 150 prisoners survived what is now referred to as the Palawan Massacre. Dr. Carl Mango, from Pennsylvania and the physician for the 17th Squadron, was one of those killed in these trenches. Mango sprang from his hole, his clothes smoldering. His arms were outstretched as he pleaded, "Show some reason, please, God, show some reason," but a machine gunner shot him down.[7]

The eleven men who lived to tell about the massacre were among those who jumped off a nearby cliff to a beach after escaping the flames. They hid there until nightfall. Japanese search parties found and executed many escapees, but these eleven later managed to swim to safety. A local guerrilla leader protected them and arranged for a U.S. Navy flying boat to pick them up and fly them to Leyte, which resulted in the U.S. Ranger raid that saved Bert Bank and his comrades at Cabanatuan.[8]

Another POW work detail was located southwest of Manila at Nichols Field. The Japanese commandant there was known as the "White Angel."

The White Angel of Nichols Field

U.S. pilots used Nichols Airfield until December 24, 1941. It soon thereafter became a Japanese Navy airbase, and POWs were sent there to repair the landing strips and do other work. Many considered it one of the worst places in the Philippines to work. The Japanese officer in charge of the POW detail was nicknamed "The White Angel" by the prisoners because he was usually immaculately dressed in a white military uniform and took great pleasure in torturing and killing POWs. They considered him to be a pure sadist. As opposed to other camps where the greatest chance of getting beaten or killed by the guards occurred during the daylight hours when actually out laboring, at Nichols the guards would come in the middle of the night and take men out unprovoked to torture or kill them.[9] The Japanese military apparently did not care how "The White Angel" handled prisoners as long as the work got done. As prisoners died or were killed, he just ordered replacements from the nearby camps.

Buck Prewett of the 27th recalled that the Japanese in the Philippines were vicious and would just as soon kill a man as look at him—"You never stared at them." He was one who did not hold back his feelings toward the guards, and since he was six feet two inches tall, he was vulnerable for many beatings. Prewett worked at Nichols Field for about five months. Each morning he walked about five to ten miles from the Pasay schoolhouse to the job. Each evening after roll call, he and the others would return to Pasay School. During one roll call, a man was discovered missing. The escapee had been with the 515th Coast Artillery and was from New Mexico. A search party was formed, and they found him in a tree. The guards viciously pulled him down and returned him to the work area, beating him the entire way. They then motioned for Prewett to get hot water and a mess cup and wash him down. Afterward the head guard reminded everyone what would have happened had the escapee not been found: ten POWs would be executed in his place. This had happened at other camps. After Prewett had finished washing the fugitive, the Japanese had the prisoner kneel on the ground, with one rifleman on each side, and on orders they shot him dead through the head and neck. Prewett still has dreams about this murder.

Not far away at Las Pinas, eight hundred prisoners were building runways over swampland to accommodate Japanese carrier planes. So brutal were the guards and harsh the labor conditions in the boiling sun that men resorted to having their arms broken by their comrades or having other injuries inflicted on themselves in order to miss work.

Mindoro Detachment

When MacArthur ordered his troops to retreat to Bataan on December 24, 1941, the fifty-two men of the 48th Materiel Squadron who were running the airfield on the island of Mindoro remained there and continued to service airplanes on their way to and from Bataan.

SSgt. Louis Kolger of the 48th was one of those who worked at the grass airfield outside the village of San Jose. He and others scattered 55-gallon metal drums all over the field so Japanese aircraft could not land there. When a U.S. plane was to land, they would move the drums to the side. They also had the edges of the field lined with beer bottles full of gasoline that they would light for nighttime landings. In early March the Japanese landed on Mindoro, and the members of the detachment retreated to a secondary base in the mountains. Most of the men by this time had malaria, and some remained hospitalized in San Jose. On May 5 or 6 they received a radio message: "This is Corregidor. We are surrendering. You are on your own." Upon this news Kolger and others retreated up into the hills and established a camp about three miles from the airfield. They buried all of their tools near a little shack in which they kept oil drums at the airfield.

According to Sgt. Crayton Burns, after Corregidor fell he suggested to 1st Lt. Warren Baggett, commanding the Mindoro Detachment, and the others that they should leave Mindoro and try to make their way down through the islands to Australia. Burns eventually made his way to the village of Pandan, on the island of Panay, about 40–50 miles away. There he met an American who referred to himself as Captain Sayre and was supposedly a U.S. Army officer. (Later it was rumored that he told others he was a colonel.) When Sayre learned about the rest of the unit, he supposedly asked Captain Raval, a

Filipino, who was an officer in the U.S. Navy, to find them and bring them to Pandan, which he did. Eventually, most of the men with Sayre used three or four outrigger canoes to travel from Catician to Magranting Island, about 120 miles away over shark-infested open water. From there they went to another small island, Cuyo, a distance of more than 70 miles.

Kolger remembered this about the outrigger canoe trip: "One of our master sergeants, Roy Wilfon, wrote a chit, which promised that the American government would reimburse the natives for the canoes. We planned to eventually sail to Australia. We sailed by night using the Southern Cross constellation to navigate." Near Cuyo one morning, a Japanese seaplane recognized who they were.

When the escapees arrived there, the natives were very helpful tending to the sick. That same morning a Japanese battlecruiser and an aircraft tender pulled into the harbor. Japanese marines boarded landing crafts and came ashore. The Americans knew they could not put up a fight because they only had nine .45 pistols and seventeen old Enfield rifles. Wilfon and Kolger discussed the situation. Wilfon decided to take a group and escape, while Kolger agreed to stay with the rest.

Years later Burns recalled other aspects of the Japanese arrival on Cuyo, though his memory about when and why they landed there differs somewhat from Sergeant Kolger's recollection. Lieutenant Baggett, Burns recalled, decided to seek out a missionary who lived nearby, and there was a good chance that he was a spy for the Japanese. He probably had a shortwave radio and contacted them about the fleeing soldiers.

The Americans soon decided that they had no choice other than to surrender. Captain Sayre and Burns walked down to the area where the Japanese were landing. Burns gave his .45 to one of the Japanese. They marched the prisoners back up to the schoolyard, which was maybe two hundred yards away. The soldier with Burns's weapon walked over and held the .45 pistol up to Burns's head and pulled the trigger. It just clicked. He then pulled the trigger another time or two. Again the trigger mechanism just clicked. He then stuck the gun in his belt and walked away. Even though the ammunition was old, Burns could not explain why he was not dead; maybe the bullets were removed. Burns later thought that his captor had decided to kill him as an example to the others of what would happen if they did not follow orders. While the men who did not escape stood there, they were told: "you will never see your loved ones and America again. One way or the other, you will all die."

As Kolger remembered, they then were taken aboard the landing craft and shipped out to the aircraft tender. But he noticed something odd about one plane onboard: the propeller and the aircraft engine were American made. The men were sent to various POW camps in the Philippines. Burns recollected that less than half of the group who surrendered on Cuyo survived the war.

Many of those from the Mindoro Detachment who did not surrender that day moved from island to island, hiding out with the help of sympathetic Filipinos. Calvin Hogg even married a Filipino woman from one of the islands and returned with her after the war. Obtaining nutritious food was often a problem, as was avoiding tropical diseases. U.S. submarines eventually rescued some escapees. Many others, however, were hunted down and captured by the Japanese. They were usually tortured and then killed, some beheaded.

The fugitive Americans always had to be vigilant because Japanese collaborators were among the Filipinos and would report them and their whereabouts. Pvt. Armand Toussaint stayed on Mindoro and was captured there after joining up with a group of Filipino guerrillas. A collaborator told the Japanese that the American knew where the airmen's mechanic tools were. After he refused to tell them the location, Toussaint was tied to a flagpole and beaten with firewood and kicked by Japanese soldiers for two hours. Some reports indicated that his eyes were gouged out as well. He was then given a second chance to tell where the tools were. He refused and was then taken beside a hole that had been dug and bayoneted until he fell in.[10]

Hell Ships to Japan

During the war, the International Committee of the Red Cross had repeatedly appealed to the Allied and Axis powers to ensure the safety of POW ships. They proposed that all such vessels be marked for clear identification so they would not be inadvertently sunk. For one reason or another, the warring countries, including Japan and the United States, chose not to comply with this recommendation, which cost the lives of many prisoners.[11] In 1944 alone more than 10,000 Allied POWs died in the Western Pacific at the hands of U.S. submariners.[12]

Many prisoners from the Philippines were sent by ship to Japan as slave laborers. Lankford, James Bollich, and Kenneth Farmer had survived the Death March, Camp O'Donnell, a brief stint at Cabanatuan, and a month and a half on a work detail repairing a bridge. They returned to Cabanatuan and then were transferred by truck to Manila with about 1,600 other prisoners and put aboard an old Japanese freighter, the *Tottori Maru,* on October 6,

1942. Described by survivors as "hell ships," the holds of these vessels were filled beyond capacity with POWs. The *Tottori Maru* carried between 1,500 and 1,900 POWs, many from the 27th Bomb Group, during this voyage. There was very little room to lie down. Dr. Hochman, the 16th's physician, had survived a month working as a doctor at U.S. Army Field Hospital No. 2 during the artillery duel between the Japanese on Bataan and the Americans on Corregidor. He then spent several months working as a prisoner-physician at Cabanatuan. He too would be shipped out on the *Tottori Maru*.

Being an officer, Hochman was allowed to stay on the deck of the ship. He was one of the lucky ones because he had sunshine and fresh air, even though he only had his summer cotton uniform and, with it being fall, was usually very cold. The *Tottori Maru* was in a convoy of about five or six ships preceded by a destroyer. One day the doctor saw the wake of two torpedoes. The Japanese captain made a sharp turn and missed them. Hochman prayed to God, "This is a hell of a way to die!"

Lankford, Bollich, and Farmer were down in the hold as the ship headed toward Formosa. Their ship steamed in and out of the harbor there several times because, apparently, there were either American airplanes going by, which could bomb the ship, or there were American submarines in the area. The men remained in the hold of the freighter for a month. The conditions were terrible. The hold was used for hauling cattle, and there was still cow manure all over when the men loaded in.

With little water and very little food, a number of the POWs died on the ship. Bodies were handed topside to fellow POWs, then thrown overboard. There was no special funeral ceremony. The men used scrap iron from the hull to tie to the bodies so they would sink.

Oryoku Maru *Nightmare*

The hell ships of 1942 at least were operating in waters that were controlled by the Japanese Navy. That was not the case in December 1944 for the 1,619 prisoners who boarded the ill-fated *Oryoku Maru*. Many POWs from the 27th were marched aboard. MacArthur was already back on Philippine soil as the prisoners were crammed into three dark, filthy, sweltering holds. As the ship slowly crept out of Manila Bay, the prisoners screamed for water and air. Many became maniacal. To find moisture, some prisoners scratched weaker comrades and began sucking their blood. Others drank urine. Fifty men died that first night, and the hell ship was only a mile off the coast of Bataan.

Jay B. Harrelson, a pilot from the 16th, said that he was "packed into the hull of the *Oryoku Maru* and the hatch was closed. We had no water, and soon, we all had difficulty breathing. Men started to go crazy. They were suffocating to death."

The next morning U.S. dive bombers attacked the convoy. A bomb dropped close to the *Oryoku Maru* killed several prisoners instantly. The hell ship, badly crippled with holes in her side, limped into nearby Subic Bay, northwest of Bataan, and ran aground twenty-one hours into her voyage. As the American planes returned to finish off the vessel, some POWs climbed on the deck and waved off the bombers.

Frank Corbi and his two friends Kolger and Burns from the 48th Materiel Squadron decided they would stick together as buddies. The ship was burning badly. Finally, one of the Japanese translators told the POWs they could leave the holds but they had to swim straight to shore—if they started to swim off in another direction, machine gunners on the beach would shoot. Those still living swam the three hundred yards and were herded to a nearby tennis court to be organized and counted; thirteen hundred prisoners were still alive. Corbi, however, decided to swim back to the ship because there were blankets and clothing that he thought the three would need.

There were still POWs coming out of the holds at that time. Because the ship was burning badly, all of the Japanese soldiers had already gotten off. After he found the clothing, Corbi went into the galley looking for food. He found some ice cream and ate it. Then he found a wooden table, pushed it over the side, and swam safely to shore, with the clothing and blankets on the table.

Two POWs on the *Oryoku Maru,* however, did escape: George Petritz, a navy ensign, and Darnell Kadolph, an army private. Both jumped into the sea and hid under wood crates. They swam about two miles down the coast away from the guards. They were rescued separately by natives. Another Filipino, Fortunato Milado, helped Petritz and Kadolph hide for about a week They then met up with guerrillas and spent a few weeks with them while they arranged for a U.S. patrol boat to pick them up, which occurred on January 29, 1945.[13]

A week after the *Oryoku Maru* grounded in Subic Bay, a truck convoy took the remaining POWs to San Fernando. After spending three days at a railroad station, the men boarded a northbound train that took them to a port on the Lingayen Gulf, the spot where Homma's 14th Army had landed in December 1941. Here they boarded two hell ships, the *Enoura Maru* and the *Brazil Maru.*

On December 18 it rained, so the thankful men at least could quench their thirst with the rainwater that trickled into the hold. Harrelson recalled that the ship had been carrying artillery and horses. They were put into the hold where the horses had been, fortunately, because they found some grain that had been left there. That served as their Christmas dinner.

By January 1, 1945, the ships reached the safety of Takao Harbor, on the southwest side of Formosa. There the survivors on the *Brazil Maru* were transferred to the *Enoura Maru*. A week later, on January 9, while still at Takao, the *Enoura Maru* was attacked by American bombers. Roll call after the attack revealed that there were now only 930 prisoners still alive. These men then were transferred to the *Brazil Maru* and again placed in the hold. Three days later the convoy sailed for Moji, Japan.

The *Brazil Maru* moved cautiously on a zigzag course toward Japan as U.S. submarines terrorized the East China Sea. As the hell ship moved north, the temperature rapidly decreased. Men were now dying at the rate of thirty a day as malnutrition, dehydration, and illness wracked their bodies. On January 30, after moving at a snail's pace, the *Brazil Maru* docked at Moji. Roll call in the hold indicated that only 435 of the original 1,619 prisoners were still alive. Many of the survivors died in the weeks and months to come—less than 300 lived to tell the *Oryoku Maru* tale after the war. Among those surviving that hell ship from the old 27th Bombardment Group was Doc Savage, the pilot Glen Stephenson left in charge of Bataan Field in January 1942.[14]

POW Camps in Japan

Dr. Hochman's hell ship arrived at Pusan, Korea, on November 8, 1942, where many of the POWs, including Bollich, Farmer, and Lankford, were taken off. Hochman continued to the city of Osaka, Japan, and was placed in the POW camp there, the first one established in that area of the country. The officer in charge of this camp was Col. Sotaro Murata. According to Hochman, the POWs were brought in for one reason—slave labor. Here they were awakened at five in the morning, fed a bowl of rice, and then sent to work. Because of various illnesses, eventually nearly half the men were sick. The POWs found it easier to stay in bed with a blanket over them than to go to work.

Hochman recognized that this was getting serious and began to get the men out of bed—forcibly—talking to them, begging them to understand that they were making a big mistake by turning their faces to the wall. With spring approaching, the weather was nicer, the sun was out, and the men needed to get outside so they could move around and exercise. He told them that perhaps they could steal some food aboard the ships they unloaded. When he first thought of this, of course, he was condemned and called a

"Jap-lover." As a result of their finally getting up and going out every day, walking, and working, the POWs began to develop muscles. They began to live again.

One could tell how the war was going when out in Osaka. The camp was located in the harbor area. There was a large volume of ships coming in and out, and the POWs worked as stevedores, stealing English-language news-papers when they could. This helped Hochman determine the progress of the war. For example, there would be enormous headlines: "American Forces Are Repulsed and Driven out to Sea." Then a week later the papers would mention that U.S. planes were taking off from the islands that they were supposedly repulsed from.

Hochman recalled treating POWs with beriberi. One type of the disease affected the lower extremities. "The men would be up all night crying with extreme pain." The other type, which affected the heart, caused tremendous swelling. "After many months of starvation and the rigors of war, their bodies swelled up unbelievably." Hochman also treated POWs with vitamin defi-ciency, which caused night blindness, scurvy, malaria, and dysentery. "The good Lord was good to me, and I'm still here. Why? I don't know. I can't answer that."

There were two hospitals in the area specifically for POWs. One was located under the concrete grandstand at Ichioka Athletic Field and was described as a "hell hole," with no windows or ventilation. It opened for patients in late 1942. Brutality was common, including frequent beatings of the patients and medical staff. POWs were frequently forced to clean up vomit and feces with their bare hands and bury it outside. Rats were everywhere. Surgery was performed with a razor and no anesthesia, nor was any medicine available to treat postoperative pain. Corpses were piled up at one end of the field and periodically burned.[15] The other treatment center was Kobe POW Hospital, coincidentally opened in June 1944, a time when the war had gone from bad to worse for Japan and its two Tripartite Pact partners. (In fact, Italy had already declared war on Germany.) Conditions at Kobe were better, and it was used as for propaganda ploy and Red Cross inspectors. Three U.S. Navy physician POWs were among its medical staff, who improved the quality of care.[16]

One day Colonel Murata called Hochman into his office and told him that he had received orders from Tokyo to make sure no POWs would ever be repatriated in case there was a U.S. landing in Japan. He was the only POW to know of this and did not tell anybody else because he was afraid the men might panic.

On June 1, 1945, at 9:00 in the morning, sirens sounded. Because of the behavior of the Japanese guards and officers, Hochman knew something big was about to happen. He recalled that "525 B-29s flew over the camp and dropped incendiaries." The Osaka camp burned to the ground.

POW Camps in Korea and China

Bollich, Farmer, and Lankford, who left Hochman at Pusan, were sent by train to a camp near Mukden in Manchuria north of Korea. Lankford thought the treatment there was better than it had been in the Philippines due primarily to the large number of POW officers there, including thirty-six generals. Lankford guessed there might have been twenty or more POWs from the 27th at Mukden.

The buildings in which they were housed were essentially underground. This was done because it was so cold in Manchuria, sometimes −30 degrees F,

27. Sixteenth Squadron men, Mukden POW Camp, Manchuria, August 1945. Front row, L to R: Charles A. Cook, Kenneth L. Farmer, Ward S. Clark, James J. Bollich, Herbert P. Lanclos. Back row, L to R: Paul H. Lankford, Sommie B. Riley, Clarence Slayton, Ben Robinson, Clarence S. Cox. They are wearing new clothes dropped by American planes at the end of the war. *Courtesy James Bollich and Kenneth Farmer*

and the dirt served as insulation. Later they built a camp specifically for POWs on about fifteen acres of land with a sixteen-foot-high concrete-block fence around it with guard stations on top.

Prisoners slept on shelves, not bunk beds. The lower one was about a foot off the ground, and the higher one about five feet above, requiring a ladder. Lankford started out working on a farm detail raising vegetables for the Japanese. The POWs stole a little bit of it for themselves. Later he went to work at a tool-and-die factory and then was transferred to a lumber mill. The Chinese and the Manchus would bring the logs in by horse cart or sometimes by train, and POWs would unload them and saw them down the middle. Some of the wood was very hard, so the prisoners were supposed to push the logs through very slowly, otherwise the band saw would break in two. Lankford would jam the logs through and break the saw intentionally—"When that happened, it would take us about a half hour to 45 minutes to fix the machine."

Cpl. Robert Wolfersberger from the 16th Squadron was also a POW at Mukden and worked at a machine shop. He said eventually the American prisoners were moved out of there because of the high sabotage rate. He said that one day the Japanese manager of the plant, who was a graduate of a college in Illinois, called in one of the other POWs and showed him a chart where the production at the factory had slowly been increasing until the time that the Americans started working there. At that point the production rate dropped off. Not all of the prisoners were kept at the main camp there. When the POWs were out on work details, they stayed at smaller subcamps.

Maj. Gen. George Parker Jr., who had commanded the II Corps on Bataan, was the camp commander of the POWs. Brig. Gen. Alfred Jones, who had commanded I Corps on Bataan, was also held there. Maj. Gen. Edward King, who had surrendered Bataan to the Japanese, was there for a short time but then moved out. Lt. Gen. Jonathan Wainwright was at the camp for only a few days, as Lankford recalled, and then was moved farther north to a prison camp at Harbin, Manchuria. According to Lankford, none of the generals or other officers were required to work because the Japanese observed the Geneva Convention rules in that regard at this particular camp. The generals ranged in rank from brigadier (one star) to lieutenant (three stars). They walked around the prison like everybody else, so the other men could just go up and talk to them, which Lankford occasionally did. He said one could get an idea on how the war was going by using the "human barometer." If the U.S. military were pushing and gaining territory and moving northward, then the Japanese would cut back on rations. If the rations increased, that meant the Americans were not advancing very fast.

Punishment—It Could Have Been Worse

Buck Prewett was one of those from the 3rd Bomb Group who volunteered in Savannah to transfer to the 27th just before the unit left on Operation PLUM. Prewett, who was looking for adventure, got more than he bargained for. He was housed in a POW camp in the mountains of northern Honshu near the town of Hanawa. According to Prewett, the prison commandant, Lieutenant Asaka, had what one might call a flaw in his personality for a military warden. The POWs sensed that he did not want to be as mean as he was supposed to be.

The Hanawa POWs underwent unprovoked beatings and were called foul names in both English and Japanese. By then the men knew enough Japanese to know what they were being called. The Christmas of 1944 was exceptionally cold, and snow piled up about twelve feet high. Prisoners in Barracks 4D had already run out of coal for their stove, and the Japanese would not give them any more coal, wood, or anything else to burn. Prewett and four others came up with the idea that they would take the wooden fire ladder, which was about fifteen feet long, and burn it for fuel. Ladders were hardly noticed by the POWs or the Japanese, so they figured it would not be missed. In February 1945 all hell broke loose when the Japanese found out that the ladder was missing. They put the entire camp on half-rations until the POWs turned in the guilty people. But the culprits could not stand to have their fellows live on half-rations. Although five had taken the ladder and used it for firewood, they drew straws to determine which two would take the rap. Even though he had a long straw, Prewett insisted on being one of the two since he was the instigator. The other was Brownell Cole. They discussed beforehand what their punishment might be—beatings, torture, or possibly death.

Cole and Prewett confessed to Lieutenant Asaka and were beaten by guards until nearly unconscious and then dropped in a three-foot trench that was similar to a grave. They were positioned on their backs next to each other with one's feet beside the other's head. The guards then placed a piece of tin over the trench and piled dirt on top. Kept there for two days and given a half ration of food once a day, the men had socks but no shoes on and would rub each other's feet to keep warm. After that they were tied up at the guardhouse. When the guards changed shifts, they would give the prisoners their best punch. On the fourth day Cole and Prewett were taken back to their barracks. They were both thankful that for punishment, Asaka had not chosen the third and final option.

Pfc. Robert Shrum of the 91st Squadron was in Camp Narumi Prison in

Japan, and Dr. Elack Schultz, the 91st Squadron physician, was the camp doctor. He performed a number of operations there using a mess-kit knife and no antiseptics, including appendectomies, hemorrhoid operations, and abscess drainage. Dr. Schultz became aware of a practice where nonsmoking POWs would trade their measly cigarette ration for future rice meals, which further contributed to a smoker's malnutrition. He held a meeting with those who were trading their cigarettes for food and got everyone to agree to discontinue the commerce.

Silvio Gasperini from Upper Michigan was one of Stephenson's close friends at West Point. He was an infantry instructor at Camp John Hay in the mountains near Baguio when the bombs started dropping on December 8, 1941. On Christmas Eve he began the 150-mile trek to Bataan and fought with the infantry until the April surrender. He survived the Death March to Camp O'Donnell. Gasperini was transferred to Japan on the same hell ship with Warren Stirling from the 27th, then to the same three POW camps. In fact, most of the prisoners on this particular hell ship and in the three camps were officers. Stirling was initially sent to work at a steel mill in Osaka and was later quartered at an all-officers camp at Zentsuji with at least seven other officers from the 27th. Known to be at Zentsuji with Stirling were William W. Bird, Samuel H. Dillard III, Arthur G. Hilley, Horace B. Patterson, John A. Ryan, and Horace A. Smith. Stirling's last three months as a prisoner in Japan were spent at Roku Rishi. Treatment at the last two camps was somewhat better than at others. For example, Gasperini received fourteen Red Cross packages at Zentsuji, said to be a "showcamp" used by the Japanese for propaganda purposes. At most camps prisoners were lucky to see a single such package.

The August 1 Kill-All Order

Lankford said the POWs did not know the atomic bomb had been dropped, but their guards did tell them that there were many, many Americans coming in big airplanes and dropping many, many bombs, killing many Japanese. They learned that the war was about to end when an American OSS officer (Office of Strategic Services—the U.S. secret intelligence agency during World War II and forerunner of the CIA) came into camp looking for General Wainwright.

Jay B. Harrelson had arrived in Japan in January 1945 on the *Brazil Maru*. In April he was transferred to Mukden POW Camp in Manchuria and met up with Lankford there. Harrelson's recollection is that one day at about sunset, he saw some Americans parachute in and land in a cabbage patch near the camp. These were OSS officers and other U.S. soldiers, and they were looking for Wainwright. They told the POWs that the war was basically over. Six feet, one inch tall, Harrelson weighed only 96 pounds when the war ended, 104 pounds less than he weighed on December 8, 1941.

Captain Kane, the adjutant for the 27th, was at a Cabanatuan POW camp on Luzon until U.S. Army Rangers liberated the prisoners on January 30, 1945. It was the belief among the POWs there that at some point the prison guards had orders to execute all the men. To further support this belief, he said they had already learned from Filipinos working around the camp about the Palawan Massacre. At many other POW camps, the guards repeatedly told the prisoners that when the United States invaded Japan, they would be executed.

In August 1944 the War Ministry in Tokyo had issued a directive to the commandants of various POW camps outlining a policy for what it called the "final disposition" of prisoners. A copy of this document, which came to be known as the "August 1 Kill-All Order," would surface during the war-crimes investigations in Tokyo after Japan surrendered. Bearing a chilling resemblance to actual events that occurred at Palawan, the directive stated:

When the battle situation becomes urgent, the POWs will be concentrated and confined in their location and kept under heavy guard until preparations for the final disposition will be made. Although the basic aim is to act under superior orders, individual disposition may be made in [certain] circumstances. Whether they are destroyed individually or in groups, and whether it is accomplished by means of mass bombings, poisonous smoke, poisons, drowning, or decapitation, dispose of them as the situation dictates. It is the aim not to allow the escape of a single man, to annihilate them all, and not to leave any traces.[17]

The Potsdam Conference was held in Germany from July 17 through August 2, 1945, with leaders from the United States, Great Britain, and the Soviet Union, to settle issues related to the occupation zones and other arrangements related to postwar Europe. Also, the United States and Britain drew up a thirteen-point document with China, which called for an unconditional surrender of Japan at once or that nation would face total destruction. This ultimatum, issued on July 26, was known as the Potsdam Declaration. The Japanese leadership discussed the ultimatum but made no official reply to the Allies. On August 4, American B-29s dropped 720,000 leaflets over Hiroshima urging everyone to evacuate because the city would soon be annihilated. At 8:15 A.M. on August 6, a lone B-29, the *Enola Gay,* dropped an atomic bomb on Hiroshima, which wiped out the city. The Americans then dropped millions of pamphlets over all of Japan calling for the nation to surrender or suffer more destruction from such bombs. The U.S. military also aimed radio broadcasts at Japan quoting Pres. Harry Truman who urged Japan to surrender or suffer additional bombings.

B-29s flew bombing missions on August 8 against the cities of Yawata and Fukuyama. That same day Russia declared war on Japan, and at 1:00 A.M. the next morning two Soviet armies crossed into Manchuria from the west while another army stationed in Vladivostok invaded Manchuria from the east. These forces would converge on the city of Harbin in Manchuria.

Japanese leaders debated the pros and cons of surrendering, but one of the factors that weighed against an unconditional surrender was the fact that they knew many of them would be held accountable for the war crimes and other atrocities they and their troops had been committing for many years. On August 9 at 11:01 A.M., while they continued debating these issues, a second atomic bomb was dropped on Nagasaki.

That day Cpl. Earl Williams from Charlotte, North Carolina, was working his twelve-hour shift in a coalmine with others from the 27th's 454th Ordnance Company. The mine had earlier been condemned by the Japanese but was reopened when the POW labor force became available. After resurfacing he and the others were told by POWs that a lone B-29 had flown over, then a brilliant flash of light came from across the bay, followed by ground tremors, a typhoon-like wind, and a big mushroom cloud rising over Nagasaki. They concluded that something incredible had just take place.

Soon messages went back and forth between Japan and the Allied nations concerning the conditions for surrender. At 11:00 P.M., August 14, the Japanese sent identical cables in English to their delegations in Switzerland and Sweden regarding their willingness to surrender, with instructions to transmit these messages to the United States, Great Britain, the Soviet Union, and China. At noon on August 15, the emperor of Japan announced over radio to his people that the nation was surrendering. Japanese military units thousands of miles away could hear this radio message from Japan, including those in Harbin, Manchuria.

After the announcement was made, sixteen captured B-29 crewmen were taken to a hill outside of the Fukuoka Prison Camp on the Japanese island of Kyushu and individually executed. This was the same place where four days earlier eight other U.S. airmen were beheaded one at a time.[18] That same day American B-29s flew their last bombing mission over Japan.

On August 16, before noon, a note accepting the surrender arrived from Washington at Imperial Headquarters. The Japanese then issued orders to their army and navy units to cease hostilities.[19] At this point the race was on for the Americans to get to POW camps before the prisoners could be executed, or at least that was what they feared might happen, either because of orders by the government, groups of soldiers acting on their own, or by Japanese citizens. In fact, many Allied POWs were executed during this period.[20] Lt. Gen. Albert Wedemeyer, who was the commanding general of all U.S. forces in China, sent airborne troops, including OSS members and Japanese American soldiers as translators, to rescue American POWs.

General Wainwright was the highest-ranking American being held as a POW. At the War Department George Marshall and his staff feared that Wainwright would be executed as a last-minute act of reprisal. The government had good reason to believe that this might happen. They were well aware of the Nanking Massacre and other atrocities in China, Manchuria, and elsewhere. They knew about the Palawan Massacre and were also aware of part of the story of the hell ship *Oryoku Maru* from the two POWs who had escaped from the vessel in December 1944.

The OSS men arrived at Hoten on August 17 and learned that Wainwright was at Si'an near Harbin, which was about one hundred miles north.[21] When they arrived there at 3:30 A.M. Sunday morning, August 19, they demanded to see Wainwright and the other POWs. After meeting with the general a few hours later, the OSS men had breakfast with about thirty-four high-ranking POW officers, who were brought up to date on various aspects of the war. This group included British lieutenant general Sir Arthur Percival; Tjarda van Starkenborgh, governor-general of the Dutch East Indies; and Maj. Gen. Edward King. There seemed to be no elation or sense of freedom among them, and the liberators were "appalled at the general lethargy that dulled the spirits of the men sitting at the table."[22]

A day or two after the OSS men had arrived at the Mukden POW camp, the Russians arrived and took the Japanese prison personnel as prisoners. One of the American POWs, Major General Parker, was put in charge of the camp. Lankford was thankful that the Red Army came in so quickly because otherwise, he thought, he would have been executed. He found the Russians to be very friendly. Once the U.S. Army Air Force knew where the POWs were located, B-29s began food drops.

After three weeks the Russians provided the former prisoners transportation to Port Arthur in Manchuria, where U.S. Navy ships were anchored. There they were ordered to take off their clothes (because they were infested with lice and fleas), took showers, and were sprayed with DDT. Each man received a new set of clothes, then all boarded a navy ship, the *Colbert* (APA-145), a 455-foot attack transport. Lankford later reminisced about boarding the ship. The chief asked his name, how long it had been since eating good food, and what he would like to eat right now. The answers respectively were, "Paul Lankford," "Three and-a-half years," and "ice cream." The chief went down to the galley to get a gallon of ice cream and a spoon. Lankford could only eat about three bites because the food was too rich. The chief said: "Okay, put Paul Lankford's name on that carton of ice cream. Anytime, day or night, he wants some ice cream, go down and get it, and let him eat all he wants."

The ship headed to Okinawa. A big typhoon hit the island, and some antiship mines came loose. The ship hit one of them and was nearly blown in half, killing a number of former POWs and sailors. Farmer recalled sailors aboard telling him at one point during the storm that the winds were 125 knots and the waves were cresting at ninety feet. They were barely able to stay afloat and had to be towed into the harbor. Lankford recalled that two frogmen dove in to examine the damage and said, "It's by a miracle from above that you people are safe."

A day or two later they were loaded onto B-24 bombers and flown to the Philippines. These aircraft had hydraulic-controlled bomb-bay doors. The aircrews had suspended some boards over the doors and told Lankford's group not to get off them because the doors could open. About halfway to the Philippine islands, the pilot announced that he had received a message from one of the airplanes with British POWs aboard. The bomb-bay doors had opened accidentally, and as a result all of the men were lost in the China Sea.

In Manila the former prisoners were given more clothes, food, and back pay. William Hipps, who had been the squadron commander of the 16th before Stephenson, happened to be stationed at Fort McKinley. He was now a colonel and director of operations for Kenney's command. When he found out that some of the 27th survivors were in Manila, he sent some big military trucks to collect the men and threw a party at his quarters.

The war ended very easily for Dr. Hochman and his comrades in Osaka, because all the Japanese disappeared, suddenly leaving the prisoners. They knew that obviously something had happened. A U.S. plane flying overhead recognized them and dropped a note telling the POWs not to move. Later two huge B-29 bombers flew over the camp, and out of the bomb-bay doors came crates attached to red, white, and blue parachutes. Inside them were clothes, food, and medicine. Hochman moved a big crate of medicine to his workplace. As he was stocking the shelves, he came across a little bottle of dry powder and a little label on the outside that read "penicillin." He had no idea what it was, no idea what to do with it. There were no instructions. He thought the medicine must be valuable. Not knowing what to do with it, he crushed over one hundred bottles of penicillin because he did not want it falling into the hands of the Japanese.[23]

Eventually, U.S. Army Rangers came into the camp and took the POWs to the Osaka Hotel. When the former prisoners left for Manila, Hochman was kept behind to look after other ill POWs. As time passed, Hochman was ordered to the port city of Wakayama to meet the U.S. 6th Fleet, which included a hospital ship to evacuate the ailing men. The doctor recalled being taken by motorboat to the battleship *South Dakota*. He got out of the boat, stepped on a little stairway, and climbed all the way to the main deck. As he got on the landing, he was "piped" aboard. He did not think it was for him. A complete U.S. Marine guard of honor and the American flag met him. Hochman said: "It was the most thrilling thing I ever experienced. They didn't tell me about this reception. I was the first POW they had ever seen. I broke down and cried. I was a basket case. I'll never forget that as long as I live. The commanding officer was Vice Admiral Ralph Riggs. He was a big husky guy. He put his arm around me. It was quite an experience."

Hanawa's Commandant, "Mr. Nice Guy"

Hanawa was relatively isolated in the mountains of northern Japan. On August 20, 1945, Lieutenant Asaka, the camp commandant, notified the POWs that the war was over. Buck Prewett recalled that about three weeks before the war's end, the civilian supervisor for his group in the copper mine had been transferred, and a young college student replaced him. On about August 18, while Prewett was down in the mine, the student told him that he wanted to talk. They went way off in an area where nobody else was. At that point he offered Prewett a cigarette. He looked him in the eye and said that America was "Number One," England "Number Two," and so forth. When he got to Japan in the rating list, he had tears in his eyes. Prewett got the point.

On about August 21, American airplanes started to arrive and drop supplies at the camp. B-29s dropped food, clothing, and medicine about every other day. Frequently, messages included with the supplies stated: "Do not leave camp! We're coming to get you!" Eventually, Lt. Col. Arthur Walker,

28. POW photograph taken September 1945 in Hanawa, Japan. Top row, L to R: Diaz Pablo, Jimmy Vaughn, Sedric Pearson, Buck Prewett, Silverstein. Middle row, L to R: Brownell Cole, S. F. Brooks, M. Vidaurri, L. Whichard, Al Lopez. Front row, L to R: M. Torres, R. Levis, Sisneros, J. Brundage, Clarence Shaw. *Courtesy Buck Prewett*

who was the highest-ranking POW in the camp and a B-29 pilot who had been shot down over Japan, decided to send some of the men into the town of Hanawa despite the messages.

Walker asked Prewett on September 10 to choose fourteen other men and go and find out the attitude of the Japanese civilians. "They may be hostile, or they may have decided to accept the surrender," he told them. The finding was that the Japanese had accepted their fate. They were not hostile in any way. Prewett noticed a shingle of a photography studio flapping in the wind and came up with the idea of having a picture taken. There was only one thing missing—money. Prewett proposed to the photographer that he would pay for the pictures when he returned to America, which was acceptable. After taking the pictures and preparing to leave, who should walk in but Lieutenant Asaka, smiling and speaking in clear English. The photographer told Asaka of their arrangement. The former commandant laughed and said, "No, no, no. I will pay for the photos." And he did.

12

"When Johnny Comes Marching Home Again"

FOR SOME WHO SURVIVED Bataan and returned home after the war: "We had been given up, surrendered; we were marked as cowards. . . . There were no banners to welcome us home, no parades to march in, no speeches, and no acknowledgment of any kind. Our folks at home had so many heroes; they were busy welcoming winners, not losers."[1]

Dr. David Hochman finally returned home after testifying about war crimes. When he arrived in San Francisco, he was still five feet, eleven inches tall but now only weighed 108 pounds. He had intestinal worms and "just about everything else you could think of," requiring four months of treatment in an army hospital.

Paul Lankford left the Philippines on October 8, 1945, aboard the Dutch ship *Clip Fontaine.* When everybody was on, the crew pulled up the anchors, the captain put the vessel in reverse, and the ship backed into a barge, breaking the propeller. It was about two more days before the propeller was replaced and the ship finally headed out into the Pacific. There were about eighty former POWs from the 27th Bomb Group aboard.

The *Clip Fontaine* was diverted to Seattle because there were too many ships in the harbor at San Francisco. Lankford was taken to the Madigan U.S. General Hospital at Tacoma, Washington. It was strange because there were German and Italian POWs there, each wearing a big letter P on the back of his fatigues, who helped care for Lankford's group.

Later the Americans were loaded on a hospital train, taking up fifteen to eighteen cars. Their clothes were put in duffel bags, and the men were given pajamas, house slippers, and a robe to wear for the rest of the trip. There was a little army nurse, a captain, assigned to Lankford's group whose job it was to see that the men traveled safely and were admitted to another army hospital near their homes.

Some of the guys stocked up on booze for the trip. When the train arrived in Salt Lake City, the drinkers slipped away in a taxi to a liquor store, loaded up, and returned to the train. The next stop was Chattanooga, Tennessee, and the same thing happened there, five of the guys slipped out to buy alcohol. When they did not come back, the nurse got frantic and tried to talk the trainmaster into waiting for them, but the train had to stay on schedule. The nurse had tears in her eyes because she just lost five of her charges. But when the train arrived at the station in Atlanta, there they were. The nurse went out, grabbed them, and gave them big hugs and kisses because she was so happy to see them returned. According to Lankford, they had hired a taxi in Chattanooga. They traveled at breakneck speed and made it to Atlanta ahead of the train.

Next Lankford was taken by train to Augusta, Georgia, and admitted to Oliver U.S. Army Hospital. He was there for about four months for treatment of various medical problems. Many of the members of the 27th, who were from the Southeast, were admitted there too. While on leave, Lankford returned to Gadsden, Alabama. His cousin, Rufus, was with him when they went into an A&P store. He saw this pretty woman with red hair at the cash register. The couple dated for about four months before he finally proposed to her. They were married on May 5, 1946. The army gave all of the former POWs from the Army Air Corps a two-week free vacation to Miami Beach, Florida. Lankford and his bride took their honeymoon there, all expenses paid.

About two months after that, Lankford had to report to Fort Bragg, North Carolina, where he ran into several other members of the old 27th. There were thousands and thousands of GIs at the base waiting to get discharged. A group of five from the 27th decided to reenlist. According to Lankford, it was surprising that a large number of former POWs from one unit decided to re-up. Most of these men stayed in for twenty years; Lankford put in thirty years and retired as a chief master sergeant. He turned eighty-seven in November 2006 in the company of his wife at their home in Maryville, Tennessee.

Dr. Hochman had been more or less out of medicine for quite a few years in the POW camps. After all, he did not even know what penicillin was. He attended lectures, did lots of reading, and then trained in internal medicine in New York City. Hochman wed, had two children, and celebrated his ninety-fourth birthday in April 2006.

War's Toll on the 27th

On November 20, 1941, Thanksgiving Day, 1,209 troops arrived in Manila from the 27th Bombardment Group and its attached units, the 48th Materiel Squadron and the 454th Bomb Ordnance Company. Perhaps as many as 40 survived from the three units who did not finish the war in POW camps. Eighteen pilots and two enlisted men from the 27th, who had made their way to Australia by one means or another and were under Lt. Col. John Davies's command, first in the 27th, then in the 3rd Bomb Group, returned home in late October and early November 1942. One of them, Pete Bender, was transferred from a hospital in Australia to one in the United States with significant injuries, having survived two B-25 crashes as pilot. A few others, including William Hipps, Reginald Vance, William Eubank, and Robert Stafford, transferred to other units shortly before or after leaving the Philippines and survived the war.

Others, such as Rocky Gause, escaped from the Japanese after being captured or surrendering, though Gause was killed later in the war. Of the fifty-two men of the 48th Squadron's Mindoro Detachment, maybe a dozen or more did not surrender on Cujo. As many as half of them may have survived the war.

The personnel records of April 3, 1942, indicate that there were between 78,000 and 79,000 Filipino and American troops on Bataan. About 2,000 of these men eventually escaped to Corregidor. Between April 10 and June 4, there were about 45,000 Filipinos and 9,300 Americans at Camp O'Donnell Prison. The difference between the April 3 numbers, minus those who escaped to Corregidor, and the Camp O'Donnell numbers indicate that more than 21,000 men had disappeared. Some escaped and others were killed during the fighting, but most died either on the Death March or from disease and starvation at O'Donnell or elsewhere.[2]

Only 43 percent of Americans who surrendered on Bataan are estimated to have ever returned home.[3] Members of the 27th estimate about 30 percent, or 240, of them survived the war. Most of the more than 560 who perished were victims of the Death March, prison camps, or hell ships, including those killed when the vessels they were on were torpedoed or bombed. Only 13 men from the 27th are known to have died in the line of duty on Luzon. Ninety from the 27th and its two attached units died at Camp O'Donnell.[4] One hundred and ninety-nine from the 27th and its two attached units died or were murdered at the infamous Cabanatuan complex, where more than 2,600 American POWs perished. The 48th Materiel Squadron lost between

111 and 149 men during the war from these same causes. At least 50 percent of the 454th did not return. By comparison, about 96 percent of all Allied solders held as POWs in German and Italian camps are estimated to have survived the war.

The Japanese General Responsible for the Death March and Camp O'Donnell

The horrors of the Death March remained secret for months as the war continued. But with the escape and rescue of Capt. William Dyess and nine others from Davao Penal Colony in Mindanao in April 1943, General MacArthur got to hear firsthand about the Death March other atrocities. Then the news of the Death March was released in the United States in early 1944, and Americans wanted the head of Lt. Gen. Masaharu Homma. His headquarters had been a mere five hundred yards from the road the weary American and Filipino troops marched on their way out of Bataan. His car traveled that road numerous times during the Death March. Although Homma, as commanding general of the Japanese forces on Luzon, had delegated authority for the evacuation of the POWs and management of Camp O'Donnell to his subordinates, he could not escape the responsibility for their actions. The American public wanted someone held accountable for these disasters and dastardly deeds.

After Japan's unconditional surrender, Homma was charged with forty-seven specific war crimes. He was found guilty by a military court of having committed war crimes and was sentenced to death. His execution by a firing squad took place on April 3, 1946. Until his last breath, Homma, known to his colleagues as the "Poet General" because of his love for painting and composing poetry during the heat of battle, held to the conviction that his trial was nothing more than "victor's justice."[5] Historians and some legal experts continue to argue about the fairness of Homma's trial and the severe sentence he received; however, a commanding officer is responsible not only for the well being of his men but also that of captured enemy soldiers. It is difficult to imagine that with a POW situation of this magnitude, the commanding officer would not have requested and received frequent detailed briefings. The Allies tried various other members of the Japanese military for crimes related to the Death March, the prison camps, and the hell ships. A number of other officers were convicted, some executed.

The Japanese commandants, Yoshio Tsuneyoshi at Camp O'Donnell and Shigeji Mori at Cabanatuan, were each sentenced during the war-crime trials in Japan to life in prison at hard labor. The infamous Col. Masanobu Tsuji escaped capture after the war and faked his own death. He was seen from time to time in various Asian countries and returned to Japan for a while, even being elected to public office. For various political reasons, the U.S. military chose not to prosecute him. He disappeared again, perhaps forever, in 1961 while in Vietnam.[6]

The 27th Remembered

Robert Shrum from the 27th became a successful architect after the war and founded his own architectural firm. He designed pro bono the Cabanatuan Memorial in the Philippines, dedicated to the Americans who lost their lives on Bataan, on Corregidor, during the Death March, in Japanese POW camps, and aboard the hell ships. The Philippine government donated the land for the memorial, which was turned over to the U.S. National Monuments Commission on May 4, 1985. The Philippine National Monument in memory of the war dead is located at Mount Samat on Bataan.

The original members of the 27th Bombardment Group who fought in the Philippines were not forgotten afterward. In 1975, alumni of the 27th, along with members of its two attached units, the 48th Materiel Squadron and the 454th Ordnance Company, began having annual reunions. Most of the hours are spent reminiscing about what might have been in the Philippines if the 27th had received its airplanes. If asked about surrendering on Bataan, each would point out that he did not surrender, rather he was surrendered.

Because the bulk of the 27th remained in the Philippines and suffered through the Death March, prison camps, starvation, disease, and the hell ships, some of the pilots who were evacuated to Australia at first had second thoughts about attending the reunions. Zeke Summers was reluctant to attend the gatherings, thinking that the others might resent his having gotten out of the Philippines and their having spent three and a half long years in terrible prison camps. But he finally went to one, and the former POWs treated him like a hero, saying: "At least you got a chance to fight. Tell us about it."

Ann Nail Stephenson

When Glenwood Stephenson left Savannah, he and Ann had been husband and wife a total of two weeks. After his departure, the theme of all of his letters to her was that the days with her were the best of his life.

In April 1942 he wrote his final letter to Ann. The sense of adventure and romance that permeated his early letters was gone. He had seen war close up by then, and the reality of death and fighting losing battles for four months had forged a pessimism that crept into his sentences. "Can't seem to say anything in a letter anymore even though our little excursions from time to time seem to make the news. Haven't been in one place over a couple of weeks since this war began and I guess that also goes for quite a while before I left the States. Sure will be glad when we can settle down together. Dream about it every night and think about it each day."

That was the last she heard about Glen until the morning of Sunday, May 3, when a knock on the door brought a War Department telegram and the tragic news of the plane crash. Stunned, Ann went to the Western Union office to telegraph Glen's father, Gordon, in Milwaukee. With Glen's body buried on Mount Bartle Frere, there could be no traditional funeral service. She felt the best thing to do would be to travel to Milwaukee to see her father-in-law. She took a train north and shared her grief with her husband's relatives. A week later, she was back home in Savannah.

By summer Ann was back into the Savannah social scene. While visiting one of the city's nightclubs, she met a soldier from New York who was stationed in the area. The couple married, and a short time later her husband was shipped to Hawaii. He was stationed there when Ann gave birth to their daughter, Sharon. With her husband stationed overseas, Ann sensed her marriage dissolving. She received a divorce.

In 1946 when the war was finally over, she married again and moved to Sacramento, California. In 1947 a daughter, Cindy, was born, followed by two sons. Ann would occasionally take out the family photo album and go through the pictures with her daughters. In the front of the album was a picture of a handsome soldier in a military uniform. When asked who he was, Ann would gaze off into space and reply, "Oh, a man I knew during the war."

Years later she shared with her daughters more about the handsome man in the military uniform in the front of the photo album. She was married to him, but he died early in the war. That, the girls thought, was the end of the story. But after enduring severe arthritis, breast cancer, and another divorce, Ann decided in 1975 to tell her daughters more about the handsome man. She had the girls get an old gray suitcase out of the closet. Inside were additional pictures of the man along with his love letters to Ann. What caught the girl's attention, however, was a beautiful gold ring that said "West Point" and "Duty, Honor, Country." On the inside was etched "Glenwood G. Stephenson, Class of 1940."

During her final months, Ann told the girls the story of her brief marriage to Glenwood, how he went off to the Philippines in 1941, and how he was killed in a plane crash in Australia in 1942. She confessed that he was her first real love, and she had a unique role for that gold ring. Meanwhile, the girls placed everything back in the suitcase and put it in the closet, finally realizing the tragic significance of the handsome man in the military uniform in the family photo album.

At the end Ann was in considerable pain as her cancer spread to her spine. She did not want any more operations. The attorney who had handled her recent divorce also looked into whether she qualified for any medical assistance from the Veteran's Bureau since her second husband, Glen, had died in the war. They started a file for her and began looking into her case. Before any action could be taken, however, Ann passed away in November 1976.

She was now at peace. Her life, like Glenwood Stephenson's, was anything but ordinary. During a span of eight years, she had been married four times. Three of those marriages ended in divorce; one in a deadly plane crash on a far-off mountain in Australia. At one point in 1941, before the war, she envisioned a comfortable, secure future married to a U.S. Army Air Corps officer.

As her casket was lowered into Sacramento's East Lawn Cemetery, on the ring finger of her left hand was the gold band that said "West Point" and "Duty, Honor, Country."

Lesson Learned

ONE HAS TO WONDER how the American and Filipino armies could have gotten themselves into such a predicament after hostilities began and how a fighting force that large could have been cut off from its sources of supply and reinforcement. What equipment and material they had at hand was often not enough, out of date, or both. In most cases the Filipino troops, who were to be a trump card, were not yet adequately trained. After the retreat to Bataan, the army was isolated without any means of adequate resupply or reinforcement. The U.S Pacific Fleet, which theoretically would have protected the supply lines to the Philippines, was significantly crippled, and the U.S. Asiatic Fleet was wholly inadequate to the challenge of the Japanese Combined Fleet. Clearly U.S. leadership at the time was partly to blame for this situation, including the president, Congress, the War Department, and the Department of the Navy, for putting troops in a situation where they had very little chance to succeed. Despite these handicaps, field commanders such as MacArthur, Brereton, and Hart could have had their troops better prepared. More than fifty years ago noted author Walter D. Edmonds, commenting on the fall of the Philippines, pointed out that the American public also needed to be held accountable:

> The poverty in the modern weapons, or in more than one case the actual and abject lack of them, had its roots in the situation here at home, and for that situation, the people of the United States must hold themselves accountable. The army of a democratic society like ours belongs to the people and the people, therefore, have an obligation to concern themselves in its affairs. . . . The men sent out to rectify the situation in the final months had neither the means nor [the] time. The reinforcements and material rushed to them were not enough, arrived too late, or did not reach the Philippines at all.[1]

Despite these shortcomings, the tenacious defenders of Bataan and Corregidor were able to significantly disrupt the timetable that the Japanese had set for their conquest of the island nations of the western Pacific. The Philippines campaign, originally scheduled to be completed in fifty days, took five months. Approximately 192,000 Japanese army and navy personnel had to be deployed, a number far in excess of the original strength allotment.[2] We know now, with hindsight, that these early defensive actions fought so fiercely by the United States and its Allies in the Philippines, Java, Australia, New Guinea, the Coral Sea, and Midway bought valuable time for America to "gear up" for war, thereby contributing to the Allied victory. If these early Japanese campaigns had gone unchecked, the Allied offensive phase likely would have begun in Hawaii or California instead of New Guinea and Guadalcanal.

Appendix 1

Twenty-seventh Bomb Group Pilots Flown from the Philippines to Australia, December 17–18, 1941

Maj. John H. Davies
Capt. Edward N. Backus
1st Lt. Harry L. Galusha
1st Lt. Ron D. Hubbard
1st Lt. Herman F. Lowery
1st Lt. Floyd W. Rogers
1st Lt. James R. Smith
1st Lt. Julius B. Summers
2nd Lt. Richard R. Birnn
2nd Lt. Oliver C. Doan
2nd Lt. Robert F. Hambaugh
2nd Lt. Gustave M. Heiss Jr.

2nd Lt. James H. Mangan
2nd Lt. Henry J. Rose
2nd Lt. Robert G. Ruegg
2nd Lt. Alexander R. Salvatore
2nd Lt. Ralph L. L. Schmidt
2nd Lt. Thomas P. Talley
2nd Lt. Francis E. Timlin
2nd Lt. Edwin C. Townsend
2nd Lt. Douglas B. Tubb
2nd Lt. Leland A. Walker
2nd Lt. Howard D. West

Appendix 2

Royce's Raid Crews

The original list was kept by William G. Hipps, who participated in the raid, and edited years later under the supervision of J. Harrison Mangan. Same names for B-25 pilots and copilots appear in the *27th Reports*. The names of other crew members are known, but the plane each flew on cannot be verified.

Former 27th Bomb Group Members in Italics
Names in brackets are variant spellings found on Hipps's list.

B-25C
Ship #41-12483
13th Squadron, 3rd Bomb Group
Davies Flight—Valencia
(P) *Lt. Col. John H. Davies*
(CP) *1st Lt. James B. McAfee*
(N) Lt. William C. Clapp
(B) *Capt. Ronald D. Hubbard*
(E) Technical Sergeant Young
(G) Cpl. Robert M. Newman
(G) Sergeant Hayes
Passengers—Del Monte to Batchelor Field
Brig. Gen. Ralph E. Royce (Mission Commander)
Lt. Col. William C. Kennard [Kinard] (USAAF, M.C.)
Nat Floyd (Civilian Reporter)

B-25C
Ship #41-12441
13th Squadron, 3rd Bomb Group
Davies Flight—Valencia
(P) *Capt. Herman F. Lowery* (C.O., 13th Sqdn.)
(CP) *2nd Lt. Leland A. Walker*

(N) 1st Lt. Joseph M. Bean
(B) TSgt. William B. Wherry
(E) Cpl. Hodges K. Rigdon [Regan]
(G) Noah Fresquez
(G) Sgt. David H. Runnager
Passengers (Del Monte to Batchelor Field)
Sgt. Edward Van Every (G, #41-2447)
Capt. Jesus Villiamor (Philippine Army Air Corps)
Lieutenant Thompson (unknown)

B-25C
Ship #41-12442
13th Squadron, 3rd Bomb Group
Davies Flight—Valencia
(P) *1st Lt. Gustave M. Heiss*
(CP) *2nd Lt. Edwin C. Townsend*
(N) Lt. John Bevan
(B) Sgt. Marlon K. Smith
(E) TSgt. Henry S. Simpers [Snipers]
(G) Sgt. James W. Miller
(G) Sgt. Lionel G. Young
Passengers (Del Monte to Batchelor Field)
Lt. Thomas P. Gerrity (USAAF)

Leander (Enlisted Man, Signal Corps)
Sgt. Arthur Komori (USA, Nisei,
Interpreter)

The only bomber not lost within a year after the raid, it is currently on display in Aitape, New Guinea.

B-25C

Ship #41-12455
90th Squadron, 3rd Bomb Group
Davies Flight—Valencia
(P) 1st Lt. Bennett G. Wilson (C.O.,
90th Sqdn.)
(CP) 2nd Lt. John J. Keeter
(N) Lt. E. T. Tisonyai
(B) TSgt. Luther D. Word
(E) SSgt. Kenneth W. Gatewood
[Wood]
(G) Sgt. Jimmy D. Morse (actually
spelled "Morris")
(G) Cpl. Stephen L. Taylor
(Flight Chief) MSgt. Firman S. Adams
Passengers (Del Monte to Batchelor
Field)
Cpl. Richard E. Nurss (USA Signal
Corps)
Lt. E. D. Benham (USAAF)
Lieutenant Burke (Unknown)

B-25C

Ship #41-12485
90th Squadron, 3rd Bomb Group
Davies Flight—Valencia
(P) *Capt Paul I. "Pappy" Gunn* (C.O.,
ATC. Archerfield)
(CP) *1st Lt. Frank Bender*
(E) "Midgett" (probably Jack Fox)
(G) SSgt. Arnold M. Thompson
(G) Pfc. Joseph A. Paradiso [Paradise]
(No Navigator, No Bombardier)

Passengers (Del Monte to Batchelor
Field)
Capt. Henry G. Thorne (C.O., 3rd
Sqdn., 24th Pursuit Group)
TSgt. Eustace M. Messor (USA, Signal
Corps)
Lt. L. H. Keys (USAAF)
Lieutenant Cox (Unknown)
Sergeant Jefferies (Stowaway)

27th Reports records the ship's number as
41-12498.

B-25C

Ship #41-12480
13th Squadron, 3rd Bomb Group
Strickland Flight—Maramag
(P) 1st Lt. Robert F. Strickland
(CP) *Maj. William G. Hipps* (Asst. Ops.
& Plans O./USAFIA Staff)
(N) Lieutenant Brindel (19th Bomb
Group)
(B) TSgt. George H. Bengel [Bengal]
(E) SSgt. William R. Crutchfield
(G) Sgt. Kenneth A. Cooper
(G) Pfc. Arthur J. White
Passengers (Del Monte to Batchelor
Field)
Pfc. Clyde L. Horn (AR, #41-2447)
Clarence Yamagata (Nisei, Interpreter)
Capt. Harvey Whitfield (USAAF)

B-25C

Ship #41-12443
13th Squadron, 3rd Bomb Group
Strickland Flight—Maramag
(P) *1st Lt. James R. Smith*
(CP) *2nd Lt. Thomas P. Talley*
(N) Lieutenant Grant
(B) MSgt. Ray A. Oliver
(E) TSgt. Aden L. Simmons
(G) Sgt. Guy E. Clanton

(G) Cpl. Alfred A. Fawe [Fall]
Passengers (Del Monte to Batchelor
Field)
Pfc. Herbert M. Wheatley (AE, #41-2447)
Lt. Col. Chih Wang [Chi Wong]
(Chinese Army Liaison)
Lt. Jack Wienert (USAAF)

B-25C
Ship #41-12511
13th Squadron, 3rd Bomb Group
Strickland flight—Maramag
(P) 2nd Lt. Harold V. Maull [Maul]
(CP) *2nd Lt. Howard B. West*
(N) Lt. William Culp
(B) Sgt. O. C. Cook
(E) SSgt. Cyril A. Moore
(G) Cpl. Francis H. Pryor
(G) Pfc. Francis M. Fowler
Passengers (Del Monte to Batchelor
Field)
Kimple (Enlisted Man)
Lieutenant Arter (Unknown)
Lt. David M. Conley (USAAF)

B-25C
Ship #41-12472
13th Squadron, 3rd Bomb Group
Strickland Flight—Maramag
(P) 2nd Lt. Malcom E. Peterson
(CP) *2nd Lt. James H. Mangan*
(N) Lieutenant Hanson
(B) SSgt. John P. Butler
(E) Sgt. Norman H. Salles
(G) Cpl. M. S. Whismett [Whinsett]
(G) Sgt. Lawrence H. Cooper
Passengers (Del Monte to Batchelor
Field)
SSgt. Kenneth A. Gradle (R, #41-2447)
Sgt. John J. Phelan (USA, Signal Corps)
Frank Hewlett (Civilian Reporter, UP)
Lieutenant Glover (Unknown)

B-25C
Ship #41-12466
13th Squadron, 3rd Bomb Group
Strickland Flight—Maramag
(P) 1st Lt. John D. Feltham [Felthan]
(CP) 2nd Lt. John R. Linn
(N) Lt. Alfred A. Heyman
(B) TSgt. Melvin E. Owens [Owen]
(E) TSgt. Norman L. Cates [Gates]
(G) Cpl. George H. Nelson
(G) Cpl. Chester L. Hatcher
Passengers (Del Monte to Batchelor
Field)
Capt. Joseph H. Moore (C.O., 20th
Sqdn., 24th Pursuit Group)
Lieutenant Wright (Unknown)
Sgt. Carl L. Card (USA, Signal Corps)

B-25C
Ship #41-12496
90th Squadron, 3rd Bomb Group
(P) *Lt. Ralph L. L. Schmidt*
(CP) *Lt. Richard R. Birnn*
(N) Unknown
(B) Unknown
(E) Unknown
(G) Unknown
(G) Unknown

Started on Philippines Mission from
Charters Towers on the morning of April 11,
but upon arrival at RAAF Station, Darwin,
a bad cut was found on one of the main
tires. No replacement tire was immediately
available. Decision made to abort mission.

B-25C
(Ship Serial Number Unknown)
(Squadron Unknown), 3rd Bomb
Group
(P) 1st Lt. Donald P. Hall (C.O., 89th
Sqdn.)

(P) 1st Lt. Christian Petrie Jr.
(N) Unknown
(B) Unknown
(E) Unknown
(G) Unknown
(G) Unknown

Hall and Petrie tried to fly a tire to Darwin for Schmidt's B-25 and got lost.

B-17E
Ship #41-2447 ("San Antonio Rose II")
14th Recon Squadron, 19th Bomb
    Group
(P) Capt. Frank P. Bostrom
(CP) Lt. Wilson L. Cook
(N) Lt. Harold E. Snider
(B) Lt. Earl Sheggrud
(R) SSgt. Kenneth A. Gradle
(AR) Pfc. Clyde L. Horn
(E) SSgt. John C. Haddon
(AE) Pfc. Herbert M. Wheatley (Tail
    Gunner)
(G) Sgt. Edward Van Every
Passenger (Townsville to Del Monte)
Brig. Gen. Ralph Royce (Chief, Air
    Staff USAFIA, Mission Com-
    mander)

Plane destroyed on ground at Del Monte
No. 1 at 5:20 P.M., April 12 while undergoing
replacement of left outboard engine.

B-17E
Ship #41-2421
14th Recon Squadron, 19th Bomb
    Group
(P) Capt. David G. Rawls
(CP) Unknown

(N) Lt. Robert T. Jones
(B) Unknown
(R) Unknown
(AR) Unknown
(E) Sgt. Robert J. Dunn Jr.
(AE) Sgt. Robert K. Palmer
(G) Unknown
Passenger (Del Monte to Batchelor
    Field)
Capt. Frank P. Bostrom

B-17E
Ship #41-2486
30th Bomb Squadron, 19th Bomb
    Group
(P) Capt. Edward C. Teats
(CP) Lt. "Ted" Greene
(N) Lt. Walter E. Seamon
(B) Lieutenant Stone
(R) Unknown
(AR) Unknown
(E) Sergeant Hopkins (?)
(AE) Unknown
(G) Unknown
Passengers (Del Monte to Batchelor
    Field)
Col. Charles A. Backes (Chief of Staff,
    Philippine Army Air Corps)
Lt. Col. Arthur S. Fischer (USA, G2,
    Quinine Expert)
Lt. John D. Bulkeley (USN, C.O.,
    MTB Sqdn. 3)
Lt. Harold E. Snider (N, #41-2447)
Lt. Earl Sheggrud (B, #41-2447)
1st Lt. Howard W. Brown (USA, Signal
    Corps)
Lt. P. S. Miller (Unknown)
Private Johnson (Unknown)

Appendix 3

*Commentary on the Mission of B-25 #41-12455 by Two Former
27th/3rd Pilots*

Richard Launder and Harry Mangan served in both the 27th and the 3rd Bomb
Groups and flew B-25s out of Charters Towers and Port Moresby. In 2004 each commented on the last flight of #41-12455.

Richard Launder
E-mail to Larry W. Stephenson, April 4, 2004

At about 7:00 P.M. on the evening of April 21, 1942, a B-25 of the 3rd Bomb
Group carrying a crew of seven, slammed into a mountain in north Queensland, Australia. The story ends there of life for the seven crew members, but
we who mourn their loss, are not content to close the book on that tragic
event. We want to know Why?

There is ample valid information about this flight that allows us to make
a reasonably accurate assessment of what happened. Official investigators
would sum it up in two words: "pilot error." Granted, but let's look behind
that remark. What led up to pilot error. A one word answer to that is
"inexperience." In my days of flying in the Southwest Pacific, I don't believe
10% of the pilots were proficient in instrument flying. I personally observed
an example of that, described on page 67 of my book, *College Campus in the
Sky.* In the case of B-25 #41-12455, several basic rules of good piloting were
violated.

1. In mountainous terrain, if you are lost, execute a 180-degree turn and
   retrace until you find yourself [definition of "lost": cannot pinpoint your
   position at any moment].
2. Never follow railroad tracks. They might disappear into the side of a
   mountain.
3. Never try to fly visually in bad weather. Get to a safe altitude and stay on
   course.

We will never know what went on in that flightdeck, but those three rules
were broken and any one of them was deadly. To give you some idea of how
difficult it is to do what they were trying to do, find their way out of a can-
yon [valley] in near darkness and bad weather—aside from the fact that they

shouldn't have been there in the first place, what could they have done? Turn around, climb to 6,000 feet and set a straight course to Charters Towers or Townsville.

Harry Mangan
Letter to Larry W. Stephenson, April 9, 2004

Causes of airplane accidents can be related to structural, mechanical, and/or outside forces. If the accident board cannot firmly establish one of these causes, then they will likely state that the cause is "pilot error." I have served on such boards and will tell you that blaming the pilot is an easy out for the board.

1. When you are lost, a 180-degree turn is an appropriate move. In the case of bomber #41-12455, however, we cannot be absolutely sure whether they knew they had crossed the coastline and were flying over land.
2. Although there was no indication that they were following railroad tracks, I have followed tracks [the pilot's "iron compass"] at altitudes so low I could read the town's name on the railroad station. But I would not recommend following railroad tracks in a mountainous area.

Appendix 4

Followup of 27th Bomb Group Pilots

Pilots Who Were Rotated Home in Late October 1942

Eighteen of the 27th Bomb Group's pilots returned to the United States in the fall of 1942. They remained in the U.S. Army Air Forces, and most, because of their combat experience, were assigned to train new pilots. Some did return to the Pacific later during the war. Many afterward had distinguished U.S. Air Force careers. They are listed below by their rank in October 1942.

COL. JOHN "BIG JIM" DAVIES taught bombing tactics in Orlando upon his return to the United States but itched to get back to the Southwest Pacific. In April 1943 he got his wish when he was appointed chief of staff of the 5th Bomber Command, headquartered at Port Moresby, New Guinea, of which the 3rd Bombardment Group was a part. A year later he was assigned to command the 313th Bomb Wing, which consisted of the 6th, 9th, 504th, and 505th Bomb Groups, with more than 105 B-29 Super Fortresses. Newly promoted Brigadier General Davies and his colleagues took the war to Tokyo and other areas of Japan thanks to the much longer range of the Super Fortresses. Davies himself led some of the massive bombing raids from the island of Tinian. In June 1945 the 509th Composite Group was assigned to his 313th Bomb Wing. The 509th consisted of specially trained aircrews and other staff as well as B-29s equipped to carry atomic bombs.[1] Davies witnessed Col. Paul Tibbets's landing of the *Enola Gay* after its historic atomic-bomb mission on August 6. Davies later changed his name from "John" to "Jim" to capitalize on the "Big Jim" nickname from the war. He ended his military career in 1957 as a major general (two stars). At that time he commanded the Alaskan Air Command, responsible for guarding and defending the northern borders of the United States. After leaving the military, Big Jim had a second successful career as a real-estate investor and developer in the Napa Valley of California. Davies died in 1976.

MAJ. RON HUBBARD returned to the United States but soon found himself back in the western Pacific working as a future-plans officer with the 5th Bomber Command. Later he was transferred to the 38th Bombardment Group and served as its deputy commander until the end of the war. Afterward he attended school at the Air Force Institute of Technology, where he earned a bachelor's degree in aeronautical engineering. He remained in the air force, and many of his assignments throughout his career were research related. He retired as a colonel, then went on to another career teaching mathematics for ten years. Hubbard and his wife currently live in Jacksonville, Florida.

Capt. Harry Galusha taught combat tactics to flyers at various airbases in the States after his return and attained the rank of lieutenant colonel. After the war he started a printing business. His son Harry Jr. recalled that his father did not talk about his wartime experiences. Galusha died in 1992.

Capt. Tom Gerrity remained in the military during the war and the U.S. Air Force thereafter. His numerous assignments included command of the 11th Bombardment Group, Strategic Air Command. He eventually attained the rank of general (four stars), and his last command was the Air Force Logistics Command. Gerrity died in 1968.

Capt. James B. McAfee, West Point Class of 1940, also survived the war. He remained in the air force but did not make it a career as many of the other 27th pilots did. He left the service in the late 1940s, after attaining the rank of colonel, and launched a successful insurance business. McAfee died in 1977.

Capt. Bob Ruegg was assigned to Wright Field in Ohio as a test pilot after returning to the States. He too stayed in the military and, after a distinguished career, retired from the air force as a lieutenant general (three stars) in 1972 at Elmendorf Air Force Base, Alaska, where he had commanded the U.S. Air Force Alaskan Command. Ruegg currently lives in Colorado Springs, Colorado.

Capt. James R. Smith from Fort Wayne, Indiana, remained in the air force after the war, retiring in 1966 at the rank of lieutenant colonel. At the time he was deputy commander of Kelly Air Force Base in San Antonio. He afterward worked for General Dynamics on their FB-111 (fighter-bomber) project. Smith died in 1985.

Capt. Julius "Zeke" Summers Jr., West Point Class of 1940, also survived the war. He retired as a colonel after thirty years in the air force. He was the one who initially told the Stephenson family in 1995 about Glen's war experiences and the fate of the 27th Bomb Group. Summers died in 1999.

First Lt. Frank "Pete" Bender, who had survived two B-25 crashes as a pilot (one in April and another in July 1942), was transferred from a hospital in Australia to one in the United States in the late fall of 1942. He recovered and remained in the military, making the air force his career. His last assignment was to command the 340th Bomb Wing at Bergstrom Air Force Base in Austin, Texas. The 340th was a Strategic

Air Command unit composed of eight-engine B-52 bombers. He later worked for International Polymer Corporation of Houston and retired at age eighty-one. Colonel Bender died in 2003.

FIRST LT. OLIVER C. DOAN from LaSalle, Illinois, remained in the air force after the war. He obtained the rank of colonel, retired in 1968, and died in 1969.

FIRST LT. ROBERT FORT HAMBAUGH, after returning home, learned to fly four-engine B-24 bombers and then was sent to England, flying bombing missions over Europe. In August 1944 he was put in charge of the newly formed 36th Bombardment Squadron (H) whose job it was to fly over enemy territory with special electronic devices and jam their radar. Squadron Leader Hambaugh flew missions in his B-24, named "Bama Bound," until the end of the war, attaining the rank of lieutenant colonel. Afterward he returned to Homewood, Alabama, and entered the business world. Hambaugh died in 1974.

FIRST LT. HARRY MANGAN returned to the United States and commanded a squadron equipped with B-26 twin-engine bombers, training combat pilots for Europe. From 1952 to 1958 he was in the Strategic Air Command, flying B-36s and B-52s. He served in the air force until 1965, retiring as a colonel. Mangan had missed the first cut at becoming a general but called the shortcoming a blessing in disguise because he turned his hobby—painting—into a career as a water colorist. He managed a chain of art stores and taught painting at the college level after leaving the military. Mangan married his high-school sweetheart, had three sons, and currently lives in Potomac Falls, Virginia.

FIRST LT. HENRY ROSE attained the rank of lieutenant colonel during the war. Afterward he left the military to complete his degree, wanting to be a petroleum engineer rather than a pilot. Ironically his first job after graduation was as a personal pilot for the CEO of an oil company, but he spent most of his postwar career solely as a petroleum engineer in the Texas Panhandle. Rose died in 2005.

FIRST LT. ALEXANDER SALVATORE from Glendale, California, like many former 27th pilots serving with the 3rd B.G., was awarded the Silver Star, the United States' third-highest decoration for valor. He received it for air combat during the battle for Kokoda Trail in New Guinea. Lt. Col. Salvatore's last assignment before retiring in 1961 was as commander of Toul-Rousieres Air Force Base in France. Afterward, he taught high school mathematics until almost the time of his death in 1971.

FIRST LT. THOMAS TALLEY from Smyrna, Georgia, was an aeronautical engineer before the war. Afterward he attended medical school and became a physician, serving out his career as a psychiatrist in the air force. Talley died in 1994.

First Lt. Francis Timlin from Shanton, North Dakota, also remained in the military and retired from the air force as a colonel. He died in 2004.

First Lt. Leland Walker of Salt Lake City, Utah, remained in the military and, during the early 1950s, briefly commanded the 3rd Bombardment Group. He retired as a colonel and passed away in 1979.

First Lt. Howard West, from Excelsior, Minnesota, taught dive-bombing tactics using the new North American A-36 (a variant of the P-51 Mustang) upon his return to the States. By the end of the war, he was training fighter pilots to fly the P-51. He remained in the U.S. Air Force afterward, attaining the rank of colonel before retiring in 1970. He currently lives in Greenwood, Minnesota.

Some of the Other 27th Pilots Who Survived Their Philippines Service
Edward N. Backus, like Stephenson, was a first lieutenant when he left for the Philippines and roomed with Stephenson aboard ship. He was in the group that left with Davies on December 18, 1941, to get the group's A-24s in Brisbane. In February 1942 Captain Backus led the 91st Provisional Squadron with Zeke Summers and Harry Galusha to Java and met Stephenson there. When Java fell, Backus left for India with Brereton as part of the general's staff. During the war, he had many combat assignments and by April 1944 commanded the 97th Bomb Wing in England. He was promoted to the temporary rank of brigadier general (one star) that August. He retired as a brigadier general in 1961 and died in 1973.

William E. Eubank too was a first lieutenant when he arrived in the Philippines as a squadron commander and a captain when he left Corregidor in 1942 with Stephenson and other 27th pilots on the submarine *Seawolf.* When Java fell, he left for India with Backus as part of Brereton's staff. He was assigned to the Strategic Air Command after the war, becoming the first to fly a B-52 into SAC's inventory. He commanded a KC-135 flight that achieved two world records—a nonstop speed record from Tokyo to Washington, D.C., of thirteen hours and forty-seven minutes and an unrefueled jet distance record from Tokyo to the Azores, a distance of 10,288 miles. That was a far cry from the several-hundred-mile range of the A-24 dive bombers. He retired in 1965 as a major general. As of 2006, Eubank and his wife reside in Shreveport, Louisiana.

Lt. Rocky Gause had escaped to Corregidor when Bataan surrendered. When the island surrendered, Gause eventually escaped in a small boat with Capt. William Osborne and sailed an estimated 3,200 miles to Australia, arriving there in October 1942. Gause was killed later during the war in Europe while flying a fighter. Osborne also returned to the war front and commanded the 1st Battalion of the famous Merrill's Marauders in Burma. He died in 1985 and was inducted into the U.S. Ranger Hall of Fame at Fort Benning, Georgia, in 1998.

PAUL "PAPPY" GUNN'S popularity and wartime exploits achieved almost legendary proportions. As MacArthur moved north from Australia to the Philippines, right there with him as General Kenney's engineering mastermind was Pappy Gunn. He, of course, had another reason for wanting the islands liberated, for his wife, Polly, and their four children were prisoners at Santo Tomas University Prison Camp in Manila. He continued converting Mitchell B-25s and A-20s of the 3rd Attack Group into deadly fighting machines, often personally testing his latest modifications during actual combat missions.[2] In 1943 U.S. Army Air Force chief Gen. Hap Arnold called Gunn to the United States to explain to factory engineers just what he was doing to the A-20s and the B-25s to make them into "Grim Reapers."

As MacArthur was closing in on the Philippines, Kenney was concerned that Gunn might take the matter of his family's incarceration into his own hands and fly alone into Manila to rescue them. Kenney grounded him. Colonel Gunn's war ended when he was wounded by bomb fragments that lodged in his shoulder, spending the duration recovering in Australia. After the war he was reunited with his family. His love for the Philippines and flying eventually brought him back to the islands, where he ran an airline company. Gunn died in a plane crash near Manila in 1957 when caught in a tropical thunderstorm.[3] Jack Heyn, a veteran of the 3rd Bomb Group, commented in 2005: "I'm an ardent fan of Pappy. He became a folk hero to most of the guys who flew with him, worked with him, or in my case, just happened to be in the same outfit with him. In the air war of the Southwest Pacific, he became a legend in his own time."

JAY B. HARRELSON was the pilot from the 16th who drove Stephenson, McAfee, and others to Mariveles for their trip to Corregidor, where they then escaped by submarine. He later endured the Death March, Camp O'Donnell, other prison camps, and the hell ship *Oryoku Maru*. At one point shortly after the war, Harrelson was stationed at Barksdale Air Force Base in Louisiana and flew B-25s. Paul Lankford from the old 16th was also stationed there. Lankford was from Gadsden, Alabama, and Harrelson was from nearby Crossville. The two would fly back to Alabama in a B-25 to visit relatives and return with consumables such as fresh vegetables, crates of live chickens, and occasionally some home brew. He flew a variety of other airplanes, including B-17s and six-engine B-47s for the Strategic Air Command. He had many duty assignments and even served in Vietnam before retiring in 1970. Colonel Harrelson and his wife currently live in Tucson, Arizona.

WILLIAM G. HIPPS, who commanded the 16th Squadron before Stephenson and flew on Royce's Raid, returned to the United States and was assigned to the War Department General Staff as an air officer, Operations Division, Pacific Area, working for Gen. George Marshall for two and a half years. By June 1945 Hipps was back in the Pacific theater as director of plans with Kenney's command. By the time he retired in 1967, he was a brigadier general. Hipps met his late wife, Juanita Redmond, a U.S. Army nurse, in Manila. She later worked on Bataan and Corregidor and escaped by navy seaplane with other army nurses about a week before the island's surrender. At the time they were married in 1946, she was a lieutenant colonel and functioned as chief nurse for the U.S. Army Air Forces. She wrote a book, *I Served on Bataan,* which became a bestseller in 1943 and was the basis for the popular Hollywood war movie *So Proudly We Hail.*[4] General Hipps died in 2007.

COLUMBUS "DOC" SAVAGE was the pilot who replaced Stephenson as leader of the 16th Squadron after he left Bataan Airfield at the end of January 1942. Savage was a survivor—the Death March, the *Oryoku Maru,* and POW life in Manchuria. He used to say that at the war's end he was the oldest second lieutenant in the military. After the war Savage remained in the service, finally retiring from the air force in 1964 as a colonel. He then worked for General Dynamics in Fort Worth on the B-36 project. He retired for good at age sixty-five and died in 2002. Savage never stopped thanking God for having survived the *Oryoku Maru.* He loved to tell his friends: "Minnie Pearl [a Grand Old Opry star] says, 'I'm proud to be here!' Me? Doc Savage. I'm proud to be anywhere. I'm a walking miracle. The Lord must have had something for me to do otherwise I wouldn't be around. [After the *Oryoku Maru* trip,] I have so much to be thankful for I'll never catch up."

ROBERT F. STAFFORD was a pilot in the 16th Squadron who served with Stephenson in the Ferrying Command during the summer of 1941. He served at the Bataan Airfield under Stephenson and escaped with him by submarine to Java. He fled Java with McAfee and Bender in a C-52 to Brisbane. He served a month or two with the 3rd Bombardment Group out of Charters Towers but then transferred to the 19th Bombardment Group, flying B-17s, and was sent home in December 1942. A year later he returned to command a B-17 squadron in the western Pacific. Retiring from the air force in 1961 as a colonel, Stafford currently lives in Sonoma, California.

WARREN STIRLING, one of four West Pointers from the Class of 1940 assigned to the 27th Bombardment Group as a pilot in March 1941, stayed behind on Bataan and functioned as an infantry officer, for which he was promoted to captain. He endured the Death March, Camp O'Donnell, hell ships, and other POW camps. While cooling his heels in these prisons, he did not enjoy the astronomical rise in rank that some members of the U.S. Army Air Forces did. "Boy" colonels were common by the end of the war, and there were even "boy" generals as the USAAF rapidly expanded. His comrades who had escaped the Philippines and survived the war were almost all lieutenant colonels and colonels when Stirling returned to the States in 1945. After the war he stayed in the U.S. Air Force and flew nineteen missions in B-29s over Korea. Stirling retired after thirty years as a lieutenant colonel and died in 2005.

REGINALD VANCE, who briefly commanded the 27th Bombardment Group before Davies, was transferred to Brereton's headquarters in the Philippines on December 8, 1941, serving as intelligence officer. When Brereton left the Philippines on December 24, he became an air officer on Corregidor. On January 31, 1942, Vance was put in charge of the pilots who left Corregidor on the submarine *Seawolf.* He then rejoined Brereton's staff in Java as his intelligence officer. After that island fell, he served in Australia and later in Europe. Like Backus, at one point he was promoted to the temporary rank of brigadier general in the Army Air Forces. After the war he held numerous air-force commands. Vance retired with the rank of colonel and died in 1981.

Appendix 5

The 27th's Wartime Legacy

The 27th had been formed at Barksdale Air Base in February 1940, when the elite 3rd Bombardment Group was split down the middle so that many of its officers and enlisted men wound up in the new unit. In late March 1942 what was left of the 27th's pilots and enlisted men (who were not POWs) were reabsorbed by the 3rd Bomb Group at Charters Towers, Australia, and many became leaders in the 3rd. Although the survivors among those 27th pilots were furloughed back to the United States in late October 1942, the 3rd Bomb Group continued to play a significant role over the next three years in the defeat of Japan. The unit preferred the name "Attack Group," which they had been called in the late 1930s. Maj. Gen. George Kenney permitted them to use that name for the rest of the war. The name of his own command soon became the U.S. Fifth Air Force.[1]

At about the time the veteran 27th pilots left for the States, Gunn, with Kenney's support, increased the armament on the B-25s of the 3rd Attack Group by installing more machine guns forward for frontal assaults. He also got rid of the useless belly turret.

It seemed that Gunn had been considering placing four .50-caliber machine guns in the nose of the B-25 for quite some time, along with two .50-caliber machine guns mounted on each side in front. He had apparently discussed this possibility with Davies and others. It is unclear whether Gunn had actually attempted to modify a B-25 before Kenney told him to start working on such a project in November 1942. The general wanted to use the B-25s, which could carry a bigger load than the A-20s, as attack aircraft. Although the aircraft was designed to be a medium bomber, he knew they were tough, very reliable, and had acceptable performance to be used as low-level attack bombers. They would be used for skip-bombing ships while the eight forward-firing .50-caliber machine guns would strafe the antiaircraft gunners on deck.

Gunn and Kenney worked closely on this project. When the general flew back to Brisbane from Port Moresby in late November, he consulted with Gunn, and they traded ideas. In mid-December Gunn twice flew his prototype B-25 up to Port Moresby for his evaluation. Further changes were made. Finally, Kenney was impressed enough to send Ed Larner, the squadron leader of the 90th, back to Brisbane so that he could learn to fly the plane and work further with Gunn on refinements. The general told Gunn to prepare enough B-25s for a full squadron. After the 90th returned to Port Moresby with these planes, he further instructed Larner to start practicing skip-bombing with them.[2]

The Aussies too began using a different brand of low-level strafer in New Guinea in September 1942, the British twin-engine Beaufighter. Some said that with its four 20-mm cannons firing forward and six machine guns in the wings, it was the most heavily armed fighter in the world. It also had a machine gun in the rear and could carry ordnance under its wings.[3] Although the Beaufighter was effective, the B-25s and A-20s used as strafers could also simultaneously carry a greater bomb load. Two missions for which the 3rd Group is particularly well known during World War II, and which General Kenney seemed to be especially proud of, occurred during the Battle of the Bismarck Sea and the air attack on Rabaul Harbor, November 2, 1943. Kenney later referred to the Rabaul Raid as "the toughest fight Fifth Air Force encountered in the whole war."[4]

Battle of the Bismarck Sea

In early March 1943 the 3rd played a major role in the Battle of the Bismarck Sea, one of the most decisive air-naval battles of World War II. A convoy of Japanese ships left Rabaul about midnight, February 28, to take supplies and reinforcements to Lae, then considered the capital of the Japanese-held areas of New Guinea, about four hundred miles away. Most sources state that the convoy consisted of eight destroyers and eight supply or troop ships, but Fifth Air Force sources claim that there were twenty-two ships, including two battlecruisers. On the afternoon of March 1, the crew of an American B-24 spotted the convoy headed westerly along the north coast of New Britain.[5]

The next day the weather was bad for Allied aircraft hunting the Japanese ships, with thunderstorms and low-hanging clouds obscuring their view of the ocean below. B-17s made three separate attacks on the convoy and claimed that they had sunk two transports. American P-38 twin-engine fighters were supposed to be flying fighter cover but had difficulty finding the bombers they were supposed to be protecting. Throughout the night of March 2–3, RAAF Catalina flying boats dogged the Japanese, sending hourly reports on their location and dropping an occasional bomb. Early in the morning on March 3, a B-17 took over the surveillance duties. Seven Australian Beaufort twin-engine bombers carrying torpedoes were sent out, but only two reached the convoy and scored no hits. Later that morning several more Allied planes assembled—U.S. B-17s, A-20s, and P-38s, as well as RAAF Beaufighters, A-20s, and Beauforts. The B-17s dropped their bombs from high altitude, causing minimal damage partly because of poor visibility through the clouds. Beaufighters came in low and strafed the convoy with machine-gun and cannon fire. B-25s from the 3rd and 38th Bomb Groups dropped their bombs from medium altitude but had minimal effect.

Then came the naval debut of the low-level strafer-attack bombers of the 3rd. Among the pilots were three who had flown earlier with the 27th, Richard Launder

29. Japanese destroyer being strafed by a 3rd Bomb Group aircraft during the Battle of the Bismarck Sea. *Courtesy Jack Heyn and Maj. Gen. John H. Henebry*

and J. B. Criswell in Java and Bill Beck around Darwin. Maj. Ed Larner's 90th Squadron led the way with twelve B-25s that had just been converted and carrying eight forward-firing .50-caliber machine guns controlled by the pilot. Each gun could fire up to eleven hundred rounds per minute. The sequence in the ammunition belts feeding the guns was made up of one tracer, two armor-piercing, and two incendiary bullets. The B-25s also carried three or four 500-pound bombs with delayed fuses.

Larner's squadron broke into three elements of four airplanes as they attacked the ships. His own group came in first in a frontal attack. Capt. John "Jock" Henebry led the second element of four planes and attacked the ships broadside, as did the last set of four. Henebry recalled seeing all those ships and feeling "scared as hell" at the thought of flying right up to their sides at water level.[6] The attackers closed on the ships between 220–260 mph, opening up with bursts from their deadly .50-caliber machine guns from about a mile out. Launder commented: "The Navy torpedo planes were committed to a straight run to the target, a skip-bomber was not. We could zig and zag all we wanted to, while at the same time spraying the target from stern to stern with .50-caliber machine guns."[7]

The 500-pound bombs were released and skipped like stones across the water into the ships. The planes pulled up at the last minute to avoid the masts. Fancy maneuvering by the helmsmen was useless against such an attack. After each plane had completed a run against their initial target, they went after other ships from the side and rear. The 3rd Bomb Group's 90th Squadron was followed by its 89th Squadron, led by Capts. Glen Clark and Ed Chudoba. They were flying twelve of the Pappy Gunn modified A-20s. The 89th and 90th Squadrons, along with other Allied aircraft, flew two missions that day and one the next. Significant damage was done by these low-level skip-bombing strafers, or as Kenney called them, "commerce destroyers."

Japanese accounts are in general agreement with each other. On March 2 two of the destroyers from the convoy rescued about 800 soldiers from a transport sunk that day. On the night of March 2–3, they slipped into Lae Harbor and unloaded these men and then raced back to rejoin the convoy early on the morning of March 3. Japanese records state that the navy lost seven transports on March 3 and three destroyers. Four of the other five destroyers, which had picked up some of the survivors from the sinking ships, headed north out of harm's way, losing contact with the fifth, which they assume sank. That night, three of those destroyers came back and rescued more troops in the water but returned to Rabaul instead of taking them to Lae. Reports indicate that the Japanese lost 3,664 troops as a result of these air attacks, with 2,427 survivors returned to Rabaul.[8]

The P-38s also destroyed many enemy fighters sent out to protect the convoy. Relatively few of the Japanese troops from those sinking ships made it to shore on New Guinea. Often they were strafed while clinging to flotsam. Some who did reach the island were alleged to have been eaten by headhunting natives.

This was the first defeat of such a numerically large naval force at sea without opposing surface vessels involved. One has to wonder if after MacArthur heard the news about the damage caused by these modified Mitchells, he reflected on the year 1925, when he served on the trial board for Billy Mitchell's court-martial.[9]

Air Attack on Simpson Harbor, Rabaul—November 2, 1943

Rabaul, with its excellent harbor, five major airfields, and a garrison of 100,000 troops, was Japan's main stronghold and staging area in the Southwest Pacific dur-

30. Third Bomb Group B-25 leaving Simpson Harbor, Rabaul, during a raid on November 2, 1943. *Courtesy Maj. Gen. John H. Henebry and Jack Heyn*

ing 1942 and 1943. The Allies conducted frequent air attacks against the airbases, harbor, and town, including one major bombing raid by the Fifth Air Force on October 12, 1943, involving about three hundred aircraft. Many of these strikes were at the request of the U.S. Navy, which was supporting marine and army operations on Guadalcanal as well as the troops that landed on Bougainville on November 1, 1943. Bougainville, another island in the Solomons, was much closer to Rabaul than Guadalcanal. That same day three hundred more Japanese fighter aircraft were sent from Truk Island farther north to Rabaul.

On November 2 General Kenney sent seventy-five B-25s against the ships in and antiaircraft guns around the harbor at Rabaul—a distance of about five hundred miles from Port Moresby and four hundred miles from the Allied airfield at Dobodura. Fifty-seven P-38 fighters were also sent as escorts. Forty-one ships were attacked during this raid, led by twenty-five-year-old Maj. "Jock" Henebry, who was then the operations officer for the 3rd Attack Group and soon to be its commander. The 3rd used its low-level strafing and skip-bombing techniques.

Here again, there is significant disagreement about the amount of damage inflicted on the ships and tonnage sunk between Kenney's Fifth Air Force people and other sources. Many enemy aircraft, however, were shot down or destroyed on the ground. One large tanker, three smaller merchant ships, a minesweeper, and two smaller boats were sunk according to the Japanese, while many others were damaged. The raid, however, took a significant toll on U.S. airplanes and aircrews. Forty-five airmen were killed or missing, with nine P-38s and eight B-25s lost. Stepped-up air attacks such as this conducted by the AAF, U.S. Navy, and RAAF, spelled the end for Rabaul as a major enemy staging area. The November 2 mission also forced Japanese aircraft to remain over the area and defend against Kenney's raiders instead of interfering with Adm. William Halsey's landing force on Bougainville.[10]

That night Australian Beauforts made another attack on Rabaul. After that the weather closed in for the next few days, but on November 5 Halsey sent ninety-seven planes from his five aircraft carriers on a raid against shipping in the harbor. One hour later twenty-seven of Kenney's B-24 heavy bombers and sixty-seven P-38s arrived from New Guinea to work over the harbor and wharves. In the weeks that followed, Allied aircraft continued to pound Rabaul, and within a few months, the base had no air support whatsoever. The Japanese then moved the bulk of their ships and planes to Truk.[11]

The 3rd moved their headquarters from Charters Towers to New Guinea in January 1943 and by 1944 were operating out of the Philippines. The men lived up to their name as the Grim Reapers as Gunn and Kenney effectively armed their planes with more machine guns and parafrag bombs. The men liked to boast that they never carried oxygen because they never flew above one hundred feet, and if they came across a cow while in flight, they flew around it.

During the war, the 3rd Bomb Group operated all sorts of aircraft—B-25s, A-20s, A-24s, and later the twin-engine A-26 attack bomber. Their low-to-the-deck aerial assaults instilled fear into Japanese ground, sea, and air forces. The unit claimed 642 ships sunk, an estimated 2,000 planes destroyed, and almost 40,000 Japanese troops killed.[12] It was awarded three Distinguished Unit Citations, one Presidential Unit Citation, and the Philippine Presidential Citation. Many members of the RAAF served in various crew positions with the 3rd during the war.[13] It is probably fair to say that few of the group's pilots at the end of the war knew little if anything about the trials, tribulations, and contributions of the men of the 27th at the start of the war, but those pioneers were just as much a part of the Grim Reapers legacy.

Over time Kenney's command had grown from the remnants of Brereton's Far East Air Force to what was called the Far East Air Forces, which included the Fifth and Thirteenth U.S. Air Forces and the Allied Air Forces, including the RAAF and the Dutch East Indies Air Forces, in the Southwest Pacific Theater.

MacArthur said of Kenney after the war, "Of all the brilliant air commanders of the war, none surpassed him in those three great essentials of combat leadership: aggressive vision, mastery of air tactics and strategy, and the ability to extract the maximum in fighting qualities from both men and equipment."[14]

Notes

Chapter 1

1. Griffith, *MacArthur's Airman,* 37. See also Melinger, *Significant Events in Air Force History,* 38–39. Just thirteen years later, an American four-engine B-29 bomber using air-to-air refueling would be the first to circle the globe nonstop in ninety-four hours.

2. Coffey, *Hap,* 177; Griffith, *MacArthur's Airman,* 40.

3. Daso, *Hap Arnold,* 34–38; Arnold, *Global Mission,* 25–29.

4. Daso, *Hap Arnold,* 101–14.

5. Ibid., 161.

6. Kreidberg and Henry, *History of Military Mobilization in the United States,* 571.

7. Hipps interview, Feb. 2002 (by A. Martin).

8. Daso, *Hap Arnold,* 162.

9. *Funk & Wagnalls Encyclopedia* (1972), s.v. "Selective Service."

10. Shannon, *Twentieth Century America,* 446.

11. Brown interview, Sept. 2003 (by L. Stephenson). Major Brown was a B-17 command pilot during World War II.

12. Griffith, *MacArthur's Airman,* 25.

13. De Seversky, *Victory through Air Power,* 43–47.

14. Smith, *Dive Bomber,* 45–56.

15. De Seversky, *Victory through Air Power,* 171.

16. Slow rolls are generally executed while flying horizontally and rolling the plane slowly over sideways, 360 degrees.

17. "Casualties: Some Boys Really Got Hurt," Big Maneuvers Test U.S. Army, Louisiana Maneuvers, 1940–44, Louisiana in World War II, http://www.crt.state.la.us/tourism/lawwii/maneuvers/LIFE_ARTICLE/Maneuvers_Life_Article.htm.

Chapter 2

1. Secret Communiqué, Jan. 13, 1942, Box T-1601, Messages AGWAR to USAFIA, RG 338, National Archives, Washington, D.C.

2. McGlothlin, *Barksdale to Bataan,* 25.

3. *Twenty-seventh Bombardment Group Reports.* This fifty-nine-page typewritten monograph was likely completed in September 1942. The authors were U.S. Army Air Forces pilots from the 27th who had gotten out of the Philippines before Bataan fell. Photographs and

many official military documents, such as troop lists, orders, and reports, are included. At the time they were writing, the authors only knew that the U.S. forces on Bataan and Corregidor had surrendered but did not know their fate, including that of most of their comrades in the 27th. This book epigraph is taken from the opening of the *27th Reports.*

4. Taylor, *Trial of Generals,* 53.

5. Ibid.

6. *Reports of General MacArthur,* 23.

7. Bartsch, *December 8,* 94.

8. *Reports of General MacArthur,* 79.

9. Morris, *Corregidor,* 24.

10. Bartsch, *December 8,* 40.

11. Kreidberg and Henry, *History of Military Mobilization in the United States,* 558–59.

12. Bartsch, *December 8,* 84–85, 104.

13. Davis, *Hap,* 21. See also Huston, *American Air Power Comes of Age,* xvii. It was not until July 1942 that the term "Army Air Forces" officially replaced "Army Air Corps."

14. Bartsch, *December 8,* 93–94.

15. Ibid.

16. Ibid, 175, 188.

17. Morton, *Fall of the Philippines,* 6.

18. Taylor, *Trial of Generals,* 35.

19. May, *Steadfast Line,* 175–84; McGlothlin, *Barksdale to Bataan,* 15–16.

20. Bartsch, *December 8,* 213.

21. Whitman, *Bataan,* 105.

22. Francis E. Timlin to Gustave Breymann, Sept. 13, 1984, in author's possession (L. Stephenson).

23. Reginald Vance to William H. Bartsch, n.d. [1980], copy in author's possession (L. Stephenson).

24. Arnold, "Conversation between General Arnold and General Marshall."

25. Morton, *Fall of the Philippines,* 7.

26. Williams, *AAF in Australia,* 3–6. B-17s were flown from California via Hawaii, Midway, and Wake; then south to Rabaul, Port Moresby, or Darwin; and finally north to the Philippines. A more northerly route, via Guam instead of Rabaul and Port Moresby, had been used by Pan American flying boats, but its value was limited by the fact that Guam was dangerously close to the Japanese-mandated Marianas and Caroline islands. In addition, the proximity of Japanese garrisons in the Marshall Islands endangered Wake in case hostilities should begin. Hap Arnold wanted a more southerly route developed, with airfields on Canton, Jarvis, and Johnston islands, so that in case of war with Japan, the long-range bombers could get to Australia and the Philippines. As recently as February 21, 1941, he had been told, "Neither the War, nor the Navy Department has any plan for operations that would require the movement of long-range Army bombardment aviation to the Orient, nor can the need for such a plan be foreseen." Williams, *AAF in Australia,* 4–5, 150n6.

27. In the McAfee diary, the *27th Reports,* and other unpublished sources, Glen Stephenson is often referred to by his West Point nickname, "Steve," which we have changed to "Glen" to avoid confusion.

28. *27th Reports,* 9.

29. "World War II: The Defensive Phase," 426.

30. *27th Reports.*

31. Bartsch, *Doomed at the Start,* 229.

32. Connaughton, *MacArthur and Defeat,* 157.

33. Gillison, *Royal Australian Air Force,* 186.

34. Brereton, *Diaries,* 25–32.

35. Wainwright, *Wainwright's Story,* 12–14.

36. Bartsch, *December 8,* 191.

37. Morton, *Fall of the Philippines,* 71.

38. Bartsch, *December 8,* 219.

39. Watson, *Army Air Action in the Philippines and Netherlands East Indies,* 43–48.

40. Toland, *But Not in Shame,* 11–12.

41. Connaughton, *MacArthur and Defeat,* 14.

42. *Reports of General MacArthur,* 59–60.

43. Ibid., 21–29, 79–80.

44. Watson, *Army Air Action in the Philippines and Netherlands East Indies,* 50.

45. Taylor, *Trial of Generals,* 52–57; Connaughton, *MacArthur and Defeat,* 128.

Chapter 3

1. Dyess, *Dyess Story,* 27.

2. Bartsch, *Doomed at the Start,* 40–41.

3. Gillison, *Royal Australian Air Force,* 200–202.

4. *27th Reports.*

5. Kreidberg and Henry, *History of Military Mobilization in the United States,* 379.

6. Young, *First 24 Hours of the War,* 60–90.

7. Prange, *At Dawn We Slept,* 539.

8. Young, *First 24 Hours,* 60–90.

9. *World Book Encyclopedia* (1983), s.v. "World War II."

10. *27th Reports.*

11. Bartsch, *December 8,* 415. The decision or nondecision to attack Japanese positions on Formosa makes interesting reading even today. See, for example, Edmonds, *They Fought with What They Had;* Manchester, *American Caesar;* Brereton, *Diaries;* and perhaps most definitive, Bartsch, *December 8.*

12. Bartsch, *December 8,* 225–27; Townsend, *Duel of Eagles,* 170, 324.

13. Bartsch, *Doomed at the Start,* 52–54. Unidentified aircraft are called "bogeys," while known enemy aircraft are termed "bandits."

14. Bartsch, *December 8,* 264–70.

15. Ibid., 425–26.

16. Ibid., 264–82.

17. Ibid., 287.

18. Romulo, *I Saw the Fall of the Philippines,* 29.

19. Smurthwaite, *Pacific War Atlas,* 39.

20. Bartsch, *December 8,* 296.

21. Bartsch, *Doomed at the Start,* 66.

22. Dyess, *Dyess Story,* 29.

23. Bartsch, *December 8,* 311.

24. Ibid., 323–27, 385.

25. Ibid., 57. Each Zero was equipped with two cannons and two machine guns.

26. Ibid., 342–43.

27. Ibid., 242–43, 283, 409.

28. Brereton, *Diaries,* 43–44.

29. Bartsch, *December 8,* 385, 409.

30. Dyess, *Dyess Story,* 32.

31. Bartsch, *December 8,* 245–46.

32. Ibid., 324.

33. Ibid., 419–20.

34. Reginald Vance to William H. Bartsch, 1980. When Brereton chose the officers to go with him to the Philippines as part of the headquarters staff for FEAF, he had already reached the limit of personnel he was allowed to take when he came to Vance, whom he also wanted. Therefore, he arranged for the major to become commander of the 27th to get him to the islands. Soon after he arrived, Vance would be transferred to Brereton's headquarters as intelligence officer and Davies would assume command of the group. After the unit reached the Philippines, Vance functioned both as the 27th's commander and as one of Brereton's staff officers until December 8.

35. *27th Reports;* Hubbard memoir; McAfee diary.

36. *27th Reports.*

37. Ibid., 15.

38. Ibid.

39. Dyess, *Dyess Story,* 32–33.

40. Shores, Cull, and Izawa, *Bloody Shambles,* 1:186.

41. Bartsch, *Doomed at the Start,* 143.

42. McAfee diary, Dec. 10, 1941.

43. Toland, *Rising Sun,* 272–79.

44. *27th Reports.*

45. Ibid.

46. Julius "Zeke" Summers to Larry Stephenson, Sept. 19, 1995, in author's possession.

47. *27th Reports.*

48. A. B. Feuer, "Pawn of Fate: The Pensacola Convoy," *Sea Classics* (July 2004), online at Find Articles, http://findarticles.com/p/articles/mi_qa4442/is_200407/ai_n16065359

49. Ibid.

50. Manchester, *American Caesar,* 212, 242.

51. Ibid., 212.

52. Morton, *Fall of the Philippines,* 150.

53. Edmonds, *They Fought with What They Had,* 281n.

54. Ibid., 281.

55. Firth, *Matter of Time,* 58.

56. MacArthur, *Reminiscences,* 123.

57. Manchester, *American Caesar,* 215.

58. Taylor, *Trial of Generals,* 35.

59. Smurthwaite, *Pacific War Atlas,* 41.

60. Toland, *But Not in Shame,* 118.
61. Manchester, *American Caesar,* 217.
62. Morton, *Fall of the Philippines,* 161–65.
63. MacArthur, *Reminiscences,* 125.
64. Whitman, *Bataan,* 44.
65. Ibid.
66. Toland, *But Not in Shame,* 150.
67. Manchester, *American Caesar,* 212–13.
68. Morris, *Corregidor,* 55.
69. Morton, *Fall of the Philippines,* 46–8.
70. Morrison, *Two Ocean War,* 39.
71. Connaughton, *MacArthur and Defeat,* 199.
72. *27th Reports.*

Chapter 4

1. Manchester, *American Caesar,* 217; Taylor, *Trial of Generals,* 64–65. MacArthur decided to declare Manila an open city on December 24 but did not officially make the proclamation until December 26. As part of this process, the Japanese consul-general in Manila, who had been interned, was acquainted with the plan so he could convey it to the Japanese military. Under international law an open city is not being used in any way for military purposes and so not subject to attack. The chief of military history for the U.S. Army later wrote, "Since Manila was used as a base of supplies, and since U.S. Army Headquarters was based in the city and troops passed through it after December 26, it is difficult to see how Manila could be considered an Open City." This subject would be debated by military lawyers during the war-crimes trials.
2. Kane, *Brief History of the 27th.*
3. *27th Reports.*
4. Edmonds, *They Fought with What They Had,* 199–200.
5. Bartsch, *Doomed at the Start,* 456n8.
6. Moody, *Reprieve from Hell,* 61
7. *27th Reports.*
8. Gerrity, "Bataan Diary," Dec. 26, 1941.
9. Miller, *Bataan Uncensored,* 116.
10. *27th Reports.*
11. Morton, *Fall of the Philippines,* 112.
12. Bartsch, *Doomed at the Start,* 205. In fairness to the Filipino deserters, many of them had not been appropriately trained or equipped to participate in battle, some of their officers had no combat training, and probably few if any who deserted had much enthusiasm for risking their lives for "Mother America." Quezon, their president, following a visit to Tokyo in 1938, began demanding that the United States accelerate the plans for Philippine independence from 1946 (as originally planned) to 1940 so that the islands could remain neutral during a possible war between Japan and the United States. When Washington refused, Quezon cut the defense budget because he said a buildup of his army would only antagonize the Japanese. Furthermore, when the victorious Japanese later set up a Filipino puppet government, about 75 percent of the prewar Philippine Senate and 30 percent of the House joined the new regime.

13. Connaughton, *MacArthur and Defeat,* 253.

14. *27th Reports.*

15. Ind, *Bataan,* 203.

16. *Reports of General MacArthur,* 98–99.

17. Gerrity, "Bataan Diary," Dec. 28, 1941.

18. *27th Reports.*

19. *Reports of General MacArthur,* 98–99.

20. The 27th Reports specifically states that the C-39 landed at Del Monte but does not mention the B-18s landing there. Yet five of the 27th Bomb Group pilots known to have flown on the B-18s mention landing at Del Monte. See Hubbard memoir; "Current Intelligence Section A-2 Interview with Colonel John Davies, November 23, 1942"; Howard West to Larry Stephenson, Oct. 11, 2007, in author's possession; and the diaries of Oliver Doan and Ralph Schmidt (Edward Rogers personal collection).

21. *27th Reports.*

22. Ibid., 14.

23. Ibid., 27.

24. Bartsch, *Doomed at the Start,* 171.

25. "Gateway to Victory Memorial Stone at Bretts Wharf," Dunn, Australia at War, www .ozatwar.com/bretts.htm.

26. *27th Reports.*

27. Ibid.

28. Hubbard memoir, 14.

29. *27th Reports.*

30. "Current Intelligence Section A-2 Interview with Colonel John Davies, November 23, 1942," 1–3; Birkett, "A24 Banshees of the 27thBG(Lt) and 3rdBG(Lt)," Feb. 20, 2004 (accessed Nov. 7, 2007).

31. According to Hap Arnold, the solenoids that controlled the firing of the guns on the A-24s were in boxes nailed to the inside of the crates, attached to each of which were packing lists of its contents. He states that the crates, after the planes were removed, were thrown on a trash pile and burned, the boxes left inside them. Thus, with the assembly complete, there were no solenoids to be found, and the pilots could not fire the guns. When the solenoids were not found, Arnold immediately received messages by radio and cable demanding them, further stating, "On almost every day, I was asked by the White House or the Secretary of War for a report on what I was doing about those solenoids." Afterward, he sent 104 solenoids by air across the Pacific to take care of all the planes, another 104 by boat across the Pacific, and another 104 by airplane across the Atlantic, Africa, and Asia. Arnold also states that the secretary of war contacted the assistant secretary of war for air, Bob Lovett, and said: "Bob, where are those things you need to make the airplanes shoot properly—oh, what's the name—hemorrhoids! Where are those hemorrhoids, anyway, Bob?" Arnold, *Global Mission,* 290.

Walter Edmonds, who had interviewed Davies and many other airmen who served in the Philippines and Java, commented on Arnold's statement about solenoids supposedly being shipped in crates with the planes, "I find it hard to accept in light of the other missing items." Edmonds, *They Fought with What They Had,* 317. According to Brereton, the lack of parts for the A-24s had been known in the States earlier, and the parts were shipped out in B-17s. But after the outbreak of war, these planes were held up in Hawaii until a new more southern ferry route was developed. Brereton, *Diaries,* 74.

But whichever version of the A-24 story is correct, the fact still remains that those army airmen best qualified to reassemble the planes were back in he Philippines, and most were doing everything except what they were trained to do.

32. Watson, *Army Air Action in the Philippines and Netherlands East Indies,* 95.

33. Francis E. Timlin to Gustave Breymann, Sept. 13, 1984.

34. Twenty-seventh Bombardment Group Reunion booklet (Apr. 4–5, 1975), 7.

35. Bartsch, *Doomed at the Start,* 206.

36. Knox, *Death March,* 43.

37. Morton, *Fall of the Philippines,* 256–58.

38. Knox, *Death March,* 100.

39. Smurthwaite, *Pacific War Atlas,* 42.

40. Toland, *But Not in Shame,* 152.

41. Ibid., 136–38, 152.

42. May, *Steadfast Line,* 71, 91. Maj. John Sewell, the 27th Bombardment Group's operations officer, was put in charge of the unit when Davies left for Australia. He also continued to command the 2nd Battalion. Capt. Mark Wohlfeld was the executive officer. Lt. George Kane was the S1 (personnel officer), Lt. Bert Bank was the S2 in charge of intelligence, and Lt. Bert Schwarz was the S3 in charge of operations. Lt. Warren Stirling commanded the 17th Squadron, and William Eubank commanded the 91st Squadron. Capt. Theodore Bigger commanded the 48th Materiel Squadron. Capt. Robert Blakeslee commanded the 454th Ordnance Company, which was elsewhere on Bataan, and Capt. John McCorkle commanded the 2nd Observation Squadron until he was wounded around January 29 while out on patrol along the outpost line of resistance. McCorkle died the following day, and Lt. Earl D. Egger replaced him as the commander of the squadron.

43. *27th Reports.*

44. McGlothlin, *Barksdale to Bataan,* 77–78.

45. Whitman, *Bataan,* 39; Edmonds, *They Fought with What They Had,* 239.

46. Bartsch, *Doomed at the Start,* 233, 237.

47. Ind, *Bataan,* 168–72.

48. Ibid., 209–10.

49. Reginald Vance to William H. Bartsch, 1980.

50. Whitman, *Bataan,* 40; Edmonds, *They Fought with What They Had,* 239.

51. Bartsch, *Doomed at the Start,* 257.

52. *27th Reports.*

53. Arnold, "Lessons of Bataan," available online at www.qmmuseum.lee.army.mil/WWII/bataan_lesson.htm.

54. McGlothin, 75.

55. *27th Reports.*

Chapter 5

1. Red Hanson (*Seawolf* crew member), interview by Clyde Stephenson, ca. 2000.

2. Manchester, *American Caesar,* 244.

3. Edmonds, *They Fought with What They Had,* 377.

4. Ibid.; Brereton, *Diaries,* 83.

5. Frank, Horan, and Eckberg, *USS* Seawolf, 64–65.

6. Ibid., 71.

7. Blair, *Silent Victory,* 173.

8. Frank, Horan, and Eckberg, *USS* Seawolf, 74–75.

9. Manchester, *American Caesar,* 244; Reginald Vance to William H. Bartsch, 1980. Later the submarine *Trout* took out the Philippine gold reserve and tons of silver coins. Another $15 million worth of silver coins were placed in sealed wooden boxes, towed out on barges at night to a carefully surveyed location between Corregidor and Caballo islands, and dumped in the bay. Serial numbers on $40 million worth of paper money were recorded, and the money burned. Wainwright, *Wainwright's Story,* 113–14.

10. Vance to Bartsch, 1980.

11. Morrison, *Two Ocean War,* 139.

12. Frank, Horan, and Eckberg, *USS* Seawolf, 81.

13. White, *Queens Die Proudly,* 257.

14. Watson, *Army Air Action in the Philippines and Netherlands East Indies,* 99.

15. Ibid., 109.

16. White, *Queens Die Proudly,* 86–87; Edmonds, *They Fought with What They Had,* 256–57.

17. Watson, *Army Air Action in the Philippines and Netherlands East Indies,* 97–98. For the Japanese advance through the Malay Peninsula, see P. Thompson, *Battle for Singapore,* 373.

18. Edmonds, *They Fought with What They Had,* 270–72.

19. Smurthwaite, *Pacific War Atlas,* 58; Edmonds, *They Fought with What They Had,* 410.

20. Edmonds, *They Fought with What They Had,* 281, 285.

21. Weller, "Luck to the Fighters," pt. 1, 274.

22. Edmonds, *They Fought with What They Had,* 251–52.

23. Ibid., 325–26.

24. Ibid, 439.

25. *27th Reports.*

26. Ibid.

27. Launder, *College Campus in the Sky,* 30.

28. *27th Reports.*

29. Ibid., 33–34.

30. *27th Reports,* 41–44.

31. Ibid., 48.

32. Weller, "Luck to the Fighters," pt. 2, 34.

33. *27th Reports.*

34. Edmonds, *They Fought with What They Had,* 347.

35. *27th Reports.*

36. Gillison, *Royal Australian Air Force,* 233. On the fall of Singapore, see also P. Thompson, *Battle for Singapore,,* 227, 323, 337, 373, 382, 507–509, 605–608; and Day, *Great Betrayal,* 255–57.

37. Bartsch, *Doomed at the Start,* 262–63.

38. White, *Queens Die Proudly,* 192.

39. Edmonds, *They Fought with What They Had,* 252–53.

40. Ibid., 361–63.

41. *27th Reports.*

42. Ibid.

43. Brereton, *Diaries,* 97.

44. Shores, Cull, and Izawa, *Bloody Shambles,* 2:209.

45. Dull, *Battle History of the Imperial Japanese Navy,* 60.

46. Edmonds, *They Fought with What They Had,* 366.

47. *27th Reports,* 44.

48. Robinson, *Fight for New Guinea,* 36; *27th Reports,* 44.

49. U.S. Army Far East Command, *Imperial Japanese Navy in World War II.*

50. Edmonds, *They Fought with What They Had,* 396.

51. *27th Reports.*

52. Weller, "Luck to the Fighters," pt. 3, 129.

53. Dull, *Battle History of the Imperial Japanese Navy,* 65.

54. Edmonds, *They Fought with What They Had,* 366.

55. Gillison, *Royal Australian Air Force,* 347–51.

56. Shores, Cull, and Izawa, *Bloody Shambles,* 2:43–126.

57. Day, *Great Betrayal,* 272.

58. Shores, Cull, and Izawa, *Bloody Shambles,* 2:239; Toland, *But Not in Shame,* 234. On the conditions of the aircraft flown by Galusha and others on the mission, see Lt. Col. Harry L. Galusha, "Synopsis of the Last Flight of the 91st Bombardment Squadron in Java," Nov. 22, 1943, Third Air Force, Tampa, Fla., in author's possession (L. Stephenson). He writes, "Summers' plane was as near to a complete wreck as any . . . in the Air Corps." Summers had repeatedly complained about the lack of maintenance help and, with his gunner, had at one time had to change an engine with little or no assistance.

59. Edmonds, *They Fought with What They Had,* 339; Watson, *Army Air Action in the Philippines and Netherlands East Indies,* 114. Days before, Hart had received orders from Washington to relinquish his command and return to the United States. This was in part because of insistent pressure by the Dutch to have one of their own in charge of ABDAFLOAT, though also because Hart had indicated to his superiors that he considered himself too old for a combat command.

60. Shores, Cull, and Izawa, *Bloody Shambles,* 2:195–96, 240–41.

61. Thomas, *Battle of the Java Sea,* 167.

62. Edmonds, *They Fought with What They Had,* 424.

63. *27th Reports.*

64. Craven and Cate, *Plans and Early Operations,* 399.

65. Edmonds, *They Fought with What They Had,* 404.

66. K. Thompson, *Thousand Cups of Rice,* 31–38.

67. Shores, Cull, and Izawa, *Bloody Shambles,* 2:322–23.

68. Toland, *But Not in Shame,* 261.

69. Craven and Cate, *Plans and Early Operations,* 401.

70. Edmonds, *They Fought with What They Had,* 441–44.

71. Weller, "Luck to the Fighters," pt. 3, 133.

Chapter 6

1. For more information on Broome, see Hugh Edwards, *Port of Pearls: Broome's First Hundred Years* (Swanbourne, W.A.: Hugh Edwards, 1984); and Sister Mary Albertus Bain, *Full Fathom Five* (Perth: Artlook Books, 1983).

2. Gillison, *Royal Australian Air Force,* 464.

3. Ibid., 465.

4. Edmonds, *They Fought with What They Had,* 437.

5. Shores, Cull, and Izawa, *Bloody Shambles,* 2:313–15.

6. Edmonds, *They Fought with What They Had,* 432–33n.

7. Ibid., 408–15.

8. Many of them were sent along with some of the 902 survivors of the cruiser USS *Houston,* who had swum ashore, to work on what became known as the "Burma-Siam Death Railway." The Japanese were building this railroad through the jungle between Thailand and Burma to supply their troops. Many British and Australian POWs from Singapore as well as local natives also worked on this project, many of them dying from malnutrition and other causes.

9. MacArthur, *Reminiscences,* 137.

10. Gilbert, *Churchill and America,* 237.

11. Edmonds, *They Fought with What They Had,* 372.

12. Ibid., 373.

13. Ibid., 385.

14. McGlothlin, *Barksdale to Bataan,* 83.

15. *27th Reports.*

16. Norman, *We Band of Angels,* 85, 94.

17. Connaughton, *MacArthur and Defeat,* 295.

18. McGlothlin, *Barksdale to Bataan,* 79.

19. Gautier, *I Came Back from Bataan,* 56.

20. Mosely, 192–93.

21. Wilmont, *Struggle for Europe,* 101.

22. Day, *Great Betrayal,* 222–23; Gillison, *Royal Australian Air Force,* 266.

23. Manchester, *American Caesar,* 254.

24. Polmar and Morrison, *PT Boats at War,* 101, 110, 115.

25. Ibid., 23.

26. Morton, *Fall of the Philippines,* 360–61; Connaughton, *MacArthur and Defeat,* 287–88.

27. Bartsch, *Doomed at the Start,* 340; Watson, *Army Air Action in the Philippines and Netherlands East Indies,* App. 9, "Interview of General Sutherland by Edmonds, June 4, 1945," 5–6.

28. Polmar and Morrison, *PT Boats at War,* 27.

29. "General Douglas MacArthur in Australia during WW2," Dunn, Australia at War, http://home.st.net.au/~pdunn/macarthur.htm.

30. Manchester, *American Caesar,* 263.

31. Wainwright, *Wainwright's Story,* 2–4, 67–68.

32. Morton, *Fall of the Philippines,* 360.

33. Manchester, *American Caesar*, 266.

34. Hipps interview, Feb. 2002 (by A. Martin).

35. "General Douglas MacArthur in Australia during WW2."

36. MacArthur, *Reminiscences*, 145. Years later MacArthur's recollection was that he had first causally mentioned his "I Shall Return" statement to reporters at Batchelor Field when he first arrived from the Philippines.

37. Morton, *Fall of the Philippines*, 364–65.

38. Connaughton, *MacArthur and Defeat*, 298.

39. Williams, *AAF in Australia*, 168.

40. Dunn, *Pacific Microphone*, 155–56.

41. Ind, *Bataan*, 366.

42. Van der Vat, *Pacific Campaign*, 164.

43. Edmonds, *They Fought with What They Had*, 348.

44. Weller, "Luck to the Fighters," pt. 1, 270; Day, *Great Betrayal*, 127–28.

45. Edmonds, *They Fought with What They Had*, 358; Gillison, *Royal Australian Air Force*, 426–32.

46. Edmonds, *They Fought with What They Had*, 359.

47. Gillison, *Royal Australian Air Force*, 426–31.

48. *27th Reports.*

49. "Current Intelligence Section A-2 Interview with Colonel John Davies, November 23, 1942," 3–4.

50. Gillison, *Royal Australian Air Force*, 469.

51. "Current Intelligence Section A-2 Interview with Colonel John Davies, November 23, 1942," 4.

52. "3rd Bombardment Group, AKA 3rd Attack Group, in Australia during WW2," Dunn, Australia at War, http://home.st.net.au/~dunn/31bg.htm.

53. Williams, *AAF in Australia*, 51. The quantity of bombers produced in the United States at that time did not permit the maintenance of two light groups in Australia, so plans had been made at headquarters, USAAF, for the withdrawal (on paper) of the 3rd Bomb Group. But in accordance with General Brett's recommendation, the 3rd was allowed to remain and to absorb the 27th Group since the 3rd was relatively complete and the 27th was not.

54. Cortesi, *Grim Reapers*, 10, 14.

55. Tunny, *Fight Back from the North*, 19.

56. "3rd Bombardment Group, AKA 3rd Attack Group, in Australia during WW2," Dunn, Australia at War, http://home.st.net.au/~dunn/31bg.htm; Tunny, *Fight Back from the North*, 19.

57. Cortesi, *Grim Reapers*, 10–11.

58. Layton, *And I Was There*, 375.

59. *27th Reports.* Lae, which is located on the southeastern coast, had been a small gold-mining town before the war and had a Qantas airstrip and hangar. That runway was the last place Amelia Earhart took off from during her attempted flight around the world in 1937.

60. Gillison, *Royal Australian Air Force*, 458–59.

61. McAulay, *Battle of the Bismarck Sea*, 9; "3rd Bombardment Group, AKA 3rd Attack Group, in Australia during WW2," Dunn, Australia at War, http://home.st.net.au/~dunn/31bg.htm.

62. Alcorn, "Grim Reapers," 15.

63. Gunn, *Pappy Gunn*, 120–22.

64. Cortesi, *Grim Reapers*, 11–12.

65. Ibid., 12.

66. Ibid.

67. Birnn, "War Diary," 42.

68. Mangan's diary (Mar. 29) states, "Col. Davies and some of the lads brought up six B-25s today." McAfee's diary (Apr. 1) states: "Flew down with 12 other guys in a C-39 to Brisbane to pick up B-25s. Got them okay."

69. Cortesi, *Grim Reapers*, 13.

70. Boer, "Early B-25C Mitchells of the ML/KNIL."

71. Cortesi, *Grim Reapers*, 14.

72. Williams, *AAF in Australia*, 58–59, 167, 167n63. U.S. Army Air Corps documents indicate that the Dutch had about 900 army and navy personnel who had been evacuated to Australia and were under the command of Maj. Gen. L. H. Van Oyen of the Dutch Air Force. Approximately 450 of them were air-force personnel, but most were students. There were, however, sufficient Dutch pilots to form one bombardment squadron. On about March 27 Van Oyen met with General Brett and agreed to turn over the twelve B-25s that had just arrived in Australia because of the urgent tactical situation and in view of the fact that an American squadron could use the planes immediately. There were another eleven en route for the Dutch that the Americans would also get. The Dutch government either would receive credit in kind in the United States or the planes would be replaced at a later date.

But Van Oyen was not yet ready to turn over control of his country's troops to the Allied command and recognized Vice Admiral Helfrich, who was then in Ceylon, as the supreme commander of all Dutch Air Force personnel in Australia. Negotiations between the Americans and the Dutch were considerably hampered by a lack of understanding as to who had authority as well as probable delays in communications in the Dutch chain of command. Perhaps it was also known at some higher U.S. headquarters that the Dutch airmen were not yet ready to give up the B-25s in their possession. Because of the urgent need for the bombers, Davies may have been instructed to "steal" them or at least get them one way or the other, and his superiors would deal with the Dutch later.

73. Avery, *B-25 Mitchell*, 95.

Chapter 7

1. Cortesi, *Grim Reapers*, 19.

2. Gaylor et al., *Revenge of the Red Raiders*, 63.

3. That same day a squadron of the U.S. 22nd Bomb Group, flying Martin B-26 "Marauder" twin-engine bombers from Townsville, staged a raid through Port Moresby on the Japanese stronghold at Rabaul. They had arrived in Townsville a few days before, and this was the unit's first combat mission. The 22nd and 3rd Bomb Groups would be involved in many coordinated missions during the months to come.

4. Cortesi, *Grim Reapers*, 22.

5. Wainwright, *Wainwright's Story*, 72, 74, 88.

6. Ind, *Bataan*, 368–69.

7. Ibid.

8. Hipps interview, Aug. 29, 2001 (by L. Stephenson).

9. Bartsch, *Doomed at the Start,* 357–58.

10. Manchester, *American Caesar,* 288.

11. McAfee diary, Apr. 7, 9, 1942. These B-25s would prove ideal for missions requiring long-range, nonstop flying, having flown from the States via Hawaii and the islands to the southwest to Brisbane. They were fitted with auxiliary fuel tanks, capable of removal and reinstallation, likely from storage in Australia. See also Boer, "Early B-25C Mitchells of the ML/KNIL."

12. Cortesi, *Grim Reapers,* 22; Williams, *AAF in Australia,* 61.

13. Bartsch, *Doomed at the Start,* 360.

14. West interview, Sept. 29, 2007.

15. Martin, *Brothers from Bataan,* 75–76.

16. *27th Reports.*

17. Bartsch, *Doomed at the Start,* 394.

18. Ibid., 394–95.

19. "Current Intelligence Section A-2 Interview with Colonel John Davies, November 23, 1942," 12.

20. Bartsch, *Doomed at the Start,* 393.

21. *27th Reports.*

22. Bartsch, *Doomed at the Start,* 395.

23. Durden, "Philippine Raid 'a Picnic,'" *New York Times.*

24. "For the Boys on Bataan," *Time,* 39:21.

25. Durden, "Philippine Raid 'a Picnic,'" *New York Times.*

26. "Raid on Philippines Thrills Flyers," *New York Times.*

27. Glusman, *Conduct under Fire,* 173.

28. Bartsch, *Doomed at the Start,* 396.

29. Durden, "Philippine Raid 'a Picnic,'" *New York Times.*

30. Bartsch, *Doomed at the Start,* 396–97.

31. Ibid.

32. "Col. Davies, Describes Blow," *New York Times.*

33. Ibid.

34. Durden, "Philippine Raid 'a Picnic,'" *New York Times.*

35. "Raid on Philippines Thrills Flyers," *New York Times.*

36. Bartsch, *Doomed at the Start,* 401, 403–4.

37. Connaughton, *MacArthur and Defeat,* 298.

38. Ind, *Bataan,* 369.

39. Harry Mangan, Roster, in author's possession; Jefferson, *Gateway to Victory,* 8.

40. "Col. Davies Describes Blow," *New York Times.*

41. Durden, "Philippine Raid 'a Picnic,'" *New York Times.*

42. Ibid.

43. Ibid.

44. "Battle of the Pacific," *Time,* 20.

45. U.S. Army Far East Command. *Imperial Japanese Navy in World War II,* 175.

46. "Provisions for Secret Base," *New York Times.*

47. Craven and Cate, *Plans and Early Operations,* 418.

48. "Raid on Manila and Cebu," *New York Times.*

49. Bartsch, *Doomed at the Start,* 400; *27th Reports,* 48.

50. Nelson, *First Heroes,* 120–56.

51. Ibid., 121.

52. Ibid., 120–56.

53. Ibid.

54. Ibid., 156.

Chapter 8

1. Toland, *Rising Sun,* 180–83.

2. Taylor, *Trial of Generals,* 83–84.

3. Whitman, *Bataan,* 453.

4. Toland, *But Not in Shame,* 193.

5. Ibid., 265.

6. Taylor, *Trial of Generals,* 84.

7. Bartsch, *Doomed at the Start,* 245.

8. Morton, *Fall of the Philippines,* 421–54; May, *Steadfast Line,* 113–20.

9. Knox, *Death March,* 102.

10. Young, *Battle of Bataan,* 290.

11. Glusman, *Conduct under Fire,* 164.

12. Sides, *Ghost Soldiers,* 41.

13. Ibid., 45.

14. Ibid., 40–46.

15. Glusman, *Conduct under Fire,* 163.

16. New Jersey Hong Kong Network, *Basic Facts on the Nanjing Massacre and the Tokyo War Crimes Trials,* http://www.cnd.org/njmassacre/nj.html

17. Knox, *Death March,* 130.

18. Toland, *But Not in Shame,* 320.

19. Gautier, *I Came Back from Bataan,* 77–78.

20. Toland, *But Not in Shame,* 326.

21. Dyess, *Dyess Story,* 94–95.

22. Toland, *But Not in Shame,* 329.

23. Connaughton, *MacArthur and Defeat,* 296.

24. Norman, *We Band of Angels,* 95.

Chapter 9

1. Day, *Great Betrayal,* 279.

2. Telephone conversation between Larry Stephenson and Ron Hubbard, Feb. 5, 2001.

3. Toland, *But Not in Shame,* 260.

4. McAulay, *Battle of the Bismarck Sea,* 15.

5. Gunn, *Pappy Gunn,* 166.

6. Toland, *Rising Sun,* 346; Gillison, *Royal Australian Air Force,* 453–54.

7. *Reports of General MacArthur,* 124.

8. Wigmore, *Japanese Thrust,* 410.

9. Layton, *And I Was There,* 370.

10. Feldt, *Coast Watchers,* 3–26.

11. Cortesi, *Grim Reapers,* 28.

12. Launder, *College Campus in the Sky,* 58.

13. Williams, *AAF in Australia,* 181n24. New pilots sometimes had difficulty identifying ship movements off New Guinea, where there were chains of small islands. At 20,000 feet, these islands resembled convoys, and inexperienced pilots reported them as such, giving the exact tonnage of each "enemy ship." Oftentimes, bombardment squadrons were dispatched based on such reports, which later led to combat units verifying such sightings by photographic aircraft.

14. Birnn, "War Diary," 43–44.

15. See Gaylor et al., *Revenge of the Red Raiders.* A memorandum by Lt. James McAfee, 3rd Bomb Group intelligence officer, "Deficiencies in the Servicing and Control of the Seven-Mile Airdrome at Port Moresby," dated May 1, 1942, states: "the weather station at Port Moresby has done nothing to acquaint the pilots of our aircraft before leaving of the weather that they might encounter en route to the mainland [Charters Towers]. In this respect, the weather has not been good at all in that area, and has been very uncertain. A prompt and accurate weather report should be available down on the runway so that pilots returning from a mission and hurriedly gassing up to leave can have an idea of what they will run into. The weather station Garbutt Field [Townsville] has not been very accurate in their reports either."

16. Jago, "Last Flight of USAAF #112455," 6.

17. Ibid., 39.

18. "Crash of a Lockheed 14, Possibly in North Queensland, on 21 April 1942," Dunn, Australia at War, http://home.st.net.au/~dunn/ozcrashes/qld120.htm.

19. Ibid.

20. Dickinson, *I Was Lucky,* 105–106.

21. "21 April 1942 Crash of a B-25 Mitchell on Mount Bartle Frere, Qld," Dunn, Australia at War, http://home.st.net.au/~dunn/ozcrashes/qld119.htm.

22. Jago, "Last Flight of USAAF #112455," 3.

23. Ibid., 6.

Chapter 10

1. *Reports of General MacArthur,* 127.

2. Launder, *College Campus in the Sky,* 67.

3. Shores, Cull, and Izawa, *Bloody Shambles,* 1:185–86. Wagner had commanded the 17th Pursuit Squadron, which flew P-40s, in the Philippines at the beginning of the war. He emerged from the defense of the islands with a larger-than-life reputation after being credited with shooting down four enemy fighters in a single flight and destroying others on the ground. Wagner had gone from being a lieutenant when he was on Bataan in January to lieutenant colonel, an increase of three ranks in three months.

4. Launder, *College Campus in the Sky,* 58. See also Spick, *Fighters at War,* 94–95. The early version of the Airacobra was underpowered for a fighter and was easily outfought by Japanese opponents. In addition, the Allison engine turned out to be unreliable and had poor access for routine maintenance. Four hundred of this early version of the interceptor had been built for the British. Some were then sent over to England, where they were tested and rejected by the RAF, which thought the P-39s were not suitable for air-to-air combat mainly because of

their slow rate of climb. Many of these models, referred to as the P-400, were then sent to the Southwest Pacific, where there was a severe shortage of Allied fighter aircraft.

5. Williams, *AAF in Australia,* 116–17. Royce's American bombers were from three bomb groups: the 3rd, still significantly lacking aircraft; the 19th, to which the four-engine heavy bombers, many of which were shot-up survivors of the Java campaign, were assigned; and the 22nd, which flew twin-engine B-26s. The 22nd Bomb Group had arrived from the United States about a month earlier and was headquartered in Townsville.

6. Lundstrom, *First Team,* 157.

7. *27th Reports.*

8. Ibid.

9. Ibid.

10. Cortesi, *Grim Reapers,* 29.

11. Ibid.

12. Morrison, *Two Ocean War,* 142–44.

13. Launder, *College Campus in the Sky,* 55–56.

14. Lundstrom, *First Team,* 298.

15. Depickere, "Battle of the Coral Sea," http://users.pandora.be/dave.depickere/Text/coral .htlm.

16. Lundstrom, *First Team,* 299.

17. Four Japanese carriers were lost at Midway, while the U.S. Navy lost one. After the battle the Pacific Fleet was truly on the offensive. In the six months since the war began, the Japanese had lost four of the six large fleet carriers that had participated in the attack on Pearl Harbor, and the other two were out of commission as a result of the Battle of the Coral Sea, which had also cost Japan a smaller carrier.

18. Gillison, *Royal Australian Air Force,* 520, 522–24; Layton, *And I Was There,* 382–413; Spick, *Fighters at War,* 94–95.

19. Alcorn, "Grim Reapers," 10.

20. Edward Rogers to Larry Stephenson, personal correspondence, Jan. 16, 2006.

21. *27th Reports,* 58.

22. Williams, *AAF in Australia,* 142

23. Ibid., 141.

24. U.S. Army Far East Command, *Imperial Japanese Navy in World War II,* 179.

25. Gillison, *Royal Australian Air Force,* 562.

26. Ibid., 567–68.

27. *27th Reports,* 56.

28. "Douglas SBD Dauntless—USA," The Aviation History Online Museum, http://www .aviation-history.com/douglas/sbd.htm.

29. Townsend, *Duel of Eagles,* 300, 337. See also Birdsall, *Flying Buccaneers,* 11. The navy's version of the A-24, the SBD "Dauntless," did have its shining moments. Marine pilots flew them in the Solomons with some success. But their greatest contribution was at the Battle of Midway in June 1942, where navy crews helped sink four Japanese aircraft carriers. It was, however, a rare navy dive bomber that made more than one flight during a carrier battle. Consequently, large losses could be accepted—once. During Midway, for example, the three U.S. carriers lost more than 40 percent of their 231 SBDs, torpedo bombers, and fighters, most

of which occurred in a single day. In ground-support missions pilots flew multiple sorties against the same targets, each offering a chance for a mishap. The latter led to some very ugly math in terms of losses.

The German Stuka Ju87 dive bomber suffered a similar fate during the Battle of Britain to the A-24s. During first months of the war, they had little difficulty in carrying out their missions over Poland, Scandinavia, and France, where the Germans had achieved air superiority with plenty of fighter support. Things were different over the English Channel and England, where the dive bombers suffered catastrophic losses. On one day alone, twenty-eight Stukas were shot down. One German fighter pilot commented, "They attracted Hurricanes and Spitfires [British fighters] as honey attracts flies." Also, German fighter pilots claimed to have difficulty escorting the sluggish Stukas, with a top speed of only 230 mph and a slower cruising speed, across the Channel. American fighter pilots had the same complaint about the A-24. In the middle of August 1940, Ju87s were withdrawn from the skies over Britain, more than a year before the 27th was sent with its dive bombers to the Philippines.

Did U.S. Army Air Corps leaders know about the Stuka being withdrawn from the British campaign, and if so, did they understand the significant difference in tactical air support provided the dive bombers over Poland and France versus England? In addition to enemy fighters, antiaircraft gunners also took a large toll on such airplanes, which swooped in low to drop their bombs. Because of this, the practice of dive bombing was debated in every air force in the world during the 1930s. The RAF and the Soviet Air Force never deployed them. Japanese dive bombers that attacked land targets suffered a similar fate to the A-24s and the Stukas.

Some A-24s saw limited combat action in other theaters, but the army found that it generally no longer had a need for dive bombers mainly because of the New Guinea experience. They had ordered navy Curtiss SBC Helldivers in 1940, but by the time the modifications specified by the army had been made and the planes tested, the generals had decided not to use them. Few if any of the approximately one thousand A-25s (the army version of the SBC) manufactured ever saw combat action. The A-36 (a variant of the P-51 Mustang) was also used by the Army Air Forces as a dive bomber. About five hundred were deployed overseas before being withdrawn from operational use in 1944. "North American A-36," Wikipedia, http:en .wikipedia.org/wiki/North_American_A-36.

30. Griffith, *MacArthur's Airman*, 56; "The Genius of George Kenney," *Journal of the Air Force Association* 85 (Apr. 2002): 1–11.

31. "Genius of George Kenney," 3.

32. Kenney, *General Kenney Reports*, 28–29.

33. Henebry, *Grim Reapers*, 200.

34. Glines, *Could Never Be So Lucky*, 274.

35. Kenney, *General Kenney Reports*, 29–30.

36. *27th Reports*.

37. Alcorn, "Grim Reapers," 12, 15.

38. *27th Reports*.

39. Griffith, *MacArthur's Airman*, 26–27.

40. Henebry, *Grim Reapers*, 87. Parafrags were twenty-three-pound fragmentation bombs that exploded on impact and sent shrapnel fragments flying in a 360-degree pattern. The parachute attached slowed the forward speed of the bomb and delayed its hitting the ground

or other objects, thus giving the low-flying A-20s time to get away. Parafrags were particularly effective against personnel, parked airplanes, and motor vehicles. General Kenney was responsible for developing the weapon before WWII.

41. Launder, *College Campus in the Sky,* 60–61.

42. Griffith, *MacArthur's Airman,* 71.

43. Gailey, *MacArthur Strikes Back,* 89–93.

44. Kenney, who did not care for most navy officers, had been part of the 1938 aircrew that had intercepted the Italian liner *Rex* 625 miles off the East Coast. This episode brought a reprimand from the navy for carrying out a mission more than one hundred miles beyond the coast.

45. McAulay, *Battle of the Bismarck Sea,* 6, 16.

46. Ibid., 17.

47. "Crash of a B-25C Mitchell into Coral Sea on 4 September 1942," Dunn, Australia at War, home.st.net.au/~dunn/ozcrashes/qld137.htm. The copilot was Australian Allan Reginald Page.

48. Alcorn, "Grim Reapers," 14.

49. Col. John Davies to Lt. Gen. George Kenney, Aug. 1, 1942, in *27th Reports.*

50. Arnold, *Global Mission,* 343–46.

51. Kenney, *General Kenney Reports,* 112.

52. Gause, *War Journal,* 171.

53. Claringbould, *Forgotten Fifth,* 14.

54. "Current Intelligence Section A-2 Interview with Colonel John Davies, November 23, 1942," 6–7.

55. Ibid, 10–11.

56. Ibid, 14.

57. Gailey, *MacArthur Strikes Back,* 126–27.

Chapter 11

1. Glusman, *Conduct under Fire,* 255.

2. Kerr, *Surrender and Survival,* 95–98.

3. May, *Steadfast Line,* 168.

4. Bumgarner, *Parade of the Dead,* 95–98.

5. Martin, *Brothers from Bataan,* 115.

6. Gautier, *I Came Back from Bataan,* 1–13, 137–44.

7. Sides, *Ghost Soldiers,* 10.

8. Kerr, *Surrender and Survival,* 212–15.

9. Martin, *Brothers from Bataan,* 115–18.

10. On May 20, 1948, Capt. Masutaro Iwasaki was sentenced by a U.S. military court to fifteen years at hard labor for ordering his troops to beat and kill Toussaint.

11. Glusman, *Conduct under Fire,* 287–88.

12. Ibid., 367.

13. Stanton, "He Thought He Would Die."

14. Lawton, *Some Survived,* 149–233.

15. Glusman, *Conduct under Fire,* 305–14.

16. Ibid., 318–21.

17. Sides, *Ghost Soldiers,* 23–24.

18. Toland, *Rising Sun,* 962.

19. Ibid., 966.

20. Glusman, *Conduct under Fire,* 435.

21. Schultz, *Hero of Bataan,* 388–89.

22. Ibid, 392.

23. Penicillin did not become generally available to U.S. troops and their Allies until 1943, and it was not widely available to the general public until 1944.

Chapter 12

1. Connaughton, *MacArthur and Defeat,* 296.

2. Whitman, *Bataan,* 605.

3. Connaughton, *MacArthur and Defeat,* 296.

4. Olson, *O'Donnell,* App. 12.

5. Sides, *Ghost Soldiers,* 59.

6. Ibid., 333–34.

Epilogue

1. Edmonds, *They Fought with What They Had,* ix, xi.

2. *Reports of General MacArthur,* 122.

Appendix 4

1. Craven and Cate, *The Pacific: Matterhorn to Nagasaki,* 707.

2. Gunn, *Pappy Gunn,* 218–19.

3. "Pappy!" Sam McGowan Home Page, http://members.aol.com/blndbat/pappy.html.

4. Hipps interview, Feb. 2002 (by A. Martin). See also "Brigadier General William Hipps," Air Force Link, http://www.af.mil/bios/bio_print.asp?bioID=5809&page=1.

Appendix 5

1. Watson, *Army Air Action in the Philippines and Netherlands East Indies,* 180; Manchester, *American Caesar,* 282. Kenney's American command had a name change, from the Far East Air Force to the Fifth Air Force, in early September 1942. Although the Fifth Air Force actually had existed on paper in Washington since February 2, when the remnants of FEAF left fighting in the Philippines became the Fifth Air Force, technically the name at that time did not include the FEAF units fighting in Java or based in Australia. MacArthur referred to the Fifth as "my air."

2. Gunn, *Pappy Gunn,* 131; Arnold, *Global Mission,* 230–31; Kenney, *General Kenney Reports,* 21, 117. The idea to use skip-bombing in the Southwest Pacific seems to have come from different sources. Pappy Gunn had learned to skip bombs across the water before the war during his days as a navy pilot. Also, during a trip to England in April 1941, Hap Arnold discovered that the RAF was having some success using light bombers flying over the water to skip bombs into enemy ships. The Germans had used a similar technique for attacking vessels. When Arnold returned, he had this technique tested at Eglin Field, Florida, before Kenney left for Australia. Kenney, however, seems to have been the real instigator for skip-bombing in the Southwest Pacific. On the way to Australia, he and his aid, Maj. Bill Benn, who was

also a pilot, borrowed a B-26 Marauder on Fiji and loaded it with dummy bombs to try out the technique against coral knobs offshore. Soon after their arrival in Australia, Kenney put Benn in charge of a squadron of B-17s, with orders to develop skip-bombing techniques for use against Japanese shipping. The technique was implemented in October 1942.

Most of the skip-bombing Benn's squadron did, however, was at night. Kenney thought that for the tactic to be effective during daylight, they needed an airplane with several .50-caliber machine guns in the front to strafe antiaircraft gunners as the bomber came in low toward the target. As the technique evolved during the war, bombs were also intentionally slammed into the side of ships without hitting the water.

Pilots soon learned a potential danger of this low-level tactic. When they dropped their bombs with delayed fuses, if a target was not hit, the bomb could continue bouncing along at about the same speed as the airplane that dropped it, "flying in formation," as the pilots called it. If the bomb exploded when it was in the air, the bomber could be damaged or brought down.

3. McAulay, *Battle of the Bismarck Sea,* 29–30.

4. Griffith, *MacArthur's Airman,* 141.

5. Cortesi, *Grim Reapers,* 42; Morrison, *Two Ocean War,* 272.

6. Birdsall, *Flying Buccaneers,* 57; Morrison, *Two Ocean War,* 272.

7. Launder, *College Campus in the Sky,* 67.

8. Dull, *Battle History of the Imperial Japanese Navy,* 278–81; *Reports of General MacArthur,* 202–5.

9. Levine, *Billy Mitchell,* 238–63. Mitchell's most impressive demonstration had been sinking the *Ostfriesland,* a former WWI German battleship. The ship was built with hardened steel armor to be as nearly unsinkable as possible. Many U.S. Navy officers claimed aircraft could not sink it. On Thursday, July 21, 1921, a group of U.S. Army bombers each dropped single 2,000-pound bombs on or near the "unsinkable" dreadnought, while U.S. military leaders, naval attaches of foreign nations, politicians, and newspaper reporters watched from nearby ships; Mitchell himself observed from the two-seat army airplane he was piloting. At 12:18 P.M. the first bomb was dropped. At 12:31 the sixth and last airplane dropped its bomb, and the big ship vanished beneath the surface. The entire sequence lasted but twenty-two minutes. The sinking of this mighty warship was eagerly reported in newspapers around the world. Whereas, most military men understood its significance, many in the navy at that time refused to change their tactical or strategic focus.

10. Griffith, *MacArthur's Airman,* 142.

11. Kenney, *General Kenney Reports,* 318–27; Griffith, *MacArthur's Airman,* 141–42.

12. Cortesi, *Grim Reapers,* 98.

13. McAulay, *Battle of the Bismarck Sea,* 26.

14. MacArthur, *Reminiscences,* 157.

Bibliography

Books, Articles, and Manuals

Airfields, Base Sections 2 & 3, S. W. Pacific, 1941–42. Canberra: AUSLIG, Dept.
  Administrative Services, [1991]. Provided by J. N. Tunny.
Alcorn, John S. "The Grim Reapers." *J. American Aviation Historical Society* (Spring
  1975).
Arnold, Capt. Harold A. "The Lessons of Bataan: The Story of the Philippine and
  Bataan Quartermaster Depots." *Quartermaster Review* (November–December
  1946). Available online at Quartermaster World War II History, U.S. Army
  Quartermaster Museum, www.qmmuseum.lee.army.mil/WWII/bataan_lesson
  .htm.
————. *Global Mission.* New York: Harper & Brothers, 1949.
Avery N. L. *B-25 Mitchell: The Magnificent Medium.* St. Paul, Minn.: Phalanx, 1993.
Bank, Bert. *Back from the Living Dead.* Tuscaloosa, Ala.: Bert Bank, 1945.
Bartsch, William. *Doomed at the Start.* College Station: Texas A&M Press, 1992.
————. *December 8, 1941: MacArthur's Pearl Harbor.* College Station: Texas A&M
  Press, 2003.
Basche, Dirk. *Pemennunde Guide through Historical-Technical Center Information
  and Environment.* Halle, Germany: Union Druck, 1999.
Birdsall, Steve. *Flying Buccaneers: The Illustrated Story of the Fifth Air Force.* Garden
  City, N.J.: Doubleday, 1977.
Birnn, Lt. Ronald *sic* [Richard] R. "The War Diary." Part 2. *Air Power Historian* 4,
  no. 1 (January 1957): 40–45.
Blair, Clay, Jr. *Silent Victory.* Philadelphia: Lippencott, 1975.
Boer, Peter C. "Early B-25C Mitchells of the ML/KNIL, Feb. 1942–June 1942."
  World War II Quarterly 3, no. 1 (2006): 3–10.
Bollich, James. *Bataan Death March.* Gretna, La.: Pelican, 2003.
Bradley, James. *Flags of Our Fathers.* New York: Bantam, 2000.
Brereton, Lt. Gen. Lewis H. *The Brereton Diaries.* New York: William Morrow, 1948.
Bumgarner, John R. *Parade of the Dead.* Jefferson, N.C.: McFarland, 1995.

Byrd, George, Delph Thorn, and Rich Wittish. *The History of Aviation in Savannah.* Savannah, Ga.: Savannah Airport Commission, 1998.

Claringbould, Michael John. *The Forgotten Fifth.* Kingston, Australia: M. J. Claringbould, 1997.

Coffey, Thomas M. *Hap: The Story of the U.S. Air Force and the Man Who Built It.* New York: Viking, 1982.

Connaughton, Richard. *MacArthur and Defeat in the Philippines.* New York: Overbrook, 1942.

Cortesi, Lawrence. *The Grim Reapers.* Temple City, Calif.: Historical Aviation Album, 1985.

Craven, W. F., and J. L. Cate. *The Army Air Forces in World War II.* Chicago: University of Chicago Press, 1948.

———. *The Pacific: Guadalcanal to Saipan, August 1942–July 1944.* Vol. 4. Chicago: University of Chicago Press, 1950.

———. *The Pacific: Matterhorn to Nagasaki: June 19, 1944 to August, 1945.* Vol. 5. Chicago: University of Chicago Press, 1953.

———. *Plans and Early Operations, January 1939–August 1942, The U.S. Army Air Forces of WWII.* Vol. 1. Chicago: University of Chicago Press, 1950.

Daso, Dik Alan. *Hap Arnold and the Evolution of American Airpower.* Washington, D.C.: Smithsonian Institution Press, 2000.

Davis, Richard. *Hap: Henry H. Arnold, Military Aviator, Air Force, Fiftieth Anniversary Commencement Edition.* Washington, D.C.: Government Printing Office, 1997.

Day, David. *The Great Betrayal.* New York: Norton, 1988.

DeSeversky, Alexander P. *Victory through Air Power.* New York: Simon and Schuster, 1942.

Dexter, George. *The New Guinea Offensives.* In *Australia in the War, 1939–45,* series 1. Canberra: Australia War Memorial, 1961.

Dickinson, Wesley E. *I Was Lucky.* San Jose, Calif.: Dilworth, 2002.

Doolittle, James. *I Could Never Be So Lucky.* New York: Bantam Falcon Books, 1992.

Dull, Paul S. *A Battle History of the Imperial Japanese Navy (1941–45).* Annapolis, Md.: U.S. Naval Institute Press, 1978.

Dunn, William J. *Pacific Microphone.* College Station: Texas A&M Press, 1988.

Dyess, William, E. *The Dyess Story.* New York: G. P. Putnam's Sons, 1944.

Edmonds, Walter D. *They Fought with What They Had.* Boston: Little, Brown, 1951.

"Evolution Chart, 27th Bomb Group (L) and 3rd Bomb Group (M)." In *United States 5th Air Force, S. W. Pacific, 1941/42.* Canberra: AUSLIG, Dept. Administrative Services, [1991]. Provided by J. N. Tunny.

"Evolution Chart, 49th Fighter Group, 17th, 3rd, 13th, 20th, & 33rd Provisional Squadrons, S. W. Pacific 1941/42." In *United States 5th Air Force, S. W. Pacific,*

1941/42. Canberra: AUSLIG, Dept. Administrative Services, [1991]. Provided by J. N. Tunny.

Falk, Stanley. *Bataan: The March of Death.* New York: Jove, 1962.

Feldt, Eric. *The Coast Watchers.* New York: Oxford University Press, 1946.

Firth, Robert H. *A Matter of Time.* Chicago: Adams, 1981.

Frank, Gerold, James D. Horan, and J. M. Eckberg. *USS* Seawolf: *Submarine Raider of the Pacific.* New York: G. P. Putnam's Sons, 1945.

Gailey, Harry. *MacArthur Strikes Back: Decision on Buna, New Guinea, 1942–1943.* Novato, Calif.: Presidio, 2000.

Gause, Damon "Rocky." *The War Journal of Damon "Rocky" Gause.* New York: Hyperion, 1999.

Gautier, James D., with Robert L. Whitmore. *I Came Back from Bataan.* Greenville, S.C.: Emerald House, 1997.

Gaylor, Walter, Don L. Evans, Harry A. Nelson, and Lawrence J. Hickey. *Revenge of the Red Raiders.* Boulder, Colo.: International Research, 2006.

Gerrity, Tom. "Bataan Diary." *Philadelphia Evening Bulletin,* June–July 1942.

Gilbert, Martin. *Churchill and America.* New York: Free Press, 2005.

Gillison, Douglas. *Royal Australian Air Force, 1932–42.* Australia in the War of 1939–45, ser. 3, vol. 1. Canberra: Australian War Memorial, 1962.

Glines, Carroll V. *I Could Never Be So Lucky Again.* New York: Bantam, 1991.

Glusman, John A. *Conduct under Fire.* New York, Viking, 2005.

Griffith, Thomas, Jr. *MacArthur's Airman.* Lawrence: University Press of Kansas, 1998.

Gunn, Nathaniel. *Pappy Gunn.* Bloomington, Ind.: Author House, 2004.

Henebry, John. *Grim Reapers.* Missoula, Mont.: Pictorial Histories Publishing, 2002.

Huston, John W. *American Air Power Comes of Age—General Henry H. "Hap" Arnold.* World War II Diaries. Vol. 2. Honolulu: University of the Pacific Press, 2004.

Ind, Allison. *Bataan: The Judgment Seat.* New York: Macmillan, 1944.

Kane, George. *Brief History of the 27th and Yearbook, 1940–1982.* Edited by Sam Moody. N.p.: 27th Bombardment Group Alumni, [1982].

Kenney, George. *The Saga of Pappy Gunn.* New York: Duell, Sloan, and Pearce, 1959.

———. *General Kenney Reports: A Personal History of the Pacific War.* Washington, D.C.: Government Printing Office, 1997.

Kerr, E. Bartlett. *Surrender and Survival.* New York: William Morrow, 1985.

Knox, Donald. *Death March.* New York: Harcourt Brace Jovanovich, 1981.

Launder, Richard. *College Campus in the Sky.* San Jose, Calif.: Writers Club, 2001.

Lawton, Manny. *Some Survived.* Chapel Hill, N.C.: Algonquin Books, 1984.

Layton, Edwin T. *And I Was There.* New York: William Morrow, 1985.

Levine, Isaac Don. *Billy Mitchell: Pioneer of Air Power.* New York: Duell, Sloan, and Pearce, 1943.

Link, Robert, Harry Fisher, and Charles Trumbull, eds. *A History of the Veterans of the United States Naval Submarine Fleet.* Vol. 4. Dallas: Taylor Publishing for U.S. Submarine Veterans of World War II, 1990.

Lundstrom, John. *First Team: Pacific Naval Air Combat from Pearl Harbor to Midway.* Annapolis, Md.: Naval Institute Press, 1984.

MacArthur, Douglas. *Reminiscences.* New York: McGraw Hill, 1964.

Manchester, William. *American Caesar.* New York: Dell, 1978.

Martin, Adrian R. *Brothers from Bataan.* Manhattan, Kans.: Sunflower University Press, 1992.

May, Mary Cathrine. *The Steadfast Line: The Story of the 27th Bombardment Group (Light) in World War II.* Tallahassee, Fla.: Kinko's, 2004.

Mayo, George. *U.S. Military Academy Class of 1940, Class Roster as of 1 May 2000.* N.p., n.d.

McAulay, Lea. *Battle of the Bismarck Sea.* New York: St. Martin's Press, 1991.

McCarthy, Dudley. *South-West Pacific Area—First Year Kokoda to Wau.* In *Australia in the War, 1939–1945,* series 1. Canberra: Australian War Memorial, 1959.

McGlothlin, Frank Emile. *Barksdale to Bataan.* Covington, La.: N.p., 1984.

Melinger, Phillip. *Significant Events in Air Force History.* Air Force History and Museums Program. Washington D.C.: Government Printing Office, 2003.

Miller, Col. E. B. *Bataan Uncensored.* Long Prairie, Minn.: Hart Publications, 1949.

Moody, Samuel B. *27th Bombardment Group History & Yearbook, 1940–42.* 1985.

Moody, Samuel B., and Maury Allen. *Reprieve from Hell.* Orlando, Fla.: N.p, 1961.

Morris, Eric. *Corregidor.* London: Hutchison, 1982.

Morrison, Samuel Elliot. *The Two Ocean War: A Short History of the U.S. Navy in the Second World War.* Boston: Little, Brown, 1963.

Morton, Louis. *Fall of the Philippines.* Washington, D.C.: Center for Military History, U.S. Army, 1989.

Mosley, Leonard. *Marshall, Hero for Our Times.* New York: Hearst Books, 1982.

Nalty, Bernard C. *Winged Shield: A History of the USAF.* Washington, D.C.: Air Force History Museum Program, 1997.

Nelson, Craig. *First Heroes.* New York: Viking, 2002.

Norman, Elizabeth. *We Band of Angels.* New York: Pocketbooks, 2000.

Odgers, George. *Air War against Japan.* In *Australia in the War, 1939–45,* series 3. Canberra: Australia War Memorial, 1957.

Official Register of the Officers and Cadets United States Military Academy for the Academic Year ending June 30, 1940.

Olson, Col. John. *O'Donnell: Andersonville of the Pacific.* N.p., 1985.

———"USMA in the Philippines, 1941–1942." *Assembly: Association of Graduates* (July 1993): 11–17, 25.

Pilot's Handbook of Flight Operating Instructions for Models B-25C and B-25D. Inglewood, Calif.: North American Aviation, 1942. Reprint, Appleton, Wisc.: Aviation Publications, 1978.

Polmar, Norman, and Samuel Loring Morrison. *PT Boats at War.* Osceola, Wisc.: MBI, 1999.

Prange, Gordon W. *At Dawn We Slept: The Untold Story of Pearl Harbor.* New York: Penguin Books, 1984.

Robinson, Pat. *The Fight for New Guinea.* New York: Random House, 1943.

Romulo, Carlos. *I Saw the Fall of the Philippines.* Garden City, N.J.: Doubleday, Doran, 1943.

Schaller, Michael. *Douglas MacArthur, Far Eastern General.* London: Oxford University Press, 1989.

Schom, Allen. *The Eagle and the Rising Sun: The Japanese American War, 1941 to 1943, Pearl Harbor through Guadalcanal.* New York: W. W. Norton, 2004.

Schultz, Duane. *Hero of Bataan: The Story of General Jonathan M. Wainwright.* New York: St. Martin's Press, 1981.

Shannon, David. *Twentieth Century America: The United States since the 1890s.* Chicago: Rand McNally, 1963.

Shores, Christopher, Brian Cull, and Yasuho Izawa. *Bloody Shambles.* Vols. 1 and 2. London: Grub Street, 1992 (vol. 1) and 1993 (vol. 2).

Sides, Hampton. *Ghost Soldiers.* New York: Anchor Books, 2002.

Smith, Peter C. *Dive Bomber.* Annapolis: Naval Institute Press, 1982.

Smith, Steven Trent. *The Rescue.* New York: John Riley and Sons, 2001.

Smurthwaite, David. *The Pacific War Atlas, 1941–1945.* London: Mirable Books, 1995.

Spick, Mike. *Fighters at War: The Story of Air-to-Air Combat.* East Grinstead, West Suffex, UK: Elephant Editions, 1997.

Stamp, Loren. *Journey through Hell.* Jefferson, N.C.: McFarland. 1993.

Stinnet, Robert B. *Day of Deceit.* New York: Free Press, 2000.

Taylor, Lawrence. *Trial of Generals.* South Bend, Ind.: Icarus, 1981.

Thomas, David Arthur. *The Battle of the Java Sea.* New York: Stein and Day, 1968.

Thompson, Kyle. *A Thousand Cups of Rice: Surviving the Death Railway.* Austin, Tex.: Eakin, 1994.

Thompson, Peter. *The Battle for Singapore.* London: Portrait, 2005.

Toland, John. *But Not in Shame: The Six Months after Pearl Harbor.* New York: Random House, 1961.

———. *The Rising Sun: The Decline and Fall of the Japanese Empire, 1936–1945.* New York: Random House, 1970.

Townsend, Peter. *Duel of Eagles.* Edison, N.J.: Castle, 2003.

Tunny, Noel. *Fight Back from the North: 3rd Bomb Group (M) 19th Bomb Gp (H) 22nd Bomb Gp (M) 49th Fighter Group—South West Pacific, 1942.* Brisbane, Australia: Myla Graphics, 1991.

———. *Gateway to Victory: The Establishment of the First U.S. Armed Forces in Australia, 1941–42.* Brisbane, Australia: Myla Graphics, 1991.

Van der Vat, Dan. *The Pacific Campaign, World War II.* New York: Simon and Schuster, 1991.

Volckmann, Russell. *We Remained.* New York: W. W. Norton, 1954.

Wainwright, Jonathan M. *General Wainwright's Story.* Garden City, N.J.: Doubleday, 1946.

Weller, George. "Luck to the Fighters." 3 parts. *Military Affairs* (Winter 1944, part 1; Spring 1945, part 2; Summer 1945, part 3): 259–96; 33–62; 124–50.

White, W. L. *Queens Die Proudly.* New York: Harcourt Brace, 1943.

Whitehouse, Arch. *Billy Mitchell: American Eagle of Air Power.* New York: G. P. Putnam Sons, 1943.

Whitman, John. *Bataan: Our Last Ditch.* New York: Hippocrene, 1990.

Wigmore, Lionel. *Japanese Thrust.* In *Australia in the War, 1939–45,* series 1. Canberra: Australia War Memorial, 1957.

Wilmont, Chester. *Struggle for Europe.* New York: Harper Dolophone, 1952.

Wright, Lt. Gen. John MacNair, Jr. *Capture on Corregidor: Diary of an American P.O.W. in World War II.* Jefferson, NC: McFarland, 1988.

Young, Donald J. *The Battle of Bataan.* Jefferson, N.C.: McFarland, 1992.

———. *First 24 Hours of the War.* Jefferson, N.C.: McFarland, 1992.

Correspondence, Diaries, Memoirs, and Personal Narratives

Arnold, Lt. Gen. Henry "Hap," to Ann Stephenson. May 15, 1942. Clyde Stephenson personal collection.

Bender, Frank "Pete." Unpublished autobiography. 1997–2000. In author's possession (L. Stephenson).

Davies, John, to Ann Stephenson. May 2, 1942. Stephenson Family Collection.

Hubbard, Ronald. Memoir. 2002. Copy in author's possession (L. Stephenson).

Mangan, James Harrison. Personal narrative. November 4, 1942. In author's possession (L. Stephenson).

McAfee, James. Diary. 1941–42. Copy in authors' possession.

McAfee, Maj. James, to Gordon Stephenson. May 22, 1943. Stephenson Family Collection.

——— to Larry Stephenson. September 1, 1995. In author's possession (L. Stephenson).

Stephenson, Ann, to Gordon Stephenson. May 17, 1942. Stephenson Family Collection.

Stephenson, Glenwood. Letters, 1922–43. Stephenson Family Collection.

———. Unpublished autobiography. 1931. In author's possession (L. Stephenson).

Stephenson, Gordon. Personal narrative. 1932–42. Stephenson Family Collection.

———, to Glenwood Stephenson. July 18, 1933. Stephenson Family Collection.

———, to Maj. James McAfee. March 14, 1943. Stephenson Family Collection.

Stephenson, Hazel, to Glenwood Stephenson. July 20, 1933. Stephenson Family Collection.

Timlin, Francis, to Gustave Breymann. Letters, 1984–85. Copy in author's possession (L. Stephenson).

Vance, Reginald, to William H. Bartsch. 1980. Copy in author's possession (L. Stephenson).

Interviews by Authors

Bank, Maj. Bert. November 16, 2003.

Bartsch, William. August 16, 2001.

Bax, Franz. May 2003.

Beck, Col. William. December 3, 2003.

Bollich, James. October 2001.

Breymann, Gustave. April 3, 2004.

Brown, Maj. Raymond W. August 11, 2003.

———. September 2003.

Burns, Crayton. November 5, 2003.

Burroughs, Dallas, Jr. November 2, 2003.

Bymers, Margaret Zwaschka. May 2001.

Cagwin, Maj. Gen. Leo G. March 2001.

Callahan, Patrick, Jr. February 24, 2004.

Chandler, Evelyn. March 10, 2004.

Connor, John. November 2, 2003.

Cook, Charles. December 28, 2003.

Corbi, Frank. January 24, 2004.

Dickinson, Maj. Wesley. February 12, 2004.

Doan, Mrs. Oliver. November 30, 2005.

Dow, G. Wayne. January 4, 2007.

Dunn, Peter. August 7, 2005.

Eubank, Maj. Gen. William. September 1, 2001.

Farmer, Kenneth. August 21, 2001.

Fisher, Janice. December 2001.

Forrester, Mrs. Randall. February 1, 2001.

Galusha, Harry Jr. September 25, 2007.

Gause, Damon L. February 7, 2001.

Gautier, James "Cajun," Jr. March 10, 2004.

Gerrity, Tom, Jr. June 29, 2005.

Gilmore, Col. John. March 2, 2004.

Gunn, Nathaniel I. February 2, 2004.

Hambaugh, Robert, Jr. November 30, 2003.

Hampton, Elbert. November 2, 2003.

Hanson, Red. Interview by Clyde Stephenson. Ca. 2001.

Harrell, Ralph. May 21, 2001.

Harrelson, Col. Jay B. August 29, 2001.

Hess, Col. Lester C. March 2001.

Heyn, Jack. April 6, 2004.

Hipps, Brig. Gen. William. August 29, 2001.

———. February 2002.

Hochman, Capt. David. October 22, 2003.

Hubbard, Col. Ronald. February 5, 2001.

Jackson, Herbert H. November 2001.

Jones, James. December 28, 2003.

Kane, Maj. George. October 3, 2003.

Keeter, Hilton. October 29, 2001.

Knowles, Jesse. November 18, 2005.

Kolger, Louis. November 6, 2003.

LaFitte, William. December 28, 2003.

Lankford, Paul. September 29, 2003.

Larson, Robert. May 2001.

Launder, Capt. Richard. April 2, 2004.

Lee, James V., Jr. May 21, 2001.

Maher, Scott. October 2003.

Mangan, Col. J. Harrison "Harry." February 1, 2001.

May, Mary Catherine. March 12, 2004.

McAfee, Julia, and Jim, Jr. September 1, 2001.

McCready, Joanne Stephenson. October 28, 1995.

Moody, Elizabeth. November 2, 2003.

Morrissey, Lt. Col. Stephen B. April 2002.

Morron, Glen C. March 1, 2004.

Myron, Lillian Stephenson. October 7, 1995.

Ott, Arlene. June 2001.

Overton, Cletus. December 28, 2003.

Patten, Col. Samuel M. March 2001.

Patterson, Cindy. March 2002.

Pedo, Marie. August 2002.

Prewett, Granville "Buck." February 16, 2004.

Rogers, Edward. March 8, 2004.

Rose, Maj. Henry. December 3, 2003

Rosen, Col. Melvin H. April 2003.

Ruegg, Lt. Gen. Robert. December 12, 2002.

Savage, Col. Columbus "Doc." August 27, 2001.

Schwarz, Capt. Bert. August 28, 2001.

Shirek, Leona. May 2001.

Shrum, Robert. December 29, 2003.

Sims, Leland. March 2001.

Smith, James D. November 30, 2005.

Stafford, Col. Robert. December 10, 2002.

Stephenson, Clyde. September 6, 1995.

Stephenson, David. October 7, 1995.

Stephenson, Willis. 2003.

Stirling, Lt. Col. Warren. February 2, 2001.

Stoflet, Malcolm. April 2001.

Summers, Col. Julius "Zeke." September 6, 1995.

Swanson, Calvin. December 28, 2003.

Thalacker, Harold. November 2001.

Timlin, Col. Francis E. February 2, 2001.

Tunny, Noel. January 21, 2003.

Underwood, R. W. December 28, 2003.

Wakeham, Allan. May 25, 2003.

West, Col. Howard B. September 19, 21, 29, 2007.

Wilson, Lt. Col. Harry. July 3, 2001.

Winton, Brig. Gen. Walter F., Jr. November 2001.

Wolfersberger, Robert. October 6, 2003.

Wood, John. December 18, 2003.

Wright, Lt. Gen. John M., Jr. August 2003.

Wundrow, Martha. May 2001.

Internet Sources

Big Maneuvers Test U.S. Army, Louisiana Maneuvers, 1940–44. Louisiana in World War II, http://www.crt.state.la.us/tourism/lawwii/maneuvers/LIFE _ARTICLE/Maneuvers_Life_Article.htm.

Birkett, Gordon R. R. "A24 Banshees of the 27thBG(Lt) and 3rdBG(Lt)." Posting in Light & Medium Bombers Forum, ArmyAirForces.com, http://www .armyairforces.com/forum/m_59827/tm.htm.

"Brigadier General William Hipps." Air Force Link, http://www.af.mil/bios/bio _print.asp?bioID=5809&page=1.

"Charters Towers." Walkabout—The Australian Travel Guide, http://www.smh .com.au/news/queensland/charters-towers/2005/02/17/1108500202239.html.

Depikere, Dave. "The Battle of the Coral Sea" (timeline based on Edwin Hoyt, *Blue Skies and Blood*). World War II, Analyzed! http://users.pandora.be/dave .depickere/Text/coral.html.

"Douglas SBD Dauntless—USA." The Aviation History Online Museum, http:// www.aviation-history.com/douglas/sbd.htm.

Dow, Gerald Wayne. "Unit History—27th Bomb Group (L)." Family History and Genealogical Research of Gerald Wayne Dow, www.lindadow.net/unit _history-27th_bomb_gp_lt.htm.

Dunn, Peter. Australia at War, http://home.st.net.au/~dunn and www.ozatwar.com.

Feuer, A. B. "Pawn of Fate: The Pensacola Convoy," *Sea Classics* (July 2004).

Online at Find Articles, http://findarticles.com/p/articles/mi_qa4442/is
_200407/ai_n16065359.

"Major General Eugene Lowry Eubank." Air Force Link, http://www.af.mil/bios/
bio_print.asp?bioID=5370&page=1.

"Major General William E. Eubank Jr." Air Force Link, http://www.af.mil/bios/
bio_print.asp?bioID=5371&page=1

New Jersey Hong Kong Network. *Basic Facts on the Nanjing Massacre and the Tokyo
War Crimes Trials,* My China News Digest, http://www.cnd.org/njmassacre/nj
.html.

"North American B-25 Mitchell." Acepilots.com: World War II and Aviation History, http://www.acepilots.com/planes/b25.html

"Pappy!" Sam McGowan Home Page, http://members.aol.com/blndbat/pappy
.html.

Texas Military Forces Museum, Lost Battalion Association, www.texasmilitary
forcesmuseum.org/lostbattalion/index.htm.

"USS *California* (BB-44)." The California State Military Museum, http://www
.militarymuseum.org/usscalif.htm.

West Point, http://www.west-point.org.

"World War II: The Defensive Phase." Chap. 20 in *American Military History.*
Army Historical Series. (Washington, D.C.: Center of Military History, U.S.
Army, 1989). Online at http://www.army.mil/cmh-pg/books/AMH/AMH-20
.htm.

Newspapers, Periodicals, and Yearbooks

Auburn. Auburndale High School Yearbook, 1929–33.

"Battle of the Pacific; North from Australia." *Time,* April 27, 1942.

"Col. Davies, Describes Blow; Shipping 'Plastered to Bits.'" *New York Times,* April
16, 1942, sec. 1.

Durden, F. Tillman. "Philippine Raid 'a Picnic'; Hope for Offensive Bounds." *New
York Times,* April 17, 1942, sec. 1.

"For the Boys on Bataan." *Time,* April 27, 1942.

Howitzer. U.S. Military Academy Yearbook, 1938–40.

"Provisions for Secret Base." *New York Times,* April 17, 1942, sec. 1.

"Raid on Manila and Cebu." *New York Times,* April 16, 1942, sec. 1.

"Raid on Philippines Thrills Our Flyers." *New York Times,* April 18, 1942, sec. 1.

Stanton, Anne. "He Thought He Would Die." *Detroit Free Press,* February 11, 2004.

Reports and Military Documents

27th Bombardment Group Reports, ca. September 1942.

27th Bombardment Group Squadron Roster, October 21, 1941.

Abington, C. Juliett. *Summary of Air Action in the Philippines and Netherlands East*

Indies, 7 December 1941–26 March 1942. Army Air Force Historical Studies 29A. Washington, D.C.: General Printing Office, 1945.

Arnold, Gen. Henry "Hap" "Conversation between General Arnold and General Marshall," Sept. 25, 1941, Memphis, Tenn. Folder 6, Container 221, Arnold Papers. Library of Congress, Washington, D.C.

"Burial Detail and Accident Report, for B-25 Crash, April 21, 1942," May 19, 1942. Headquarters, Third Bombardment Group (L), Army Air Forces, Charters Towers Air Base, Charters Towers, Queensland.

"Current Intelligence Section A-2 Interview with Colonel John Davies, November 23, 1942," 142, 052, Davies John, 23 November 1942, Archives Branch, Maxwell Air Force Base, Ala. Typescript.

Davies, Maj. John, to Commanding General FEAF, Manila, P.I. Secret Cypher Message (RAAF Form A.14), December 21, 1941, Darwin.

Denno, Bryce. "USMA Class of 1940 in the Defense of the Philippines." Unpublished manuscript, n.d. U.S. Military Academy Library, West Point, N.Y.

Jago, Robert. "The Last Flight of USAAF #112455," February 1, 2001. Draft of report self-published in Australia.

Kreidberg, Marvin A., and Merton G. Henry. *History of Mobilization in the United States Army, 1775–1945.* Department of the Army Pamphlet 20–212. Washington D.C., November 1955.

"Officers and Enlisted Roster for Personnel to Assemble and Move Airplanes, Headquarters 27th Bombardment Group," December 13, 1941.

"Officers Roster, 27th Bombardment Group (L), Air Force Combat Command, Fort McDowell, San Francisco," October 29, 1941.

"Officers Roster by Squadron, Headquarters, 27th Bombardment Group (L), Far East Air Force, Fort McKinley, P.I.," December 8, 1941.

Reports of General MacArthur: Japanese Operations in the Southwest Pacific Area, Vol. 2, Part 1. Compiled from Japanese Demobilization Bureau Records. Washington, D.C.: U.S. Army Center of Military History, 1994.

"Royce's Raid—Crew and Passenger Roster."

Secret Communiqué, January 13, 1942. Box T-1601. Messages AGWAR to USAFIA. Record Group 338. National Archives, Washington, D.C.

U.S. Army Far East Command. *Imperial Japanese Navy in World War II: A Graphic Organization of the Japanese Naval Organization and List of Combatant and Noncombatant Vessels Lost or Damaged in the War.* Special Operational Monograph Series 116 (JOMS). Tokyo: Military History Section, 1952.

U.S. Army Roster of General Officers, War Department ASF. Registration 31-WDGA. Office of the Adjutant General. Washington, D.C., August 1, 1945.

U.S. War Department War Crimes Office, Judge Advocate General's Office. File 41–9, "Torture and Bayoneting of Pfc. Toussaint, San Jose, Mindoro, P.I.," May 30, 1948. Copy in author's possession (Stephenson).

BIBLIOGRAPHY

Watson, Richard L., Jr. *Air Action in the Papua Campaign, 21 July 1942 to 23 January 1943.* Army Air Force Historical Studies 17. Washington, D.C.: Government Printing Office, 1944.

————. *Army Air Action in the Philippines and Netherlands East Indies, 1941–42.* Army Air Force Historical Studies 111. Washington, D.C.: Government Printing Office, 1945.

Williams, E. Kathleen. *The AAF in Australia to the Summer of 1942.* Army Air Force Historical Studies 9. Maxwell Air Force Base, Ala.: Historical Division, Air Force Research Agency, 1944.

Index

Pages shown in *italics* represent illustrations

ISBN-13: 978-1-60344-019-6
ISBN-10: 1-60344-019-4

52995